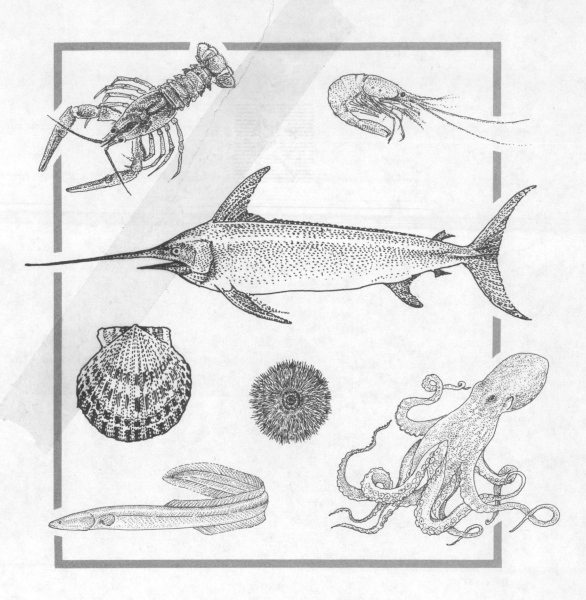

SIMON AND SCHUSTER
New York   London   Toronto   Sydney   Tokyo   Singapore

F·I·S·H

The Basics

SHIRLEY KING

Illustrations by Glenn Wolff

Also by Shirley King
Saucing the Fish
Dining with Marcel Proust

———————————

Simon and Schuster
Simon & Schuster Building
Rockefeller Center
1230 Avenue of the Americas
New York, New York   10020

SIMON AND SCHUSTER and colophon are registered trademarks
of Simon & Schuster Inc.

Designed by Nina D'Amario/Levavi & Levavi
Manufactured in the United States of America

1   3   5   7   9   10   8   6   4   2

Library of Congress Cataloging in Publication Data

King, Shirley.
Fish, the basics / Shirley King.
p.   cm.
1. Cookery (Fish)   2. Cookery (Seafood)   I. Title.
TX747.K52   1990
641.6'92—dc20   90-9732
                                                      CIP

ISBN 0-671-65052-1

Dedication

I dedicate Fish: The Basics *to Lyn Stallworth who worked tirelessly with me on the first steps of this book. Her editorial skills and friendly advice were generously given and I am most grateful.*

I also dedicate this book to my family, friends, students, and all those who find seafood cookery somewhat of a mystery. I hope I have explained it well and that by reading and using this book all becomes clear.

Acknowledgments

MANY PEOPLE HELPED ME TO GARNER INFORMATION FOR THIS BOOK. RICHARD LORD, WHO IS a walking reference book on seafood (now writing his own book), is the Fulton Fish Market Information Services. His joy in life comes from collecting new species of seafood to photograph and write about. He gave me invaluable help on the fish profiles and lots of other information.

Ken Gall of the New York Sea Grant Extension Program at Deer Park collected and gave me information, especially on the fat, cholesterol, and omega-3 content of the fish and shellfish written about in this book.

Susan Herrmann Loomis sent me exquisite fish and shellfish from Seattle (when she lived there—Susan now lives in New York) to cook and taste. Jon Rowley and Peter Redmayne, also of Seattle, have made invaluable contributions to this book, for which I thank them.

Lawrence Skrivanek of Mister Wright (a liquor store in New York City) and my dear friend Stephen R. Lawrence, both wine connoisseurs, have kept me up to date on many fine wines that I enjoy with fish.

I am also most grateful to those friends who shared in the creation of many of the recipes and to my students who (unknown to them) gave me much invaluable input during my seafood workshops.

Very many thanks to Nach Waxman, owner of the Kitchen Arts and Letters bookstore in New York City, for his continuing support and for brilliantly suggesting the title for this book.

My thanks to Carole Lalli, my editor at Simon and Schuster, who has always been inspiring, and to Kerri Conan, her assistant, for the meticulous follow-ups on the editorial details.

Contents

Preface

THERE IS NO GREAT TRICK TO COOKING SEAFOOD. WHAT YOU NEED IS A GOOD PIECE OF FRESH fish and a good recipe. The same holds true for shellfish.

This book will show you how easy it is to master the simple techniques necessary to produce perfectly delicious seafood dishes. You will learn how to select that choice piece of fish at the store. You will also learn about the forms in which fish and shellfish are available, the seasons when they are at their best, the best methods of preparation, and the variety of accompaniments, seasonings, and sauces that especially enhance their flavor.

This book is designed to present basic information and then send you on your way, to confidently prepare seafood well and to learn to create dishes on your own. With the help of this book, seafood cookery will become as fascinating as you choose to make it.

Part I is an introduction to the kinds of fish and shellfish available today. In this part of the book you will become familiar with seafood nomenclature and learn to distinguish among the varieties of seafood you encounter at the market. You will learn how to buy seafood and what to do with it once you get it home. Learning how to fillet a fish and alternative ways of cutting fish and their fillets will help you either to direct the fish store personnel to do it for you, or to do it yourself. You will also learn how to be sure you are getting the many health benefits of seafood.

Part II consists of some 57 basic recipes and methods for preparing the seafood you buy. Most of the methods and recipes can be used with many different kinds of seafood, and you will find that once you know them, your own inventiveness will lead you to create new and exciting taste experiences. In this part of the book you will also find recipes for sauces and salads, as well as advice on which vegetables, herbs, and spices are best for different kinds of seafood and which wines are the most suitable to drink with them.

9

Finally, Part III is an alphabetical listing that gives a profile of virtually every kind of seafood you may find in your fish market or supermarket, with references to the basic recipes useful for each. I want you to be able to enjoy all the seafood available to you today.

Fish: The Basics is meant to become one of the cookbooks you use constantly, a great resource and aid in preparing dishes based on the wonderful fruits of the sea.

How to Use This Book

ALL THE INFORMATION THAT YOU NEED TO IDENTIFY, CHOOSE, STORE, PREPARE, AND cook fish and shellfish is in the three parts of this book. These sections work both independently and together.

Part I includes general information on seafood. Begin by examining seafood's health benefits: There are tables that list lean and fat seafood varieties, and others that list amounts of cholesterol and omega-3 fatty acids in seafood. You will find drawings of the different structures of fish and shellfish as well as illustrated filleting, boning, and skinning techniques. How do you select and buy the freshest seafood? What forms of which species are commonly available? What's the best way to store seafood until you are ready to cook it? After reading Part I, handling fish and shellfish will be natural.

In Part II, I discuss cooking seafood. First, learn to recognize proper doneness. Then browse through the descriptions of the various seafood cooking methods. For each method there is at least one specific recipe, and each recipe includes a list of all the fish and shellfish suitable to that particular method. Tables of additional information help you adjust the serving quantities, cooking times, and temperatures. The recipe for broiled fish fillets, for example, is so basic that it applies to all fish (except minnows!), as well as numerous shellfish. Part II emphasizes the versatility of fresh seafood.

Each common fish and shellfish species is profiled in Part III. This is your chance to get to know all sorts of seafood—both the familiar and the less so. Here is information about availability—where to find each kind of seafood and when—as well as discussions of cooking methods and recipes that are suitable to the profiled seafood. These alphabetized entries include illustrations and, if necessary, specific handling instructions.

It's simple to use this book: You may begin by selecting a particular fish or a specific cooking method.

Let's say, for instance, that you want to cook salmon, because you like it. If you don't often go to the fish store, you might first want to read through Part I and get an idea about how to select the freshest fish. Next, look up the salmon profile in Part III. While scanning the entry, you will see that salmon is usually available whole, in steaks, or in fillets, and you will learn how much of each form is needed per person. A list of recommended salmon preparations follows.

Suppose you choose to broil a salmon fillet. Turn to Part II and read first about broiling, then go to the broiling recipe that catches your eye. By reading the instructions, you note a couple of other fish that are suitable for this same preparation. Now you are ready to go to the fishmonger, certain to leave with the right amount of the freshest fish possible.

Or suppose you fancy a particular fish preparation—say, poaching, for example, because you crave a plainly cooked fish accompanied by a healthful sauce. Begin by looking up poaching in Part II. Reading through the text, you decide to poach a whole fish (rather than a fillet), and you note several fish you can poach. Perhaps you leaf through a couple of profiles—in Part III, remember—to become acquainted with the fish mentioned. Again, it's off to the fish store, and you're ready to select the freshest fish possible to bring home and poach. You can even clean it yourself if you wish—easy instructions are in Part I.

Don't forget to plan the rest of the meal. There's information on sauces and condiments, as well as discussions of side dishes and wines. Have fun, because it's easier than you think—and so satisfying—to cook seafood well.

Part
I

BASIC
INFORMATION

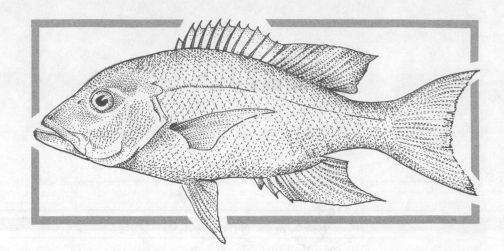

About Fish and Shellfish Cookery

IF YOU GO TO THE FISH STORE WITH A PRECONCEIVED NOTION OF THE FISH OR SHELLFISH YOU want to cook, you may end up going home with something less than fresh; it is better to be flexible in your choice, once you've learned how to judge freshness. And once you've become familiar with the textures and tastes of different kinds of fish and shellfish, it will be easy to choose a recipe or make up one of your own. Even if you are not familiar with some of the "new" fish that are appearing in the markets, you need not avoid them, for undoubtedly they are similar to other fish that you know. The profiles at the end of this book will help you distinguish all sorts of seafood, so don't be afraid to try a "new" fish.

In the fish store you can find fish and shellfish in a wide variety of forms— whole fish as well as fish cut into steaks, fillets, and chunks (chunks are also known as roasts). Whole fish are "drawn," "dressed," and "pan-dressed." Fish fillets cut from whole fish are practically boneless, and for that reason appeal to many. Steaks are convenient for individual portions, and chunks (weighing 1½ to 5 pounds, cut from a whole fish) can easily be stuffed and served to several people. Once you learn to recognize the advantages of the different forms, you can make better choices when planning your meals.

Although frying, broiling, grilling, and baking are popular ways of preparing fish, there are as many cooking methods for fish as there are for meat. In fact, cooking is not always necessary to enhance the flavor of fish. Some fish, like tuna and yellowtail, taste great raw, as attested by the popularity of sushi and sashimi—raw fish as served by the Japanese.

Cooking fish is really simple, since it is naturally tender and needs only to be cooked through to attain its fullest flavor and texture. We will be concerned with cooking fish so that it does not overcook or fall apart in the cooking utensil, but cooks just long enough that it is still juicy and practically melts in your mouth. Elaborate sauces are not necessary, as you will see. Nowadays it isn't considered essential to "sauce" a fish; we know that the natural juices from both fish and vegetables are enough to flavor and moisten the fish. Times have changed and our cooking tastes have evolved; if you want sauces, see the sauce recipes in Part II. Also see my earlier book *Saucing the Fish* (Simon and Schuster, 1986).

The taste of cooked fish ranges from delicate-mild-bland (flounder, sole) to flavorful (mackerel). Adjectives such as *nutty* and *sweet* can be applied to the taste of many fish. Most lean white-fleshed fish not only need to be enhanced but are perfect vehicles for subtle seasonings. They are cooked with little added fat, mild herbs, spices, seasonings, vegetables, and, if necessary, some liquid such as wine or stock. Fish with higher fat content such as salmon, mackerel, herring, whitefish, tuna, eel, sturgeon, sablefish, and trout can be cooked with stronger-flavored accompaniments, such as the more emphatic herbs and spices. These fish are also excellent for smoking.

For shellfish, freshness and proper cooking methods are of the utmost importance. In addition, you will need to learn several simple techniques—for opening oysters and clams, cleaning mussels, and so on. These techniques are described in the profiles in Part III of this book.

Some shellfish is expensive, while some cost less than most finfish. If you live near the coast, of course, you may garner some shellfish on your own for free! Always be sure to check your sources with the local fisheries department to avoid bad effects from contaminated waters and to make sure it is the legal season to gather shellfish. Also be sure to store them properly. Under those circumstances, picking your own is the best way to ensure absolute freshness.

Shrimp are the most popular shellfish—practically every restaurant across the country serves shrimp in some form or other. Just think of how many shrimp dishes there are! Though relatively expensive, small shrimp cost less per pound than flounder fillet. Blue crabs, mussels, squid, conch, octopus, and periwinkles are just some of the shellfish that are cheap. To my mind, the best shellfish in the world are the lobsters from the East Coast, stone crabs from Florida, blue crabs from the Chesapeake Bay area, Dungeness crabs from the Pacific Northwest, and crawfish from Louisiana, California, and Oregon. But each to his own taste.

Shellfish had better be cooked properly! There is nothing as awful as rubbery shrimp or tough, dried-out lobster. Nowadays, perhaps as a reaction against dreadful cooking habits, many seem to like their shellfish nearly raw. This is not to my taste, but I do want my morsels moist, tender, and sweet. As stated earlier, this shouldn't be difficult once you are familiar with the simple methods explained in this book. Fortunately, the endless variety of seafood and recipes for it means that every palate is sure to be satisfied.

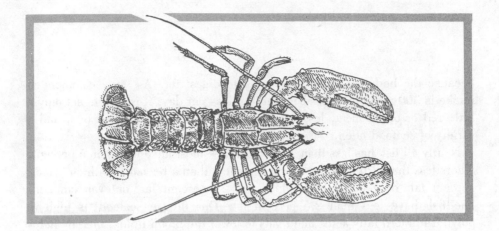

Seafood and Health

SEAFOOD IS GREAT FOOD FOR OLD AND YOUNG, SINCE IT IS SO EASILY DIGESTED, AND SO healthful. Fish and shellfish are variously rich in vitamins; high-quality protein; major minerals such as calcium, phosphorus, magnesium, and potassium; and trace minerals such as iron, copper, zinc, iodine, vitamin B_{12}, folic acid, fluoride, and selenium. Calcium is found in those fish having bones that we eat, bones that are soft and harmless when cooked—I refer especially to canned sardines, salmon, anchovies, and pickled shad and herring. Unsaturated omega-3 fatty acids found in seafood are useful in combating high blood cholesterol levels and in preventing some other diseases. Generally speaking, fattier fish have higher levels of omega-3s—such as salmon, whitefish, and mackerel; the exception is eel with low omega-3s.

Fish and shellfish are low in calories (most have fewer than 150 calories in 3½ ounces of cooked flesh), sodium (except canned seafood preparations and smoked and cured seafood), saturated fats, and cholesterol (most have less than 100 milligrams of cholesterol in 3½ ounces of raw flesh). Recently there have been many studies on the subject of the link between high cholesterol and heart disease. The outcome is that the American Heart Association and the National Heart, Lung and Blood Institute recommend that we lower the level of cholesterol in our blood. Primarily they recommend lowering fat intake

17

because the body produces cholesterol to digest fat. As the recommended intake is 300 milligrams of cholesterol or less per day, it is best to eat only a little red or organ meat, less dairy products and high saturated oils, and a variety of seafood often.

Nearly all fish has less than 20 percent fat—most have less than 5 percent, others less than 2.5 percent, which is far less than a beefsteak, which has 37 percent fat, or a pork chop, which has 21 percent fat, or even chicken. Shellfish have less than 2.5 percent fat. This fat (in seafood) is high in polyunsaturated fatty acids and tends to lower the blood lipids, thereby helping to prevent blood clots from forming. It also helps combat arthritis, asthma, multiple sclerosis, diabetes, lupus, psoriasis, migraine; cancer of the breast, colon, pancreas; and prostate tumors.

Studies have found that the omega-3 fatty acids in seafood have been found to be of benefit to those people who eat a lot of fish. The Japanese have had very little incidence of heart disease until recently because their normal diet included fish most days. Now that they are beginning to eat like Westerners, heart disease is on the rise. In Greenland heart disease was nearly unknown, even though the Eskimo diet was not all fish, but also seal and whale. The Dutch were found to benefit from eating a fair amount of fish—even though the fish was mostly lean fish. It seems that even the smallest amount of omega-3s taken regularly combats heart disease.

Fish taste best when simply prepared—broiled, grilled, roasted, or baked in the oven, cooked in a microwave oven, poached or steamed. In general, except for the oil necessary to keep fish from sticking to a pan or grill, little added fat is needed, and of course, all the vegetable oils, including olive oils, are cholesterol free. What varies among the vegetable oils is the saturated fat. For instance, olive oil is monounsaturated. Safflower, corn, sunflower, soybean, and cotton seed oils are polyunsaturated, while coconut and palm oils are saturated. The more saturated a fat, the more cholesterol your body will produce.

Don't deep-fry or sauté *high-fat* fish (in fat) for it does nothing for their taste or your health.

Recently mussels, oysters, scallops, and clams have been discovered to have far less cholesterol than previously thought because the plant sterols in them (which work against cholesterol) had been erroneously counted as cholesterol. Crab and lobster have about the same cholesterol count as chicken with its skin removed (75–90 milligrams per 3½ ounces). As a point of reference for all fish and shellfish, two large egg yolks have 550 milligrams of cholesterol.

Despite the common fallacy that shellfish is high in cholesterol, you should know that:

• All shellfish have less than 2.5 percent fat when raw. The percentage of fat will alter depending on the cooking method and vary according to the season and other factors.
• It is all right to eat moderate amounts of shellfish when on a low-cholesterol diet because shellfish is low in saturated fat, but when on a strict low-cholesterol diet, stick to small portions taken infrequently.
• Most important—shellfish and fish are low in fat. A low-fat diet lowers cholesterol production in our bodies. You can safely eat a variety of seafood, which is what most people do naturally, without raising your cholesterol level. Even though some seafood are high in cholesterol, many are high in omega-3s, which combat it. You can consider cutting down your fat intake in other foods so that you can benefit from the fattier fish and their omega-3 fatty acids.

The following tables on fat, cholesterol, and omega-3 content have been compiled from several sources, which are listed in the bibliography on page 450.

I have found that various sources may give slightly different figures. There are three main reasons for this: there are natural variables that occur between individual fishes; there are differences within each fish tested (some sections are more fatty than others, for instance); and modes of testing vary somewhat. However, the following tables give us relatively accurate and valuable guides.

FAT CONTENT OF RAW FISH
Lean Fish (less than 5 percent fat)

FISH	PERCENTAGE OF FAT	FISH	PERCENTAGE OF FAT
Anchovy, fresh	4.8	Mullet	3.8
Bass		Perch	
black sea	2.0	ocean	1.6
freshwater	2.0	yellow	0.9
striped	2.3	Pike	
white	3.7	northern	0.7
Blackfish (tautog)	0.2	walleye	1.2
Blowfish (cooked)	0.7	Pollock	0.9
Catfish		Porgy	2.7
freshwater	4.4	Redfish, red drum	1.0
ocean	2.9	Rockfish	1.6
Cod and scrod		Roughy, orange	0.3
Atlantic	0.7	Salmon	
Pacific	0.6	chum	4.2
Croaker	3.2	pink	3.4
Cusk	0.7	Sea robin	not
Dolphinfish (mahi-			available
mahi)	0.7	Sea trout	3.6
Drum, black	1.5	Shark	4.5
Flounder	1.2	Sheepshead	2.4
Groupers	1.0	Skate	1.3
Haddock	0.7	Smelt	2.4
Hake	0.7	Snappers	1.3
Halibut	2.3	Sole	1.2
Jacks	2.2	Sunfish	0.7
Kingfish, southern and		Swordfish	4.0
northern	1.8	Tilapia	2.5
Lingcod	1.1	Tilefish	2.3
Mackerel, king	2.0	Trout	
Monkfish	1.5	rainbow	3.4
		brook	2.5

FISH	PERCENTAGE OF FAT	FISH	PERCENTAGE OF FAT
Tuna		Weakfish (sea trout)	3.6
bigeye	1.6	Whiting	
bluefin	4.9	Atlantic	1.3
skipjack	2.7	Pacific	1.3
yellowfin	0.9	Wolffish	2.8

Fish with Moderate (5 percent to 10 percent) or High (more than 10 percent) Fat Content

Fish with high fat content are also high in omega-3 fatty acids.

FISH	PERCENTAGE OF FAT	FISH	PERCENTAGE OF FAT
Amberjack	8.7	Sablefish, blackcod	14.2
Anchovy, canned or		Salmon	
salted	9.7	Atlantic	6.3
Bluefish	6.5	coho	6.0
Buffalofish	16.6	sockeye	8.6
Butterfish	8.0	king	10.4
Carp	5.6	Sardines	6.8
Dogfish, spiny	11.4	Shad	13.8
Eels (other than con-		Spot	6.1
ger eel)	15.8	Sturgeon	5.2
Herring		Trout, lake	9.4
Atlantic	9.0	Tuna	
Pacific	13.9	albacore	7.2
Mackerel		bonito	5.5
Atlantic	13.9	Whitefish	5.9
Spanish	6.3	Yellowtail, farmed in	
Pompano, Atlantic	9.5	Japan	9.9

CHOLESTEROL CONTENT OF SHELLFISH

The numbers indicate the cholesterol content (in milligrams) of 3½ ounces (100 grams) raw flesh. The recommended daily cholesterol intake is 300 milligrams or less. Here in order of least to most.

SHELLFISH	MILLIGRAMS OF CHOLESTEROL IN 3½ OUNCES (100 GRAMS) RAW FLESH	SHELLFISH	MILLIGRAMS OF CHOLESTEROL IN 3½ OUNCES (100 GRAMS) RAW FLESH
Soft-shell clam	25	Spiny lobster	70
Mussel	28	Blue crab	78
Scallop	33	Abalone	85
Quahog clam	34	Northern Atlantic	
Sea scallop	36	lobster	95
King crab	42	Razor clam	107
Pacific oyster	47	Crawfish	139
Octopus	48	Shrimp	152
Eastern oyster	55	Squid	233
Dungeness crab	59	Sea urchin	498
Conch and whelk	65		

OMEGA-3 CONTENT OF SHELLFISH

The numbers indicate the omega-3 content (in grams) of 3½ ounces (100 grams) raw flesh. Only EPA (eicosapentaenoic acid) and DHA (docosahexaenoic acid) are included in the omega-3 values. Here in order of most to least.

SHELLFISH	MILLIGRAMS	SHELLFISH	MILLIGRAMS
Pacific oyster	0.68	Razor clam	0.26
Squid	0.49	Belon oyster	0.24
Shrimp	0.48	Quahog clam	0.24
Olympia oyster	0.45	Soft-shell clam	0.24
Mussels	0.44	Northern lobster	0.20
Eastern oyster	0.44	Sea scallop	0.19
Spiny lobster	0.37	Crawfish	0.17
Snow crab	0.37	Octopus	0.16
Blue crab	0.32	Bay and calico scallops	0.13
Dungeness crab	0.31	Abalone	0.04

SAFE SEAFOOD

It almost goes without saying that the first criterion when cooking and eating seafood is that it be fresh. Simply put, bad seafood smells bad and should not be eaten.

We know that bacterial growth hastens contamination, and we have to learn how to combat it.

Tips for Careful Seafood Cookery

• Handle seafood properly, making sure that utensils and boards are clean to prevent cross-contamination that can provide a breeding ground for salmonella. For instance, always clean a board well after it has had chicken on it.

• Always buy from a reputable source. If you catch fish, treat it scrupulously well from the moment you catch it.

• If you garner your own shellfish, check with the department of fish and game or local health authorities to be sure that the water is safe.

• Be extra careful when eating raw fish and shellfish, particularly raw bivalves. When buying bivalves, you may ask to see the tag held at the fish store that verifies that the shellfish came from clean, tested waters. The waters are identified on the tag.

• Eat a variety of seafood rather than one kind exclusively.

• People who are already suffering from disease or are otherwise debilitated should limit their seafood intake to once a week.

• Cook seafood to 140 degrees F or freeze it for two days to kill parasites.

• Contaminants can collect in the viscera of a fish, in some of its fatty areas (such as the belly flaps), in the dark fat muscle that runs along its lateral line, and to some extent in its skin. Avoid eating these parts if there is any possibility that the fish may be contaminated.

Besides the natural spoiling process, the environment can compromise the safety of even otherwise fresh fish. Bivalves such as clams, mussels, and oysters, which are sedentary creatures, filter their food from the water, so they may be infected by pollutants in the water. Among the polluting effects is red tide, a natural phenomenon that occurs worldwide. Though called red tide, it is neither red nor a tide, but a combination of nutrients, carbon dioxide, cool waters flowing into warm, and sunlight that all contribute to an algae bloom. Red tide is of much concern in Maine and around San Francisco, especially during the summer months. Though not all red or brown tides are toxic for fish and shellfish, the creatures are poisonous to humans and can cause paralytic shellfish poisoning (PSP), which is usually lethal. The various potential dangers are greatest when bivalves are eaten raw. But I must emphasize that waters are tested regularly and advisories are put out when there is any danger.

Pollution may also be in the form of harmful chemicals or pesticides that drain into water. Such chemicals include PCB—polychlorinated biphenyl

—deposits of which are found in rivers where fish spawn; PCBs concentrate in the guts of a fish, especially in the liver, the strip of dark fat found along the lateral line, and the fatty flesh of the belly. There are advisories (in New Jersey) against eating large bluefish because they are at the top of the food chain and have probably eaten contaminated fish. No such advisories exist regarding small blues, those up to 6 pounds. Striped bass from the Chesapeake Bay area and around New York also are banned. Restrictions on their catch were instituted a few years ago, partly because they have been over-fished, and also because they spawn in rivers and thus have been affected by PCBs. Paradoxically, sportsmen are allowed to keep bass that are at least 36 inches long—those that are probably the most highly affected by the PCBs.

Parasites, tiny worms of the Anisakidae family are sometimes found in saltwater fish, such as mackerel, herring, rockfish, cod, and haddock. As a precaution, a fair amount of cod and haddock is candled—fillets are laid on top of light boxes so the parasites can be seen and removed. Other parasites of the diphyllobothrium species can be present in freshwater fish, such as pike, perch, and salmon. Salmon, although most often caught in the sea, do (in the wild) spend time in streams, rivers, and lakes. Lightly smoked or cured fish may also be affected. The tiny worms can be killed by cooking fish to 140 degrees F or freezing them for two days. Very few people have been affected; only fifty cases have been reported in the United States since the records began, back in the 1960s, with no deaths.*

Most poisons are resistant to heat, so cooking will not guarantee safety.

Scombroid or saurine poisoning can occur in jack, mackerel, tuna, swordfish, and dolphinfish (mahi-mahi), fish that are usually perfectly safe to eat. This poisoning develops when the fish are left in warm temperatures and not chilled when caught. A bad smell is a clue to scombroid poisoning. Symptoms are headache, skin rash, and upset stomach. Saurine poisoning may be combated with antihistamine drugs.

Ciguatera poisoning is due to a toxin that concentrates in large fish that probably get it by consuming smaller fish that eat affected phytoplankton. Jacks, snappers, groupers, and parrot fish are some of the fish that are affected. The toxin can't be discerned, for it concentrates in the liver and viscera. Ciguatera is a much greater problem in the Caribbean than in North American waters.

---

* *The Dangers of Eating Raw Fish* by Peter M. Schantz, V.M.D., Ph.D. The New England Journal of Medicine, April 27, 1989.

Botulism occurs in canned or vacuum-packed seafood. In normal processing these fish are heated to specific temperatures for specific times in order to kill the organism that produces the botulism toxin. If botulism does occur, it is most certainly because the can or box has the smallest of holes in it, which allows the organism to enter and grow.

In short, relatively few people get sick from eating fish and shellfish and most cases probably are due to poor food handling, since waters are monitored often and fish and shellfish are tested.

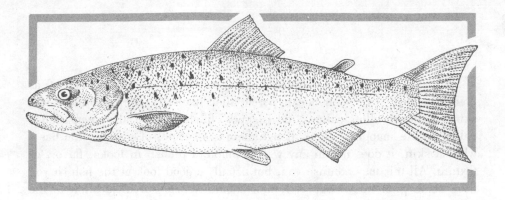

Buying and Storing Fish and Shellfish

SOME NAMES FISH GO BY

IDENTIFYING FISH MAY, AT FIRST GLANCE, SEEM TO BE DIFFICULT. THERE ARE MANY SPECIES within each family of fish or shellfish and a species known by one name may be given other, perhaps confusing, names in the fish store. Sometimes these are colloquial names used in particular localities, which may differ from the names you are used to. Sometimes a fish with an uncatchy name—such as pollock—will bear a grander label, such as "Boston bluefish," although a pollock in no way resembles a bluefish. Fish stores may give a species a more becoming name or the name of a similar, possibly more popular, fish. Or a fishmonger may aim to pass off a cheaper fish as a more expensive one. This is illegal, of course; the Food and Drug Administration has a list of approved market names.* In the fish-by-fish profiles in Part III of this book, you will find the vernacular and local names given to the different species as well as the approved market names.

---

* The Food and Drug Administration's Guide to Acceptable Market Names for Food Fish Sold in Interstate Commerce, 1988. Superintendent of Documents, U.S. Government Printing Office, Washington, D.C.

Many fish with even the slightest tinge of red on the skin are passed off as "red snapper." I've seen ocean perch fillets called "snapper" fillets and skinned tilefish fillets called "red snapper" fillets. I have also seen tilefish called "white snapper," and although there is a species of snapper that has a whitish skin, it does not in any way resemble a tilefish in looks, flavor, or texture. All this may confuse you, but usually a good look at the fish (if you have some prior knowledge of how it should appear) or a question to the fishmonger will help you figure out the correct name.

In using the word *correct* I mean the common or usual name established by law. Each species and its family have scientific Latin names, and fish stores and suppliers may use their own market names for different species. Monkfish, for example, is called "belly fish" by fish purveyors. Monkfish is often referred to by its French name, *lotte*, especially in restaurants.

The word *squid* is subject to translation as well, and squid are often known as *calamari*, the Italian name, or as *calmar*, the French, or as *calamar*, the Spanish.

Peter Redmayne, editor and publisher of *The Seafood Leader*, a seafood magazine published in Seattle, Washington, writing in an editorial for that magazine (Spring 1987), noted some name changes he had seen in restaurants. The New Zealand fish called permit had been served as "New Zealand pompano," but there are no true pompano in New Zealand waters. Another restaurant offered "Chesapeake Bay pollock" because the manager said it was trying to give the "poor pollock some pizzazz." (Pollock is not available as far south as the Chesapeake Bay). Redmayne also heard about some Alaska pollock that was being passed off as "Georges Bank cod" by a distributor. Another distributor took arrowtooth flounder—a fish with little going for it because it cooks up soft and thus is usually used as mink food or fertilizer—repacked it in boxes marked "petrale sole," and marked it up two dollars a pound.

Very likely you will see labels that say "fresh fish." Well, it had better be fresh; or if it was frozen, it should have been frozen properly, and if defrosted, defrosted properly. (More about frozen fish later.) I have seen the word *fancy* on some labels in Seattle markets. This in fact means previously frozen, now defrosted. Hah! Other markets are more honest and use labels that read "previously frozen."

On the positive side, more and more markets are identifying the source of seafood—the name of the lake, river, bay, ocean, or state it was fished from.

This is a good practice and tends to increase our interest in all seafood. And the FDA is now insisting that fish stores and suppliers use correct nomenclature.

When you are at the fish store you see a great variety of fish and shellfish in many different forms on display. It's often easiest to look for a familiar fish in a familiar form, but there are more adventurous ways to buy fish. It is possible to group fish according to their different forms (fillets, steaks, etc.) and according to their textures and tastes, each of which suggests cooking methods that are most suitable for it.

Once you've become familiar with the cooking methods and the fish and which is most appropriate for which, shopping for seafood and cooking it will become very simple. For instance, you may decide on a mild-tasting fish that is easy to sauté or a more emphatically flavored fish to broil. Or you will soon learn that when you see a fresh-looking, firm, and flavorful fish you can grill or blacken it.

USEFUL TERMS YOU WILL NEED TO KNOW

Drawn fish: Fish that have been gutted.

Dressed fish: Whole fish that have been gutted and scaled and from which the gills have been removed. They are ready to cook. Usually the fins have been cut off as well, which I don't like. Cook whole fish with their fins, for they are part and parcel of the fish.

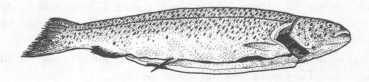

Pan-dressed fish: A pan-dressed fish is a fish that has been gutted and scaled. Its head and fins have been cut off and the tail has been trimmed. Pan-dressing is usually done to small fish that will fit in a medium-sized frying pan.

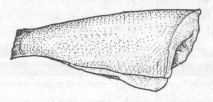

Fillets: Fillets are boneless sections or pieces of fish flesh, cut from both sides of the fish. Fillets are just the ticket for those who want the pleasure of eating boneless fish.

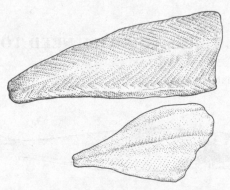

Filleted fish abound at the fish store. The fillets may be skinned or not. Fillets come in varying sizes. You can, for example, buy a whole large salmon fillet or part of one.

Fillets are conducive to all sorts of cooking methods, and you will learn the many different ways of handling and cutting fillets from this book.

Butterflied or split fish: These fish that have been split open and boned out or not, producing two sides of the fish joined by the belly skin or the back (see pages 67 and 68).

Steaks, loins, wheels, and center cuts: Steaks come near to solving the bone problem too. They make fine individual portions.

The flesh of a steak is cut against the grain, sliced straight through the backbone, and only a small cross section of the backbone is left attached to the flesh.

Most large roundfish—salmon, cod, and tilefish, for example—can be cut into steaks, as can halibut, a large flatfish. Steaks from these fish should be cut 1 inch thick. Other smaller flatfish may also be cut into steaks to good effect, though these should be smaller—¼ to ½ inch thick.

Tuna are cut into large fillets off the central bone, called "loins," and then into boneless, skinless steaks. Sharks and swordfish are cut into "wheels" and "center cuts" from which steaks are then cut; this practice is unique to these large varieties. To stay moist, tender, and attractive when cooked, these steaks should be cut 1 to 1¼ inches thick.

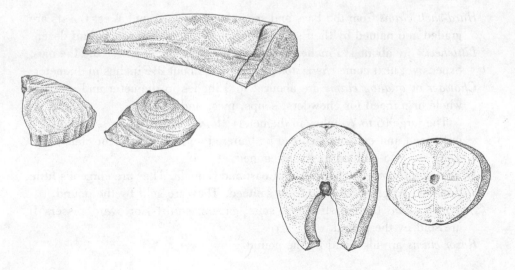

Chunks (*roasts*): Chunks, also known as roasts, may not be visible to you when you visit the fish store. Chunks are cut from the heaviest part of a large fish which typically weighs between 5 and 10 pounds. These are fish that the fishmonger cuts steaks from, such as salmon, lingcod, cod, pollock, and tilefish.

You can ask the fishmonger to cut you a chunk weighing 1½ to 4 pounds or more. You can also ask him to bone it out or you can do this yourself by following instructions on page 69. The chunk can be stuffed with vegetables, herbs, and a fillet of another fish (for contrast) and then baked, roasted, poached, or cooked on an outdoor grill.

HOW SHELLFISH ARE GRADED AND SOLD

Clams

Hard-shell clams from the bays and seas along the East and West Coasts are graded and named by their size. They are sold by the dozen or half dozen.

Littlenecks are about 1½ inches in diameter and are the smallest and the most expensive; next come *cherrystones*, which are about 2½ inches in diameter.

Chowder or *quahog clams* are about 4 to 5 inches in diameter and are sold whole or minced for chowders, soups, pies, and fritters.

The large (6 to 7 inches in diameter) *Atlantic surf, bar,* or *sea clams* are processed and cut into strips to be battered and deep-fried for clam rolls. They are also minced and sold canned.

Manila clams come from the West Coast and Canada. They are gorgeous little thin-shelled clams that are best sautéed. They are sold by the pound.

Soft-shell clams (called steamers, softs, gapers, squirts, or even "pissers"!) are sold by the pound.

Razor clams are also sold by the pound.

Geoduck clams (pronounced "gooeyduck") from the northwest Pacific are very large, weighing 2 pounds or more each. They are sold by the pound, and their neck and strip flesh is also sold by the pound.

Conch

Conch are sold by the piece when alive in their shells. Conch meat, cooked or raw, is often frozen. Conch meat is sold by the pound.

Crabs

Crabs are sold alive or cooked. Crabmeat picked from cooked crabs is sold in different grades as follows:

Lumpmeat or *backfin crabmeat* consists of large whole lumps from the body and the backfin.

Special crabmeat consists of lumpmeat and flakes from the rest of the body.

Flake or regular crabmeat consists of all the meat from the whole body, except the choice lumpmeat.

Claw crabmeat consists of only the meat from the claws.

　　All the above is sold by the pound; most is pasteurized and canned.

Cocktail claws are cooked crab claws with shells partially removed. They are usually available frozen and are sold by the pound.

Soft-shell crabs from Maryland are graded according to size and sold by the piece. They are sold both live and frozen, but I think soft-shell crabs should still be alive when you buy them. Often the fish stores clean them in advance, thereby killing them. I prefer to view the live crabs and have the fishmonger clean them in front of me, or do it myself.

　　Crabs may not be graded by the following names at your fish store but these are the names most commonly used by processors. Generally speaking, the larger they are the more expensive they are.

Whales: over 5 inches.

Jumbos: 4½ to 5 inches.

Primes: 4 to 4½ inches.

Hotel or primes: 3½ to 4 inches.

Mediums: 3 to 3½ inches.

Hard blue crabs from Maryland are known as "jimmys." The females are called "sooks." Jimmys and sooks are sold by the dozen or half dozen. Jimmys are graded by size, the largest are #1 jimmys, then come mediums.

Stone crabs are found in waters from the North Carolina coast to the Gulf of

Mexico. Claws are all that is sold of the stone crab. The claws are always previously cooked and some are frozen. Stone crabs are graded by the number of claws that make up a pound. The largest claws are the most expensive.

Dungeness crabs are sold by the pound, either live, cooked, or cooked and then frozen. Picked crabmeat is also available from these crabs, as are crab claws and legs, either attached to the body or not.

King crabs have two claws and six long walking legs. These and the shoulder meat are what is sold. Seldom sold fresh, most king crab meat is frozen or canned. The legs, some of which have the shell split open for easy eating, and the claws are sold by the pound, the larger pieces fetching higher prices. Claws, legs, and shoulders are also sold in clusters. The most expensive picked king crab meat is from the upper part of the legs (called the *merus meat*), followed by the meat from the claws and the lower part of the legs, which are edged in red; the least choice meat is the white meat from the shoulder and other body meat. *Fancy meat* refers to a mixture of these three. *Salad meat* consists of chunks of red-edged and white meat and the smaller pieces from the body.

Snow crabs, also called tanner crabs, have ten legs, two of which end in claws. The shells are much smoother than those of the king crab. The claws, legs, and shoulders are sold in clusters, as is the case with the king crab. Meat picked from cooked snow crabs is canned or frozen. Leg meat is the most expensive.

Jonah, rock, and *red crabs,* all from the northern Atlantic Ocean, are not often sold in fish stores at the moment, because they yield less meat than other crabs. The claws are processed and usually sold frozen, or in cans as picked meat.

Other Shellfish

Crawfish or *crayfish*, which are bought alive, are graded by size—the larger they are, the higher their price. Whole live crawfish are sold by the pound. The tail meat is sold fresh or frozen by the pound.

Gooseneck barnacles, mostly found off the coast of the Pacific Northwest, are sold by the pound, live.

North Atlantic lobsters are sold by the pound, live, or cooked. Cooked meat from these lobsters, sold by the pound, is expensive, as is canned meat. Live these lobsters are graded by size: *Chicks* or *chicken lobsters* weigh around a pound; *culls* have one claw and are less expensive. Lobsters weighing 1 to 2½ pounds usually cost the same per pound, although prices vary according to the season or at holiday times. Very large north Atlantic lobsters may cost less per pound.

Spiny or *rock lobsters*, from cold and warm waters, have no claws, so mainly the tails are sold. The tails are mostly frozen and are graded by their weight, which ranges from 2 ounces to 2 pounds. Many are imported from South Africa, Australia, and New Zealand. They are also available from Florida and farther south.

Northern Atlantic mussels are sold by the pound. The number per pound ranges from 8 to 18, approximately. They are not graded by size.

New Zealand green-tipped mussels are also sold by the pound, usually cooked and frozen.

Octopus are usually frozen; they weigh 1 to 4 pounds. They are sold by the pound.

Oysters are sold in shell or shucked. They are also shucked, breaded, and frozen, or shucked and canned. Live in-shell oysters are sold by the dozen, sometimes by the pound. Suppliers grade them by size, but you may not see them graded in the store. Different species and different-sized oysters command different prices.

Periwinkles are sold by the pound. There may be as many as 60 to the pound.

Scallops are sold by the pound in the United States. The adductor muscle is all we eat of the scallop here. The shell and the rest of the animal are thrown away at sea when the scallop is shucked. In Europe scallops are sold by the piece, most often with each scallop still lying on its bottom flat shell. *Sea scallops* are the largest: there are 6 to 25 per pound. There are 50 to 80 *bay scallops* per pound. *Calico scallops* are smaller: there can be 100 to the pound. (Beware—these are sometimes called bay scallops.)

Sea urchins are sold live by the piece or by the pound. Japanese sources sell the meat (*gonads* or *roe*) of these animals already shucked, lying on little wooden boards. Each board holds about 20 pieces, equal to half a pound.

Shrimp are sold by the pound, except of course when canned. They are graded by size. Most shrimp are previously frozen; they come headless with shell on or off. They are defrosted before being sold and are sometimes cooked, peeled, and deveined for your convenience.

The largest, 8 to 15 to the pound, are the most expensive, and they may be called anything from *extra-colossal*, to *colossal*, to *jumbo*. There is no hard and fast rule about how fishmongers name the sizes—the names are given quite arbitrarily. Other grades available in stores are *large* (16 to 35 per pound), *medium* (36 to 50 per pound), and *small* (51 to 60 per pound). There can be as many as 400 to the pound. Fresh head-on prawns (freshwater shrimp) are sold by the pound: there are about 12 to the pound.

Squid are available both fresh and frozen, although most are cleaned and frozen at sea. Fresh squid may have been cleaned at the fish store. Squid are sold by the pound. Heads, tentacles, and bodies are sold.

FRESHNESS

How to Recognize It

First of all, it is best to go to the fish store with no set idea of the fish or shellfish you want to prepare in mind, for it is pretty obvious that the freshest seafood is the one you want to buy and eat. I hardly ever plan a seafood meal ahead; the freshest is what I buy and serve. The whole experience of eating fresh fish is quite different from eating something that was taken from the water a few too many days ago and then was not carefully gutted or, most importantly, thoroughly chilled. Oddly enough, such fish are often called "old" fish, even though they may have been quite young when they were caught! Ideally, fish should be enjoyed within 48 hours after capture.

Americans and Canadians live in large countries. Fishing boats in these countries, in order to realize a large enough catch for their huge markets, must stay at sea a day or more at a time. What fishmongers then call "fresh" may already be a week—or more—out of the water. However, there are many day fishing boats, especially on the coast of Massachusetts, New York, Connecticut, and New Jersey.

The depressing fact is that most of our fish reach us after many days out of water, but if fish are properly handled they can still be excellent. Many fish companies are making the right sort of effort to get fish to the consumer in less time nowadays, and consumer tastes are forcing the suppliers to ensure better quality. An example of this is the recent innovation of bleeding, gutting, icing down, and boxing fish on board fishing vessels, initiated some time ago in Europe and Japan and now in New England. This method results in delivery of superior cod and haddock.

Optimum handling begins the moment the fish is caught. Fish guru Jon

Rowley, who helps restaurants and fish stores buy the best seafood, describes the process: "The fish must be stunned and bled immediately after it is caught. Then it must be drawn—that is, gutted, washed, and chilled—*before* rigor [stiffness] sets in. The fish must go into rigor slowly and come out of rigor slowly. A fish kept in rigor for six days is the same as if it came right out of the water." If you catch your own fish, dress it before rigor sets in and you will be amazed at how wonderful it tastes.

All fish have some bacteria on their skin, in their gills, and in their guts. The flesh of a fish is slightly acidic during rigor, so bacteria growth is inhibited, but bacteria spread into fish quickly after rigor passes. The growth of bacteria is greatly reduced when fish are gutted and properly iced or refrigerated by the supplier at 32 degrees F (0 degrees C). Unfortunately, our home refrigerators are set at around 39 degrees F (4 degrees C), so, once home, fish should not be stored uncooked longer than a day. Some markets sell ungutted fish, which is not a good idea if they are kept for any length of time, even if properly chilled. (Exceptions include farmed fish such as striped bass, which have a good shelf life. Also note that freshwater fish have a longer shelf life than marine fish; the fact that they are bred in warm water means that the bacteria are better controlled when the fish are iced and refrigerated.) Ask the fishmonger to gut the fish for you right there and then, or follow the simple directions on page 55 and page 73.

Buy from reliable stores where the fish are displayed on a lot of ice or in a good refrigerated state. The place should smell fresh and be well patronized by the local community so that there is abundant turnover.

Some live shellfish, such as lobsters and Dungeness crabs, should be kept in tanks of running salt water. Live clams, oysters, mussels, crawfish, sea urchins, periwinkles, conch, and abalone should be refrigerated, preferably in airy sacks, so that they stay alive. They are displayed on ice. Soft-shell crabs are kept on a bed of seaweed in flat boxes. Hard-shell blue crabs are kept in bushel baskets.

The store display should look bright and lively, with sparkling ice, glistening skins, brilliant fish eyes, and translucent fish fillets and steaks.

Ideally, to tell the freshness of a fish you would use smell, sight, and touch. Even if you cannot use all your senses in a store—for sanitary reasons, your server should not let you touch fish or bring it up to your nose to smell it—your eyes can tell you a lot.

The questions that follow are clues to freshness—if the answers to most of the questions are yes, then we can assume that you have chosen well:

Whole Fish

Smell Does the fish have an aroma of the sea?

An ammonia smell might be found in the cartilaginous species such as sharks, rays, and skates, but this can usually be gotten rid of by soaking methods. See the methods desired in the fish profiles in Part III of this book.

The iodine smell and flavor sometimes found in flounder and brown shrimp can be attributed to their diet.

Sight Does the fish look fresh?

Are its eyes clear and bright and flush with the surface of the head?

Are the scales (if any) shiny and intact, coated with a clear, glossy, thin mucous layer?

Are all the fins in good shape, so you know that the fish has not been mishandled?

Are the gills of a strong red color and not gray, discolored, or misshapen? A thick, gray, viscous coating is a bad sign. *Note:* Some fish are bled through the gills and this process will turn the gills pale.

Touch Is the flesh firm?

Does the flesh bounce back if you make an indentation with your finger?

Does the fish feel rigid when you pick it up? The flesh (muscles) around the backbone should still be in rigor. When the fish is first out of the water it is supple, but when rigor sets in the muscles stiffen. Later, when the fish loses this stiffness, bacteria start to invade the flesh, and the peak of freshness has passed. *Note:* Rigor can last from a few hours up to one week; if a fish struggles during capture, rigor will last a very short time.

Fillets, Steaks, and Other Cuts of Fish

Smell Does the fish have an aroma of the sea?

Sight Is the flesh unblemished with no traces of bruises or blood spots? Does it have a translucent look?

Does the flesh look firm, not flaking or falling apart due to a condition called "gaping"?

Touch Is the flesh firm?

Does the flesh bounce back if you make an indentation with your finger?

Packaged Fish

If buying packaged fish, use the above criteria as much as you can. You can smell bad fish and shellfish right through the packaging!

Smoked Fish

Smoked fish, whether packaged or not, should look moist and firm to the touch with no telltale excretions of oil or salt. They should not be dry—dryness denotes an old article. Keep them well refrigerated.

Frozen Fish and Shellfish

Frozen fish and shellfish, whether labeled "frozen" or "thawed," should look much like any packaged fresh fish. You must use the same criteria as for fresh fish when choosing it. The package must be intact, with no sign of freezer burn—drying out caused by dehydration. Freezer burn turns the flesh white and opaque, and it becomes soft and spongy. Solidly frozen fillets should look glossy, and whole fish should be carefully packaged and unblemished. *Note:* Frozen fish will turn rancid in long-term frozen storage; it has a characteristic smell and taste that is not appetizing.

Preparing and Storing Fish

If you catch fish yourself, or others bring you fresh fish, be sure that they are gutted as soon as possible and stored properly. Follow the simple instructions on page 55 and page 73 if your friends did not gut the fish. If they have been well handled—that is, if they have not been allowed to bruise themselves on the deck of the boat or on the dock, their skin has not been broken, and they have been bled, gutted, and iced down promptly—the length of time that they will taste their best has been extended. As a rule of thumb you can then keep the fish in the refrigerator up to three days before you eat them.

For a whole, drawn, dressed, or pan-dressed fish, put crushed ice into its belly cavity and use more ice to cover the outside skin. Place the fish, in an upright position as if it were still swimming, in a draining pan with holes, in a colander, or on a rack, and put this container on top of another pan so the ice moistens the skin and removes bacteria as it melts and drains away.

Restaurants use this method and I recommend it, especially if you have a big fish or a big catch. You can also store a whole dressed fish, fillet, or steak in a plastic bag (or cover it with plastic wrap) and place it in the refrigerator.

Remember that seafood should be eaten as soon as possible. It is not like beef, which can improve with age, although fish probably does improve for up to 48 hours after capture—the sweetness of the flesh intensifies in that time and then fades.

Shellfish Freshness

If you buy live shellfish, be sure they are *still* alive when you cook them.

Lobsters, crawfish, and crabs should be lively. Lobsters picked out of marine tanks should splay their legs, claws, and tails or curl their tails in. At any rate they should react! Blue crabs from the East Coast are not kept in marine tanks but Dungeness crabs from the West Coast are. Both hard- and soft-shell blue crabs are kept chilled in baskets or boxes of seaweed while crawfish are kept in sacks or boxes in a moist but cool place. All should definitely show signs of life before cooking.

Bivalve mollusks—that is, those sea creatures with two shells, such as clams, mussels, and oysters—must not have broken shells, gaping shells, empty shells, or heavy shells that might be filled with mud or sand. If they do, they should be discarded. Bivalve mollusks must have tightly closed shells. The exceptions are geoduck clams, razor clams, and soft-shell steamer clams whose siphons protrude so that they can never totally close their shells. Touch these siphons or necks, and if they retract or move a little, the creatures are alive. With clams, mussels, and oysters, if the shells are slightly open but close after a hard knock, you may be sure they are alive. When oysters, clams, and mussels are sold shucked, the plump creatures should lie in plenty of their own clear, natural liquid.

The sea scallop we buy is the round adductor muscle that fastens the two beautiful shells of the scallop together. Scallops are mostly shucked at sea and are therefore dead when we buy them. They must glisten, be firm, and smell sweet. This applies also to the smaller bay and calico scallops. If they are packaged, put the package to your nose.

Univalves, such as periwinkles, conch, and abalone, each have only one shell. They are considered sea snails because each has a single foot that rests on rocks. A periwinkle or conch has an *operculum;* a hard protective shield that covers the opening to the shell when its foot is withdrawn. When you touch the foot or operculum it should move slightly, showing that the creature is alive.

Sea urchins have spherical shells, called *tests*, covered with spines. If the prickly spines move when touched, the urchins are alive. You can buy sea urchin roe or gonads (*uni*) packaged on little wooden trays from Japanese markets. There are five little tongues of roe, colored bright orange-yellow, within each sea urchin. They should look and smell fresh.

Most shrimp are sold frozen; 65 to 70 percent are imported. Most are sold as raw frozen tails (with shells), and in fish markets they are called green (raw) headless shrimp. Some farmed freshwater prawns—colorful blue shrimp from the South, the Caribbean, Hawaii (the largest domestic producer), and Brazil—are beginning to appear in New York markets with lingering signs of life, if garnered the night before you meet up with them. In California and Hawaii some are kept alive in tanks. Some live white shrimp are now available in New York City's Chinatown. It is essential that *fresh* shrimp and prawns be eaten as soon as possible because their flesh disintegrates quickly and becomes soft and mushy.

Whole raw shrimp with heads on come from Maine and the Gulf of Mexico at different seasons of the year and should look fresh, colorful, and in pristine condition. The deterioration of a head-on shrimp is quick—pull off the head and it will last longer. However, when cooked you will miss sucking out the "fat" (liver, roe, and pancreas) in the head, which tastes so good!

Most of the shrimp we eat have come from the warm-water oceans of the world, and nearly all are frozen headless, but with shells on. Whether in their shells or not, they must look shiny, moist, translucent, all of a piece, uncrushed, and bright. Some raw shrimp have such pink shells that they may be mistaken for cooked shrimp. Cooked shrimp must look firm to the touch, no longer translucent but not dried out—a dry appearance denotes overcooking and toughness. This also applies to cooked lobster and crabmeat.

Squid, cuttlefish, and octopus are sold fresh, frozen, or defrosted. One must look for good color—that is, a creamy white flesh under the outer membrane, which is brown on the summer Illex (short-finned) squid and is white on the winter Loligo (long-finned) squid but turns purple with age; look for the same creamy white flesh when the squid are cleaned. Cuttlefish have varied colored membranes, ranging from a brownish beige to sepia to a dark bluish tinge. Under the membrane should be the same creamy white flesh as the squid. On the octopus look for gray skin (which turns white when cooked) and white flesh.

All packaged crabmeat is cooked before it is sold, and the shells are picked clean. Fresh crabmeat should be kept very cold and used as soon as possible. Canned *pasteurized* crabmeat lasts several months in the refrigerator.

Dungeness crabs from the West Coast are sold live from tanks, but they are mostly sold whole cooked, in sections, or as picked meat. Some Dungeness crab meat is frozen, as are whole crabs.

Snow crab (also called tanner and marketed as queen crab in Atlantic Canada) and king crab are cooked and sold mostly frozen in the shell or as picked crabmeat. It is hard to tell when shell-on crab legs are of good quality for obvious reasons—you can't see the flesh inside. However, when they are sold split open, you can see whether the flesh is moist and shows no signs of freezer burn.

Red, rock, and Jonah crabs from the Atlantic are mostly used for picked crabmeat, although they are sometimes available alive. Red rock crabs from the West Coast are very similar to Jonah and rock crabs.

Claws are all that is sold of the stone crab. Either the left or right claw is picked off a live crab, which is then thrown back into the water to grow another claw. These picked claws are immediately cooked, cooled, and chilled. A good deal of the crop is also frozen. Buy only claws that look freshly caught and cooked. Barring breaking open the shell, the only way to know their freshness is by smell. You want no odor, or at best one of the sea.

How to Store Live Shellfish

Live shellfish need air and moisture. Store them in the refrigerator in open plastic or paper bags, preferably with seaweed or wet paper towels to keep them moist. Cook lobsters the day you buy them. You can pretty safely keep mussels, oysters, and clams refrigerated one or two days before eating.

Freezing Tips

It is hard for me to be enthusiastic about freezing seafood unless it is flash-frozen in supercold commercial freezers at −40 degrees F (−40 degrees C); the home freezer proves inadequate. The Japanese freeze tuna fish and may keep it frozen for a year before thawing it for sashimi. The home freezer that only reaches 0 degrees F (−18 degrees C) can be used to store previously frozen seafood or to store fresh seafood for a short time—a week for fatty fish, a month for lean fish and shellfish. If you plan to eat raw fish, freeze it for two days to kill any parasites it may have. Few fish have parasites—for further information see page 17.

Defrost seafood slowly in the refrigerator. Don't hurry the process, except by defrosting in the microwave oven. Don't defrost the seafood all the way through in the microwave, however, otherwise it will start to cook on the outside edges. Complete the defrosting at room temperature.

Before freezing fish, all you need to do is clean it (gut it and remove the gills). Then wrap it well with freezer wrap or put it in a heavy plastic Ziploc bag, making sure it is airtight to prevent freezer burn. Push or suck the air out before sealing the bag. Put shellfish, such as scallops and squid in Ziploc bags also. Don't freeze previously frozen shrimp.

Another good method of freezing fish is to glaze it with several layers of water. Dip the fish in water and lay it on a tray in the freezer, and when it has frozen, dip it again. Repeat this operation several times until the fish has an ⅛-inch ice coating on it. Store it in the freezer in a Ziploc bag.

Yet another way to freeze an appropriately sized cleaned fish is to put it in a clean milk carton and fill the carton with water. Freeze the container, fish and all.

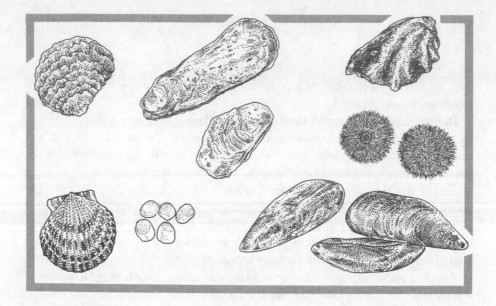

How Much to Buy

THE AMOUNT OF FISH YOU BUY DOES, OF COURSE, DEPEND MUCH ON APPETITE. WHEN BUYING whole fish with head and tail, you need 10 ounces to 1¼ pounds per portion. Portions of filleted fish can vary from 3 ounces to ½ pound per person. Some fish lose more water than others in cooking, particularly skinned filleted fish, and one has to compensate for this loss by buying more than usual.

The fishmonger can usually help you with the amount to buy for a certain number of people, but when buying whole fish you need to be aware of those fish that lose water in cooking, those that are heavy with bones, and those with large, heavy heads. In general you do not need to buy as much of rich and flavorful fish as you do of milder and leaner fish. The amount you buy is your choice; however, you can refer to the guide below and, of course, to the different recipes.

FISH	PAN-DRESSED OR WHOLE	FILLET	STEAK	CHUNK
	AMOUNT PER PERSON			
Anchovy	¾–1 lb.			
Bass:				
black sea, white sea, white (fresh water)	1 lb.	5–8 oz.		
smallmouth, large-mouth	1 lb.	6–8 oz.		
striped (both wild and fresh water)	1 lb.	6–8 oz.	6–8 oz. (wild)	¾ lb. (wild)
Blackfish (tautog); also called hardhead, black trout, steelhead)	1 lb.	6–8 oz.		
Blowfish (sea squab, chicken of the sea)		6–8 oz. (tail ends)		
Bluefish (snapper, tailor, chopper)	¾–1 lb.	6–8 oz.		¾ lb.
Buffalofish		6–7 oz.		
Butterfish, Pacific and Atlantic	8–10 oz.			
Carp		6–7 oz.	6–7 oz.	
Catfish (channel, white, brown, bullhead, flathead)	¾ lb.	6–10 oz.		
Cod and scrod:				
Atlantic cod and scrod	¾ lb.	6–8 oz.	6–8 oz.	
Pacific gray cod	¾ lb.	6–8 oz.	6–8 oz.	
salt cod in dry state	¾ lb.	3–4 oz.		
Croaker	¾ lb.			
Cusk	¾–1 lb.	6–10 oz.		
Dolphinfish (mahi-mahi)		4–8 oz.		
Drum (croaker)	¾ lb.	6–10 oz.		
Eel	2–3 oz.	7 oz.	7 oz.	

FISH	AMOUNT PER PERSON			
	PAN-DRESSED OR WHOLE	FILLET	STEAK	CHUNK
Flounder (summer, Southern, Gulf, black-back, fluke, yellowtail, etc.)	1–1¼ lbs.	6–8 oz.		
Grouper	¾–1 lb.	6–8 oz.		¾ lb.
Haddock	¾ lb.	6–8 oz.	6–8 oz.	
Hake, white	¾ lb.	6–8 oz.	6–8 oz.	
Hake, red (ling)	¾ lb.	4–8 oz.		
Halibut	¾–1 lb.	6–8 oz.	6–8 oz.	
Herring, Atlantic and Pacific	½–¾ lb.	8 oz.		
Kingfish, Atlantic and Gulf (croaker)	¾ lb.	6–8 oz.	6–8 oz.	
Lingcod	¾ lb.	6–8 oz.	6–8 oz.	
Mackerel:				
Atlantic, Pacific	¾–1 lb.	6–8 oz.		
king mackerel (king-fish)	¾ lb.		6–8 oz.	
Spanish mackerel		6–8 oz.	6–8 oz.	
jack mackerel	¾ lb.			
chub mackerel	¾ lb.			
Japanese mackerel	¾ lb.			
Mahi-mahi (dolphin-fish)		4–8 oz.		
Marlin		4–8 oz.		
Monkfish (anglerfish, bellyfish, etc.)	¾ lb.	8 oz.		
Mullet, striped	¾–1 lb.	6–8 oz.		
Ocean perch, Atlantic		6–8 oz.		
Perch, yellow	½–1 lb.	6–8 oz.		
Pike	¾–1 lb.	6–8 oz.		
Pollock, Atlantic, Pacific, Alaskan	¾–1 lb.	6–8 oz.		

FISH	AMOUNT PER PERSON			
	PAN-DRESSED OR WHOLE	FILLET	STEAK	CHUNK
Pompano	¾–1 lb.	6–8 oz.		
Porgy (scup)	¾–1 lb.	6–8 oz.		
Redfish		6–10 oz.		
Rockfish:				
Atlantic (redfish, ocean perch)	¾–1 lb.	6–8 oz.		
Pacific (black, canary, orange, yellow, widow, blue, yellowtail bocaccio, rock cod)	¾–1 lb.	6–8 oz.		
Roughy, orange		6–8 oz.		
Sable (black cod—butterfish when filleted)	¾ lb.	6 oz.	7 oz.	⅔ lb.
Salmon:				
Atlantic, chinook (king), chum (keta), coho (silver), pink (humpback), sockeye	½–¾ lb.	6–8 oz.	6–8 oz.	½–¾ lb.
baby coho (salmon)	8–10 oz.			
Sardines	¾–1 lb.	6–8 oz.		
Sea robin	½–1 lb.	6–8 oz.	6–8 oz.	
Seatrout, spotted	6–8 oz.			
Shad and roe		4–7 oz.		
Shark:				
Atlantic and Pacific, mako, thresher, silky, dusky, shovelnose, nurse, blacktip (spinner)			6–10 oz.	
sand shark (dogfish)		4–8 oz.	6–8 oz.	

FISH	AMOUNT PER PERSON			
	PAN-DRESSED OR WHOLE	FILLET	STEAK	CHUNK
Sheepshead	¾–1 lb.	6–10 oz.		
Skate (ray)	½–¾ lb.	6–8 oz.		
Smelt (surf)	½–¾ lb.	5–8 oz.		
Snapper, red, American red, gray (also called mangrove), lane, silk (also called yelloweye, day, red day, longfin, pargo de la alto), yellowtail, vermilion (beeliner)	¾–1 lb.	6–10 oz.		1 lb.
Sole:				
Pacific (Dover, English, petrale, rex, rock, sand, yellowfin)	¾–1 lb.	4–8 oz.		
Atlantic (gray)—see Flounder	¾–1 lb.	4–8 oz.		
European Dover sole	¾–1 lb.	4–8 oz.		
Spot (Norfolk)	¾ lb.			
Sturgeon, Atlantic and lake		6–8 oz.		
Sunfish, various	¾–1 lb.			
Swordfish (broadbill, billfish)			7–10 oz.; cubes: 4–8 oz.	
Tilapia (also called St. Peter's fish)	¾ lb.	6 oz.		
Tilefish (blueline, gray, golden, rainbow)	¾–1 lb.	6–8 oz.	10–12 oz.	
Trout:				
freshwater (rainbow, lake, brook, brown, steelhead)	8–10 oz. (bone in or out)	6–8 oz.		

FISH	AMOUNT PER PERSON			
	PAN-DRESSED OR WHOLE	FILLET	STEAK	CHUNK
sea (spotted and speckled, weakfish)	¾–1 lb.	6–8 oz.		
Tuna:				
bigeye, bluefin, skip-jack, yellowfin, blackfin			6–10 oz.	
albacore, bonito, lit-tle tunny	¾–1 lb.		6–10 oz.	
Wahoo		4–8 oz.		
Weakfish—see Drum or Trout (sea)	¾–1 lb.	6–8 oz.		
Whitebait (silversides)	6–8 oz.			
Whitefish, freshwater	¾ lb.	6–8 oz.		
Whiting (silver hake, New England hake)	¾ lb.	4–8 oz.		
Wolffish (ocean catfish)		6–8 oz.		
Yellowtail to eat raw		3–4 oz.		
Cooked		6–8 oz.		
Yellowtail snapper—see Snapper				
Yellowtail flounder—see Flounder				

FISH	AMOUNT PER PERSON
Fish roe, various	4–6 oz.

CRUSTACEAN, MOLLUSK, OR CEPHALOPOD	NUMBER PER PERSON	AMOUNT PER PERSON
Abalone	½–1	4 oz. (flesh)
Clams:		
littleneck, cherrystone	6–9	
soft-shell (steamers)		¾–1 lb.

CRUSTACEAN, MOLLUSK, OR CEPHALOPOD	NUMBER PER PERSON	AMOUNT PER PERSON
manila		6–8 oz.
geoduck		4 oz. (flesh)
Conch		6–8 oz.
Crabs:		
hard-shell blue (depending on size)	2–6	
soft-shell blue (depending on size), red, rock, jonah	2–4	
king, snow (tanner), queen		½–1 lb. (legs) or 4–8 oz. (flesh)
Dungeness	1	1 lb.
stone crab claws		¾–1 lb.
crabmeat (various kinds)		4–8 oz.
Crawfish:		
whole	6–12	½–1 lb.
tail meat		6–8 oz.
Gooseneck barnacles		½–¾ lb.
Langostinos		½ lb.
Lobsters:		
Atlantic	1	1–2 lbs.
spiny (tails)	1–2	6–8 oz.
cooked meat		4–6 oz.
Mussels, northern Atlantic		¼–1 lb.
Octopus		6–8 oz.
Oysters:		
in shell	6–9	
shucked		½ pint
Periwinkles		4–8 oz.
Scallops (sea, bay, calico)		4–8 oz.
Sea urchins	1	1–4 oz.
Shrimp:		
in shell		6–8 oz.

CRUSTACEAN, MOLLUSK, OR CEPHALOPOD	NUMBER PER PERSON	AMOUNT PER PERSON
cooked meat		5–6 oz.
Squid:		
uncleaned		6–8 oz.
cleaned		4–6 oz.

Smoked seafood such as trout, salmon, tuna, mackerel, mussels, bluefish, chub, haddock, eel, scallops, sable, and sturgeon is usually used for an appetizer or salad and only a few ounces need be bought for each person—I suggest 2 to 4 ounces per person.

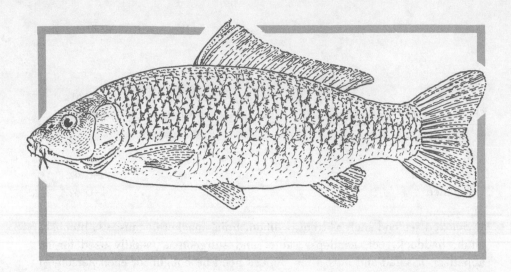

Methods of Preparation

AN UNDERSTANDING OF ANATOMY IS NECESSARY FOR COMPLETE MASTERY OF FISH COOKING. Once you know the anatomy of a fish you can cut it in various ways, such as into steaks, chunks, or fillets, and make different cuts from fillets, such as medallions, escalopes, or slivers. With this knowledge you can create a variety of dishes and also ensure even cooking, which is so important to fish. Becoming familiar with the bone structure of fish also allows you to separate the flesh from the bones easily, once it is cooked.

ROUNDFISH

Anatomy

When we refer to a *roundfish*, we mean any fish, whether with a rounded or compressed body, *that swims in a vertical position and has eyes on both sides of its head*. By contrast, a flatfish has a compressed body (hence the name), swims horizontally, and has both eyes on the top of its head.

52

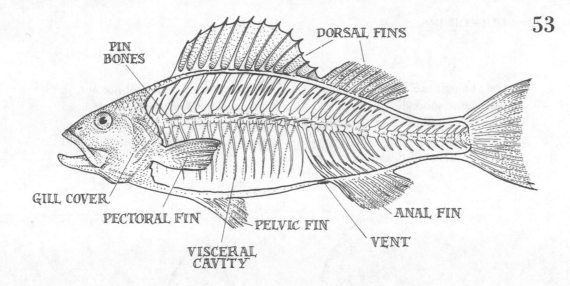

The skeleton of a roundfish consists of a central backbone with a row of straight bones reaching upward to the dorsal fins and two rows of curved rib bones that enclose the visceral cavity—that is, the stomach cavity.

Most roundfish have another row of bones, called *pin bones,* sticking outward at a right angle from the backbone. In general pin bones of small fish are few, feathery, thin, and short, and extend only along the backbone above the rib cage. When a roundfish is filleted, these bones remain in the center of the fillets, but are easily removed.

Not all roundfish are round! Their shapes vary from round to oval to compressed. If we look at cross sections of different parts of a roundfish, we learn

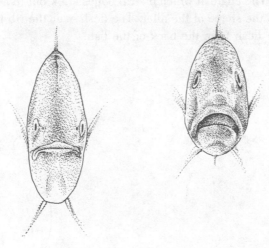

that, though the fish is roundish in shape, the cross sections will not always produce a solid disk of flesh. A cross section of the flesh behind the head shows the hollow of the visceral cavity; it is shaped somewhat like a horseshoe. Cross sections taken beyond the visceral cavity, nearer to the tail, will be solid disks of flesh.

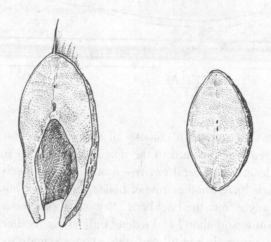

The rib bones of roundfish jut out from the backbone either at a curve or—as in the case of cod, whiting, and eel—at a sharp, nearly right angle. It is said that the Mercedes-Benz symbol derives from the cross section of an eel's backbone. The angle at which the rib bones stick out in a particular fish, of course, alters the shape of the fillet. The flesh over the rib bones is always thinner than the flesh from the back of the fish.

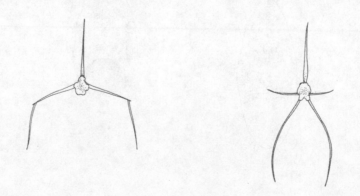

Utensils Needed

• A hard plastic chopping board, perhaps used only for fish.
• For any size fish: a boning or filleting knife. I prefer to use a boning knife with a nonflexible 5½-inch-long blade. For a smaller fish, you can use a sharp paring knife with a 4-inch-long blade. Some people (including fishmongers) use a flexible filleting knife with an 8- to 10-inch long blade.
• A chef's knife with an 8 or 10-inch-long blade.
• For fish with sturdy pin bones: a pair of pin-nose or needle-nose pliers. For fish with thin, feathery pin bones: a pair of tweezers.

Gutting

It is important that a fish be gutted as early as possible to prolong its shelf life. The gills must also be removed before cooking. Usually a fish has been gutted when you see it, either at sea or by the fishmonger. However, if you catch a fish or a friend gives you an undrawn fish, you must gut it, scale it, and remove its gills yourself.

To gut a fish, take a sharp-pointed knife and insert it in the anal vent. Make a slit up the belly to the head, cutting around the pelvic fins or between them.

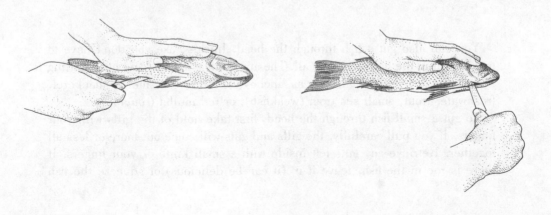

Empty out the visceral cavity. The dark secretion of blood (the kidney) on the backbone can give a bitter taste to the fish; this blood is often hidden, covered by a skinlike lining along the backbone. Cut through the lining if necessary, scrape the blood away, and rinse out the inside of the fish. The blood is often present in a cleaned fish too—remove it.

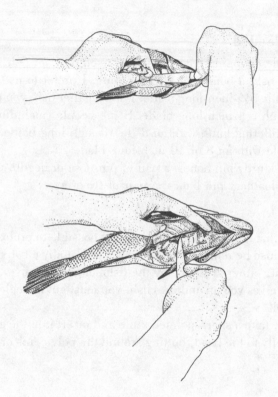

You can also gut a fish through the head. In this case you don't have to make a slit in the belly cavity at all. The appearance is neat, and head gutting is suitable for such small fish as anchovies, sardines, smelts, mackerel, freshwater trout, small sea trout (weakfish), or red mullet (*rouget*).

To gut a small fish through the head, first take hold of the gills with your fingers. If you pull carefully, the gills and guts will come out more or less all together. Retrieve any guts left inside with a small knife or your fingers. If there is roe in the fish, leave it in (it can be delicious) or squeeze the fish carefully (like a toothpaste tube) to extrude the roe. Rinse the inside of the fish.

It is more difficult, but not impossible, to gut a large fish through the head, for the gills are large and strong.

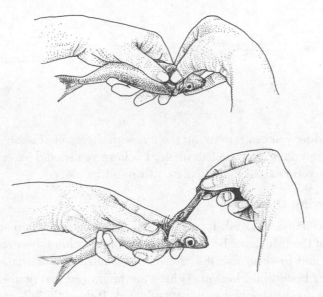

Scaling

Not all fish need to be scaled. Some, such as catfish, monkfish, wolffish, and swordfish, are scaleless. On others, such as mackerel and pompano, the scales are very small, fine, and negligible.

Scale a fish with a fish scaler, a dull kitchen or table knife, or a spoon. You want to avoid splitting the skin, so don't use too sharp a knife. Holding the fish by the tail, put it headfirst in a large plastic bag, such as a Baggie or Ziploc bag, or directly into a garbage pail or a sink full of water, so that the scales do not fly all over. If it is a large fish, handle it without bending it too much, so that you do not break the backbone.

Start removing the scales from the tail end by inserting the knife under the scales and pushing them off in short strokes, working up to the head. Be careful of the dorsal fins, for the spiny ones can puncture your skin easily.

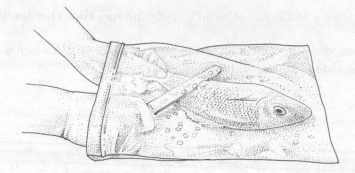

Before scaling you can remove all the fins with shears or scissors, if you like, but if you intend to cook the fish whole, I believe you should leave the fins and tail on, so you can see the complete fish in all its glory.

Removing the Gills

The gills must be removed, for they contain bacteria and blood and can spoil the taste of the fish. They lie under the gill covers behind the eyes. Gills, the breathing and in some fish the filtering mechanism, are J-shaped pieces of cartilage or bone with filaments (which are bright red and feathery when the fish is very fresh) attached to the outside and, frequently, gill rakers—a row of little "bones"—protruding from the inside. (In herbivorous fish the gill rakers behind each gill arch prevent food from escaping out of the gill opening and direct food down the gullet; large carnivorous fish often lack gill rakers.) There are four gills on each side of a fish's head.

The gill nearest to the head is attached by a membrane and must be freed by cutting alongside it. Lift up the gill cover and with a sharp knife or kitchen shears cut along the innermost gill to free it from the head. Cut the gills free at each end also. Use a cloth to pull them out so that the gill rakers don't stab you. Discard. Rinse the inside of the fish and pat the outside dry with a paper towel. (Even fish supposedly cleaned at the store may retain some of the gills; if so, remove them.)

When making stock with fish "frames" (skeletons, heads, tails, and skin), be sure to remove the gills, as they might impart a bitter taste to the stock. Also, rinse any traces of blood from the bones before using them.

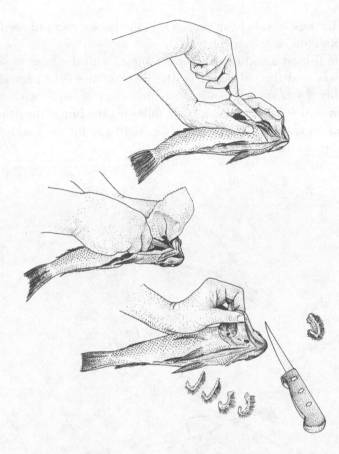

Filleting

Now let's learn about filleting and what can be done with fillets once they are free of the bones. The aim in filleting a whole fish is to take as much flesh from the bones as possible, while producing a beautiful fillet. A roundfish produces two fillets, one from each side of the body.

Take the time to examine the fish *before* filleting. Look inside the visceral cavity and acquaint yourself with the angle of the rib bones and the shape and size of the cavity. You shouldn't see any pin bones sticking out of the backbone at this point. At any rate, the knife will cut through them without much difficulty, unless they are very large and strong. They can be removed afterward.

Your knife must always be in contact with the bones, and you need to make long, smooth strokes as you cut.

Place the fish on a cutting board at an angle, with the head to your right pointing away and the top dorsal fin (the back of the fish) nearest to you. (Reverse this if you are left-handed.)

Cut downward with your boning knife, following the line of the head behind the pectoral fin and the armored gill cover, until you hit the backbone. Also cut down through the flesh just above the tail.

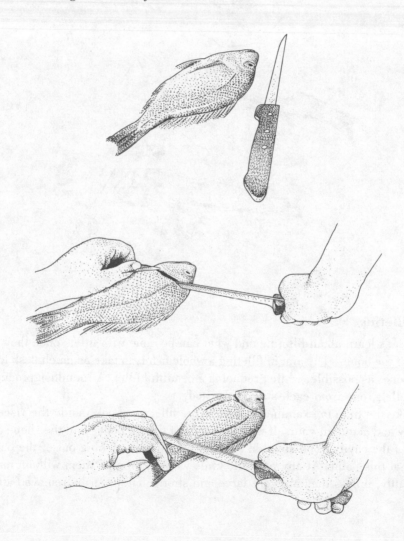

Now, take your knife and insert it just behind the head, and with one hand on the fish (but of course out of cutting reach) make a cut through the skin along the back, close to but avoiding the dorsal fins, all the way down to the tail. Cut in long, continuous strokes, not with a jiggedy motion. Then, following the same cut, cut deeper into the fish until you reach the backbone. You will feel a slight or substantial bump, depending on the size and kind of fish.

Now, fold back the flesh so you can see what you are doing.

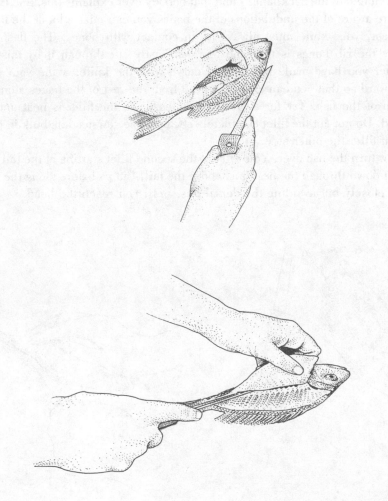

Again, take your knife to the head end to complete the cutting of the fillet. Your next cut must curve slightly upward and then down over the rib bones to release the flesh. You will be cutting through the pin bones that extend from the backbone as you do this. Even if you can't see the pin bones, you will hear your knife going clickety-click as it severs them. Look inside the cavity to check the angle of the rib bones so you can tell how sharply your knife must curve upward. (The rib bones of some fish that have large visceral cavities, such as cod, protrude greatly, and so the knife must curve upward, nearly at a right angle to the backbone. I find that nobody ever explains this, and unless you are aware of the undulations of the bones you can miss a lot of the flesh.) I repeat, your knife must always be in contact with bones. The flesh that covers the rib bones is thin and one can easily cut through it by mistake.

After you have made the upward curve with the knife, angle your knife downward so that you can clean the flesh from the rest of the bones along the length of the fish. Try for a clean cut, please, so the fillet is neat and not jagged. Do not cut the fillet completely off, because you need its bulk in place as you fillet the other side.

Now turn the fish over. You will cut the second fillet starting at the tail end.

Cut down through the flesh just above the tail. Cut as before along the back skin, closely but avoiding the dorsal fins, until you reach the head.

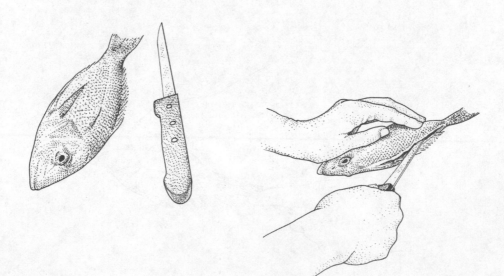

Now make another deeper cut, following the previous cut, until you reach the backbone.

Make a diagonal cut behind the pectoral fin and gill cover. Gently pull back the flesh and angle the knife slightly downward, slicing to free the flesh above the straight bones near the tail.

As you reach the rib bones, curve the knife upward and over them, until you reach the head.

Free this fillet entirely from the bones. Turn the fish over and free the other side as well.

Check to see whether any rib bones are still attached to the fillets. Insert your knife under them to release them.

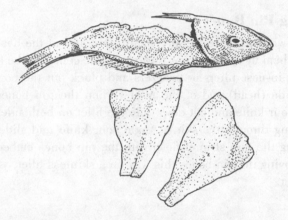

Skinning a Fillet

You can skin a fillet if you wish. To do so, take the fillet and place it on the board, skin side down, so the tail end is nearest to you. Pin the tail end to the board with the fingertips of one hand. Take a chef's knife with an 8- or 10-inch blade (no other knife works as well) and slip the blade at an angle between the fillet and the skin just in front of your fingertips. Saw gently back and forth, separating the flesh from the skin all the way up. Lift the fillet as you work to make sure that it is coming smoothly off the skin. You can pull on the skin as you are cutting. Discard the skin, or save it to make a stock. Trim any raggedy edges off the fillet.

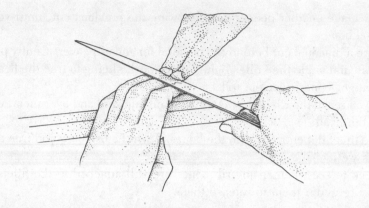

Removing Pin Bones

Check to see whether there are any small pin bones at the head end of each fillet, or find them by running your finger over the center of the fillet. If a fillet is thin, take pin-nose pliers or tweezers and pluck out the bones by pulling toward the wide (head) end of the fillet. When the pin bones are big and strong, take your knife and cut down into the fillet on both sides of the bones (without cutting through the skin). Angle your knife and slide it across the skin, removing the thin strip of flesh with the pin bones embedded it it.

When removing the pin bones this way on a skinless fillet, you will have a V-shaped fillet.

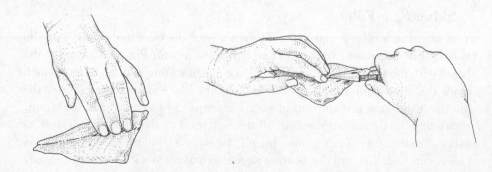

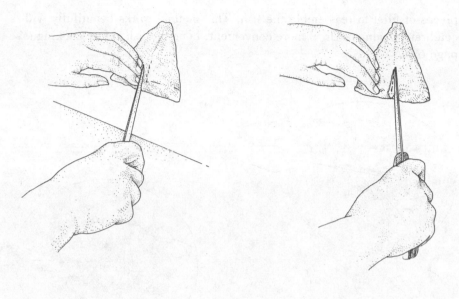

Filleting a Cooked Whole Roundfish

It is not as easy to lift a *whole* fillet from the top side of a whole cooked fish as it is to remove one from a raw fish. The easiest way is to cut the top fillet down the middle, above the backbone, and lift it off the fillets in two sections.

Make a cut down the middle of the flesh on top of the backbone and lift off the skin, if desired. Gently lift one half of the upper fillet off the bone, then slide the other one off, taking care to lift it free of the rib bones, which sometimes want to stick on. If the rib bones come away with the flesh, slide your knife under them to remove them. When the skeletal bones are exposed (with the other fillet underneath), pull the tail up all the way to the head, lifting the backbone away from the flesh. The whole bone structure, including the head, should come away in one piece if the fish has been cooked through properly. Discard the skeleton or put it to the side of the plate. The entire bottom fillet is now free too. Eat and enjoy.

When serving a large cooked fish, you may find it convenient to bone the fish completely and then reassemble it. Do this in the manner described above, taking large *pieces* of the fish fillets off with a long metal spatula. Put the pieces aside, neatly and in order, and remove the backbone. Put back the pieces of fillet to reassemble the fish. This method works beautifully with a celebratory salmon. Or, if more convenient, bone the fish before cooking (see page 69).

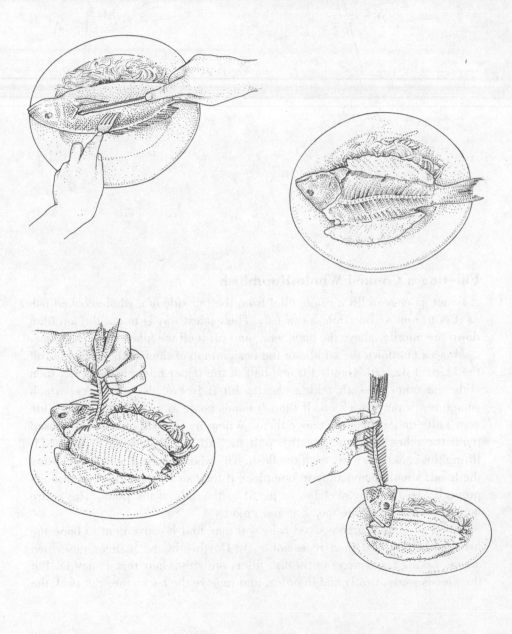

Butterflying or Splitting

To *butterfly* a fish is to make two fillets from it that are connected by either the belly skin or the back. Incidentally, it is not possible to butterfly a flatfish because the fillets are not joined together anywhere. They are separated by bones.

One method of butterflying a roundfish is to split it open from its back and bone it at the same time, producing two fillets joined by the belly skin. Be sure there is no belly slit. This can only be done to an ungutted fish or a fish that has been gutted through the head. It makes a pleasant variation in presentation and is used mainly for smaller fish that are served as individual portions, such as herring, sardines, mackerel, trout, whiting, black sea bass, flying fish, and other fish that weigh 1½ pounds or less.

To butterfly using this method, first scale the fish and cut off its head and fins. Then cut into the back of the fish, first on one side of the dorsal fins, then on the other, down and over the rib bones until you reach the visceral cavity. Do not cut through the skin at the bottom of the fish! Lift out the viscera. Spread the joined fillets open and remove any remaining bones.

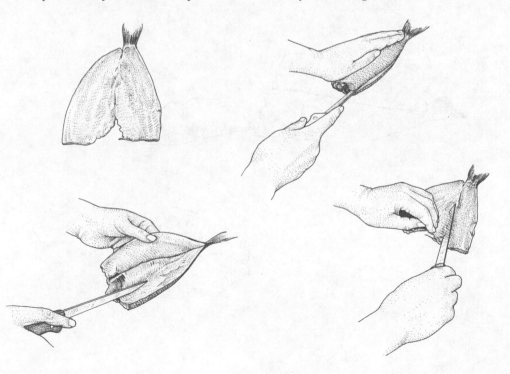

Another method produces two fillets connected by the back. Follow the directions for boning out on page 69. You can leave the head and tail on if you like. Spread the fish open. This method is good for small fish such as trout, herring, mackerel, sardines; baby coho salmon is usually prepared this way by processors. You can create little butterflies from these fish that have been butterflied. Spread the fish open. Cut off the head and tail. Then cut down across the fish to make four butterflies, from 1½ to 2 inches wide.

You can also butterfly filleted fish. For this method, see page 86.

In cooking, butterflied fish are treated as fillets.

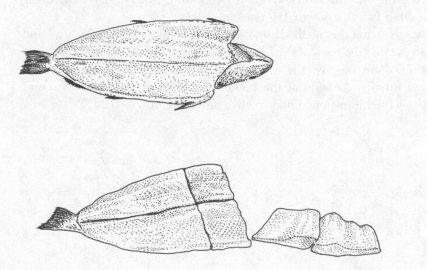

Boning Out

Boning out is useful when you are stuffing a chunk or "roast," or when you just want to make a nice presentation of a whole fish such as a bake-poached or roast salmon for a party, so that you do not need to deal with the bones when serving.

For a whole fish, once it is scaled and gutted, continue the cavity cut all the way to the tail. Spread the fish open a little and cut through the rib bones and up toward the back on either side of the backbone (first one side, then the other), without actually cutting through the skin along the back of the fish. Do not cut off the dorsal fins if you are going to close the fish up again for the final presentation. Find the tops of the rib bones at the point where they were attached to the backbone and strip them clear of the flesh with your fingers or insert a knife under them to loosen them, then discard them. Try to keep the flesh intact. Then cut or detach the central backbone (kitchen shears are good for this) at both the head and the tail and pull it free. Most likely you will not be able to remove the row of smaller bones near the dorsal fins unless you have a large fish. Don't worry about them—they are easily avoided when the fish is cooked.

Trout and baby coho salmon are usually prepared this way by processors. Whole fish such as large salmon, bluefish, tilefish, groupers, and red snappers can certainly be prepared this way before they are roasted, bake-poached, or stuffed and then roasted.

Bone out a chunk or "roast" in the same way. The chunk will most likely come already scaled and cleaned and won't have the head or the tail.

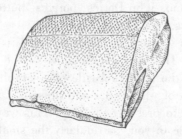

(continued)

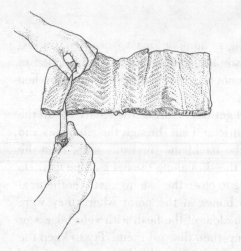

Another Way to Dress a Roundfish That Weighs Two Pounds or Less

A whole fish is cut in half lengthwise to separate the two halves, producing two fillets with half the head attached to each.

Take, for instance, a whole pompano, whose beautiful skin should be shown to advantage. (Incidentally, pompano, though technically a roundfish, has a compressed flat body.) Gut it and then slice it in half lengthwise. Here's how: Starting at the head, place the knife at a right angle across the mouth, cut into the mouth, then cut through the head and body, following the backbone from head to tail. One side of the fish will still contain the backbone, so loosen it with a sharp knife and also remove the rib bones from each fillet. Trim the edge of each fillet. This method works best for fish with fairly compressed bodies, such as pompano, John Dories, porgies, butterfish, and small black sea bass or striped bass.

A fish prepared this way can be bake-poached in the oven or broiled or grilled on a barbecue. The skin should show for the presentation, so either bake-poach the fish in the oven skin side up, or broil it skin side down in a pan filled with ⅛ inch of white wine and present it skin side up. Grill the halves flesh side down to preserve the skin. This way you do not waste any flesh—it is all available to you, particularly the small amount of delectable flesh in the head (the cheek), which is lost when filleting.

It is also a good way for two to share a fish.

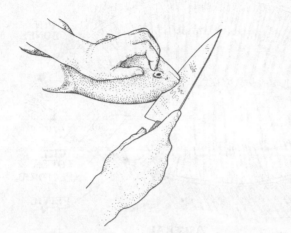

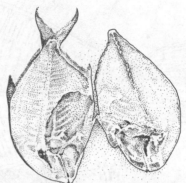

FLATFISH

Anatomy

The flatfish group includes all flounder, sole, dab, fluke, plaice, Greenland turbot, and halibut, as well as Dover sole, turbot, and brill from Europe.

Flatfish have flat, compressed bodies. They swim in a horizontal position and look like oval plates as they swim. The skin on the top side of a flatfish is dark, acting as camouflage so the fish will not be easily seen from above and will blend in with the sandy bottom of the ocean where flatfish like to live. The underside is usually white or nearly white. (The underside of the gray sole is gray and that of the Greenland turbot is black.) The scales on a flatfish are not large; on small fish they are negligible and only a gentle scrape is necessary to remove them.

The dorsal and anal fins of a flatfish run the length of its body. Its relatively small visceral cavity and anal vent lie near the head, just behind the gill cover, like a little pocket. If there are any gonads (male and female roe sacs), they lie along both sides of the fish and next to the straight bones behind the visceral cavity.

A flatfish starts life with an eye on either side of its head and the same coloring all over. When it is but half an inch long it begins to flatten out, and one eye joins the other on the top of its head. The eyes can be on the right or

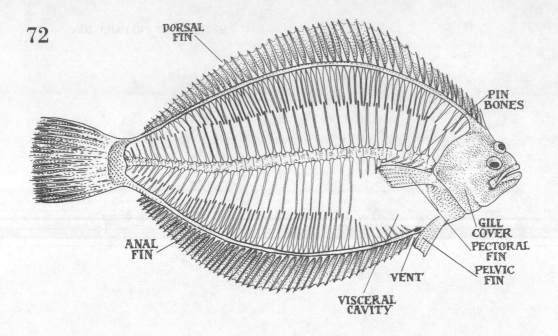

left side of the head, depending on the species, but most flatfish from U.S. waters are right-eyed, although most flukes, Southern flounder, and sand dabs from Florida waters and the Gulf of Mexico are left-eyed. How do you tell whether a flatfish is right-eyed or left-eyed? With the dark skin facing upward, place the fish horizontally in front of you with the visceral cavity, pelvic fin, and mouth nearest to you. A right-eyed flatfish has its eyes to the right of the visceral cavity; a left-eyed flatfish, to the left. Recognizing right- and left-eyed flatfish will help you to identify different fish and also make it easier to follow instructions on filleting those fish.

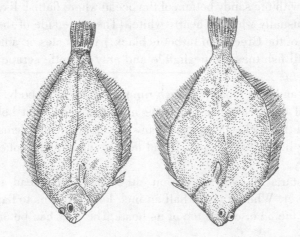

The skeleton of a flatfish is very simple. It consists of a central backbone with straight bones extending out to the little bones supporting the dorsal and anal fins. The basic skeletal structure is so simple and strong that if you remove the fillets and let the skeleton dry, you can use it to comb your hair! But we won't do that. Instead, we will learn how to gut a flatfish and how to cut fillets and steaks from it.

Utensils Needed

• A hard plastic chopping board, perhaps used only for fish. This board can easily be scrubbed with bleach.
• A boning or filleting knife. (I prefer a boning knife with a nonflexible 5½-inch blade.)
• A chef's knife with an 8- to 10-inch blade.

Gutting

Note: It's not necessary to gut a flatfish before filleting it, but it is necessary before cooking a flatfish whole.

Insert the tip of the boning knife in the anal vent. Cut a slit toward the head, between the two pelvic fins. Empty the cavity with your fingers, loosening the guts with the knife and pulling the remainder away. Rinse.

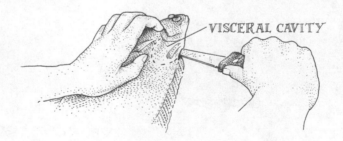

VISCERAL CAVITY

Filleting

Roundfish fillets (see page 74) taper at the tail end and are usually very thin over the rib bones. Flatfish fillets are of a more even thickness, therefore they cook more evenly, although the top fillet of a flatfish is a little thicker than the bottom one. Flatfish fillets are boneless, save for a few pin bones at the head

end, which can easily be removed. These bones are all that remains of the rib cage when the fish is filleted. (They can also be left in, if they are very fine for they will be harmless when cooked.) Flatfish fillets are simplicity itself to eat, for they are easily lifted off the flat bone structure.

At the fish store we see double fillets of flatfish that have been deftly cut by processors—or, preferably, have been cut by the fishmonger that day. When filleting flatfish ourselves, we can take either two or four fillets from each fish.

To Produce Two Fillets Place a right- or left-eyed fish, dark skin uppermost, diagonally on the cutting board, with the head to your left and the tail pointing away to the right.

Take your knife and first make a slit across the flesh next to the tail, then cut into the skin along the fins, starting at the tail and finishing just before the head. You should feel the little bones that support the fins all the way along. Make a cut behind the head, the pectoral fin, and the visceral cavity.

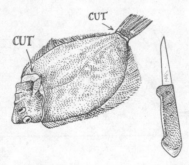

Now cut in deeper with long strokes until you reach the slight bump of the backbone. Again, you should feel the bones at all times with your knife.

Gently fold back the fillet, ease your knife over the backbone, and continue to cut, slightly downward at first, then flatten out the knife to free the rest of the fillet from the bones. Do not free the fillet completely, for you need its bulk in place as you fillet the other side.

Turn the fish over and place it with the head to your right.

Repeat the above operation, starting at the head end.

Free this fillet completely from the bones and turn the fish over to free the other fillet.

Trim the edges of each fillet. Trim any pin bones from the head end.

Now you have two nice fillets.

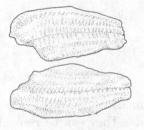

To Produce Four Fillets Place the fish on the cutting board, underside up, with the head away from you and the tail toward you.

Take your knife and make a cut down the middle of the fish, above or just to one side of the backbone (you can feel the backbone with your fingertips) from the head to the tail.

Cut the left-hand fillet away starting at the head end, using long strokes to obtain a smooth fillet, with the knife at an angle to free it from the bones. Do not cut the fillet completely off, because you need its bulk in place as you fillet the other side of the fish.

Turn the fish around with the head toward you and cut the other fillet away, but again not completely off.

Turn the fish over and repeat the procedure, cutting the two fillets from this side completely free from the skeleton. Release the fillets on the other side of the fish.

Trim the edges of the fillets. Trim any pin bones from the head end.

Now you have four nice fillets.

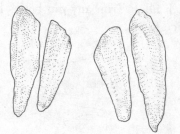

Note: If you should find gonads (roe sacks) in these fish during filleting, lift them up and put them aside. They can be cooked with the fillets or served separately. They can also be used to make a sauce, a custard, or a mousse.

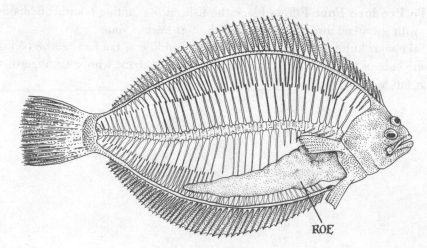

ROE

Skinning a Fillet

This method is the same as for roundfish fillets: Take the fillet and place it on the board, skin side down, so the tail end is nearest to you. Pin the tail end to the board with the fingertips of one hand. Take a chef's knife and slip the blade at an angle between the fillet and the skin just in front of your fingertips. Saw gently back and forth, separating the flesh from the skin all the way up. Lift the fillet as you work to make sure that it is coming smoothly off the skin. Discard the skin, or save it to make a stock.

In Europe the white underskin is often left on because its color does not offend and because it tastes good (as does the dark skin).

Filleting a Cooked Whole Flatfish

Make a cut down the middle of the flesh to the central backbone and gently lift one side—that is, one half—of the fillet off the bone, then slide the other side off. When the skeletal bone is exposed (with the other fillet underneath), lift it up from the tail end all the way to the head. The whole bone structure including the head should come away in one piece if the fish has been cooked properly. Now you are free to eat the rest of the fish.

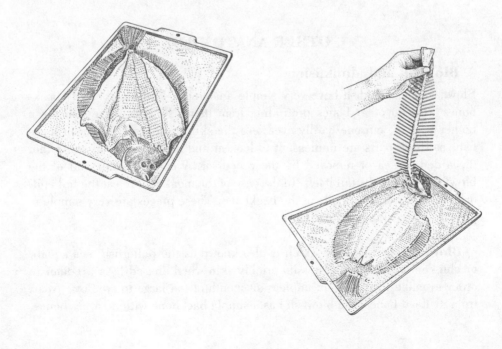

Flatfish Steaks

The halibut, a large flounder, is most often cut into steaks by processors or fishmongers. Halibut steaks should be cut 1 inch thick for best cooking results. As halibut are usually very large fish, weighing up to 750 pounds, they have strong backbones that are best cut with a cleaver or a saw. Leave this job to an expert if the fish is very large.

Smaller flatfish such as sole, flounder, brill, and turbot can be cut into steaks for variety also. To do this, cut down against the grain of the fish as you would for roundfish, in slices about ⅜ to ½ inch thick. You will need a heavy chef's knife or a cleaver and a mallet to get through the backbone. A few little steaks look marvelous on a plate, arranged in a star pattern.

OTHER ANATOMIES

Blowfish and Monkfish

Blowfish and monkfish have very simple anatomies: Both have sturdy backbones with no other bones protruding from them. Both of these fish are a bother to skin, but one hardly ever sees the skin or heads of either of these fish, as these parts are unpleasant to look at and touch, and thus are either discarded at sea or removed by the processor. We eat the tail end of the blowfish, but not the tail itself. In the case of the monkfish we eat the tail end, or fillets cut from each side of the backbone. These pieces are very simple to prepare for cooking and eating.

Blowfish The blowfish, which is also known as the pufferfish, sea squab, or chicken of the sea, inflates its prickly skin when chased by a predator in order to make itself into an unpleasant mouthful too large to swallow. Apart from its head bones, the blowfish has a simple backbone with no other bones.

When the head, tail, skin, and guts of a blowfish have been removed, what remains is a firm, glistening piece of tail flesh surrounding the backbone. In Japan, where there are fifteen varieties of blowfish (*fugu*), it is important that a professional do the skinning and gutting because tetrodotoxin, which is highly toxic, can be present in the liver, ovaries, and viscera and can contaminate the flesh. Sushi chefs with ten years' experience are the only ones entrusted with this task. By contrast the United States species of blowfish is harmless. If you catch your own blowfish, cut off the head and tail with a boning or filleting knife and then pull off the skin, using a cloth or pliers so you don't get scratched. The skin comes off easily, the guts spill out, and you are left with a tender morsel of blowfish meat, ready to cook.

Blowfish tails are sold already prepared for cooking; they are usually small, weighing 2 to 6 ounces each, so that several pieces are required for a helping. They are delicious quickly sautéed, barbecued, or broiled, and they can be picked up and eaten much like chicken drumsticks.

Monkfish The monkfish tail has wonderful sweet flesh surrounding a simple backbone resembling a rod. Under the silky skin is a layer of pinkish-purplish tissue covering the white flesh. This must be cut off so that the pure white flesh is all that you see. The dark layer must be removed because, although tasty enough, it shrinks around the flesh as it cooks and distorts the shape, and it turns even darker when cooked. You have to be ruthless when cutting off the dark tissue, and some of the white flesh may come away with it as you cut.

If you buy an unskinned monkfish, cut the skin loose with a boning or filleting knife and throw it away (most of it can be pulled off). Cut the fins off the top and bottom of the fish. Insert your boning or filleting knife under the dark tissue, starting at the head end. Following the rounded shape, curve the knife around and under the dark flesh to free it from the white flesh. Do the same on the other side of the fish.

You can cook the whole tail end very successfully. Cutting the tail end into steaks is useless because in cooking the flesh tightens up and the bone tends to pop out, making it impossible to cook on the other side, but you can cut fillets from each side of the backbone easily. You will find some tough white flesh on the side of the fillet that was next to the backbone. Trim this away. Cook the fillets whole, or cut them, on a strong diagonal, into medallions (thick slices), escalopes (thin slices), or cubes.

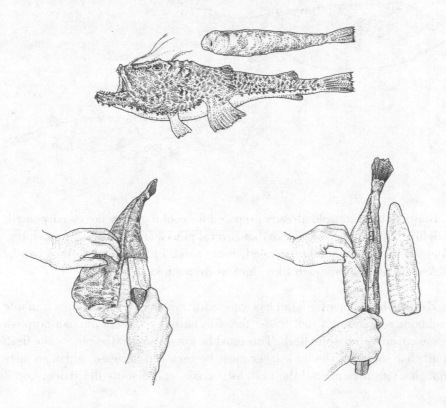

Tuna

Tuna weighing up to 1,400 pounds are caught, and apart from small bonitos and little tunnies we never see a whole tuna in a fish store. Skilled cutters carve large tuna into "loins" from which we cut steaks (preferably 1 to 1¼ inches thick) or cubes (1 to 1¼ inches square). The skin is easily removed, and must be, as it is as tough as leather. The dark, nearly black part of the flesh is muscle rich in myoglobin, a blood pigment. It has a stronger taste than the rest of the tuna and can be cut off or not, as you prefer. I personally find it perfectly delicious, as do the Japanese. Try it in a hand roll.

Swordfish

Swordfish weighing up to 1,000 pounds are caught commercially. The head, fins, and guts are usually removed at sea and at the fish store we see center cuts and wheels, which are cross sections of the fish. All cuts can be made into steaks (1 to 1¼ inches thick) or cubes (1 to 1¼ inches square). The skin is thick and can be removed before cooking if desired. The flesh color ranges from gray to white to pink-orange. The dark part is the red muscle. Apart from the red muscle, the flesh turns white when cooked.

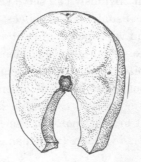

Shark

There are 350 species of sharks, but those we see the most of are mako, thresher, and (soon, I hope) sand sharks (also known as dogfish). Sharks weigh up to several thousand pounds. They never cease to grow as long as they have food to eat. Sharks have cartilaginous skeletons that are easily broken by handling, and the fragility of these skeletons makes it difficult to catch sharks in a way that allows them to be kept alive. Sharks are marketed, much like swordfish and tuna, in loins, center cuts, and wheels, and then cut into steaks. When available the smaller sand sharks are sold filleted or cut into steaks.

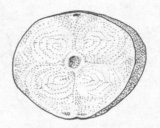

DIFFERENT CUTS POSSIBLE FROM FILLETS

Now that you have learned to fillet fish—or even if you haven't learned but are used to buying fillets—you can choose to leave the fillets as they are (with pin bones removed before cooking) or cut them into a variety of shapes.

The decision whether to cut a fillet or cook it whole depends to a large extent on the size of the fillet. If fillets are left whole, a small one (6 to 8 ounces) will be enough for an individual helping, while a whole fillet from the side of a 6- to 9-pound fish obviously can serve several people. (The amount you want for each portion is usually 6 to 8 ounces, depending on appetite and choice of fish—perhaps you will opt for a lesser amount if you choose a rich or expensive fish. See page 44 for suggested amounts to buy.)

Whole fillets can be broiled, baked, fried, deep-fried (if small), poached, steamed, or grilled. The cooking method will depend on the size of the utensils you have at hand. For instance, you can easily fry a small fillet in a small frying pan, but if you want to cook more than one you may have to fry them in batches, placing the fillets in a large frying pan with sufficient space around them. If you want to bake a whole large fillet, you must have a large enough baking or roasting pan.

Thin or thick slices, either on the diagonal or straight across the grain, can produce escalopes, medallions, or slivers, while other cuts can produce butterfly shapes or cubes. You have undoubtedly noticed that fillets, especially from roundfish, are usually of uneven thickness. Some of the cuts I describe here ensure even cooking and all of them will help you to attain neat and attractive presentation.

Before cutting a fillet, skin it if desired (see pages 63 and 77), then remove the pin bones, if any, with pin-nose pliers, your fingers, or tweezers, or cut them out.

Roundfish

Slices Take your boning, filleting, or chef's knife and cut even-sized portions right down against the grain of the fillet, 2 to 3 inches apart, or make diagonal cuts for a sleeker, more generous look. To make diagonal cuts, place the fillet with the head end at your right. Hold your knife at an angle so the sharp edge is closer to the tail end and the top of the knife is closer to the head end. Cut toward the tail end. Repeat for the other portions. Remember to cut the tail portion wider than the other portions, because it is thinner. Of course, it is possible to cut more than one slice for each portion, making the slices 1½ inches wide. If the slices are narrower than that, they may fall apart in cooking.

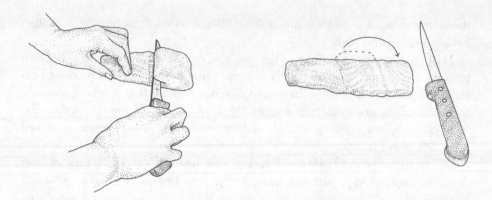

To even out thick fillets, take your knife and cut through the thickest part of the fillet, crosswise, nearly all the way through. Fold back the top piece to level the fillet out.

Escalopes and Rosettes Escalopes are slices cut against the grain, ¼ or ½ inch wide. When they are laid flat on a broiler pan, they will cook to perfection—that is, perfectly evenly. When you serve them, you can lay them out concentrically like rosettes, in rows or in a star shape.

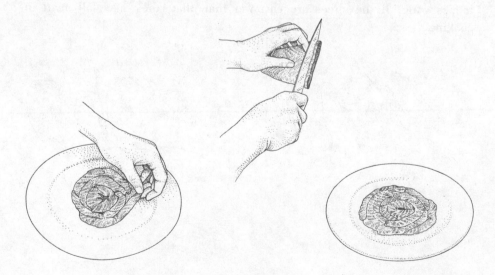

Medallions A medallion is thicker than an escalope. Cut the slices 1 inch thick straight down against the grain of the fillet. Each medallion will have a thin "tail," rather like a lamb chop. Lay each slice out, then curl the thin part of the slice around the thick part until you have a nice, neat, round medallion. Insert toothpicks to keep them together if necessary. These medallions, when cooked, can be placed on the plate in different designs—three in the center of the plate, in a row, whatever you fancy.

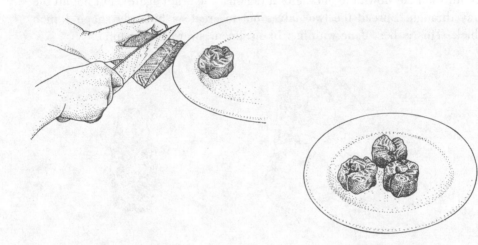

Slivers Fillets of fish with brightly colored skin, such as red snapper, pompano, John Dory, salmon, and black sea bass, can be cut into slivers on a strong diagonal angle and bake-poached, skin side up, to show off their perfectly beautiful skins.

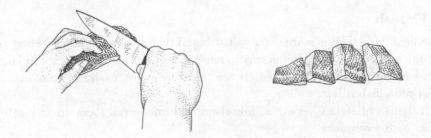

Place a fillet in front of you with the head end, where you will start your cuts, at your right. Hold your knife at a strong diagonal angle with the sharp edge of the blade facing you. Make slivers about 1 to 1½ inches wide. These slivers show both flesh and skin. Then use a wide spatula to transfer the slivers onto a baking dish or baking pan.

Butterflies To make butterfly-shaped portions of fish another way, take a skinless fillet or loin and cut a slice 2 inches thick straight down against the grain, then cut down the middle of it (against the grain again), but not all the way through. Spread the two halves out to create a butterfly shape 1 inch thick. This is best done with fish like salmon, swordfish, or tuna.

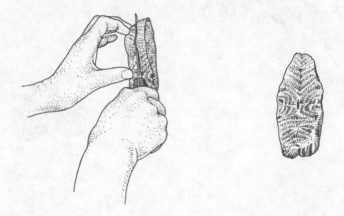

Cubes Cubes taken from filleted fish are used for brochettes, kebabs, soups, and salads. They are obtained from thick fillets of firm-fleshed fish such as swordfish, monkfish, tuna, and shark.

Cut your fillets into slices 1 to 1¼ inches thick, then tailor the cubes.

Flatfish

The flesh of flatfish is more evenly distributed than that of roundfish—that is, no one part of a flatfish fillet is very much thicker than the rest, except in large fish such as halibut. Flatfish fillets are therefore much easier to cook evenly than roundfish fillets.

If flatfish fillets are very thin, fold them in thirds or roll them up and fasten them with toothpicks.

Strips If you want variety, you can cut flatfish fillets into diagonal strips, which are then deep-fried (these are called *goujonettes* in French) or prepared as seviche, for instance.

You will need the complete fillet from each side of the fish for this preparation. Feel for any small pin bones at the head end of each fillet and cut them out. Slice each fillet every ¼ or ½ inch straight down against the grain on a strong diagonal.

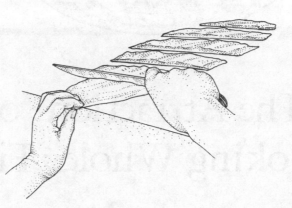

Cubes Halibut and large turbot can be cubed. Follow the instructions on page 86 for cubing roundfish.

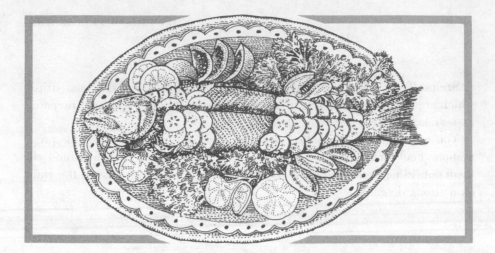

The Attraction of Cooking Whole Fish

IT IS MY STRONG BELIEF THAT FISH TASTES AND COOKS BETTER ON THE BONE. THE BACKBONE is an excellent heat conductor and the skin keeps the moisture in.

Cooked whole fish, whether large or small, look marvelous. You can cook small fish as individual portions and display large fish on a big platter for a more formal and dramatic presentation.

Many fish have beautifully colored skins. The skin of red snappers, black bass, trout, pompano, porgies, and salmon should be displayed to advantage. If you don't like to eat the skin, which can be delicious, show it anyway, since it can be easily lifted off with a knife at the table. In any case, to keep in moisture, do not remove the skin before cooking, but by all means scale it.

By cooking whole fish we are sure of eating all the flesh without wasting any, and there is the delight of eating the cheek muscles of the fish—delicious morsels that are fought over by some! The eyes can be removed easily when the fish is cooked, and the head made a little more glamorous with sprigs of parsley or small pieces of cut vegetables inserted in the hollows where the eyes were.

Fear of getting a bone in the mouth does discourage some from eating a cooked whole fish. However, once you know a little fish anatomy and can choose a fish with a *simple* bone structure (one that is easy to fillet off the bone once it is cooked and on your plate), you will have greater confidence and be able to better enjoy fish prepared this way.

This is not to say that all fish should be cooked whole, for this would be impractical. Swordfish, tuna, and most sharks are too large by far.

Of the fish featured in this book I recommend cooking the following fish whole, gutted, gilled, and scaled for individual servings: when they weigh 1½ pounds or less: black sea bass, striped bass, bluefish, catfish, flounder, sole, whiting, trout, sardines, mackerel, monkfish tails, pompano, porgies, rockfish, entire ray or skate wings, smelts, red snappers, whitefish, and weakfish (also known as sea trout). All these fish have very simple bone structures and their flesh can be easily lifted off as fillets with your knife and fork.

Large fish of these species can also be served whole. You can poach, bake-poach, roast, broil, steam, or grill them.

Part
II

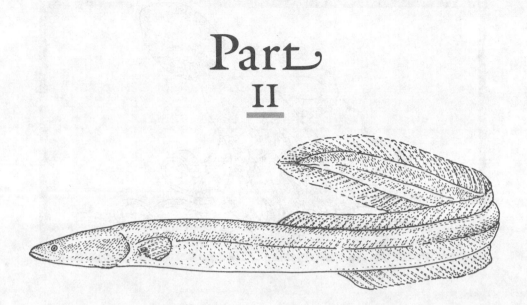

Basic
Cooking Methods,
Techniques, and
Recipes

Introduction

ON THE FOLLOWING PAGES I HAVE PROVIDED EASY-TO-UNDERSTAND DESCRIPTIONS OF THE different methods of cooking seafood, as well as basic recipes for each method. From the descriptions you will learn which kinds of seafood are suitable for different methods of preparation and which herbs, spices, and seasonings are best for different kinds of fish and shellfish. You will also learn about cooking times, temperatures, ways of recognizing when seafood is cooked, and health benefits. All the recipes given are for main courses, unless otherwise noted, and since all are suitable for several different kinds of seafood, I have noted the best choices for each. Also provided are lists of vegetables, herbs, spices, and seasonings that can be used in place of those in the recipes. Feel free to mix and match as you like or as the market dictates.

The recipes include *approximate* preparation times; I know that everyone works at his or her own speed, and I cannot correctly gauge yours! You will

92

also find approximate cooking times and whether all or some of it can be done beforehand. A large number of fish and shellfish have been listed with each recipe in alphabetical order. When you see generic names such as salmon, rockfish, flounder, sole, or bass listed, feel free to use any one of the species.

Broiling, grilling, frying, deep-frying, and baking are the most common ways of cooking seafood, but there are many more methods. To benefit from the health-giving properties of fish and shellfish, we are now tending to devise ways of cooking them so that added fats (such as oil, butter, and margarine) and coatings (such as bread crumbs and batter) do not significantly decrease the health benefits. Of course, sauces play a good part in enhancing the flavor of seafood, but they need not be fattening. Using vegetables, herbs, spices, and seasonings to flavor seafood can lead to highly satisfactory—and delicious—results, as you will see. Healthful and, happily, nonfattening ways of preparing seafood are poaching, steaming, broiling, grilling, baking, and roasting.

There are many quick ways to cook fish and shellfish. Since most seafood is naturally tender and need only be cooked through—that is, until the flesh turns opaque all the way through—only large whole fish, octopus, and large squid require long cooking. The rest take minutes—individual portions of seafood take only 3 to 15 minutes to cook, depending on thickness—and don't forget that seafood continues to cook as it makes its way to the table.

Since the purpose of this book is to teach you *how* to cook seafood, precise cooking times are rarely given. Some kinds of seafood cook faster than others because of the density of the flesh or its thickness, but rather than relying on hard and fast rules about how long seafood should cook per inch of thickness, you will find that it is better to learn how to recognize when it is cooked and then check for yourself to see whether it is done. With a little practice you will learn the approximate times and temperatures for cooking different kinds of seafood. Then you can apply this knowledge to a seafood recipe from any cookbook!

In the recipes you will notice that you are required to distinguish the *skin side* of a fillet when the fillet has been skinned. Often the instruction reads, "Lay the fish skin side down in the pan." You can tell the skin side because it is not as translucent as the side carved from the skeleton. It is usually not a clear white, as with most fish fillets, and you can see the darker fatty flesh that lies along the central lateral line along the fillet. There may even be shiny thin remains of the skin left on.

Checking for Doneness

• Use your finger to feel whether the flesh is firm but bouncy. Feel the tip of your nose with your finger—that's it, firm but bouncy!

• Insert a fork or knife into the thickest part of the flesh and pull it apart to see if it is opaque all the way through.

• Insert a small, thin instant-read thermometer (Taylor makes a good one) into the thickest part of the flesh; if it reads 130 degrees F, the fish is cooked.

• If you can easily pull out a spine from one of the fins when roasting or poaching a whole fish, the fish is cooked.

• For shellfish, cut a piece in half to see whether it is opaque all the way through.

• Mussels and clams should be cooked only until they open, or they will toughen.

Note that overcooked fish produces white fat globules on the opaque flesh. If you oversalt the fish, the fat will rise to the surface faster.

So, let's take the cooking methods one by one and see the advantages of each.

One more tip: Before you start to cook, take the fish or shellfish out of the refrigerator for a little while. This will take the chill off so it will cook more evenly.

Avoiding Fishy Smells

People often ask me how to avoid getting a fishy smell in the kitchen when cooking fish. Well, fish is not naturally smelly when fresh and belief in this "smell" is probably not based on fact. I cook fish nearly every day, and I would say that the only smell that knocks me for a loop is that of the guts of some fish. The guts and any bits of fish garbage should be enclosed in separate garbage bags or plastic bags and thrown out immediately.

Some say that putting a piece of bread in the oven when baking, roasting, broiling, or bake-poaching will help to eliminate smells. Another possibility is to place a piece of bread on the edge of the pan when poaching.

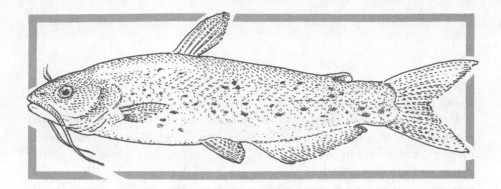

Baking, Bake-Poaching, Oven Steaming, and Casserole Baking

BAKING*

Baking is a healthful and easy way to cook fish. You can bake fillets, steaks, and butterflied fillets of many fat and lean fish. Shellfish, such as clams, can be baked in foil and oysters can be warmed through (on the half shell) in the oven.

Oils and butter need not be used in great quantities, if at all. You need these fats only to add flavor, to help nonfatty fish brown nicely, or to provide a glaze. Sometimes the broiler should be used briefly to brown the fish, either

---

* *Note*: For clarity, I suggest that we talk about *baking* fillets or steaks of fish and *roasting* whole fish and large chunks. (See page 113 for information on roasting.)

95

before or after baking. You may also sear the fish in some fat in a skillet or frying pan before baking, to produce a light brown glaze.

Herbs, spices, and seasonings play an important part in baking. Generally, you will want to use stronger-tasting herbs like thyme, rosemary, marjoram, oregano, and savory in recipes for oily, strong-tasting fish, along with zestier spices and seasonings such as allspice, ginger, chili peppers, paprika, cumin, coriander, garlic, and mustard. Add such flavorings as dill, tarragon, basil, parsley, chervil, and lemon juice to light, lean-fleshed fish. (See page 243 for a more detailed discussion of herbs.)

Use a baking pan, a casserole, or a gratin dish for fillets. Lay them on a bed of chopped or sliced vegetables—the vegetables make a rack for the fish and provide added flavor. Finely slice or chop the vegetables so that they cook in the little time it takes to bake a fillet. Vegetables that take longer, such as carrots and potatoes, must be cooked until just tender before being baked with the fish—you can bake, sauté, or blanch them beforehand.

Pouring dry white wine or water to a depth of ⅛ inch keeps the fish from sticking to the baking pan and produces a tasty piece of fish.

Baked fish dishes rarely need to be sauced, as the moisture from the fish and vegetables is usually adequate and all that's needed is a squeeze of lemon juice. If you want a sauce, by all means look at the sauce recipes on pages 225–234; some casserole and gratin dish recipes do require sauces.

BAKE-POACHING AND OVEN STEAMING

Bake-poaching is an easy way to poach a piece of fish without submerging it in a liquid. No added fat is used in this method and the fish will not brown. All that is needed is some dry white wine or water in the bottom of a shallow baking pan and a covering of some sort to keep the moisture in. The covering can be a wilted lettuce leaf that you discard afterward, a piece of parchment paper, or even aluminum foil.

This is a very plain way of cooking fish—it will taste quite bland and you will certainly get the true unadulterated taste of it. It will be your choice as to whether you will enhance it with a sauce or with accompanying vegetables, herbs, spices, seasonings, or even liquor.

You can use this method to show off fillets of fish with beautiful, edible skin. Such fish include black sea bass, bluefish, mackerel, pompano, rockfish, smelt (butterflied), red snapper, salmon, tilefish, tilapia, trout, weakfish, and whiting. Of course, not only fish with good-looking skin can be bake-poached—use any fish you like.

You can take advantage of this method to cook a whole large fish for a special occasion. All the juices will be retained inside the foil, and they can be clarified and made into a flavorful aspic when you are decorating the fish. Large fish can also be poached in a fish poacher, but the bake-poaching method obviates the need for a poacher, and to my mind is much more satisfactory, for there is no chance of the fish juices and their flavors seeping away into the poaching liquid. Of course, a flavorful poaching liquid does enhance the flavor of a dull tasting fish.

In the oven-steaming method the seafood is cooked in a tightly closed paper package. This is called cooking *en papillote*. This method is a good one, for all the moisture is retained in the package and a wonderful aromatic steam escapes as the package is opened. Serve this as a romantic meal for two! You can mix vegetables and seafood together and, if you like, bake a potato to go with them; you will have a potless meal and very little washing up.

CASSEROLE BAKING

Seafood can be combined with vegetables or a sauce in a shallow earthenware, Pyrex, or ovenproof china casserole dish, then simply baked in the oven until done. Vegetables may have to be sautéed or blanched in advance because the seafood takes little time to cook, and a coating sauce must be prepared beforehand as well.

You can assemble a casserole several hours before cooking. Cover it with plastic wrap and refrigerate it until you are ready to cook. Take it out of the refrigerator 10 to 15 minutes before baking, to take the chill off, or, if you want to cook it straight from the refrigerator, lengthen the cooking time in the recipe. Most casseroles can be prepared and cooked in little more than three quarters of an hour.

For variety, cut fish fillets on a strong diagonal into ¼- to ½-inch-thick slices or slice large sea scallops across into wafers. Intersperse them with sliced cooked vegetables, such as potatoes. Add a few herbs or a basil leaf or coriander pesto, as well as some seasonings and chopped tomatoes, to finish the dish. Or put a layer of toasted bread, fresh bread crumbs, mashed potatoes, or sliced cooked potatoes on the bottom of the dish. Lay the fish or shellfish on top of the bread or vegetables and pour an appropriate sauce on top. This way the bread or vegetables absorb the delicious juices of the seafood.

I recommend using a hot oven (400 to 475 degrees F), as I prefer to sear the fish rather than letting it "sweat" in the oven and lose moisture. This temperature assures quick cooking.

HEALTH

The methods described here require that very little fat be added to the fish or shellfish. As we have noted, little or no oil, butter, or margarine is needed to give oily fish a nice glaze. The same can be said about sprinkling on bread crumbs to give a fine crust: few are needed.

BASIC BAKING RECIPES

BAKED FATTY FISH FILLETS

Preparation time: 15 minutes
Baking time: 10 to 20 minutes

SPECIAL EQUIPMENT: Baking pan or sheet with ½-inch-high edges

The preparation can be done ahead of time and the fish can be refrigerated until you are ready to bake it. Remember to bring it to room temperature before putting it in the oven.

Choose fillets of fish such as

bluefish • buffalofish • lake trout • mackerel • salmon • shad • sturgeon • whitefish

or see the list of fatty fish on page 21.

Dry white wine or *water*
1 medium onion, thinly sliced
*2 tablespoons chopped fresh or 1
    tablespoon dried rosemary*
*2 tablespoons mild olive oil or
    unsalted butter or margarine,
    melted*
Salt to taste
*Freshly ground black pepper to
    taste*

*1½ to 2 pounds fish fillets with
    skin on and pin bones removed*
Juice of ½ lemon or lime (¼ cup)
*1 tablespoon diced sweet red,
    yellow, or green pepper
    (optional)*
4 rosemary sprigs for garnish

1. Preheat the oven to 475 degrees F.
2. Pour wine or water to a depth of ⅛ inch into a shallow baking pan or baking sheet with ½-inch-high edges.
3. Mix sliced onion with half the rosemary; half the oil, melted butter, or melted margarine; and salt and pepper to taste in a bowl.
4. Lay the onion mixture in the middle of the baking pan.
5. Place the fillets on top of the onion mixture, skin side down.
6. Brush the fish with lemon juice and the rest of the oil.
7. Sprinkle with remaining chopped rosemary and diced pepper (if desired).
8. Bake for 10 to 20 minutes, depending on the thickness of the fish.
9. Check for doneness after 7 minutes (see page 94).
10. If the fish has not taken on enough color to suit you, quickly heat the broiler and brown it a little. This should take less than a minute. Keep in mind that you don't want to overcook the fish.
11. Sprinkle with salt and pepper to taste.
12. Use one or two wide spatulas to lift the onion mixture and fish onto a serving platter or individual plates. Pour any juices that are left in the baking pan over the fish.
13. Garnish with rosemary sprigs.

Variations: Use the same amounts of shallots or scallions in place of the onion. Use the same amount of thyme, mint, basil, or savory in place of the rosemary.

SERVES 4

BAKED LEAN FISH FILLETS

Preparation time: 10 minutes
Baking time: 7 to 20 minutes

SPECIAL EQUIPMENT: Baking pan or sheet with ½-inch-high edges

   Choose fillets of fish such as

bass • catfish • dolphinfish (mahi-mahi) • gray sole • grouper • haddock • lingcod • mullet • petrale sole • pike • red snapper • rockfish • scrod, cod • spotted sea trout • tilefish • weakfish (sea trout)

or see the list of lean fish on page 20.

Dry white wine or *water*
1½ to 2 pounds fish fillets with skin on or off and pin bones removed
½ stick (2 ounces) unsalted butter or margarine, melted

Juice of ½ lemon (¼ cup)
Salt to taste
Freshly ground white pepper to taste
2 tablespoons finely chopped parsley
4 lemon wedges

1. Preheat the oven to 450 degrees F.
2. Pour wine or water to a depth of ⅛ inch into a shallow baking pan or baking sheet with ½-inch-high edges.
3. Place the fish skin side down onto the pan.
4. Brush the fish with the melted butter or margarine.
5. Bake for 7 to 20 minutes, depending on the thickness of the fish.
6. If fillets are very thin, check for doneness after 3 minutes (see page 94).
7. If the fish has not taken on enough color to suit you, quickly heat the broiler and brown it a little. This should take less than 1 minute. Keep in mind that you don't want to overcook the fish.
8. Use one or two wide spatulas to lift the fish onto a serving platter or individual plates. Pour some or all of the juices from the pan over the fish and sprinkle it with lemon juice, salt, pepper, and chopped parsley.
9. Garnish with lemon wedges.

Variations: Use ground cumin or paprika in place of the white pepper. Use chervil, tarragon, or dill in place of the parsley.

SERVES 4

BASIC BAKE-POACHING RECIPES

BAKE-POACHED FISH FILLETS

Preparation time: 15 minutes
Bake-poaching time: 8 to 10 minutes

SPECIAL EQUIPMENT: Baking pan with ½-inch-high edges
Optional: parchment paper *or* aluminum foil (see ingredients list below)

Choose fish fillets, preferably with attractive, edible skin, such as

black sea bass • bluefish • haddock • freshwater striped bass • mackerel • mullet • pompano • red snapper • rockfish • salmon • tilapia • tilefish • weakfish (sea trout) • whiting

*2 6 to 8-ounce fish fillets with skin
 on and pin bones removed*
Dry white wine or *water*
*½ small fennel bulb, very finely
 sliced (¾ cup); save a piece of
 the green fennel frond for
 garnish (fennel is called anise in
 some stores)*

Salt to taste
*4 lettuce leaves (outer leaves of
 romaine) or parchment paper or
 aluminum foil*
¼ teaspoon paprika or white pepper

1. Preheat the oven to 425 degrees F.
2. Cut each fillet through the skin on a strong diagonal, to make 8 slivers in all. (For method, see page 85.)
3. Pour wine or water to a depth of ⅛ inch into a baking pan with ½-inch-high edges.
4. Put the sliced fennel in the pan. Sprinkle the fennel with salt to taste. Bake the fennel for 10 minutes or until nearly tender.
5. Remove the pan from the oven and place the slivers, skin side up, on top of the fennel.
6. Cover the fish with the lettuce leaves.
7. Bake for 8 to 10 minutes, until fish is just cooked through (see page 94).
8. Discard the lettuce leaves.

(continued)

9. Using a wide spatula, serve the fennel, fish, and juices on individual plates and sprinkle with paprika or white pepper.
10. Garnish the fish with the fennel fronds.

Variation: You can use celery, red onion, or sweet pepper (red, green, or yellow) in place of the fennel.

SERVES 2

BAKE-POACHED WHOLE FISH

Preparation time: 10 minutes
Bake-poaching time: 35 minutes to
   1¼ hours

SPECIAL EQUIPMENT: Heavy-duty aluminum foil
Baking pan or sheet with ½-inch-high edges

This method of preparing fish is a good one, for instance, when you want to make a showy piece for a buffet. For such an occasion it is best to buy a large fish (over 6 pounds), but for other occasions you can use any size whole fish. You will skin the fish after it is cooked and display the flesh in all its glory, or partially cover it with razor-thin slices of cucumber to resemble fish scales. Have fun with the decoration!

Note: Adjust the number served, as listed in the table below, according to the weight of the fish's head (buy a heavier fish if the head is large, a lighter fish if the head is small). Also note that salmon has the greatest yield of the fish listed below.

Choose a fish weighing 6 to 9 pounds, such as

**bluefish • grouper • red snapper • salmon • tilefish •
weakfish (sea trout)**

NUMBER SERVED	AMOUNT OF FISH NEEDED	APPROXIMATE BAKE-POACHING TIME AT OVEN TEMPERATURE 425°F
6 to 8	1 fish weighing 6 pounds	40 minutes
8 to 10	1 fish weighing 7 pounds	50 minutes
9 to 11	1 fish weighing 8 pounds	1 hour, 5 minutes
12 to 14	1 fish weighing 9 pounds	1¼ hours

*4 tablespoons mild olive oil or un-
    salted butter or margarine,
    melted*
*1 whole fish weighing at least 6
    pounds, gutted and scaled, with
    gills removed and head, tail,
    and fins left on*
4 tablespoons lemon juice (¼ cup)
Salt to taste
*Freshly ground white pepper to
    taste*
*1 large or 2 small bunches dill
    weed or parsley*

For decoration:
*1 seedless (European hothouse)
    cucumber*
*1 bunch chives or tarragon or 1
    scallion*
2 lemons, quartered
*1 sweet red, yellow, or green pepper
    cut in rings and/or fennel cut in
    quarters and/or tomato wedges*
1 cup mayonnaise (see page 227)

1. Preheat the oven to 425 degrees F.

2. Measure out a length of heavy-duty aluminum foil 8 inches longer than the fish (double this if the foil is lightweight).

3. Pour some of the oil, melted butter, or melted margarine down the middle of the foil lengthwise, and lay the fish on it.

4. Pour the rest of the oil, melted butter, or melted margarine inside and outside the fish.

5. Pour lemon juice all over the fish, and sprinkle the inside and outside with salt and pepper. Lay 12 dill or parsley sprigs inside the cavity.

6. Bring the two sides of the foil up over the fish and make a double fold down the middle and at both ends of the fish, so the juices cannot escape.

7. Pour water to a depth of ⅛ inch into a baking sheet or baking pan with ½-inch-high edges and place the wrapped fish in it.

8. If the fish is too long to fit in the oven, place it diagonally on the baking pan so that its head is in a corner of the oven and the tail is curved up against the oven door.

9. Bake-poach the fish for as long as necessary, depending on its size. Halfway through cooking, turn the fish over, so it cooks evenly. Remove the fish from the oven, open up the foil, and check to see that it is cooked all the way through (see page 94). If it is not cooked, wrap it up and cook it a little longer.

10. When the fish is cooked, open up the foil and let the fish rest 15 minutes at the side of the kitchen sink.

11. Put a bowl in the sink and tip the fish so the juices go into the bowl. Don't let the fish fall into the sink, as once happened to me!

12. Strain the juices through a fine sieve into a bowl. Put aside.

13. Now carefully lift off the skin, using your fingers or a blunt knife. Turn the fish over on the foil to skin the other side. Keep the head and tail intact.

14. If you like, remove the dark flesh that appears along the lateral line of the fish. It is fatty and distasteful to some, although this is where many of the healthful omega-3 fatty acids come from.

15. Lift the fish by the aluminum foil onto a platter, then rip one side of the foil away from under the fish; hold the fish in place and pull the other side of the foil away neatly.

16. If you would like to bone the fish and return it to its original shape, follow the instructions on page 69.

17. If you wish to decorate the fish, use a sharp knife to cut slices of cucumber very fine, nearly transparent. Dip them in the fish juices and overlap them so that they look like scales. Cut the chives into 2- to 3-inch lengths and stretch them from the middle of the fish outward so that they resemble the bone structure. If using tarragon, pull the leaves from the stalks. If using a scallion, cut the green part lengthwise in very thin strips to resemble chives and then cut in 2- to 3-inch lengths. Put little sprigs of dill down the natural lateral division.

18. Clean the platter with a paper towel and surround the fish with more dill; cucumber slices; pepper rings, fennel, and/or tomato wedges; quartered lemons; and mayonnaise piped into rosettes. Finally, remove the fish eye and insert some dill or a piece of lemon in the cavity. Serve warm or cold.

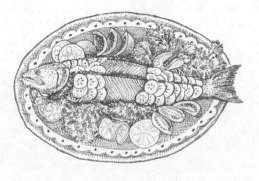

Variation: The fish can also be cooked on an open fire (see page 134). Follow the above instructions except steps 1, 7, and 8.

OVEN-STEAMED SEAFOOD *EN PAPILLOTE*

Preparation time: 25 minutes
Cooking time: 20 minutes, or 10 to 12 minutes in microwave on high setting

SPECIAL EQUIPMENT: Aluminum foil *or* parchment paper (baking sheet, 24 x 16 inches)

The preparation can be done ahead of time and the package can be refrigerated. Take the package out of the refrigerator 10 minutes before baking, to take the chill off.

Choose butterflied fish such as **baby coho salmon, rainbow** or **brook trout** or fillets of fish such as

blackfish · black sea bass · bluefish · gray sole · mackerel · ocean perch · perch · pompano · red snapper · scrod, cod · shad · sheepshead · sole · tilapia · tilefish · weakfish (sea trout) · whitefish

or shellfish such as large butterflied **shrimp** or **sea scallops.**

1 tablespoon unsalted butter or
margarine, melted
2 tablespoons coarsely grated carrot
1 small leek with some of the green
leaves cut off, finely sliced in
thin julienne strips 3 inches long
½ celery stalk, finely sliced in thin
julienne strips 3 inches long
Salt to taste
Freshly ground white pepper to
taste

8 to 10 ounces butterflied fish or 6
to 8 ounces fish fillet with skin
on or off and pin bones removed,
or 4 to 6 ounces butterflied
shrimp (16 to 20 per pound), or
4 to 6 ounces sea scallops, small
tough muscle removed, cut in
½-inch-thick wafers
1 tablespoon chopped or 1 teaspoon
dried dill weed
2 tablespoons lemon juice
1 egg white

1. Preheat the oven to 400 degrees F.
2. Fold the parchment paper in half. Draw half a heart shape, beginning at the fold and going out to the edge. Use scissors to cut it out. Unfold the paper. If you are using a microwave oven, cut the heart shape small enough that it will fit inside the oven.

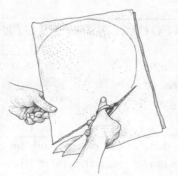

3. Rub a little melted butter or margarine over one half of the paper heart.
4. Mix the vegetables together and place three quarters of the mixture on the buttered side of the heart.
5. Pour a little butter over the mixture on the heart and add salt and pepper to taste.

6. If you are using a butterflied fish, spread it open, cut off the head and tail, and then cut across it in three places, making four slices. If you are using a fish fillet, do the same: cut across it in three places, making four slices.

7. Place the fish slices skin side down, or the shrimp or scallops on top of the mixed vegetables on the heart.

8. Place the rest of the vegetables on the fish, then sprinkle the fish with the rest of the butter, the dill weed, and the lemon juice.

9. Brush the empty half of the paper heart with egg white and also all around the edges. Fold the paper over and crimp the edges together well. Fold the edges over twice, ending with a twist at the bottom of the heart.

10. If you are using a conventional oven, place the package on a baking sheet and bake for 20 minutes. If you are using a microwave oven, put the package on a plate and microwave for 10 to 12 minutes on High. (Here you have to be precise about the time, for there is no way to tell whether all is cooked until you open the package.)

11. After the cooking time recommended in step 10, when the paper is nicely puffed up and starting to brown, remove the package from the oven and transfer it to a warm serving plate.

12. You will need sharp pointed scissors to pierce the package and then cut around the edge. Slide the contents of the package onto the plate and discard the paper.

Variations: You can use sweet red, yellow, or green peppers or tiny green beans in place of the carrots. You can use scallions (cut in thin strips) or chives (cut in 3-inch lengths) in place of the leeks. You can use basil, coriander, thyme, or parsley in place of the dill.

SERVES 1

BASIC CASSEROLE RECIPES

BAKED FISH FILLET CASSEROLE

Preparation time: 25 minutes
Baking time: 20 to 30 minutes

SPECIAL EQUIPMENT: Oval earthenware, Pyrex, or ovenproof china casserole dish (about 12 inches long)

The preparation can be done ahead of time and the casserole can be refrigerated until you are ready to bake it.

Choose thick fillets of fish such as

blackfish • catfish • cod • dolphinfish (mahi-mahi) • grouper • haddock • halibut • lingcod • red snapper • rockfish • sand shark (dogfish) • shad • tilefish • weakfish (sea trout) • wolffish

or see the list of lean fish on page 20.

*3 tablespoons mild olive oil or un-
    salted butter or margarine,
    melted*
*3 pounds thick fish fillets
    (2 1½-pound fillets) with skin on
    or off and pin bones removed*
*1 small onion, sliced lengthwise
    (from top to bottom) very finely*
*3 medium fresh tomatoes, sliced
    lengthwise (from top to bottom)*

*1 small yellow squash or zucchini,
    sliced on the diagonal into 5
    ¼-inch-thick slices*
Salt to taste
*Freshly ground black pepper to
    taste*
*3 tablespoons basil or coriander or
    parsley, chopped at the last
    moment*

1. Preheat the oven to 425 degrees F.
2. Brush the casserole dish with 1 tablespoon oil, melted butter, or melted margarine.
3. Lay the fillets skin side down in the casserole dish with the thick parts of the fillets toward the outside of the dish (where they will get the most heat).
4. Sprinkle the sliced onion over the fish.
5. Lay the tomato slices, alternating with the yellow squash or zucchini slices, down the middle of the fish.
6. Place more tomato slices around the side of the casserole dish.

7. Brush the fish and vegetables with remaining oil, butter, or margarine.
8. Bake about 20 minutes or longer, depending on the thickness of the fillets. Check for doneness (see page 94).
9. Sprinkle with salt, pepper, and chopped basil, coriander, or parsley.

SERVES 6 TO 8

BAKED FISH FILLET CASSEROLE
WITH LIGHT TOMATO SAUCE

Preparation time: 20 minutes
Baking time: 10 to 20 minutes

SPECIAL EQUIPMENT: Oval earthenware Pyrex, or ovenproof china casserole dish (about 12 inches long)

This casserole can be prepared ahead of time and refrigerated until you are ready to bake it.

Choose fillets of fish such as

bluefish • buffalofish • cod, scrod • mackerel • ocean perch • perch • red snapper • rockfish • salmon • sand shark (dogfish) • tilapia • weakfish (sea trout) • whitefish

or see the lists of lean and fat fish on pages 20 and 21.

4 tablespoons mild olive oil
1½ to 2 pounds fish fillets with skin on or off and pin bones removed
1 medium onion, finely chopped (1 cup)
3 cloves garlic, finely chopped
4 medium peeled, seeded, and chopped fresh tomatoes or 2 cups drained, seeded, and chopped canned tomatoes

Salt to taste
Freshly ground black or white pepper to taste
Nutmeg
¼ cup dry white wine
12 fresh basil leaves, finely chopped at the last moment

1. Preheat the oven to 425 degrees F.
2. Brush the casserole dish with 1 tablespoon of the oil.

3. Lay the fillets skin side down in the casserole dish with the thick parts of the fillets toward the outside of the dish (where they will get the most heat). Set aside.

4. Heat the remaining 3 tablespoons of oil in a frying pan over moderate heat.

5. Add the onion and sauté until it begins to brown, stirring occasionally.

6. Add the garlic, stir, and cook for 20 seconds.

7. Add the tomatoes, salt, pepper, and 10 rasps of nutmeg.

8. Add the wine and cook, stirring occasionally for 5 minutes. You want a fairly dry sauce, for the fish will exude some juice as it cooks.

9. Chop the basil and add all but 1 tablespoon to the sauce.

10. Pour this sauce over the fish and bake it for 10 to 20 minutes, depending on the thickness of the fillets. Check for doneness (see page 94).

11. Sprinkle with the rest of the basil and serve.

SERVES 4

BAKED CAJUN FISH CASSEROLE

Preparation time: 10 minutes
Baking time: 20 to 30 minutes

SPECIAL EQUIPMENT: Round or oval earthenware, Pyrex, or ovenproof china casserole dish (about 10 inches in diameter or 12 inches long)

Choose thick fillets of fish such as

blackfish • bluefish • catfish • dolphinfish (mahi-mahi) • gray sole • grouper • halibut • lingcod • orange roughy • redfish • rockfish • sand shark (dogfish) • sheepshead • spotted sea trout • tilefish • wolffish

3 tablespoons mild olive oil or vegetable oil
1½ to 2 pounds fish fillets with skin off and pin bones removed
1 tablespoon chili powder
1 tablespoon paprika
⅛ teaspoon cayenne pepper
½ teaspoon freshly ground white pepper
½ teaspoon freshly ground black pepper

Pinch ground cloves
1 teaspoon dried thyme
1 teaspoon dried oregano
¾ teaspoon salt
1 small onion, finely sliced
½ sweet red pepper, cored, seeded, with veins removed, and finely sliced lengthwise from top to bottom

1. Preheat oven to 425 degrees F.
2. Brush the casserole dish with 1 tablespoon oil.
3. Lay the fillets in the casserole skin side down overlapping each other, and brush them with oil.
4. Mix the spices and seasonings together in a bowl.
5. Sprinkle 3 to 4 tablespoons of the spice mixture over the fish.
6. Toss the onion and red pepper strips with 1 tablespoon of oil in a bowl and scatter them over the fish. Place the casserole in the oven to bake.
7. Bake about 20 minutes or longer, depending on the thickness of the fillets. Check for doneness (see page 94).

SERVES 4

CASSEROLE OF FISH FILLETS OR LARGE SEA SCALLOPS WITH POTATOES AND CORIANDER PESTO

Preparation time: 30 minutes
Baking time: 20 to 25 minutes

SPECIAL EQUIPMENT: Round or oval earthenware, Pyrex, or ovenproof china casserole dish (about 10 inches in diameter or 12 inches long)

Choose fillets of fish such as

**blackfish • catfish • dolphinfish (mahi-mahi) • fluke • lingcod
petrale sole • spotted trout • trout • weakfish (sea trout)**

or shellfish such as large **sea scallops.**

1½ pounds red-skinned potatoes
1 tablespoon mild olive oil
*1½ to 2 pounds fish fillets or large
    sea scallops (9 to 12 per pound,
    similar in diameter to the
    potatoes if possible)*

1 recipe coriander pesto (page 234)
*1 medium-large tomato, peeled,
    seeded, and chopped (page 241)
    (½ cup)*
*Freshly ground white pepper to
    taste*

1. Wash the potatoes and boil them for about 15 minutes, until they are just tender. Cool them under cold running water.
2. Preheat the oven to 425 degrees F.
3. Brush the casserole dish with half the olive oil.
4. Cut the potatoes into ¼-inch slices.
5. If using fish, cut it into ⅜-inch-thick slices on a strong diagonal (starting at the tail ends of the fillets). If using sea scallops, remove the tough part on the side of each and cut them crosswise into wafers ⅜ inch thick.
6. Place alternate pieces of sliced seafood and potatoes all around the casserole dish. They should fit snugly.
7. Spread the coriander pesto all over and sprinkle with chopped tomato, pepper, and the rest of the oil.
8. Bake for 25 minutes. Check doneness after 20 minutes (see page 94).

SERVES 4 TO 6

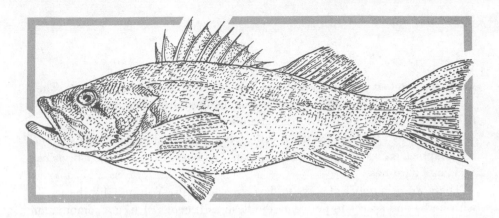

Roasting

WHOLE FISH AND LARGE CHUNKS ARE *ROASTED*. FILLETS AND STEAKS ARE *BAKED*. YOU CAN ALSO roast some shellfish.

FISH

Chef Felipe Rojas-Lombardi, my friend and colleague, helped me to appreciate roasted fish. I love this method. I find roasted fish to be hugely popular with everyone, and now that I have perfected this cooking method, I hope you will share my enthusiasm.

Roasting a large whole fish or several small whole fish takes little effort. The fish does not need constant attention, and cooking time does not need to be as exact as with some other cooking methods. The skin encasing the flesh keeps it moist and flavorful, and the central backbone acts as a heat conductor.

Large roasted fish are wonderful for buffets and dinners for eight or more. They may be served hot from the oven or at room temperature. Any number of small fish can be roasted for individual servings.

The best fish to roast are those with richly colored skins, such as salmon, red snapper, grouper, porgy, spot, pompano, all bass, tilefish, bluefish, mackerel, and sardines.

There are a number of ways to flavor roasted fish. You may fill the cavity with herbs and spices to permeate the flesh as it cooks. I like a combination of fresh thyme, finely chopped ginger, and garlic, perhaps with some ground cumin and salt, or a combination of fresh dill weed, grated lemon rind, black pepper, and salt. You may also sprinkle the fish with a drop or two of dry white wine, dry vermouth, or Pernod. And you may also use sliced vegetables as a bed for the fish to lie on. A roasted fish, surrounded by the vegetables it was cooked on, with its colored skin slightly browned and a little crisp, is irresistible.

Large fish or chunks (roasts) can be boned out and stuffed; a particularly dramatic presentation is a fish stuffed with a fillet of another fish that has flesh of a contrasting color—for example, a pollock stuffed with salmon or a salmon stuffed with flounder. When a roasted stuffed fish is sliced, it looks like a terrine or sandwich, with contrasting colorful layers.

SHELLFISH

You can treat scallops the same way as fish—that is, place them on a bed of vegetables and flavor them with herbs, spices, and seasonings. Coat them with a little oil or butter to produce a nice glaze.

Small unpeeled shrimp roasted in the oven are delicious. The roasted shells impart a wonderful flavor. The shell of a small shrimp is certainly edible; if the shrimp are large, equip your guests with napkins and finger bowls and let them take the shells off themselves. No doubt some of you will be kind enough to shell each shrimp for your guests, but leave on the tail and the section of the shell nearest to it. Peeled shrimp can also be roasted to good effect.

TIMES AND TEMPERATURES

To roast a fish you will want a relatively high temperature. Preheat the oven to 425 degrees F. A smaller fish—one that weighs a few ounces to a pound—will take 10 to 20 minues. A 3-pound fish serving four people will take about 35 minutes. A large fish weighing 9 pounds will take 1 hour or more. Obviously, the thicker the fish, the longer it will take to cook. But remember that the central spine will conduct heat and speed the cooking.

Shellfish need a higher oven temperature, 450 to 470 degrees F, and take 10 to 20 minutes to cook, depending on size and thickness.

A roasted fish really needs no sauce to accompany it, as a fish cooked with the skin on retains all its moisture if it is not overcooked. If you do want a sauce, however, there are many suggestions beginning on page 225.

HEALTH

From the above you will have gathered that there is no real need to use a lot of oil or fat to roast seafood. There are some stuffings that will need a little butter or oil for flavor, but otherwise the fish should be free of added fat. Roasting is a simple and clean way to cook seafood and the flavor is completely retained.

BASIC ROASTING RECIPES

ROAST WHOLE FISH

Preparation time: 20 minutes
Roasting time: 35 minutes to 40 minutes

SPECIAL EQUIPMENT: Aluminum foil
Baking pan or sheet with ½-inch-high edges

This basic method is the same no matter what size fish you use; only the cooking time will differ (Remember, domestic ovens will only be able to handle a fish weighing up to 9 pounds.) Large roasted fish can be served at a dinner or as part of a buffet. Choose fish with colorful skins and decorate the finished plate with fresh vegetables and herbs.

If the baking pan or the oven does not quite take the length of the fish, have no fear—you can curl the tail up to fit behind the door of the oven or even against the wall of the oven. *It is best to put the fish into the oven headfirst because the back of the oven is usually hotter than the front and the head end will need more cooking than the tail end.*

Choose whole fish such as

black sea bass • bluefish • croaker • freshwater striped bass • grouper • herring • ling • lingcod • mackerel • mullet • pike • pollock • pompano • porgy • red snapper • rockfish • salmon • sardines • scrod, cod • sheepshead • smelt • sunfish • tilapia • tilefish • trout • walleye • weakfish (sea trout) • whitefish • whiting

NUMBER SERVED	AMOUNT OF FISH NEEDED	APPROXIMATE ROASTING TIME AT OVEN TEMPERATURE 425°F
1	2 or 3 fish weighing a few ounces each *or*	15 minutes
	1 fish weighing ½ pound	20 minutes
2 to 3	1 fish weighing 1½ to 2 pounds	30 minutes
4 to 5	1 fish weighing 3 pounds	35 to 40 minutes
6 to 8	1 fish weighing 6 pounds	45 minutes
12 to 14	1 fish weighing 9 pounds	1 to 1¼ hours

1 large onion, finely sliced
2 carrots, scraped and very finely sliced
2 tablespoons mild olive oil, plus more for coating
2 bunches parsley (2 tablespoons chopped and the rest for decoration)
1 tablespoon finely minced garlic
2 tablespoons finely chopped ginger
1 teaspoon finely grated lemon rind
½ teaspoon salt

1 3-pound fish, gutted and scaled and with gills removed or 3 pounds of small fish weighing a few ounces each—leave the tail and fins on (even if spiny) intact for they are part of the final presentation
Dry white wine
parsley sprigs
2 sliced lemons
2 tomatoes cut in wedges

1. Preheat the oven to 425 degrees F.
2. Lay the onion and carrots on a baking sheet and sprinkle with 2 tablespoons of olive oil.

3. Roast for 10 minutes while you get the fish ready. *Note:* There is no need to precook the vegetables if you are roasting a fish weighing 6 pounds or more, for they will take the same time to cook.

4. Chop 2 tablespoons of parsley (save the rest for the decoration).

5. Add the chopped parsley to the garlic, ginger, lemon rind, and salt in a small bowl and mix together.

6. Place this mixture in the cavity of the fish.

7. When the vegetables have cooked for 10 minutes, take them out of the oven and place the fish on top.

8. Rub olive oil all over the fish (to protect the skin and keep it moist).

9. Wrap the head and tail of the fish with aluminum foil so they don't burn: Take an 8-by-12-inch piece of foil, lift up the head, and slide the foil under it. Bring the edges of the foil together and pinch or fold them together, leaving a space of 2 to 3 inches above the head. (This space is necessary so the heat will circulate but not burn the head.) Don't let the foil touch the top of the head, for it will stick to the head and ruin its looks. Fold another piece of foil over the tail. (*Note:* Small fish such as smelts, sardines, herring, and small mackerel do not need the foil; they will take less time to cook and thus won't have time to burn.)

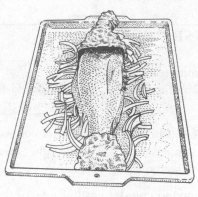

10. Sprinkle the fish with white wine and roast it in the oven for as long as necessary, depending on the size of the fish. In the case of a 3-pound fish check to see if it is cooked after 35 minutes.

11. Using one or two wide spatulas, lift the fish onto a platter and decorate it with the onions and carrots (if they are not burned and look good enough to

eat). Also use parsley sprigs, lemon slices (curled into twists), and tomato wedges.

12. If the skin is thick, cut across the fish skin behind the pectoral fin and along both the top and bottom of the fish. Put the tines of a fork in the skin and roll the skin back off the fish as if you were rolling up a window shade.

Variations: You can use shallots, scallions, fennel, celery, bok choy, or leeks in place of the onions and carrots. You can use chopped scallions, basil, thyme, and ground coriander in place of the garlic, ginger, parsley, and lemon rind. For the final presentation, you can buy whatever takes your fancy at the market. You can use bunches of scallions, chives, dill, carrot tops, beet tops, fennel tops, spinach leaves, kale, turnips, yellow squash, zucchini sliced on the diagonal, sliced limes.

SERVES 4 TO 5

ROAST STUFFED FISH CHUNK

Preparation time: 20 minutes
Roasting time: 50 minutes to 1¼ hours

SPECIAL EQUIPMENT: Baking pan or sheet with ½-inch-high edges or other ovenproof pan

You want to stuff the fish with a skinned fillet of contrasting color. This dish is best eaten at room temperature or chilled; either start the preparation the day before or at least 5 hours before needed.

Choose a 1½- to 4-pound chunk (roast) of a large fish, such as

bluefish • cod • lingcod • pollock • "tail end" halibut • sablefish • tilefish • wild striped bass

stuffed with a skinned fillet of salmon or baby coho salmon or choose a 1½- to 4-pound chunk of salmon stuffed with a skinned fillet of one of the following:

cod • lingcod • sole, flounder • tilefish

3-pound chunk, boned out from the belly but with the back intact (ask the fishmonger to do it or follow the instructions on page 69)

Salt to taste

Freshly ground black pepper to taste

Juice of ½ lemon or lime (¼ cup)

1 small onion, very finely sliced

2 cloves garlic, finely sliced lengthwise

1 large tomato, sliced from top to bottom in ¼-inch-thick slices

10 basil leaves, rinsed if necessary, dried and sliced thinly, plus a few for decorating the plate

8-ounces thin-skinned fish fillet with pin bones removed

3 tablespoons mild olive oil

Dry white wine

1. Preheat the oven to 400 degrees F.
2. Open up the chunk of fish and lay it flat on a board.
3. Sprinkle the inside of the chunk with a little salt and pepper and half the lemon juice.
4. Place half the onion, all of the garlic, tomato slices, and basil leaves on one half of the chunk. Season with salt and pepper and then place the fish fillet on top.
5. Fold the other half of the chunk over the fillet. Take string and tie it like a roast, once around every inch or so.

6. Arrange some of the remaining onion in a baking pan, sprinkle it with oil and pour white wine to a depth of ¼ inch in the pan. Place the chunk on top of the onions and brush with oil. Place the rest of the onion on top of the chunk and sprinkle with the rest of the lemon juice.

7. Roast for 50 minutes, basting occasionally with the juices in the pan. Add with more wine or water, if necessary. Be generous with the basting for the fish tends to dry out around the edges, before the inside is cooked. Check for doneness (see page 94). If using an instant-read thermometer, the chunk should be removed from the oven when the inside reaches 120 degrees F; it will continue to cook even as it cools.

8. Cook the fish longer if necessary. When it is cooked, remove it from the oven.

9. With wide spatulas, lift the fish and vegetables out of the baking pan and onto a platter. Pour over the juices. After 15 minutes cut the string and remove it carefully. Let the chunk cool to room temperature—this will take at least 3 hours. (If you want to eat it chilled, wrap it in aluminum foil and put it in the refrigerator after it has cooled. Always take it out of the refrigerator 30 minutes before serving, so it is not icy cold.)

10. Decorate the plate with basil leaves.

11. Cut the chunk into ½-inch slices with a very sharp knife.

Variations: You can use scallions or shallots in place of the onion. You can use coarsely grated zucchini or carrot in place of the tomato. You can use parsley, coriander, dill, or mint in place of the basil.

SERVES 5 TO 6

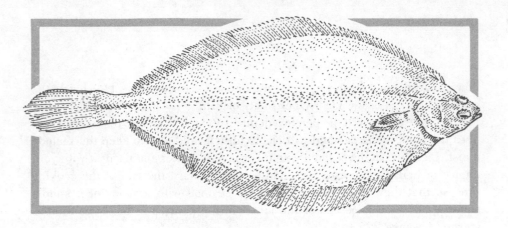

Broiling

BROILING IS ONE OF THE MOST POPULAR METHODS FOR COOKING FISH, AND IT PRODUCES THE MOST satisfactory results. The fish is seared by the heat from above so that a nice crust is formed with moist flesh underneath. You can broil whole fish, fillets, steaks, and of course all sorts of shellfish. I can't think of a single fish or shellfish that cannot be broiled, except for tiny fish like whitebait (silversides); even mollusks such as oysters, clams, and mussels can be broiled if stuffed or cooked on the half shell.

Turn the broiler to its fullest heat to do the job well, and always preheat the broiler for 5 to 10 minutes before cooking. Place the seafood on a metal pan about 3 to 6 inches away from the heat (closer if the heat is not sufficient), for it is important to sear the flesh. The heat will reach the metal pan and the flesh will cook from the bottom upward as well as from above, so there is no need to turn the seafood over.

Here is a tip: To get the seafood close to the broiler, lay another pan upside down underneath the pan you are using, or use some other object to elevate the seafood. This is useful for thinner fillets of fish.

Pour wine or water in the pan to a depth of ⅛ inch to ensure that the seafood does not stick to the pan and will easily lift out, and also to keep the seafood moist. Lightly coat the seafood with oil or melted butter and flavor it with your choice of herbs and seasonings, adding them toward the end of the cooking time so that they do not burn. Serve the seafood with a sauce or a simple squeeze of lemon juice and/or the juices in the pan. (See the sauce recipes starting on page 225.)

If you broil a thick fish or fillet, its surface may very well burn before it cooks through, so you will need to finish cooking it in the oven or the microwave oven after broiling it. Check doneness at 5-minute intervals.

Add herbs just before the fish is done so that they do not burn, but give flavor to the fish.

You can broil brochettes (shellfish or skewered cubes of fish and vegetables) rather than grilling them on an open fire. To broil them, lay the brochette sticks inside or on the edges of a baking pan. Cook them for 10 minutes, basting and turning them every 2 minutes. The recipes for brochettes are included with the grilling recipes.

Before you broil a lobster, you must split it down the middle lengthwise. The fishmonger can do this for you if you are too tenderhearted, or you can kill it by putting it into boiling water for 2 minutes, then split it down the middle. (See the method on page 342.) Lay the lobster on the broiler pan, split side up, and gently broil it about 5 inches below the heat. You may add fresh herbs and some butter or oil. It is fairly tricky to broil lobster, because it tends to dry out. However, do try—it tastes so good when you are successful.

Restaurant broilers can often act like grills. Although their heat comes from above, they have grilling rods below that retain heat so well that they make grill marks on the food being cooked. If you have such a broiler and you want the grill marks, be sure to preheat the broiler for some 15 minutes so the rods get very hot. Oil the rods lightly before putting the seafood on to cook.

TIMES AND TEMPERATURES

Broiling a small whole fish, fillet, butterflied fish, medallion, steak, and most shellfish is fast, as long as the broiler is capable of giving off efficient heat.

Depending on the thickness of the seafood, it should take 2 to 10 minutes. A ¼-inch-thick escalope will take as little as 1 minute to cook. Large whole fish and lobsters will take quite a bit longer.

BASIC BROILING RECIPES

BROILED WHOLE FLATFISH

Preparation time: 10 minutes
Broiling time: 5 to 15 minutes

SPECIAL EQUIMENT: Broiler pan or baking pan or sheet with ½-inch-high edges

For large broiled flatfish (those weighing more than 1½ pounds), it may be necessary to finish the cooking, after the fish is well browned, in either a conventional oven or a microwave oven. If you have separate units, preheat the broiler and the oven at the same time. If the broiler is located under the oven or inside the oven at the top, the broiler will heat the oven somewhat, so when you turn the oven on it will only be a few moments before it reaches the required temperature of 425 degrees F. A microwave oven can be used at the High setting. Check doneness at 5-minute intervals.

Choose whole flatfish such as

flounder, sole • sand dabs

or see the flatfish profiles on page 320.

NUMBER SERVED	AMOUNT OF FLATFISH NEEDED	APPROXIMATE BROILING TIME
1	2 or 3 flatfish weighing approximately 4 ounces each	5 to 10 minutes
	or	
	1 flatfish weighing 1 pound	10 to 15 minutes
2 or 3	1 flatfish weighing 2 pounds	20 to 25 minutes
4	1 flatfish weighing 3 pounds	30 to 35 minutes

(continued)

1 1-pound flatfish or 2 or 3 flatfish weighing approximately 4 ounces each, gutted and scaled, with skin on or off
Dry white wine or water
2 tablespoons unsalted butter or margarine, melted

Freshly ground white pepper to taste
2 tablespoons lemon juice or lime juice
1 teaspoon chopped parsley, thyme, dill, tarragon, or basil

1. Preheat the broiler to its highest setting.
2. Place the fish, dark skin side up, on a board. Make a slit down the middle of the fish, above the backbone, from head to tail.
3. Cut under the fillets close to the bones to loosen them. Do not cut all the way to the edge of the fish.
4. Pour white wine or water to a depth of ⅛ inch in the broiler pan.
5. Place the fish in the wine or water. Spread the fillets open, pour 1 tablespoon of melted butter or margarine between them, and sprinkle them with pepper.
6. Broil the fish 5 to 6 inches away from the broiler until the edges brown, about 10 minutes.
7. Check after 7 minutes to see whether the fish is cooked (see page 94).
8. If the fish is browned but undercooked, finish it in a conventional oven set at 425 degrees F or a microwave oven set on High. Check doneness at 5-minute intervals.
9. With the aid of one or two spatulas, place the fish on a serving plate.
10. Pour the remaining butter and lemon or lime juice into the juice in the pan. Give it a swirl or stir it with a spoon, then pour it over the fish.
11. Sprinkle the fish with chopped herb.

Variation: Read the instructions on page 77 to see how easy it is to fillet a cooked whole flatfish. Enjoy!

SERVES 1

BROILED WHOLE ROUNDFISH

Preparation time: 10 minutes *Broiling time:* 5 to 35 minutes including the time needed to finish cooking in the oven	SPECIAL EQUIPMENT: Broiler pan or baking pan or sheet with ½-inch-high edges

Choose whole fish such as

anchovies • black sea bass • bluefish • croakers • freshwater bass • freshwater striped bass • grouper • lingcod • pompano • porgy • red snapper • sardines • weakfish (sea trout) • whitefish

NUMBER SERVED	AMOUNT OF FISH NEEDED	APPROXIMATE BROILING TIME*
1	2 or 3 fish weighing 3 to 4 ounces each *or*	5 to 10 minutes
	1 fish weighing 1 pound	7 to 15 minutes
2 or 3	1 fish weighing 2 pounds	20 to 25 minutes
4	1 fish weighing 3 pounds	30 to 35 minutes
6 to 8	1 fish weighing 6 pounds	45 to 55 minutes

* Includes the time needed to finish cooking the fish in the oven after it has browned under the broiler.

1 3-pound whole fish or *several small fish with a total weight of 3 pounds, gutted and scaled with gills removed, but with heads, tails, and fins left on*
2 cloves garlic, minced
3 scallions, trimmed of roots and some of the green part, cut in quarters lengthwise and then into 3-inch-long pieces

1 tablespoon finely grated ginger
2 tablespoons soy sauce
1 tablespoon dry white wine, plus enough to fill the broiler pan to a depth of ⅛ inch
2 tablespoons molasses
2 tablespoons vegetable oil
1 bunch parsley
1 lemon

1. Preheat the broiler to its highest setting. If you have a separate oven unit, preheat it to 425 degrees F when you are cooking a fish weighing over 1½ pounds.

2. Make three diagonal slashes in the skin on both sides of the fish.

3. Insert garlic, scallion strips, and ginger inside the fish and then in the slits. (If you are cooking small fish, put some of these ingredients inside the fish and scatter the rest on top.)

4. Whisk the soy sauce, 1 tablespoon of the white wine, molasses, and oil together in a bowl.

5. Pour the dry white wine to a depth of ⅛ inch into the broiler pan and lay the fish in the wine. Brush the fish with some of the mixture of soy sauce, molasses, oil, and wine.

6. Broil for 10 minutes, brushing more of the mixture on the fish after 5 minutes. Check to see whether the fish is nice and brown.

7. When the fish is browned, carefully turn it over using two wide metal spatulas and brush the exposed side with more of the mixture.

8. When the fish is nicely browned, check to see whether it is cooked all the way through (see page 94).

9. If the fish needs further cooking, finish it in a conventional oven or microwave oven (see page 123).

10. Place the fish on a serving plate using wide metal spatulas and garnish it with parsley and lemon curls. (Cut the lemon into slices, make a cut from the center of each slice outward, then twist each slice into a curl.)

Variations: You can use a julienne of carrots, leeks, or chives in place of the scallions. You can use finely chopped celery or fennel in place of the ginger. You can use Lea & Perrins original or white wine Worcestershire sauce in place of the soy sauce.

SERVES 4

BROILED FILLETS, BUTTERFLIED OR SPLIT FISH, STEAKS, ESCALOPES, OR MEDALLIONS

Preparation time: 5 minutes
Broiling time: 2 to 10 minutes

SPECIAL EQUIPMENT: Broiler pan or baking pan or sheet with ½-inch-high edges

Choose *any* filleted fish, butterflied or split fish, steaks, escalopes, or medallions (for instructions on escalopes and medallions, see page 84), or see lists of fat and lean fish on pages 20 and 21, or choose ready-to-cook shellfish such as

octopus (previously cooked—see page 360) • scallops • shrimp • soft-shell crabs

Dry white wine or *water*
2 6- to 8-ounce fillets or 1¾-pound fillet with skin on or off and pin bones removed
or
2 6 to 8 ounce steaks
or
2 butterflied or split fish weighing 8 to 10 ounces each
or
escalopes or medallions weighing ¾ pound
or
¾ pound shrimp or octopus (cooked) or scallops
or

4 soft-shell crabs, cleaned
2 tablespoons (¼ stick) unsalted butter or *margarine, melted,* or *2 tablespoons mild olive oil*
1 tablespoon finely chopped fresh thyme or *parsley*
Salt to taste
Freshly ground black or white pepper to taste
1 lemon, cut in 6 wedges
Sauce of your choice (optional—see page 225)

1. Preheat the broiler to its highest setting.
2. Pour wine or water to a depth of ⅛ inch into the broiler pan.
3. Lay the fish or shellfish in the wine and brush with melted butter or margarine or oil.
4. Broil the fish or shellfish for 2 minutes if cooking very thin fillets or 1 minute for escalopes, or up to 10 minutes if cooking thicker fillets; sprinkling

the fish with the chopped herb just before the end of the cooking time. Check for doneness (see page 94).

5. Sprinkle with salt and pepper to taste.

6. With the aid of wide spatulas, place the fish or shellfish on a plate and pour over any juices left in the pan.

7. Garnish with lemon wedges and serve with optional sauce, or none at all! It will be delicious as is.

SERVES 2

BROILED LOBSTER

Preparation time: 8 minutes
Broiling time: 15 to 20 minutes

SPECIAL EQUIPMENT: Broiler pan or baking pan or sheet with ½-inch-high edges

Special care is needed in the cooking, but it *is* worth it, for the lobster takes on an especially wonderful flavor when broiled in its shell. The lobster must be killed before broiling. The preparation is not for the squeamish. See page 342 for instructions on how to kill lobsters humanely, or ask the fishmonger to do this for you (but, in this case, you will have to cook the lobsters almost immediately). Otherwise, always buy live shellfish and cook them promptly. It may be necessary to finish the cooking, after the lobster is well browned, in either a conventional oven or a microwave oven. If you have separate units, preheat the broiler and the oven at the same time. If the broiler is located under the oven or inside the oven at the top, the broiler will heat the oven somewhat, so when you turn the oven on it will only be a few moments before it reaches the required temperature of 425 degrees F. A microwave oven can be used, set at High. (Crack the lobster claws first.) Check doneness at 5-minute intervals.

NUMBER SERVED	SIZE OF LOBSTER	APPROXIMATE BROILING TIME
1	1 pound	10 to 15 minutes
1	1¼ pounds	15 to 20 minutes
1	1½ pounds	20 to 30 minutes
1 or 2	2 pounds	30 to 35 minutes
2 or 3	3 pounds	35 to 45 minutes

2 1¼-pound lobsters
½ stick (2 ounces) melted unsalted
    butter or margarine, or 2
    tablespoons mayonnaise
Salt to taste

Freshly ground black pepper to
    taste
3 tablespoons chopped scallions or
    shallots or tarragon or chives
1 lemon, halved

1. Ask the fishmonger to kill the lobsters or follow the instructions on page 342.

2. Put each lobster on its back and cut through the middle of its body lengthwise. *Do not cut all the way through the back shell.* Use kitchen scissors to cut through the middle of the shell on the underside of the tail. Spread the two halves apart with your hands, leaving each lobster partly joined together at the back.

3. Remove the little sac from behind the eyes of each lobster. Leave the pale green tomalley (liver) and the dark green coral (roe), if there is any, inside each body. Try to remove the vein that runs along the back of the tail meat by the methods on page 343. If you don't succeed, don't worry—it can easily be discarded as you are eating.

4. Preheat the broiler to its highest setting.

5. Put the lobsters in a broiler pan. Inside the bodies and tails of the lobsters, spread the melted butter, margarine, or mayonnaise; the salt and pepper; and the scallions, shallots, tarragon, or chives. Detach the lobster claws and tilt them against the edge of the broiler pan.

6. Place the lobsters 5 to 6 inches below the broiler heat and broil until they begin to brown. Turn the claws over after 10 minutes and turn the pan around. Tails usually curl up, so crack each shell across (using oven gloves or pot holders) halfway through cooking to straighten it out. Be conscientious! You must look often so you will know when to remove the lobsters from under the broiler. You don't want them to burn.

7. The lobsters may not fully cook under the broiler, so when their flesh is brown, check to see if they are cooked all the way through: Insert a fork or knife into the thickest part of the tail meat and pull it apart to see if it is opaque all the way through.

8. If the lobsters are not cooked through, crack the claws and then put the lobsters in a conventional oven set to 425 degrees F or a microwave oven set to High to finish cooking. (The total cooking time in the broiler and the oven should be approximately 20 minutes.) Serve with lemon halves.

SERVES 2

BROILED MUSSELS WITH GARLIC, BASIL, AND TOMATO BUTTER

Preparation time: 10 minutes, plus 20
    minutes to make the butter
Broiling time: 2 to 3 minutes

1 recipe Steamed Mussels
  Marinière, see page 178

1 recipe Garlic, Basil, and Tomato
  Butter, see page 237

1. When the steamed mussels are cool enough to handle, pick them out of their shells, saving one half shell for each mussel. Pick out any remaining bits of beard that you see and place each mussel on a half shell.
2. Spread each mussel with a little flavored butter and put them on a broiler tray. They can be covered with plastic wrap and refrigerated until you are ready to broil them.
3. Preheat the broiler to its highest setting.
4. Broil the mussels just until the butter melts and the mussels brown very lightly.

SERVES 6 AS AN APPETIZER

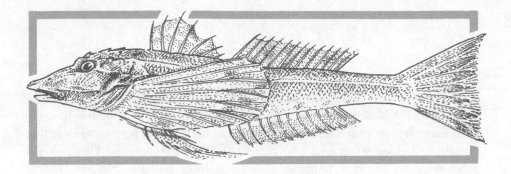

Open-Fire and Indoor Grilling

GRILLING IS QUITE SIMPLY ONE OF THE EASIEST AND MOST DELICIOUS WAYS TO COOK ALMOST ANY fish or shellfish. An open fire gives great flavor to all seafood. Grilling is very similar to broiling except that the fish is cooked by direct heat from *below*. The combination of direct heat and smoke gives a particularly good taste to fish and shellfish.

Both the grill and the seafood should be lightly oiled so the seafood does not stick to the grill. Most of the oil will disappear as the seafood cooks.

The heat source for grilling and barbecuing can be wood, charcoal (preferably hardwood charcoal), or gas. I dislike charcoal briquettes, for the flavor they give off seems chemical. I also recommend that you avoid using charcoal lighter fluid; though it is convenient, it contaminates the taste of delicate fish. For the same reason, avoid buying charcoal with lighter fluid already in it. Hardwood charcoal is undoubtedly the best heat source to use.

The fire must be very hot, with ash-covered coals or embers if it is of charcoal or wood. Leave enough time before the meal to get the heat source ready. I find that a charcoal fire takes anywhere from 20 to 45 minutes to reach the desired state. However, if you use a small chimney with newspaper at the bottom and charcoal on top, it will take only 10 to 20 minutes. These chimneys are available from hardware stores and from Williams-Sonoma, which sells one called the Easy Embers Charcoal Starter for about thirteen dollars. Gas-fired coals take less time to heat. The time it takes to heat wood depends on its density and size. If the wood is not very dense, remember that it will not give out prolonged heat.

When the fire is ready, you can mix the charcoal (if that's the heat source you're using) with a small amount of cherry, hickory, sugar maple, or mesquite wood chips; grapevines; corncobs; or dried wild fennel stalks that have been soaked in water for an hour or so. Let them smoke and char and begin to turn to ashes before laying the seafood over the heat. Throw strong herbs such as rosemary, thyme, sage, or savory onto the fire for flavor, and also sprinkle them on the seafood. If the seafood has been in a marinade, it should be drained before cooking to prevent flare-ups.

If the seafood begins to burn, take if off the fire immediately. (It may be that you have over oiled the seafood or placed it too close to the fire, or that the fire is still too hot.) Wait until the heat has subsided or finish cooking the seafood in a conventional oven that you have prudently preheated to 425 degrees F, or a microwave oven set on High. Check doneness at 5-minute intervals. Another reason to heat an oven for backup is that the fire may fade on you before the seafood finishes cooking. When a fire has faded there is not much use trying to revive it by adding more charcoal or wood, because of the time it would take for the fire to burn down and the flare-ups that are likely to occur.

A little salt and pepper and a large wedge of lemon are all that is needed to accompany grilled seafood.

You can also grill seafood using a grill pan, which is a cast-iron pan with raised ridges on the bottom. This is a fast, easy, nonfattening method of cooking seafood indoors. I find, in the city, that I use my grill pan more often than any other utensil. The ridges should be lightly brushed with oil and the pan should be preheated before cooking. You can easily make grill criss-crosses on seafood: Let the hot ridges sear the flesh, then, after a few moments, move the seafood 90 degrees for the second set of marks.

Oily fish such as tuna, mackerel, sardines, bluefish, and salmon are per-

fectly suited to grilling—the fish oils baste the flesh from within. White, lean-fleshed fish such as weakfish, monkfish, porgies, snapper, and bass are enhanced by grilling too. Wrap soft-fleshed fish, such as mature bluefish, in aluminum foil (with a few holes poked in it) and cook them over the fire—you will still get a good taste of smoke in the fish.

It is best to put small fish such as baby bluefish (snappers) in an oiled, two-sided hinged grill with a handle, which is simple to turn. Whole fish can be cooked in a fish basket, which can also be turned over.

You can turn a whole fish to cook on both sides, but a fillet, especially one of a flaky fish, cannot be turned with much success, so be especially careful. If possible, use firm-fleshed skin-on fillets. Place them skin side up on the grill, then turn them skin side down. Griffo-Grill, a new fine-mesh stainless-steel grill makes it very easy to grill thin flaky fillets such as flatfish fillets and any other seafood. A whole flounder can be grilled beautifully, and you can also place fillets on foil with holes in it, or wrap them in foil before being put on the grill.

Fish steaks are excellent cooked on the grill or in the grill pan.

Firm-fleshed fish cut into 1¼-inch cubes and shellfish can be skewered on wood or steel brochette sticks, oiled or marinated, and then grilled.

Shellfish—such as shell-on shrimp and lobster—is delicious cooked on the grill. The cooked shell heightens the taste of the meat.

You can grill lobster successfully if care is taken to prevent it from drying out. It should be killed as for broiling (see page 342) and split down the middle before being put on the grill. Cook it shell side down first, then turn it and cook it for a few seconds flesh side down.

Hard-shell crabs and crawfish, which also have to be killed before cooking, are wonderful on the grill. Octopus (previously cooked) and squid can be skewered on steel brochette sticks and grilled.

Forget about cooking mollusks such as clams, mussels, and oysters on a grill, except to open them. Clams and mussels steamed in foil over an open fire are fabulous. When you open the package the steam from the clams and herbs will delight you.

TIMES AND TEMPERATURES

Apart from the time it takes to get the fire going and in a perfect state to grill seafood, grilling is swift. The time depends on the thickness of the seafood and the temperature of the fire. Additional time may be needed to finish cooking the seafood in a conventional oven or microwave oven.

HEALTH

Very little oil is used in grilling seafood. Although the seafood and grill have to be oiled, the oil tends to disappear into the fire.

SPECIAL EQUIPMENT NEEDED

Outdoor grill, hardwood charcoal, newspaper chimney, two-sided hinged grill, fish basket, fine-mesh Griffo-Grill, aluminum foil, wood chips, grapevine cuttings, pastry brush, spatulas, pronged forks, skewers (wood or steel), baby bottle with water to put out flare-ups *or* a cast-iron grill pan.

BASIC GRILLING RECIPES

GRILLED WHOLE FISH OR SHELLFISH

Preparation time: 10 minutes, plus 20 minutes marinating time
Open fire preparation time: 20 to 40 minutes
Grilling time: 10 to 35 minutes

SPECIAL EQUIPMENT: Two-sided hinged grill for small fish or shellfish
Fish basket for a whole fish weighing 3 pounds or more
Outdoor grill and heat source

If you use a whole dressed fish, it must be gutted and scaled and the gills must be removed. Leave the fins on, even if they are spiny, for they are part and parcel of the final presentation.

Choose whole dressed fish such as

anchovies • baby coho salmon • blackfish • black sea bass • blowfish • bluefish or baby bluefish (snapper) • butterfish • croaker • freshwater striped bass • gray sole • grouper • herring • largemouth bass • mackerel • petrale sole • porgy • rockfish • sea robin (skinned) • sheepshead • smallmouth bass • spot • sunfish • trout • weakfish (sea trout) • white bass • whiting

or ready-to-cook shellfish such as

scallops • shrimp • soft-shell crabs

NUMBER SERVED	AMOUNT OF FISH NEEDED	APPROXIMATE GRILLING TIME
1	2 or 3 fish weighing a few ounces each	15 minutes
	or	
	1 fish weighing ½ pound	20 minutes
2	1 fish weighing 1½ to 2 pounds	30 minutes
4	1 fish weighing 3 pounds	35 to 40 minutes
8	1 fish weighing 6 pounds	45 minutes, plus time to finish cooking in the oven

12 sprigs fresh thyme or *1 tablespoon dried thyme*
2 tablespoons minced garlic
3 pounds small or large dressed fish
    or
8 soft-shell crabs
    or
1½ to 2 pounds sea scallops
    or

1½ to 2 pounds large shrimp (16 to 35 per pound)
½ cup lime juice or *lemon juice*
½ cup mild olive oil
Salt to taste
Freshly ground black pepper to taste
2 limes or *lemons cut in half for garnish*

(continued)

1. Prepare the open fire.

2. Pull the leaves off 6 thyme sprigs. Mix the fresh or half the dried leaves with the garlic and stuff the cavities of the fish, or, if grilling shellfish, sprinkle them with the mixture.

3. Put the lime or lemon juice and the olive oil in a shallow pan and marinate the seafood in it for 20 minutes. Turn a couple of times.

4. Oil the hinged grill or fish basket.

5. Lift the seafood out of the marinade and drain it a little before putting it in the oiled grill or fish basket. Reserve the marinade.

6. Sprinkle the seafood with salt and pepper and close the grill or fish basket.

7. Throw 4 sprigs or the rest of the dried thyme on the fire before grilling.

8. Put the seafood on the grill and cook it until done, turning it halfway through. See the table above for approximate grilling times for fish; scallops, shrimp, and soft-shell crabs will take 7 to 10 minutes. Check doneness (see page 94). *Note:* If the seafood needs further cooking but is browning too quickly on the grill and will burn if left on, or if the fire dies out, finish the cooking in a conventional oven set at 425 degrees F or a microwave oven set to High. Check doneness at 5-minute intervals.

9. Carefully take the seafood off the grill or out of the hinged grill or fish basket—you want to avoid tearing the fish skin. Put the seafood on a platter. Pour some or all of the reserved marinade over it.

10. Decorate the platter with some thyme sprigs and halves of lime or lemon.

Variations: You can use rosemary, oregano, tarragon, or mint in place of the thyme. You can use chopped scallion, shallot, or onion in place of the garlic.

SERVES 4

GRILLED FISH FILLETS, BUTTERFLIED OR SPLIT FISH, STEAKS, MEDALLIONS, OR SHELLFISH

Preparation time: 5 minutes
Open fire preparation time: 20 to 45 minutes
    or
Time needed to preheat the cast-iron grill pan: 2 minutes
Grilling time: 5 to 30 minutes

SPECIAL EQUIPMENT: Outdoor grill and heat source *or* cast-iron grill pan
Two sided hinged grill
Fine-mesh grill (optional)

Choose any filleted fish, butterflied or split fish, steaks, or medallions. Avoid very flaky fish (such as flounder or sole) unless you have a fine-mesh grill. Or choose shellfish such as

previously cooked conch or octopus (see pages 297 and 360) • scallops • shell-on shrimp • soft-shell crabs

Glaze for shell-on shrimp:
    ¼ cup oil
    pinch cayenne
    1 tablespoon fresh thyme
2 tablespoons mild olive oil
6 to 8 ounces fish fillet with skin on and pin bones removed
    or
1 1-inch-thick fish steak
    or
6 to 8 ounces previously cooked conch or octopus; scallops (small tough muscles removed) or shell-on shrimp
    or

2 to 4 soft-shell crabs, cleaned
Salt to taste
Freshly ground black pepper to taste
½ lemon
Flavored butter or spicy sauce (see pages 235 and 225) (optional)
1 parsley sprig for garnish

1. Prepare the open fire or preheat the grill pan over moderately high heat for 2 minutes. *If you are grilling shrimp,* mix it with its glaze in a bowl. Otherwise, pour 1 tablespoon of olive oil on a plate and coat both sides of the fish or shellfish with it.

(continued)

2. Brush the grill or grill pan with 1 tablespoon of oil. The oil should smoke slightly when you brush it on the grill pan, indicating that the pan is now hot enough to use.

3. When the grill or grill pan is hot, lay the fish (skin side up) or shellfish (drain shrimp of any glaze) on it and cook.

4. Using a wide metal spatula, move the fish 90 degrees to make attractive crisscross grill marks on the fish.

5. Cook the fish or shellfish until it is nearly cooked through, then turn it over and repeat the procedure on the other side until it is just cooked through. The cooking time depends on the thickness of the fish or shellfish. Check for doneness (see page 94). (*Note:* If the open fire dies out before the fish or shellfish is cooked, finish the cooking in a conventional oven set to 425 degrees F or a microwave oven set to High. Check doneness at 5-minute intervals.)

6. Place the fish or shellfish on a plate. Sprinkle it with salt and black pepper. Squeeze lemon juice over it and serve it with the optional flavored butter or sauce. Garnish it with a parsley sprig.

Variations: You can use a vegetable oil such as safflower, peanut, corn, or Oriental-style sesame oil in place of the mild olive oil. You can use a pinch of cayenne, white pepper, cumin, ground coriander, or paprika in place of the black pepper. You can use lime juice in place of the lemon juice. You can cook a few vegetables on the grill or in the grill pan at the same time you are cooking the fish. Use trimmed and sliced scallions; thin slices of sweet red, green, or yellow peppers; sliced tomato, zucchini, or yellow squash; or previously par-cooked and sliced potatoes.

SERVES 1

GRILLED OR BROILED SEAFOOD BROCHETTES

Preparation time: 5 minutes plus 20 minutes marinating time

Open fire preparation time: 20 to 45 minutes

Broiler preheating time: 5 minutes

Grilling or broiling time: approximately 10 minutes

Soaking time: ½ hour

SPECIAL EQUIPMENT: 4 12- to 13-inch-long metal or wooden skewers (if wooden, they should be soaked in water for ½ hour)
Outdoor grill and heat source

Choose firm-fleshed fish such as

dolphinfish (mahi-mahi) • **halibut** • **monkfish** • **salmon** • **shark** •
swordfish • **tuna**

or shellfish such as

sea scallops • **shrimp**

½ cup sesame oil (Oriental style)

¼ cup lime juice

½ teaspoon salt

Freshly ground black pepper to taste

1½ to 2 pounds fish fillets or steaks, cut 1¼ inch thick, with skin off
or
1½ to 2 pounds large shrimp (16 to 20 per pound) peeled and deveined
or
1½ to 2 pounds sea scallops, small tough muscle removed

2 teaspoons finely chopped fresh chives

½ cup sesame seeds

2 bunches scallions, green part cut in 1½-inch lengths, reserve white parts for another use

1. Prepare the open fire.
2. Mix a marinade of the sesame oil, lime juice, salt, and pepper in a medium bowl.

3. Cut the fish into 1¼-inch cubes. (*Note:* Be sure not to cut the fish any smaller—you will have trouble keeping it moist as it cooks.)

4. Place the seafood in the marinade for 20 minutes only. (*Note*: Do not marinate longer than 20 minutes or the seafood will begin to "cook" in the marinade and become mushy.)

5. Preheat the broiler, if you will be using it.

6. Mix the chives and sesame seeds in a shallow pan.

7. Skewer the fish, or shellfish, alternating 5 pieces of scallion with each piece. Reserve the marinade.

8. Grill or broil the brochettes for about 10 minutes, 5 to 6 inches away from the heat, turning and basting them with the marinade every 2 minutes.

9. After 6 minutes, baste again and coat the brochettes completely in the chive and sesame seed mixture. Finish the cooking. Check for doneness (see page 94). (*Note:* Firm-fleshed fish tends to lose moisture quickly, so be very careful not to overcook it.)

Variations: You can use vegetable oil, such as peanut, safflower, or corn oil, in place of the sesame oil. You can use lemon juice or dry white wine in place of the lime juice.

SERVES 4

GRILLED OR BROILED SEAFOOD AND VEGETABLE BROCHETTES

Preparation time: 30 minutes
Open fire preparation time: 20 to 45 minutes
Broiler preheating time: 5 minutes
Grilling or broiling time: 10 minutes
Soaking time: ½ hour

SPECIAL EQUIPMENT: 2 12-inch to 13-inch long metal or wooden skewers (if wooden, they should be soaked in water for ½ hour)
Outdoor grill and charcoal

Choose firm-fleshed fish such as

dolphinfish (mahi-mahi) • halibut • monkfish • salmon • shark • swordfish • tuna

or shellfish such as

sea scallops • shrimp

¼ cup dry white wine
2 tablespoons molasses
2 tablespoons soy sauce
Freshly ground black pepper to taste
½-pound skin-off fish steaks or fillets, cut 1¼ inches thick
or
½ pound large shrimp (16 to 20 per pound), peeled and deveined
or

½ pound sea scallops, small tough muscle removed
6 cherry tomatoes (or 1 tomato cut into 6 1-inch pieces)
1 medium onion, cut in 1¼-inch pieces
1 tablespoon mild olive oil
6 bay leaves
½ lemon

1. Prepare a *charcoal* fire or preheat the broiler.
2. Make the marinade: Mix the wine, molasses, soy sauce, and black pepper together in a small bowl with a wire whisk.
3. If you are using fish steaks or fillets, cut them into 8 1¼-inch cubes. (*Note:* Be sure not to cut the fish any smaller—you will have trouble keeping it moist as it cooks.)

4. Put the cubed fish or shellfish in the marinade and stir to cover all the surfaces. Leave for 5 minutes. (*Note:* The marinade is used to glaze the seafood.)

5. Put the tomatoes, onion, and oil in a small bowl and stir until they are covered with oil.

6. When the fish or shellfish has marinated 5 minutes, skewer it with the vegetables and bay leaves like this: onion, seafood, onion, tomato, bay leaf—three times in all per skewer, ending each with onion, seafood, onion (4 pieces of seafood per skewer).

7. Put the skewers on the grill (or, if broiling, on a broiler pan) and cook for 10 minutes, 5 to 6 inches away from the heat.

8. Turn the skewers every 2 minutes or so until the seafood is cooked through. Check for doneness (see page 94). (*Note:* Firm-fleshed fish tends to lose moisture quickly, so be very careful not to overcook it.)

9. Place the skewers on plates and squeeze lemon juice on them.

Variations: In place of the tomato you can use sliced sweet red, yellow, or green pepper; 1-inch pieces of zucchini or yellow squash or corn on the cob; or small mushrooms. You can use mint, rosemary, savory, tarragon, or thyme in place of the bay leaves.

SERVES 2

GRILLED LOBSTER

Preparation time: 8 minutes
Open fire preparation time: 20 to 45
   minutes
   or
*Time needed to preheat the cast-iron
   grill pan:* 2 minutes
Grilling time: 15 to 20 minutes

SPECIAL EQUIPMENT: Outdoor grill and heat source *or* cast-iron grill pan

The lobster must be killed before grilling. The preparation is not for the squeamish. See page 342 for instructions on how to kill lobsters humanely, or ask the fishmonger to do this for you (but, in this case, you will have to cook the lobsters almost immediately). Otherwise, always buy live shellfish and cook them promptly.

NUMBER SERVED	SIZE OF SHELLFISH	APPROXIMATE GRILLING TIME
1	1-pound lobster	10 to 15 minutes
1	1¼-pound lobster	15 to 20 minutes
1	1½-pound lobster	20 to 30 minutes
1 or 2	2-pound lobster	30 to 35 minutes
2 or 3	3-pound lobster	35 to 45 minutes

2 1¼-pound lobsters

½ stick (2 ounces) unsalted butter or margarine, melted or 2 tablespoons mayonnaise

Salt to taste

Freshly ground black pepper to taste

4 tablespoons chopped scallions, shallots, tarragon, or chives

Optional coating for lobsters:

2 tablespoons vegetable oil

⅛ teaspoon cayenne

1 tablespoon paprika

½ teaspoon salt

½ teaspoon white pepper

1 lemon, halved

1. Prepare an open fire if you are using one.
2. Follow instructions on how to kill a lobster. Let them rest 10 to 15 minutes.
3. Put the lobsters on their backs and cut through the middle of their bodies lengthwise. *Do not cut all the way through the back shells.* Use kitchen scissors to cut through the middle of each shell on the underside of the tail. Spread the two halves apart with your hands, leaving each lobster partly joined together at the back. Remove the little sac from behind the eyes. Leave the pale green tomalley (liver) and the dark green coral (roe, if there is any) inside the body. Try to remove the vein that runs along the back of the tail meat, by the methods on page 343. If you don't succeed, don't worry—it can be easily discarded as you are eating.
4. If you want to use the coating, put the oil, cayenne, paprika, salt, and pepper into a bowl and mix with a spoon. Coat the outside shells, claws, and legs of the lobsters with this mixture.
5. If you are using a grill pan, preheat it over medium-high heat for 2 minutes.

6. Spread the melted butter or margarine, salt, pepper, and scallions, shallots, tarragon, or chives inside the body and tail meat of each lobster. Detach the lobster claws.

7. Put the lobsters on the grill or grill pan, with the lobsters shell side down and the claws beside them. (You may only be able to fit one lobster at a time on the grill pan. In this case cook them one at a time.) Turn the lobster on the grill as it cooks.

8. When the lobsters have cooked for three quarters of the required time (in this case 15 minutes), see whether their tail meat is becoming opaque all the way through. (See page 94.) If a lobster is nearly cooked, turn it over, flesh side down, for 5 minutes and press down on the tail so that it can take some color and flavor from the fire or grill pan.

9. Serve with lemon halves. Have nutcrackers, little picks (or lobster forks), and napkins ready for the feast.

SERVES 2

WHOLE FISH STEAMED IN ALUMINUM FOIL ON THE GRILL

To cook whole soft flaky-fleshed fish such as bluefish or weakfish (sea trout) in foil on the grill, follow the instructions for bake-poaching whole fish on page 102, *except* put the packaged fish (with a few holes poked in it) on the *grill* instead of in the oven to cook it. Turn the packaged fish every so often, for 40 minutes to 1¼ hours, depending on the size of the fish and heat of the fire.

Note: The open fire must be substantial enough to last for 40 minutes to 1¼ hours. If the fire dies out, use the microwave or a conventional oven to finish the cooking.

FISH FILLETS STEAMED IN ALUMINUM FOIL ON THE GRILL

Preparation time: 10 minutes
Open fire preparation time: 20 to 45 minutes
Grilling time: 5 to 10 minutes

SPECIAL EQUIPMENT: Outdoor grill and heat source
Aluminum foil *or* fine-mesh stainless-steel grill

Fillets of sole and flounder cannot be grilled directly on an open fire because all but the most sturdy, such as petrale sole and gray sole, will fall apart. However, such fish *can* benefit marvelously from the flavors of fire and smoke if they are wrapped in foil or laid on foil that has a few holes in it, *or if you use the fine-mesh stainless-steel Griffo-Grill.*

Choose fillets with soft flaky flesh such as

cod, scrod • flounder • gray sole • lemon sole • petrale sole • sole

1 recipe basic topping I or 1 recipe
basic topping II (see page 232)
2 tablespoons mild olive oil or soft
unsalted butter or margarine
1½ to 2 pounds fish fillets, skin off
and pin bones removed

2 tablespoons lemon juice
Salt to taste
Freshly ground white pepper to
taste

1. Prepare the open fire.
2. Cut 4 pieces of aluminum foil into 12-inch squares and poke a few holes in them with the point of a knife or a skewer.
3. Lightly oil or butter the foil.
4. Place the fillets on the foil and put equal amounts of the topping down the middle of each fillet.
5. Brush the fillets with the remaining oil or butter.
6. Sprinkle the fillets with lemon juice and salt and pepper to taste.
7. Fold the foil over the fish and put the packages on the grill, *or* place the foil, with a few small holes in it, on the grill and cook the fillets on the foil, *or* put the fillets directly on an oiled fine-mesh stainless-steel grill.
8. Check for doneness after 5 minutes (see page 94). (*Note:* Some fillets are so thin that they will cook in a very short time, so be careful not to overcook them.)

SERVES 4

CLAMS OR MUSSELS STEAMED IN ALUMINUM FOIL
ON THE GRILL OR IN THE OVEN

Preparation time: 20 minutes
Open fire preparation time: 20 to 45
    minutes
    or
Time needed to preheat oven: 10 min-
    utes
Steaming time: 15 to 25 minutes

SPECIAL EQUIPMENT: Aluminum foil 18
inches wide
Outdoor grill and heat source

The preparation can be done ahead of time and the packages can be refrigerated until you are ready to cook.

18 littleneck or *small cherrystone*
    clams
    or
2 *pounds manila* or *butter clams* or
    cleaned mussels
1 *small onion, finely chopped*
2 *cloves garlic, minced*
2 *sticks celery, finely chopped*
½ *sweet red* or *green pepper, finely*
    diced

¼ *cup lemon juice* or *dry white*
    wine
2 *tablespoons finely chopped parsley*
1 *tablespoon fresh thyme leaves* or
    ¼ *teaspoon dried thyme*
2 *slices bacon, fried until crisp and*
    then crumbled (optional)

1. Prepare the open fire *or* preheat the oven to 450 degrees F.
2. Cut 4 pieces of aluminum foil into 18-inch squares. Use double foil for each package.
3. Place cleaned clams or mussels on each double thickness of foil, then sprinkle with equal amounts of onion, garlic, celery, pepper, lemon juice or wine, parsley, thyme, and bacon if desired.
4. Fold the foil over the clams loosely to give the shells room to open.
5. Fold the edges of the foil together several times to seal the packages properly.
6. When the fire is ready or the oven is hot, place the packages on the grill or on the middle oven rack and cook them for 15 to 25 minutes, until the clams or mussels open. (*Note:* Cook them a little longer if the packages have been

taken straight from the refrigerator. Mussels will take less time than clams to open. Cook only until the shells open. You can unfold the foil to see whether the mollusks are open.)

7. Eat the clams or mussels out of the foil or empty the contents of the packages onto plates.

SERVES 3 AS AN APPETIZER OR 2 AS A MAIN COURSE

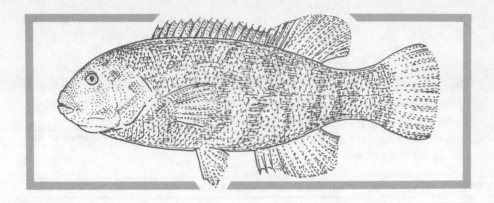

Frying and Sautéing, Including the Blackened Method

FRIED OR SAUTÉED SEAFOOD

Note: The words *frying* and *sautéing* are used more or less interchangeably here. Both methods are similar in that the food is cooked with fat, be it butter and oil, butter or clarified butter, or oil alone in a shallow frying pan or skillet over moderate to high heat. Margarine is fine too. I recommend that you use butter and oil together, so that the butter will have less chance to burn, or clarified butter (see page 242), which will not burn. The hot fat should just cover the bottom of the pan so it sears the outside of the food quickly. Frying should not be confused with deep-frying, where the food is totally immersed in very hot fat.

In frying and sautéing be sure the fat is hot enough, otherwise it will be absorbed and produce a soggy, oil-filled piece of seafood. If the fat is too hot, it will burn the outside of the fish or shellfish before the inside has a chance to cook through. You should heat the fat over moderate to high heat to sear the flesh, then lower the heat to finish the cooking. Don't crowd the fish or fillets in the pan, because the temperature of the fat will cool. The flesh will become crisp on the outside and remain moist inside when cooked properly.

Make sure you have a nice wide spatula to turn fillets over and to lift them out in one piece. Use tongs or a slotted spoon to lift out smaller pieces of seafood.

You can fry small whole fish such as trout, whether or not they have been previously boned out. They can be stuffed with herbs such as tarragon, dill, basil, mint, and garlic. The fish need only be garnished with a lemon wedge and, like many fried fish dishes, can be served with a light tomato salsa. (For the salsa recipe, see page 225.)

Pan-dressed fish are easy to fry indoors or outdoors on a camp fire.

Small skinless fillets of flounder or sole, lightly coated with flour, are very easy to fry. Sole à la Meunière continues to be a very popular dish (see page 151 for recipe.) Fillets of oily fish such as herring and mackerel are better baked or broiled. Although fried or sautéed fillets of salmon are acceptable, there are better ways to cook this fish, such as broiling, roasting, and bake-poaching. A quick sauté of shrimp, scallops, soft-shell crabs, or squid are delicious. Croquettes of all kinds of fish are easily fried.

I recommend using heavy aluminum (Wearever) frying pans for good frying and sautéing results. Nonstick Teflon coated frying pans are useful for they require less fat. They are reasonable in cost and when they lose their coating just throw them away.

To sauté successfully, use moderate to high heat to begin with and always add the food when the fat is hot, nearly smoking. After the initial searing turn the heat down slightly to cook the item through. To become a good sauté person, you need a lot of practice!

Frying and sautéing are quick cooking methods. Depending on the size and thickness of the item of seafood you are cooking, it can take 2 to 20 minutes.

BLACKENED FISH

And now we get to blackening, which is, and probably will continue to be, a favorite way to prepare fish, although the hot and spicy flavorings that are used tend to obliterate fish's character. I do enjoy the zesty taste now and again, and the method is a good one—because the fish is seared in a very hot skillet, it gets a good crust but remains moist inside.

Take any firm-fleshed fish, cut into fillets or steaks—for example, tuna, blackfish, grouper, or redfish if you can find it. (The famous blackened redfish became so popular that redfish was just about fished out and a preservation order had to be imposed.) Fillets and steaks should be at least ¾ inch thick to withstand this aggressive way of cooking! Coat the fish with a fairly thick mixture of herbs, spices, and seasonings. Then heat a heavy cast-iron skillet over high heat for 5 minutes or so until it is very hot. When the pan is hot, coat the fish lightly with a little oil, melted unsalted butter, or margarine, and place it in the pan. It will char on the outside and a crust will form. Turn it over to cook on the other side. When there is a crust on both sides, turn the heat down a little to ensure that the fish cooks through.

The herbs, spices, and seasonings used on blackened fish include thyme, oregano, marjoram, paprika, chili powder, cayenne, salt, and pepper. The coating has to be dry, so real garlic and onion cannot be used, since they will burn. Some people add garlic and onion powders or salts or granulated garlic and onion, but I simply cannot do this—what with the preservatives and, often, MSG (monosodium glutamate) in them, they stick in my mouth, leaving an unpleasant taste and ultimately causing bad breath.

HEALTH

Depending on the coating and the amount of butter and/or oil you use, fried or sautéed fish might end up with more calories than you want in your meal. However, if the fat is at the correct temperature, the fish will not absorb it.

A heavy nonstick frying pan can be used to good advantage. Less fat is needed and the fish browns easily, as long as the pan is no larger than 8 to 12 inches in diameter. A pan larger than this can't get hot enough on a domestic burner; the heat is dispersed across the pan and the fish cannot sear.

In blackening, a negligible amount of fat is absorbed by the fish, so this is a relatively healthful method.

BASIC FRYING RECIPES

FRIED FISH FILLETS, FISH STEAKS, SKATE WINGS, OR ABALONE OR GEODUCK CLAM SLICES *À LA MEUNIÈRE*

Preparation time: 5 minutes
Frying time: 2 to 10 minutes
Choose fillets or 1-inch-thick steaks preferably lean fish such as

abalone slices • blackfish fillets • cod steaks • flounder or sole fillets • freshwater striped bass fillets • geoduck clam slices • grouper fillets • largemouth bass fillets • monkfish fillets (cut into medallions) • mullet fillets • ocean perch fillets • perch fillets • pike fillets • red snapper fillets • rockfish fillets • sand shark (dogfish) steaks • shad fillets • skate wings • smallmouth bass fillets • smelt fillets • sturgeon fillets or steaks • tilefish fillets or steaks • weakfish (sea trout) fillets • whiting fillets • wolffish fillets

(*Note:* Tuna, swordfish, mako shark, salmon, and halibut steaks are best broiled or grilled, but if you choose to fry these fish, there is no need to coat them with the seasoned flour called for in this recipe.)

½ cup all-purpose flour
1 teaspoon salt
Freshly ground white pepper to taste
1 teaspoon fresh (or ½ teaspoon dried) thyme or oregano or marjoram or dill (optional)
⅛ teaspoon cayenne (optional)
1 teaspoon paprika or chili powder or cumin (optional)
3 tablespoons unsalted butter or margarine
2 tablespoons mild olive oil or vegetable oil or 3 tablespoons clarified butter (see page 242)

¾ to 1 pound fish fillets, skin on or off, pin bones removed or steaks
or
¼ pound abalone or geoduck clam slices
2 tablespoons cold butter or margarine
1 teaspoon lemon juice
2 lemon quarters
2 sprigs parsley
Sauce of your choice (optional—see page 225)

(continued)

1. In a bowl mix the flour with the salt, pepper, and any of optional herbs and seasonings you like, then spread the mixture out on a plate.
2. Put a medium-sized frying pan over moderate to high heat.
3. Add 1 tablespoon butter (or margarine) and oil or clarified butter.
4. Coat the fish in the seasoned flour and shake off the excess.
5. When the fat is hot, but before the butter or margarine has a chance to turn brown, put the fish in to fry.
6. When you see the fish getting opaque and crisp on the edges, take a wide metal spatula and turn it over. Cook only until it is opaque all the way through. This will take from 2 minutes to 10 minutes, depending on the thickness of the fish. Abalone and geoduck clam slices will take barely 60 seconds to cook. (*Note:* When a thick piece of fish is browned on both sides and is still not cooked through, turn the heat down to finish cooking.) Check for doneness (see page 94).
7. Lift the fish out of the pan using a wide metal spatula and drain it briefly on a double layer of paper towels.
8. Optional—for an extra special something! Throw away the remaining oil and butter or margarine. Clean the pan with paper towels (without burning yourself!) and put it back on the heat. Melt 2 tablespoons of cold butter or margarine in the pan, and when it bubbles up and gets frothy, add 1 teaspoon lemon juice. Swirl the sauce around the pan and pour some over each piece of fish.
9. Serve with lemon wedges and garnish with parsley sprigs.

Variations: You can use lime in place of the lemon. You can use watercress in place of parsley.

SERVES 2

FRIED WHOLE FISH OR PAN-DRESSED FISH

Preparation time: 5 minutes
Frying time: 5 to 20 minutes

Choose small whole dressed or pan-dressed fish that have somewhat compressed bodies (not too thick or rotund!) and that weigh from a few ounces each to 1 pound or so, such as

butterfish • croaker • perch • porgy • sheepshead • small freshwater or saltwater bass • spot • sunfish • tilapia

or boned out, butterflied, or split fish, gutted and scaled, such as

black sea bass • brook trout • rainbow trout • red snapper • rockfish • weakfish (sea trout)

Proceed exactly as in the previous recipe for Fried Fish Fillets and Steaks, but buy about twice as much fish (1½ to 2 pounds) and know that these whole fish will take longer to cook than fillets.

And try this coating:

½ cup all-purpose flour
¼ cup fine cornmeal
¾ teaspoon salt

¼ teaspoon freshly ground black pepper
1 teaspoon paprika
⅛ teaspoon cayenne

SERVES 2

FISH CROQUETTES AND CRAB CAKES

Preparation time: 20 minutes
Frying time: 25 minutes, plus 15 to
    30 minutes to cook fish, if cooked
    fish is not available

Choose cooked fish (leftovers are handy) such as

**blackfish • catfish • cod • halibut • lingcod • mullet • orange
roughy • perch • porgy • rockfish • salmon • salt cod (rehydrated
and cooked) • sea robin • tilefish • various bass • walleye • weakfish
(sea trout) • whitefish**

or

crabmeat

*4 cups roughly flaked cooked fish,
    with any skin and bones re-
    moved
      or
2 pounds steamed or baked fish
    fillets with any skin and pin
    bones removed
      or
4 pounds steamed or bake-poached
    whole fish, with any skin and
    bones removed
      or
2 pounds crabmeat, picked over for
    any cartilage
2 cups fresh bread crumbs, made
    from 6 slices white bread (cut
    crusts off and pull apart, then
    process in the food processor
    until fine crumbs appear)*

*½ cup mayonnaise (see page 227)
2 tablespoons lemon juice
2 eggs, beaten
1 jalapeño pepper, seeded and
    finely chopped
2 scallions, finely chopped
2 tablespoons chopped parsley
1 clove garlic, minced
Salt to taste
Freshly ground white pepper to
    taste
1 cup all-purpose flour
6 tablespoons vegetable oil
1 recipe tomato salsa or aioli (see
    pages 225 and 229) or 2 lemons
    cut in wedges*

1. Flake the fish into a bowl and add the rest of the ingredients except the flour, oil, and salsa. Mix well but lightly.
2. Put one cup of flour on a board or counter. Flour your hands and form

croquettes about 3 inches in diameter and ¾ inch thick. Mix a little flour into the mixture as you work if the mixture is very sticky. The stickiness depends on the moisture of the fish.

3. Heat the oil in a skillet over moderate heat.

4. When the oil is hot, cook a few fish croquettes at a time, being sure not to crowd the pan.

5. After they start to brown at the edges, turn them over with a wide spatula. Fry each side about 3 minutes.

6. Drain on paper towels and serve with salsa, aioli, or lemon wedges.

MAKES 12 CROQUETTES

SAUTÉED SHRIMP, SCALLOPS, SOFT-SHELL CRABS, SQUID, OR BLOWFISH

Preparation time: 5 to 20 minutes
Sauté time: 4 to 12 minutes

2 tablespoons unsalted butter or margarine
2 tablespoons mild olive oil
¾ pound large shrimp (16 to 35 per pound), peeled and deveined
  or
¾ pound sea or bay scallops, small tough muscle removed
  or
4 to 6 cleaned soft-shell crabs (see cleaning instructions on page 304 or ask the fishmonger to do it for you)
  or
¾ pound squid, cleaned by you or the fishmonger, cut into

¼-inch rings
  or
1 pound blowfish tails, cleaned
Salt to taste
Freshly ground white pepper to taste
2 cloves garlic, finely minced
1 scallion, finely sliced
3 tablespoons lemon juice
2 tablespoons finely chopped parsley

1. Heat 1 tablespoon of butter or margarine and the oil in a 12-inch-wide frying pan over high heat.

2. When the fat is hot, but before the butter or margarine has had a chance to turn brown, add the seafood in one layer. (*Note:* Both sea and bay scallops

and squid must have lots of space around them as they are sautéed, otherwise they lose moisture. Cook them in batches if necessary.)

3. When you see that the seafood pieces (all except the soft-shell crabs) are becoming opaque on one side, turn them over with tongs or a wide spatula so they will cook on the other side. Check for doneness (see page 94). Soft-shell crabs should be turned over when they start to crisp and turn golden. (Incidentally, they pop and crack as they cook, so stand back!) You can tell soft-shell crabs are cooked when they feel a little more solid in the body and have turned dark brownish red. A medium-size crab takes about 8 to 10 minutes to cook.

4. Now quickly throw on some salt and pepper, add the rest of the butter, the garlic, and the scallion, and turn the seafood around in this mixture.

5. Finally, add the lemon juice and chopped parsley, stir, and turn out on to a serving platter.

SERVES 2

BLACKENED FISH FILLETS

Preparation time: 5 minutes
Frying time: 2 to 7 minutes

SPECIAL EQUIPMENT: Cast-iron frying pan or heavy skillet that you don't mind discoloring (reserve one of your skillets just for cooking blackened fish)

This cooking method was devised by the famous chef Paul Prudhomme of New Orleans. He found that searing fish with a highly seasoned coating in a "white-hot" pan gives it a delicious moist interior and a crusty exterior. But this method can hardly be called his anymore because practically every seafood chef in the country has cooked fish this way since Chef Paul first put the method on the map! This is my version.

A word of caution: Cooking fish in a very hot cast-iron frying pan may not be for the novice.

Choose fillets at least ¾ inch thick from any large, fairly firm-fleshed fish, such as

blackfish • bluefish • catfish • dolphinfish (mahi-mahi) • grouper • lingcod • red snapper • redfish • rockfish • sablefish • sheepshead • tuna

½ teaspoon dried thyme

½ teaspoon dried oregano or
    marjoram

1 tablespoon paprika

1 teaspoon chili powder

½ teaspoon freshly ground black
    pepper

½ teaspoon freshly ground white
    pepper

¼ teaspoon cayenne pepper

1 teaspoon salt

3 tablespoons vegetable oil or
    unsalted butter or margarine,
    melted

2 8- to 10-ounce fish fillets with
    skin off and pin bones removed

1. Put a cast-iron frying pan over high heat.
2. Mix the herbs and seasonings together and place them on a plate.
3. Pour the oil, butter, or margarine on another plate.
4. When the pan is extremely hot—that is, smoking and looking gray with heat—coat the fish thoroughly on both sides with the seasonings. Then moisten the fillets with the oil, butter, or margarine.
5. Lay the fillets in the pan. They will splatter and pop and smoke, so it is best to stand back! The fish will char and get a fine crust in 2 minutes or so. Be prepared to turn the fish over when it is charred on one side and remove it after you have checked that it is cooked all the way through (see page 94).
6. Enjoy!

SERVES 2

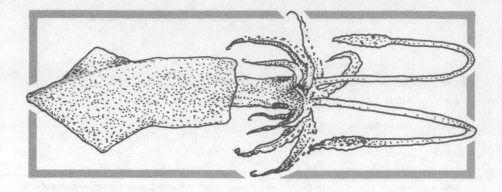

Deep-Frying

DEEP-FRIED SEAFOOD CAN BE MOST DELICIOUS, AND IT IS NOT NECESSARILY VERY FATTENING. IF it is made correctly—that is, if you use a light coating and a good-quality oil that is hot enough—the oil will not penetrate the fish or shellfish, so it will be perfectly cooked, not soggy or oily, but crisp on the outside and moist on the inside.

You will need an electric deep fryer with temperature control, a deep saucepan, or a wok. You will also need a frying basket or a large slotted spoon to retrieve the fish from the hot oil.

Use 1 or more quarts of oil, depending on the amount of seafood you want to fry and the size of the cooking receptacle. As a rule, the oil should be at least 2 inches deep in the pan.

The quality of the oil and the temperature are the important factors in deep-frying. The oil must be good-quality vegetable oil—use corn, sunflower, peanut, or safflower oil. The temperature of the oil must be 375 degrees F. The best way to test the oil's temperature is with a deep-fry thermometer; these thermometers are cheap and easy to come by. If you don't have one, test the temperature of the oil by dropping in a 1-inch cube of bread. If it turns golden brown in 20 seconds, the oil is ready to cook with.

The coating of deep-fried seafood is the first thing to hit the hot oil, and it seals the flesh. The coating can simply be seasoned flour (a mixture of flour, salt, pepper, paprika, and a pinch of cayenne), or you can make a heavier coating by dipping the fish in seasoned flour, then in beaten egg or milk, and lastly in bread crumbs or cornmeal. You can coat the fish with a plain batter made by mixing seasoned flour, egg, and milk, or you can use a tempura batter made with flour, egg, water, or beer plus, if you like, a beaten egg white folded in to lighten it. Fresh or dried herbs and spices such as paprika, chili powder, cayenne, salt, and pepper can be added to the coating. (See recipes for coatings and batters below.)

The color of the coating will alert you to when the seafood is cooked. You will want a good, appetizing golden color, not a burnt dark-brown coating.

You may have to fry the seafood in batches to avoid a steep drop in temperature; be sure the oil has time to regain the correct temperature after frying each batch. If you have to do this, have a warm oven (200 degrees F) ready to receive the seafood. But try to eat the seafood as soon as possible before it loses its delicious crispness.

Have a rack or paper towels ready on which to lay the seafood so that the excess oil will drip off.

Have plenty of lemon wedges around to squeeze over the seafood, and maybe a fresh salsa (see page 225) or the ever-popular tartar sauce if you wish.

The oil can be used two or three times, until it becomes dark or odorous. When it is cool, strain it through cheesecloth or a fine sieve and pour it back into the original bottle or container through a funnel and store it covered.

Lean fish, shrimp, scallops, squid rings, and clams can be deep-fried. Whole fish, from the smallest (whitebait and silversides) to black sea bass and skinned catfish, are also fine for deep-frying.

Fish such as sole and flounder can be deep-fried, but need to be filleted first. Cut sole or flounder fillets on the diagonal ½ inch to 1 inch wide, and squid rings ¼ inch wide, and dip them in seasoned flour a few at a time. Then put them in a sieve to shake off the excess flour before you fry them. When coating fish with batter, let some of the excess drip off before deep-frying.

Fritters made with finely chopped or flaked fish or shellfish can be deep-fried. They are likely to absorb a little oil between the flakes.

TIMES AND TEMPERATURES

Be sure to leave enough time for the oil to get to the right temperature, 375 degrees F, before starting to fry. Deep-frying times vary: Squid rings take no more than 30 seconds to cook, while a whole catfish, depending on size, will take from 10 minutes to 30 minutes.

HEALTH

The heavier the coating or batter, the more fattening the dish. If you are on a diet, forget about deep-frying—you don't need the oil or the coating at all.

BASIC DEEP-FRYING RECIPES

DEEP-FRIED SEAFOOD: VARIATION I

Preparation time: 5 to 10 minutes
Deep-frying time: 10 seconds to 3 minutes
Time to heat oil: approximately 7 to 10 minutes

SPECIAL EQUIPMENT: Electric deep fryer with a temperature control *or* deep saucepan *or* wok
Frying basket *or* large slotted spoon
Deep-fry thermometer

You can use corn oil, peanut oil, safflower oil, or sunflower oil to fry with. It can be used two or three times. When it is cool, strain it back into the original container and keep it in the refrigerator. If you are using a deep saucepan or wok to cook with, you will be able to control the required heat more easily if you have a deep-fry thermometer, which is easy and cheap to buy.

Choose 6 to 8 ounces of one or an assortment of the following:

anchovies, very small, gutted through the head • cod or tilefish fillet, cut in 1-inch slices or cubes • crawfish tails, peeled and deveined (available frozen) • shrimp, peeled and deveined • smelt, gutted through the head • sole fillet, cut in diagonal ½-inch-wide strips • squid, cleaned and cut in ¼-inch rings • whitebait, rinsed and drained

Seasoned flour (enough for 4 serv-
ings):
½ cup all-purpose flour
1 teaspoon salt
½ teaspoon freshly ground
pepper
Herbs and seasonings
(optional—see page 343)
1 quart or more vegetable oil (at
least 2 inches deep)

6-to-8 ounces seafood
2 lemon wedges
2 parsley sprigs
Flavored mayonnaise
(optional—see page 229)
Tomato salsa (optional—see page
225)

1. Make the seasoned flour in a medium bowl.
2. Heat the oil to 375 degrees F. The oil must be at least 2 inches deep.
3. Place some seafood in the flour and coat well.
4. Then put it in a sieve above the bowl and shake off excess flour. Be sure all the pieces are separate from one another.
5. When the oil is at 375 degrees F, fry the seafood (in batches if necessary, because overcrowding will lower the heat considerably) for just over a minute (taste a squid ring after 10 seconds).
6. Check the other seafood for doneness (see page 94).
7. Drain on paper towels. Keep in a warm oven if you are making several batches. Always let the oil reach 375 degrees F before adding another batch.
8. Serve with lemon wedges, parsley sprigs, and a flavored mayonnaise (like tartar sauce) or a tomato salsa.

SERVES 1

DEEP-FRIED SEAFOOD: VARIATION II

Preparation time: 5 to 10 minutes
Deep-frying time: 10 to 20 minutes
Time to heat the oil: approximately 7
    to 10 minutes

SPECIAL EQUIPMENT: Electric deep fryer with a temperature control *or* deep saucepan *or* wok
Frying basket *or* large slotted spoon
Deep-fry thermometer

See Variation I for suggestions on type of oil and control of heat.

Choose lean whole fish such as

black sea bass • ling • whiting

or choose shellfish such as

soft-shell crabs

*¾ to 1-pound whole fish, gutted and
    scaled and with fins removed*
        or
2 or 3 soft-shell crabs, cleaned
*Flour and cornmeal coating
    (enough for 4 servings):*
    ½ cup all-purpose flour
    ¼ cup fine cornmeal

1 teaspoon salt
*¼ teaspoon freshly ground black
    pepper*
1 teaspoon paprika
⅛ teaspoon cayenne
1 quart or more vegetable oil
2 lemon wedges
2 parsley sprigs

Proceed just as in Variation I, except that frying the whole fish may take 20 minutes and frying the soft-shell crabs 10 minutes. Check for doneness (see page 94). (*Note:* Soft-shell crabs will feel more solid and should be a lovely golden-red color.)

SERVES 1

DEEP-FRIED SEAFOOD: VARIATION III

Preparation time: 1¼ hours
Deep-frying time: 2 to 20 minutes
Time to heat oil: approximately 7 to
    10 minutes

SPECIAL EQUIPMENT: Electric deep fryer with a temperature control *or* deep saucepan *or* wok
Frying basket *or* large slotted spoon
Deep-fry thermometer

See Variation I for suggestions on type of oil and control of heat.

Choose seafood such as

catfish • oysters • soft-shell clams

Beer Batter:
  ¾ *cup all-purpose flour*
  ½ *cup fine cornmeal*
  1 *teaspoon salt*
  ½ *teaspoon freshly ground white*
    pepper
  2 *teaspoons paprika*
  2 *large eggs, separated*
  1 *cup light beer at room*
    temperature
  1 *tablespoon mild olive oil*

2 *12-ounce catfish on the bone,*
  skinned, with head, tail, and
  fins removed
  or
24 *oysters, shucked and drained*
  or
24 *soft-shell (steamer) clams,*
  shucked and drained
2 *lemon wedges*
1 *recipe tomato salsa (see page*
  225)

1. Put the flour, cornmeal, salt, pepper, and paprika in a medium bowl and stir well.
2. Make a well in the mixture and add the egg yolks, beer, and oil. With a wire whisk, gradually mix until the wet ingredients are incorporated into the dry. Let stand 1 hour.
3. Before coating the seafood, beat the egg whites until stiff and fold into the batter.
4. Now proceed just as in Variation I. The catfish will take about 20 minutes to cook. The oysters and steamer clams take only 1 minute for each side. For the catfish, check doneness as on page 94; oysters and clams must be crisp on the outside and juicy in the middle.
5. Serve with lemon wedges and a tomato salsa.

Variation: You can add 1 teaspoon fresh (or ½ teaspoon dry) thyme, oregano, marjoram, or dill; ¼ teaspoon cayenne, 1 tablespoon paprika, chili powder, or cumin to any of the coatings.

SERVES 2

FRITTERS

Preparation time: 20 minutes
Cooking time: 20 to 30 minutes
Time to heat oil: approximately 7 to
    10 minutes

SPECIAL EQUIPMENT: Electric deep
fryer with a temperature control *or*
deep saucepan *or* wok
Frying basket or large slotted spoon
Deep-fry thermometer

See page 160 for suggestions on type of oil and control of heat.

Choose seafood such as

conch • crabmeat • salt cod

¾ cup all-purpose flour
1 teaspoon baking powder
1 large egg
½ cup milk
1 pound crabmeat, picked over for
    any cartilage
        or
1 pound conch, precooked and
    chopped by hand, or ground
    through the fine cutting blade of
    a meat grinder
        or
1 pound salt cod, previously soaked
    (*see page 290*) and shredded
    (*cod weighs more when it is
    rehydrated, so put ½ cup aside
    for another use*)
2 cloves garlic, finely minced
1 jalapeño pepper, seeded and
    finely chopped (*1 tablespoon*)

3 tablespoons finely chopped parsley
¼ cup lemon juice
2 tablespoons white wine
    Worcestershire sauce
8 drops Tabasco sauce
1 teaspoon salt (or less, depending
    how salty the seafood is)
¼ teaspoon freshly ground black
    pepper
Pinch cayenne
1 quart or more vegetable oil (*corn
    oil or safflower oil preferred*)
1 lemon or lime, cut in 6 wedges
1 recipe tomato or tomatillo salsa
    (*optional—see pages 225 and
    226*) or 1 recipe aioli
    (*optional—see page 229*)

1. Sift the flour and baking powder into a medium-sized bowl.
2. In another bowl, whisk the egg and the milk together with a wire whisk.
Add this mixture gradually to the flour mixture, whisking all the time.

3. Add the seafood, garlic, jalapeño pepper, parsley, lemon juice, Worcestershire sauce, Tabasco sauce, salt, black pepper, and cayenne to the egg-flour mixture and combine well with a large spoon. Let stand 5 minutes.

4. In the meantime, heat the oil (at least 2 inches deep) in an electric deep fryer, deep saucepan, or wok to 375 degrees F (or until a 1-inch cube of bread browns in 20 seconds' time). Preheat the oven to 200 degrees F.

5. Using a teaspoon, drop about 9 or 10 teaspoonfuls of the mixture into the hot oil and fry for 1 to 2 minutes on each side, or until golden brown.

6. Drain each batch of fritters on paper towels and put them in a baking pan in the oven while you fry the rest. (*Note:* Always wait until the oil has reached 375 degrees F before adding another batch.)

7. Serve the fritters with lemon or lime wedges, one of the salsas, or aioli, if desired.

MAKES ABOUT 40 TEASPOON-SIZED FRITTERS

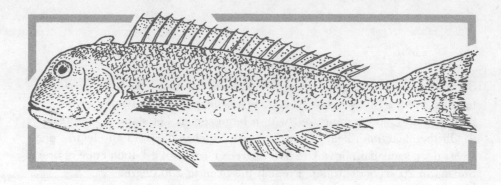

Poaching

TO POACH SEAFOOD IS TO COOK IT IN WATER, WHICH IS FLAVORED WITH VEGETABLES, HERBS, seasonings, and wine. Poached seafood can be ordinary daily fare or a special dish for a special occasion. You can serve it hot or at room temperature, garnished or not; if it is to be served at room temperature, you can, of course, prepare it beforehand. Poaching and boiling are similar in that the food is cooked in hot liquid; when poaching the liquid must simmer.

Poaching is a time-honored practice, but I have the feeling that it causes some of the flavor of the seafood to disappear into the poaching liquid. However, it has its uses, as you will see from the recipes in this section, especially if the poaching liquid is flavorful. When tackling a large whole fish I personally prefer bake-poaching (see page 96), for it prevents the flavors and juices from escaping.

If you are poaching a large fish, prepare the poaching liquid in a fish poacher. This is a long pan 4 to 8 inches high with a lift-out tray; it may be

166

so large it will stretch over two burners on your stove. For small whole fish, fillets, or shellfish you can use a large pot or baking pan with 4-inch sides. Fill the utensil you are using with enough liquid to cover the seafood. Add cut aromatic vegetables, fresh herbs such as thyme, oregano, marjoram, basil, coriander, tarragon, and bay leaves. Fennel and lemon or orange peel can also be added. The liquid should be barely simmering when you lower the seafood into it. You can wrap the fish in cheesecloth, tying at both ends before immersing it in the poaching liquid, so that it can be easily lifted out of the liquid. Otherwise, be prepared to lift it out with wide metal spatulas.

You can poach many kinds of whole fish, although it is best to poach fish with firm flesh. Poached salmon is a classic, of course, but a whole poached trout, blackfish, or cod can also look very attractive. Poach a whole fish for 10 to 45 minutes, depending on its size and thickness. You can skin a poached whole fish for better presentation, leaving the head and tail intact. Cover it with tiny thin slivers of cucumber and decorate it with dill or tarragon for a pleasing look.

With the exception of salmon, it is not a good idea to poach fish with dark or oily flesh such as mackerel, sable, herring, sardines, and bluefish. Poaching does nothing for their flavor.

Poaching is a plain way of cooking seafood, so it is a good idea to serve poached seafood with accompanying vegetables, perhaps those that were cooked in the poaching liquid. A whole poached fish with skin on can be garnished with these vegetables.

A coating of aspic will enhance a cold poached fish.

When you want to make a seafood salad by poaching shrimp, scallops, and squid for a few minutes, immerse them in a strainer or colander, so that they can be quickly retrieved and not overcooked. You can also use a slotted spoon to retrieve them.

To poach individual portions from fillets, lay them in a large baking pan and heat the oven to 350 degrees F. Pour boiling hot poaching liquid over the fish, cover the top of the pan with aluminum foil, and put it in the oven for 10 to 20 minutes, depending on the thickness of the fillets. This is a good way to poach salmon slices (see page 170). Fish fillets can be poached with skin on or off, but there will be less shrinkage if you leave the skin on.

You may also choose to liven up poached seafood with a flavorful sauce or mayonnaise. If so, there are plenty of sauce recipes to choose from (see page 225). When serving warm or cold poached individual portions, such as slices, serve the sauce on the plate under the fish or present it on the side.

TIMES AND TEMPERATURES

After the poaching liquid has simmered for 25 minutes or so, the seafood can be added to it, or it can be added to the seafood. Depending on the thickness, the seafood will be cooked after 10 to 30 minutes. When poaching in the oven, slices of fish will be cooked between 10 and 15 minutes at 350 degrees F.

HEALTH

No fat is used in this preparation method, so unless you prepare a rich sauce to accompany the seafood—which, of course, your guests can choose to eat or pass up—the dish will be fat free and therefore very healthful.

BASIC POACHING RECIPES

POACHING LIQUID

Preparation time: 10 minutes
Cooking time: 20 to 25 minutes

SPECIAL EQUIPMENT: Fish poacher *or* saucepan or baking pan with 4-inch sides
Cheesecloth (optional)

The amounts of ingredients listed below are approximate; different amounts will be needed for different amounts of seafood. Let your judgment be your guide.

On those occasions when you are going to serve the vegetables with the seafood, cut them in a uniform and decorative fashion.

Water to cover the seafood
¼ to ½ bottle of dry white wine
2 to 4 carrots, scraped, thinly sliced
2 to 4 celery stalks, sliced in 1-inch lengths
5 to 10 sprigs of thyme or *marjoram* or *basil* or *coriander* or *tarragon*
6 parsley stems
2 to 6 bay leaves

1 or 2 medium onions, roughly
  chopped
2 to 6 cloves garlic, crushed with
  the flat of a chef's knife
1 or 2 leeks with most of the green
  leaves removed and discarded,
  trimmed, halved, rinsed, and
  chopped in 2-inch lengths
  (optional)

1 or 2 lemon halves
2 or more tablespoons salt to taste
  (I mean it—taste the water!)
1 teaspoon to 1 tablespoon black
  peppercorns

1. Fill the poacher, pot, or pan with enough water to cover the seafood. (In order to be sure that the liquid will cover the seafood you are poaching, start by placing the seafood in your poacher or pot. Pour enough cold water over the seafood to cover it, then remove the seafood. This will show you exactly how much poaching liquid you need.)

2. Add the wine.

3. Lower the vegetables and herbs into the water. (*Note:* you can first tie all the vegetables and herbs in cheesecloth. This is an especially good idea when cooking sliced fillets so that the vegetables and herbs do not get mixed up with the seafood, and so that they can be easily removed.)

4. Add the salt and peppercorns.

5. Bring the liquid to a boil over high heat.

6. Turn the heat down to moderate low and simmer for 25 minutes, so the liquid is full of flavor.

POACHED WHOLE FISH

Preparation time, including time to cook poaching liquid: 30 to 35 minutes
Poaching time: 20 to 45 minutes

SPECIAL EQUIPMENT: Fish poacher *or* saucepan *or* baking pan with 4-inch sides
Cheesecloth (optional)

Poached whole fish can be presented much like bake-poached whole fish, that is, decorated so that it makes a showy piece for a buffet and served hot or cold. See page 102 for these directions.

Choose whole fish such as

blackfish • **grouper** • **red snapper** • **rockfish** • **salmon** • **tilefish**

NUMBER SERVED	AMOUNT OF FISH NEEDED	APPROXIMATE POACHING TIME
4	1 fish weighing 3 pounds	20 minutes
5	1 fish weighing 4 pounds	30 minutes
6	1 fish weighing 5 pounds	35 minutes
8	1 fish weighing 6 pounds	45 minutes

1 whole fish weighing 3 to 6 pounds, gutted and scaled and with gills removed but with head and tail left on

1 recipe poaching liquid (see page 168)

1 recipe appropriate sauce or mayonnaise (see page 225)

1. Prepare the poaching liquid.
2. While the poaching liquid is cooking, make the appropriate sauce.
3. When the poaching liquid is barely simmering, lower the fish (wrapped and tied in cheesecloth if you want) into it. Check for doneness (see page 94) 5 minutes before the end of the recommended poaching time.
4. Either use the fish poacher tray or wide spatulas to lift the fish out of the liquid onto a platter.
5. Skin the fish or not, depending on the look you want (see page 102).
6. Use a slotted spoon to retrieve the vegetables from the stock and surround the fish with them if you like. Serve with sauce or mayonnaise.

SERVES 4 TO 8

POACHED SMALL WHOLE FISH OR FISH PORTIONS

Preparation time, including time to make the poaching liquid: 35 to 40 minutes
Poaching time: 10 to 15 minutes

SPECIAL EQUIPMENT: Cheesecloth (optional)
Plastic wrap (optional)
Small baking pan

It is a good idea to poach small individual portions cut from fillets or small whole fish in a small baking pan instead of a large fish poacher.

In this recipe, when you are making the poaching liquid, I would recommend tying the vegetables, herbs, and seasonings in cheesecloth so they can be removed easily. Alternately, if you wish, you can strain the liquid over the fish. Small whole fish can also be wrapped in cheesecloth or plastic wrap so that they will stay in perfect shape. Tie the wrap at both ends.

Choose fish fillets such as

lingcod • salmon

or choose small fish such as

baby coho salmon • bass, various • brook trout • rainbow trout

1 recipe poaching liquid (see page 168)	*or*
1 recipe appropriate sauce or mayonnaise (see page 225)	*4 whole fish, weighing 8 to 12 ounces each*
Oil or butter for coating	*1 bunch chives, cut in 2-inch pieces*
4 7- to 8-ounce portions fish from fillet (see page 83), pin bones removed, cut on the diagonal	*1 tomato, peel only*
	1 bunch parsley
	1 lemon, cut in curls

1. Prepare the poaching liquid. Tie the vegetables, herbs, and seasonings in a cheesecloth bag or be prepared to strain the liquid over the fish.
2. Make the sauce or mayonnaise to be served with the fish.
3. Preheat the oven to 350 degrees F.
4. Lightly oil or butter a baking pan that will fit the fish, so the fish doesn't stick to the bottom of the pan.
5. Place the fish in the pan and pour over the poaching liquid. Discard the vegetables.
6. Cover pan tightly with sheets of aluminum foil and put in oven.
7. Cook for 10 to 15 minutes, checking for doneness after 7 minutes (see page 94).
8. Lift out the fish with a wide metal spatula onto serving plates or a platter.
9. Decorate the fish fillets with a crisscross of chives and a small round of tomato peel. Skin the small whole fish if you like and decorate it with chives and tomato peel (cut in thin strips) laid on the side of the fish body. Place parsley sprigs and lemon curls around the fish. Serve the fish hot or at room temperature, with an appropriate sauce or mayonnaise.

SERVES 4

SHELLFISH SALAD I

Preparation time, including time to make the poaching liquid: 45 minutes to 1 hour

Poaching time: 30 seconds (scallops, squid) to 2 minutes (shrimp)

SPECIAL EQUIPMENT: Cheesecloth

This simple salad requires seafood that has been previously poached (mussels can be poached or steamed). A variety of seafood is listed below; you may, of course, include more of one kind and less of another, as you like.

The salad can be served as an appetizer or a main course. You need 6 to 8 ounces for each person if you are serving it as a main course and 3 to 4 ounces if you are serving it as an appetizer.

Choose shellfish such as

mussels • scallops • shrimp • squid

1 recipe poaching liquid (see page 168)

1 recipe Lime and Dill Vinaigrette (see page 230)

¾ pound medium shrimp, peeled and deveined

¾ pound bay scallops

¾ pound squid, clean and cut in ¼-inch slices

1½ pounds mussels, steamed (see page 178) or poached and picked from their shells

Ice water for cooling seafood

3 tablespoons chopped dill or tarragon or basil or parsley or coriander

Boston lettuce or radicchio or endive leaves

1. Prepare the poaching liquid in a pot. Tie the vegetables, herbs, and seasonings in cheesecloth.
2. In the meantime, make the vinaigrette.
3. If possible, find a strainer or colander that fits inside the pot. Place the shrimp in it. When the poaching liquid is ready and barely simmering, immerse the shrimp. Poach until opaque all the way through.
4. Remove the shrimp with a slotted spoon (if you didn't use a strainer or colander) and throw them into ice water.
5. Repeat with scallops and squid, but check them after 30 seconds.
6. If mussels have not been steamed, add them to the poaching liquid and cook until the shells open. Shuck them when they are cool enough to handle.

7. Drain all the seafood well in a colander.

8. Put the seafood in a bowl and add the vinaigrette and chopped herb. Refrigerate until ready to serve.

9. Place salad leaves around a platter and put the seafood salad in the middle.

Variation: Also use this method to poach shrimp, when serving them hot or cold, with a spicy sauce or aioli.

SERVES 6 AS A MAIN DISH OR 12 AS AN APPETIZER

BOILED CRAWFISH

Preparation time, including time to make the poaching liquid: 30 to 45 minutes
Cooking time: 15 minutes
Time needed for cooling in liquid: 10 minutes

1 to 2 heads garlic, cut in half crosswise
1 to 2 lemons, cut in half
2 to 4 tablespoons Old Bay Seasoning (optional)
1 or more tablespoons salt to taste (*I mean it*—taste the water)

⅛ to 1 teaspoon cayenne
20 to 40 basil leaves, cut in thin strips
1 to 5 pounds crawfish, cleaned as per instructions (*see page 308*)

1. Fill a pot with enough water to cover the cleaned crawfish.

2. Add garlic and lemon halves, having squeezed their juice into the water.

3. Add Old Bay seasoning, if desired, salt, and cayenne.

4. Bring to a boil and after 10 minutes add the basil and the crawfish. Cover, but check to see when the liquid comes to a boil again.

5. When the liquid boils again, cook the crawfish for 1 minute, then turn off the heat and let them cool in the liquid for 10 minutes.

6. Drain.

SERVES 1 TO 6

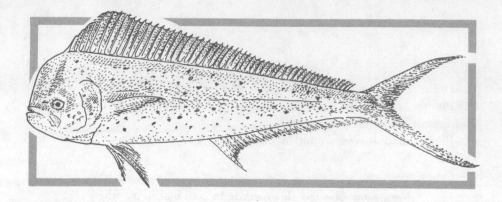

Steaming

STEAMING IS ANOTHER HEALTHFUL WAY TO COOK SEAFOOD. IT IS A PLAIN METHOD, THOUGH THE seafood can be enlivened with vegetables, herbs, and seasonings. Small whole fish (such as bass and porgies) and fillets of fish can be steamed, as well as shrimp, lobsters, and scallops.

Steaming is done over water and/or wine in a utensil such as a basket steamer that fits closely on top of a saucepan or wok, or a metal steamer that fits inside a saucepan. The utensil must be covered with a lid so that the seafood cooks in the steam. If you use a metal steamer or fold-out steam basket, put a plate in the steamer and lay the seafood on it (of course, if you use a fold-out steam basket, you must remove the center post, if it has one). Keep the liquid under the seafood at a medium boil over moderate heat and add more only if necessary; this is hardly ever necessary because seafood takes such a short time to steam.

When steaming seafood, place a bed of vegetables, such as onions or

174

fennel, or a julienne of leeks and carrots on the plate in the steamer tray under the fish. Alternately, you can lay the mixture on top of the fish. Sprinkle fillets with fresh herbs such as thyme, dill, parsley, or mint. Suitable seasonings are a little butter, a squeeze of lemon juice, and paprika, cumin, pepper, or grated ginger. Rub small whole fish with a little oil and one of the aforementioned seasonings. Whole fish will better retain their shape and skin if they are wrapped lightly in cheesecloth. They can be pulled out of the steamer more easily this way too.

Steaming (on a fold-out vegetable steamer over 1 inch of water in a large pot) is a better way to cook lobster than boiling. One advantage is that you can count the cooking time from the moment you put the lobster on the steamer over the boiling water, instead of waiting for the water to begin boiling again after you place the lobster in the pot. Also, a steamed lobster does not get quite as waterlogged as one that is boiled.

To steam clams and mussels, put some wine and/or water and some fresh herbs in a large shallow skillet or saucepan with a fitted lid. Cook over high heat, shaking the pan from time to time until the mollusks are all open. Mussels should take 5 minutes maximum. The juices are retained when you steam this way, whereas if you use the above steaming method you discard the liquid after the lobster is cooked.

It is not advisable to steam oily fish such as mackerel, herring, sardines, sable, or bluefish because steaming does nothing for their taste.

TIMES AND TEMPERATURES

It takes no longer to steam a fish or a fish fillet than it does to poach one: 3 to 30 minutes, depending on the thickness of the fish. Times for lobster steaming are given in the recipe on page 179. Other shellfish take from 3 to 10 minutes.

The steaming liquid must be kept at a medium boil over moderate heat.

HEALTH

Like poaching, this method gives you a fat-free dish, unless you serve a rich sauce.

BASIC STEAMING RECIPES

STEAMED SEAFOOD

Preparation time: 15 minutes
Steaming time: 3 to 10 minutes

SPECIAL EQUIPMENT: Chinese basket-weave steamer with a lid that fits on top of a wok or saucepan *or* a metal steamer that fits on top of a saucepan with a lid *or* a fold-out vegetable steamer that fits flat in a saucepan with a lid
Cheesecloth

Choose fillets of fish, preferably with skin on, such as

blackfish • black sea bass • catfish • cod • dolphinfish (mahi-mahi) grouper • lemon sole • lingcod • monkfish • ocean perch • orange roughy • petrale sole • red snapper • salmon • sea robin (skinned) • sheepshead • skate • tilapia • tilefish • trout • whitefish • wolffish

or choose shellfish such as

gooseneck barnacles • bay or sea scallops • shrimp • squid

2 teaspoons mild olive oil or vegetable oil

2 6 to 8-ounce fish fillets with skin on and pin bones removed
or
¾ pound scallops (small tough muscles removed), shrimp (shelled and deveined), or squid, cleaned

1 carrot, very thinly sliced or finely julienned (like matchsticks)

2 small celery stalks, very thinly sliced or finely julienned

2 bok choy leaves (finely sliced) or ¼ fennel bulb (finely sliced) or ⅛ savoy cabbage with the hard core cut off and discarded, very finely sliced, like a chiffonade

2 scallions, sliced on the diagonal in 3-inch pieces

Salt to taste

Freshly ground white pepper to taste

1 tablespoon finely chopped dill, tarragon, parsley, or thyme

1 recipe Basic Topping I or II (see page 232), or appropriate flavored butter or sauce such as Sweet Red Pepper Sauce, Honeycup Mustard Sauce, or Anchovy Butter (see pages 230, 233, and 236), or a sauce of melted butter with lemon and parsley

1. Fill a saucepan halfway with water. (If using a flat fold-out vegetable steamer, use only 1 inch of water.) Bring the water to a boil over high heat.

2. Put the oil on a plate (one that will fit on or in the steaming utensil) and coat both sides of the seafood with the oil. Put the seafood aside.

3. Put the vegetables, salt, pepper, and three quarters of the chopped herbs on the plate. Lay a piece of cheesecloth on the steamer, with some of it hanging over the edge, and place the plate on top of it. (When the seafood is cooked, you can lift the hot plate out of the steamer with the cheesecloth.)

4. (If you are cooking fillets that are less than 1 inch thick, put the lid on and steam the vegetables for 5 minutes before laying the fish on top of them.) Now lay the fish (skin side down) or shellfish on top of the vegetables, turn heat to moderate, and cover with the lid.

5. Steam from 3 to 10 minutes until the fish or shellfish is opaque all the way through. Check after 3 minutes to see if it is cooked (see page 94).

6. When the seafood is cooked, turn off the heat. Lift the plate out with the cheesecloth or use pot holders to remove the plate.

7. Serve from this plate, sprinkling the seafood with a little salt and pepper, the remaining chopped herbs, and the butter or sauce of your choice.

Variation: Simple steaming for gooseneck barnacles and fish for salads. Steam as above, but there is no need to use a plate or steam vegetables with the seafood. Oil the surface of the steamer before placing the seafood on it. Two pounds gooseneck barnacles serves 2 and takes 3 to 5 minutes to steam. Serve gooseneck barnacles with aioli sauce (see page 229) or melted butter. Two to 4 pounds fish fillets for salad, skin on or off, takes 5 to 15 minutes to steam.

Variation: Steamed Small Whole Fish

Choose whole dressed fish, small enough to fit in the steamer such as

bass • blackfish • porgies • trout

Steam as above, without vegetables, but add one of the toppings on page 232 halfway through steaming.

SERVES 2

STEAMED MUSSELS OR SOFT-SHELL CLAMS *MARINIÈRE*

Preparation time: 15 minutes
Standing time: ½ hour
Steaming time: 3 to 5 minutes

SPECIAL EQUIPMENT: 12-inch skillet with a fitted lid
Finger bowls

¾ cup dry white wine
4 tablespoons finely chopped
    shallots (about 3 shallots) or
    finely chopped scallions or finely
    chopped onion
1 tablespoon finely chopped garlic
2 pounds mussels, cleaned and left
    to stand ½ hour (see page 355)
    or
2 pounds soft-shell clams (steamer
    clams), cleaned and left to stand
    ½ hour (see page 285)

1 tablespoon fresh thyme leaves or
    ½ teaspoon dried thyme
2 tablespoons finely chopped parsley
1 tablespoon unsalted butter or
    margarine or heavy cream
    (optional)

1. Put the wine, shallots, and garlic in the skillet. Cover and cook over high heat for 2 minutes.
2. Add the mussels or soft-shell clams. They should lie in one single layer in the pan.
3. Cover the pan and cook, shaking the pan every ½ minute or so, until the mussel shells open (3 to 5 minutes). Discard any that do not open. (*Note:* Soft-shell clam shells are already slightly open; when they cook, their shells gape further apart.)
4. Pick the mussels or soft-shell clams out of the pan with tongs or a slotted spoon and put them in soup bowls.
5. If you are serving mussels, add the thyme and parsley (and the butter, margarine, or cream if desired) to the wine, shallots, and garlic in the skillet. Swirl the mixture around over high heat and, when it is foamy, pour it over the mussels. Have fun! Use a pair of empty mussel shells as a pincer to pick the rest of the mussels from their shells.

If you are serving soft-shell clams, add the butter, margarine, but not cream to the wine, shallot, and garlic in the skillet. When the butter has melted, strain the sauce through a fine mesh into little pots or ramekins and dip the soft-shell clams (out of their shells) in this sauce before eating.

Have a bowl ready for the empty shells and finger bowls to rinse your fingers.

SERVES 2 AS A MAIN COURSE OR 4 AS AN APPETIZER

STEAMED LOBSTER

Preparation time: 5 minutes
Steaming time: 10 to 55 minutes

SPECIAL EQUIPMENT: Large (16-quart) lobster pot with a lid
Flat fold-out vegetable steamer (remove the center post, if it has one)
Nutcrackers or a hammer (for large lobsters)
Lobster picks or forks

NUMBER SERVED	SIZE OF LOBSTER	STEAMING TIME
1	1 pound	10 minutes
1	1¼ pounds	12 minutes
1	1½ pounds	15 minutes
1	1¾ pounds	18 minutes
2	2 pounds	20 minutes
2	2½ pounds	25 minutes
2	3 pounds	30 minutes
4	5 pounds	55 minutes

1 or 2 cans of lager-type beer
Lobster or lobsters as needed
1 to 2 ounces (2 to 4 tablespoons)
  unsalted butter or *margarine per*
  person

Salt to taste
Lemon juice to taste
Lemon wedges

1. Pour the beer and enough water to measure 1 inch in your pot, and bring to the boil.

2. Lay the vegetable steamer in the pot and place the lobster or lobsters on

top. You should always hold a lobster by its body, near the head, not the tail, and get its claws and head in first. Cover the pot. *Count the cooking time from this point. You have to be precise because there is no way to tell if a lobster is cooked without breaking the shell open.*

3. In the meantime gently heat the butter or margarine in a small pan until it is melted.

4. When cooked, place each lobster in the kitchen sink right side up.

5. Run a little cold water over each lobster to stop the cooking and let lobster(s) stand 5 minutes.

6. Using a dishcloth to protect you from the heat, turn each lobster on its back and cut it down the middle with a chef's knife. Use scissors to cut down the middle of the underside of the tail, if you want the tail meat in one piece.

7. Find the little sac behind each lobster's eyes and remove it.

8. Detach the claws and crack them in several places with nutcrackers, or with a hammer if they are large.

9. Arrange all the pieces on a platter in a decorative way.

10. Mix the salt and lemon juice with the melted butter or margarine and place the mixture in little pots or ramekins.

11. Serve the lobster(s) with lemon wedges and melted butter.

STEAMED CRABS

Preparation time: 30 minutes in the freezer *Steaming time:* 20 to 30 minutes	SPECIAL EQUIPMENT: Large (16-quart) lobster pot with a lid Flat fold-out vegetable steamer *or* rack Wooden board (optional) Wooden mallet (optional) Nutcrackers

The crabs must be bought alive—you've just got to keep out of the way of their claws. The best way to do this is to grab the crabs from behind or by the rear swimming legs, or use long-handled tongs, after the crabs have been tranquilized somewhat by a half-hour stay in the freezer.

Steaming time does depend somewhat on the shape of the utensil you use. If you can fit the crabs in a large, wide pot in one or two layers, the steaming time will be as listed below. If you have to make more than two layers of crabs, of course the steaming will take longer, so please compensate. Also know that the crabs at the bottom will cook faster than those at the top.

NUMBER SERVED	CRABS NEEDED	APPROXIMATE STEAMING TIME
2	6 to 8 large blue crabs	20 minutes
4 or 5	12 large blue crabs	25 minutes
2	2 large Dungeness crabs	20 minutes
4	4 large Dungeness crabs	30 minutes

8 large blue crabs
  or
2 1- to 1½-pound Dungeness crabs
1 cup white vinegar
3 tablespoons crab boil, obtainable in bottled form in fish stores (optional)

4 tablespoons crab seasoning (store-bought or made from ½ teaspoon white and black pepper, 1 tablespoon paprika, ½ teaspoon cayenne, ¾ teaspoon salt, and 1 teaspoon dried oregano or thyme)

1. Put the crabs (in the bag they came in) in the freezer for 30 minutes. This is to calm them down somewhat.
2. Bring an inch of water to the boil in a large pot and add the vinegar and, if you like, the crab boil.
3. Lay a flat fold-out vegetable steamer or rack in the pot and place the crabs in one layer on top.
4. Sprinkle the crabs with crab seasoning, then add a second layer of crabs and sprinkle again.
5. Put the lid on and cook for 20 minutes.
6. Remove the crabs from the pot, place them on a platter, then take your time to enjoy this treat. It's best to crack the crabs on a wooden board with a wooden mallet and a nutcracker.

SERVES 2

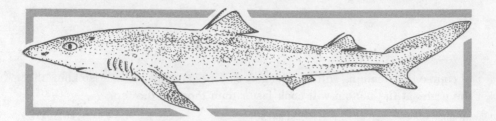

Braising

BRAISING IS A COMBINATION OF COOKING METHODS. FIRST YOU BRIEFLY SEAR OR SAUTÉ THE seafood in a pan on top of the stove, then you add additional ingredients such as a mixture of vegetables; flavorings like onion, garlic, and herbs; and broth or wine. Next, depending on the size of the seafood, you can either transfer it to a baking dish and put it in the oven or leave it in its original pan and finish cooking it on top of the stove.

This is a particularly good method for seafood that tends to be bland, for the taste of the added ingredients is somewhat absorbed by the seafood. Large, fairly firm-fleshed fillets can be braised, as well as slices or cubes of fish. Monkfish, sand shark, shrimp, squid, raw lobster in shell (cut into sections), scallops, and cooked octopus also braise well. You can also use this method for smaller pieces of fish, such as thickly sliced fillets, medallions, or steaks.

182

TIMES AND TEMPERATURES

When you braise fish or shellfish, sear it just long enough to give it some color—a few minutes on each side. The oil or fat should be hot, so the pan must be set over moderate to high heat. If you are going to finish cooking it in the oven, preheat the oven to 425 degrees F. Depending on the size of the seafood, it will be cooked in 40 to 50 minutes.

HEALTH

Use just enough fat or oil to sear the fish and brown it. After that is accomplished, you can leave the fat behind and transfer the fish to another pan before you add the additional ingredients and liquid to finish cooking. The braised fish ends up with little fat or oil.

BASIC BRAISING RECIPES

BRAISED MONKFISH TAIL, DOLPHINFISH (MAHI-MAHI) FILLETS, OR SAND SHARK

Preparation time: 20 minutes
Cooking time: 40 to 50 minutes

SPECIAL EQUIPMENT: Earthenware casserole dish or Pyrex or other ovenproof china dish

With thanks to the Minchelli brothers, chef-owners of restaurants in Paris, Geneva, and the Seychelles, who shared the idea for this recipe.

2 tablespoons mild olive oil
6 slices thick bacon, cut in 1-inch pieces
12 whole garlic cloves, peeled
3 pounds monkfish tail or tails on the bone, skinned (see page 79)
or
3 pounds sand shark (dogfish) in a piece, skinned and cut in 3-inch-thick steaks
or

2 pounds dolphinfish (mahi-mahi) fillets
1 cup dry white wine
3 medium tomatoes, skinned, seeded, and coarsely chopped (2 cups)
1 teaspoon fresh (or ½ teaspoon dried) thyme or basil or savory
Salt to taste
Freshly ground black pepper to taste

1. In a frying pan large enough to hold the fish, heat the oil over moderate heat.

2. Add the bacon pieces and garlic cloves. Separate the bacon pieces so they cook evenly.

3. Preheat the oven to 425 degrees F.

4. When the garlic is nearly brown and the bacon crisp, move them to the side of the pan. Add the fish and brown it on one side and then the other. This will take between 3 and 5 minutes for each side.

5. Place the fish in an earthenware casserole dish or a Pyrex or other ovenproof china dish.

6. Remove the bacon and garlic cloves from the pan with a slotted spoon and put them to one side.

7. Pour off the fat from the pan, put the pan back on the heat, and deglaze it with a cup of white wine.

8. Add the tomatoes, herb, salt, and pepper and cook 1 minute.

9. Place the tomato mixture on and around the fish with the bacon and garlic cloves scattered on the top.

10. Braise in the oven for 20 to 30 minutes, until the fish is just cooked through (see page 94).

11. Remove the fish from the oven, baste it with the juices, and serve.

SERVES 4

BRAISED FISH FILLETS OR STEAKS WITH PROVENÇALE SAUCE

Preparation time: 20 minutes
Cooking time: 20 to 25 minutes

The Provençale sauce described with this recipe can be made separately and used with any fish of your choice. Adding optional chopped jalapeño pepper (not typically Provençale) gives this sauce a different dimension—it will have heat in it!

Choose seafood such as

blowfish (tails) • carp (1-inch-thick steaks) • cod (1-inch-thick steaks) •
eel (1-inch-thick steaks) • lingcod (1-inch-thick steaks) •
lobster (sections in shell) • monkfish (fillets, sliced into medallions 2
inches thick) • salt cod (fillets, dehydrated) • sand shark (dogfish)
(1½-inch-thick steaks) • sturgeon (1-inch-thick steaks) • tilefish
(1-inch-thick steaks) • tuna (2-inch-thick steaks)

4 tablespoons mild olive oil
1 medium onion, finely chopped
    (1 cup)
3 cloves garlic, minced
1 or 2 jalapeño peppers, seeded and
    finely chopped (optional)
1½ to 2 pounds fish steaks or
    monkfish fillets or blowfish tails
    or
2 2- to 2½-pound lobsters (cut in
    pieces)
4 medium tomatoes, skinned,
    seeded, and chopped (2 cups)

3 tablespoons tomato paste
Salt to taste
Freshly ground black pepper to
    taste
1 cup dry white wine
3 tablespoons balsamic or red wine
    vinegar
20 fresh basil leaves, cut in strips
    at the last moment
12 black olives (Niçoise or
    calamata or Californian)
4 anchovies, cut in 1-inch pieces
    (optional)

1. Heat 3 tablespoons of oil in a shallow casserole dish or skillet over medium heat.
2. Add the onions and sweat them until they are transparent.
3. Add the garlic and chopped peppers, if desired, and cook, stirring for 2 minutes.
4. Push the vegetables aside, add 1 more tablespoon oil, and brown the seafood briefly on all sides. There is no need to cook it through.
5. Add the tomatoes, tomato paste, salt, pepper, and dry white wine. Stir and cover.
6. Lower the heat and cook for 7 to 10 minutes, depending on the thickness of the seafood. Check for doneness (see page 94).
7. When the seafood is cooked, stir in the vinegar and the basil strips.
8. Scatter black olives and anchovy pieces, if desired, over the seafood and sauce. Serve from the casserole dish or skillet, or place in a serving dish.

SERVES 4

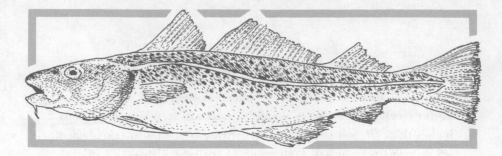

Soups and Stews

TO MAKE A FISH *SOUP*, IN WHICH THE SEAFOOD IS VISIBLE, FIRST PREPARE A FLAVORFUL BROTH, then add seafood at the last moment; the broth is made with sautéed vegetables, wine, and a stock made from fish bones, or even lobster or shrimp shells (which of course are strained off). Or you can make a smooth soup by liquefying the ingredients in the blender or pushing them through a food mill.

To make a fish *stew*, sauté seafood and then add flavorings such as vegetables, herbs, wine, and stock. A stew can be extended (with liquid) to make a sauce for pasta. You can cook a stew on top of the stove in a sauté pan, frying pan, or saucepan.

You can use fish, shellfish, or a mixture of both in a stew. Keep in mind that fish and shellfish will not take long to cook—unlike meat—so the basic liquid and flavorings should be cooked in advance for a little while before you add the seafood.

Thick fish fillets are suitable for soups and stews, although very oily fish such as mackerel and herring should be avoided unless you like strong tastes in a soup or stew. Skin (if you want) and debone fish fillets and cut them across

186

the grain into 1½-inch-thick slices. Firm-fleshed fish such as monkfish, black-fish, snapper, sea robin, and the basses are more suitable than flaky fish, which tend to break up in a soup or stew; however, with careful timing and handling, lean white fish that flakes easily such as cod can be used.

All shellfish are suitable for soups and stews, including mussels, clams, lobster pieces, and thinly sliced squid. Scrub any mollusks before using them.

TIMES AND TEMPERATURES

Whether you add seafood to a flavored broth or add flavors and broth to seafood, the fish and shellfish cook for only a few minutes. (The broth will take half an hour to prepare at the most and must be simmering when the seafood is added, or when added to the seafood.)

HEALTH

Soups and stews are usually made with little oil or fat, and so they are a nonfattening way to eat seafood. Any fat used to sauté the fish or vegetables can be skimmed off before serving. The Creamy Seafood Chowder on page 190 is the exception.

BASIC SOUP AND STEW RECIPES

FISH STOCK

Preparation time: 15 minutes
Cooking time: 25 minutes to 1 hour, 5
   minutes

SPECIAL EQUIPMENT: Cheesecloth

This is a great recipe for a quick, light fish stock.

Remember, all the fish must be scaled (if you are using the skin) and the gills must be removed—the scales can cloud the stock and the gills can impart a bitter taste. Rinse off the bones if they are at all bloody. Also remember that this stock can be frozen for later use.

In a pinch you can substitute bottled clam juice for the fish stock.

Choose the bones, heads, and skin of lean fish such as

**black sea bass • cod • flounder • haddock • hake • halibut •
monkfish • Pacific cod • red snapper • rockfish • sea robin •
sole • whiting**

or see the list on page 20, *or* buy whole **whiting** or **sea robin** and cut it into steaks.

2 pounds fish bones, heads, and skin	*1 leek, cut in half lengthwise, rinsed and chopped*
1 small onion, quartered	*½ fennel bulb, chopped (optional)*
2 stalks celery, roughly chopped	*2 cups dry white wine*

1. Put all the ingredients and 4 cups of water into a saucepan and bring slowly to the boil. Skim with a tea strainer if you want a clear stock.
2. Turn down the heat so the stock just simmers, and cook it for 25 minutes.
3. Sniff the stock. If it smells good and of fish, take it off the fire.
4. Strain the stock through cheesecloth.
5. If you want a stronger stock, simmer and reduce it for another 40 minutes.

MAKES 4½ TO 5 CUPS

FISH SOUP (*BOURRIDE*)

Preparation time: 45 minutes
Cooking time: 40 to 45 minutes*

This soup, a mixture of fish, shellfish, and vegetables cooked in a fish stock, is a marvelous meal for a special occasion. Once you have prepared the stock, the dish is easily made and costs little, and most of the preparation can be done beforehand.

You serve the soup with slices of French bread that have been rubbed with garlic and smeared with a garlic mayonnaise called aioli. Some of the aioli is stirred into the soup to flavor and thicken it. You can serve a salad before or after eating the soup.

---

* Steps 1–4 can be done beforehand. Then you only need to cook the soup for 15 minutes.

Specific seafood is listed in the recipe; however, you may substitute as you like, as long as you use some fish, some crustaceans, and some mollusks.

Choose lean fish fillets such as

blackfish • black sea bass • cod • grouper • lingcod • mako shark • monkfish • red snapper • scrod • sea robin (skinned steaks) • swordfish • tilefish • wolffish

and shellfish such as

clams • hard- or soft-shell blue crabs or crabmeat • mussels • oysters • scallops • shrimp • squid

½ cup mild olive oil
1 medium onion, finely chopped (¾ cup)
2 stalks celery, finely chopped (¾ cup)
1 small fennel bulb, trimmed and chopped (¾ cup)
1 small carrot, scraped and coarsely grated (½ cup)
3 cloves garlic—2 finely minced, 1 cut in half crosswise
1 medium leek, cut in half lengthwise, rinsed, and finely chopped
4 medium to large tomatoes, peeled, seeded, and chopped
Salt to taste
Freshly ground black pepper to taste
1 teaspoon fresh thyme leaves or ½ teaspoon dried thyme

Pinch cayenne pepper
4½ cups fish stock (see page 187)
Zest of ¼ orange cut in a piece
Zest of ¼ lemon cut in a piece
4 small red-skin potatoes (½ pound), rinsed
1 long loaf French bread
4 tablespoons dry vermouth
8 littleneck clams, scrubbed
1 pound mussels, cleaned
½ pound monkfish or red snapper fillet, cut in 1½-inch chunks
½ pound fillet of cod or scrod, cut in 1½-inch chunks
½ pound medium or large shrimp, with shells on or off
½ pound cleaned squid, cut in ¼-inch rings
1½ cups aioli (see page 229)
1 scallion, finely sliced
2 tablespoons finely chopped parsley

1. Heat the oil in a large casserole dish or pot over medium heat.

2. When the oil is hot, add the onion, celery, fennel, carrot, minced garlic, and leek, stirring occasionally until the onion is transparent.

3. Add the chopped tomatoes, salt, pepper, thyme, and cayenne and stir.

4. Add the fish stock, the zests, and the potatoes and cook until the potatoes are very nearly cooked through, about 15 minutes. If you are preparing the soup in advance, refrigerate it now and reheat it before proceeding.

5. Slice the French bread into ½-inch-thick slices and toast them lightly in a 400 degree F oven. Rub them with the halved garlic. Put aside.

6. Add the vermouth to the hot soup.

7. Put the clams in and watch to see when they open—they usually take 5 minutes or more.

8. Add the rest of the seafood. If using monkfish, put it in first because it takes longer to cook than the other seafood. Take the pot off the heat as soon as the mussels open.

9. Stir in half the aioli and sprinkle with a mixture of scallions and parsley.

10. Encourage your guests to spread the bread with aioli and dip it into the soup as they eat.

SERVES 4

CREAMY SEAFOOD CHOWDER

Preparation time: 15 minutes
Cooking time: 20 to 25 minutes

For a really special chowder, try to use fish stock made from the bones and heads of the same species of fish you are going to use in the chowder—for instance, cod bones if you choose to use cod in the chowder. Remember, if you choose to make the chowder with shellfish, you can use two 8-ounce bottles of clam juice instead of the fish stock.

Choose skin-off fillets of lean flaky fish such as

blackfish • cod, scrod • haddock • halibut • lingcod • mako shark • pollock • rehydrated salt cod, pollock, or cusk (see page 290) • rockfish • swordfish

or see list on page 20; *or* choose shellfish such as

cherrystone or razor clams • conch (see page 297) • crabmeat • geoduck clam (see page 286) • sea or bay scallops • medium shrimp

or choose smoked seafood such as

chub • haddock (finnan haddie) • mussels • sablefish • sea scallops • sturgeon • trout • whitefish

2 cups fish stock (see page 187) or clam juice

3 ounces (6 tablespoons) unsalted butter or margarine

2 cups milk

1 cup half-and-half

1 medium onion, finely chopped (1 cup)

¼ pound bacon (5 slices), cooked until crisp and roughly chopped (optional)

1 clove garlic, finely minced

1 pound potatoes, peeled, coarsely grated, and kept in cold water until ready to use

3 tablespoons cornstarch

½ cup cold water

1 pound lean fish fillet or salt cod or smoked fish with skin off and pin bones removed

or

12 ounces sea scallops, small tough muscle removed, cut in thin wafers

or

12 ounces medium shrimp, peeled and deveined

or

12 ounces crabmeat, picked over for cartilage

or

2 cups shucked cherrystone or razor clams, minced in grinder or food processor

or

2 cups geoduck or conch strips, chopped

Salt to taste

Freshly ground white pepper to taste

2 tablespoons chopped parsley or thyme leaves

1. If you are using fish stock, make it as you are gathering the rest of the ingredients together.

2. Heat 3 tablespoons butter or margarine, the milk, and the half-and-half in a double boiler over moderate heat.

3. Heat the rest of the butter or margarine in a large saucepan over moderate heat. When it is hot but not brown, add the onion.

4. Cook the onion until translucent.

5. Add the bacon (optional), garlic, potatoes, and fish stock or clam juice. Cover and bring to a boil, then turn the heat down to simmer and cook until the potatoes are nearly tender (about 5 minutes).

6. In the meantime whisk the cornstarch into the cold water in a small bowl.

7. When the mixture of butter (or margarine), milk, and half-and-half is hot, whisk the cornstarch mixture into it to thicken it.

8. Add the fish or shellfish to the stock or clam juice in a large saucepan. If you are using fish, cook until it is opaque all the way through, and stir the chowder so that the fish flakes. If you are using shellfish, pick a piece out of the soup and cut it to see if it is opaque all the way through.

9. Pour the mixture of butter (or margarine), milk, half-and-half, cornstarch, and water into the soup and stir. Remove from the heat as soon as it comes to a boil.

10. Add salt and pepper to taste and sprinkle with parsley or thyme.

SERVES 6

SEAFOOD STEW OR PASTA SAUCE

Preparation time: 20 minutes
Cooking time: 10 to 15 minutes

Specific seafood is listed in the recipe; however, you may substitute as you like. I suggest that you select a fish and a few shellfish.

Choose lean fillets or 1-inch-thick steaks of fish such as

blackfish fillets • black sea bass fillets • cod, scrod fillets • grouper fillets • lingcod • mako shark steaks • monkfish fillets • porgy fillets • red snapper fillets • sand shark (dogfish) fillets • sea robin steaks • tilefish fillets • wolffish fillets

and shellfish such as

clams • crabmeat • mussels • scallops • shrimp • sliced cooked conch • sliced cooked octopus • soft-shell crabs • squid

4 tablespoons mild olive oil or vegetable oil
3 stalks celery or ½ bulb fennel, trimmed and chopped in ¼-inch dice
1 carrot, scraped and coarsely grated
½ pound bay scallops
½ squid, cleaned and cut in ¼-inch rings
⅔ cup dry white wine
1 teaspoon fresh thyme or ½ teaspoon dried thyme
Salt to taste

3 cloves garlic, minced
½ pound monkfish fillet, cut in
   1¼-inch diagonal slices
2 soft-shell crabs, cut in half
½ pound mussels, cleaned

Freshly ground black pepper to
   taste
3 tablespoons finely chopped
   scallions
4 tablespoons finely chopped parsley

1. Heat the oil in a large frying pan or shallow casserole dish (with a fitted lid) over moderate heat.

2. When the oil is hot, add the celery, carrot, and garlic and cook 2 minutes, turning occasionally.

3. Add the monkfish and soft-shell crabs and cook for a minute or so before adding the mussels. Lower the heat, cover the pan, and cook until the mussels open.

4. Add the bay scallops and squid and stir them around in the pan.

5. Add the wine, thyme, salt, and pepper and raise the heat to hot for 1 minute. The seafood should all be cooked by this time. Check for doneness (see page 94).

6. Finally, sprinkle the stew with chopped scallions and parsley. The dish may be served hot or at room temperature.

7. If serving as a pasta sauce, add a little of the pasta water to thin the stew to a sauce!

SERVES 4

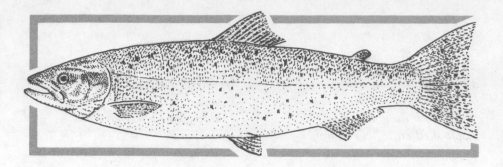

Smoking

SMOKING CAN ENLIVEN THE FLAVOR OF MANY A DULL PIECE OF SEAFOOD AND, SOME THINK, improve delicious ones—think of cold-smoked salmon!

Seafood is either cold-smoked (the usual commercial method) or hot-smoked, easily done by the amateur. The finished product is seafood flavored by brine and smoke—the different methods have different shelf lives. Hot-smoking generally must be eaten within a shorter period.

Commercially smoked seafood is usually cold-smoked—that is, it is first marinated in a brine and then smoked for a long time at low temperatures, 65 to 115 degrees F. Cold-smoked seafood can be kept, refrigerated, for weeks or months as long as it is vacuum-packed and stored at a temperature below 38 degrees F or frozen at −20 degrees F. When you buy smoked seafood, eat it within a couple of days unless it is kept under the above conditions.

Hot-smoking or smoke-cooking at home is a useful method of preservation when you have a glut of seafood. Many different utensils are available with which you can hot-smoke seafood at home—L. L. Bean and Sears stock several smoke-cookers—and, in addition, there are books available that teach you how to make your own smoke-cooker. Smokers that you can make include primitive setups that use an old-fashioned icebox, an old refrigerator, or a large drum barrel; commercially available smokers are covered barbecues fueled by electricity, charcoal, wood, and gas; small portable smokers you can put on top of a burner on your stove or on an outdoor grill, using sawdust made from hardwoods as the source of smoke; and electric smokers such as the Little Chief, some of which also use hardwood sawdust as the smoke source. I recommend that you carefully follow the directions given with your smoker until you can use it with confidence.

Hot-smoked seafood is usually marinated in brine from an hour to 24 hours, depending on how strong a flavor is desired and how thick the seafood is. (Of course, if you want to smoke-cook the seafood and eat it right away, there is no need to marinate it in brine.) The brine or marinade for hot-smoked seafood consists mainly of water and salt. Salt is important, for it slows down or stops the growth of bacteria. Sugar can be added, if you want, as well as a little paprika or ground chili powder (for color and flavor) and Cajun or Creole seasonings. You can also add flavor by adding herbs such as rosemary and thyme to the marinade. Mixtures of paprika, ground chili powder, coriander, cumin, cloves, salt, black and white pepper, cayenne, and garlic are currently in vogue, and they are delicious!

After brining, rinse and dry the seafood and then smoke it from 10 minutes to 8 hours at temperatures ranging from 100 to 250 degrees F. Seafood smoked at lower temperatures demands longer smoking time, and of course the size and thickness of the seafood or portion will determine the smoking time, just as in cooking. You can choose to have smoked seafood that is moist and soft or dry and firm and adjust smoking time accordingly.

Depending on your smoker, you may want to dry-smoke your seafood, which will help preserve it for a longer time, or water-smoke it with a pan of water in the smoker, which will produce a beautifully moist and flavorful piece of seafood that must be eaten within a day or so. Either way, with or without water, a pan in the smoker can catch any fat that may drip.

To obtain different flavors in smoking, use chips of hardwoods such as hickory, apple, oak, alder, peach, cherry, mesquite, maple, or pecan; dried corncobs; grapevines; or dried fennel sticks. These should be soaked in water for half an hour to a few hours before being drained off and added to the main fuel. This damp fuel will smoke rather than burn and give a delicious flavor to the seafood. You will need a fair amount to produce a nice, strong, smoky flavor, and you need to close down any openings in the smoker almost completely to concentrate the flavor and slow the cooking process. In some smokers, hardwood sawdust and chips are put in a pan above the main source of heat, and in others the chips are put directly on the source of heat; the fuel must be replenished as the seafood smokes. You can also scatter herbs such as rosemary and thyme directly on the heat source for flavor. Have fun! Experiment with the flavors of the brine and the wood or vines.

Hot-smoked seafood can be eaten right away, either warm from the smoker or cold. Once cooled, you can store it in the refrigerator, for a day or so, well wrapped up in plastic wrap. Do not keep it any longer than this for it must be treated like any conventionally cooked food. Hot-smoking is not usually a cure, just a fine way to cook and flavor seafood with heat and smoke. *If you want to store smoked seafood up to four weeks, I recommend that you either freeze it or smoke it to an internal temperature of 180 degrees F for 30 minutes to make sure all bacteria have been killed.*

Hot-smoked shellfish is done when the flesh has a good glaze on the outside and is firm but still fairly moist inside. Insert an instant-read thermometer in the thickest part of the flesh—140 degrees F is fine if you are not concerned with preserving the seafood for longer than a day or so, but the thermometer must read 180 degrees F for 30 minutes if you want bacteria-free seafood that can be preserved in the refrigerator for four weeks. Or you can freeze it.

When smoking, use good fresh seafood. Generally, oilier fish such as bluefish, eel, mackerel, sablefish (black cod), salmon, sturgeon, whitefish, and trout smoke better. Other fish that can be and are smoked are shad and its roe, swordfish, mako, marlin, tuna, monkfish, carp, catfish, mullet, porgy, and croaker. Actually, any firm-fleshed fish can be smoked carefully. You can smoke whole dressed, butterflied, or split fish, as well as fillets or steaks. Leave the skin on and cut the fish fillets into portions as you like. It is advisable, for obvious reasons, to make similar-sized whole fish or fish portions at the same time.

Most shellfish—clams, mussels, shrimp, scallops, and oysters—smoke well.

TIMES AND TEMPERATURES

It's impossible to give precise times and temperatures for smoking because so many factors are involved: the strength of the fire, the size of the seafood and how much you are going to smoke, the strength of flavor you want, the differences in the smokers and how they function, the outside temperature, the wind, and so on and so on. . . . Generally, marinate seafood in brine anywhere from an hour to 24 hours, depending on how strongly you want it to be flavored. Hot-smoke for 10 minutes (for small, thin fillets) to 8 hours at temperatures ranging from 100 to 250 degrees F.

HEALTH

There are not too many health advantages to smoked seafood! But it tastes so good; the salt content can be high. Still, who can resist smoked salmon, eel, trout, sturgeon, sablefish, chub, and whitefish?

BASIC SMOKING RECIPE

HOT-SMOKING (SMOKE-COOKING)

Fish preparation time: 5 to 30 minutes

Brining time: 1 to 24 hours
Rinsing time: 5 minutes
Drying time: 10 to 30 minutes
Total preparation time: approximately 1⅓ hours to 25½ hours
Smoking time: 10 minutes to 8 hours

SPECIAL EQUIPMENT: Smoker

Brining times, drying times, and smoking times are dependent on so many variants that you must refer to the explanations above or follow instructions for your particular smoker-cooker. I give very general guidelines below.

Choose whole, butterflied or split, or fillets or steaks of fish, such as

bluefish fillets • butterfish (whole) • carp fillets • catfish fillets • eel (whole) • haddock split or fillets • mackerel fillets or split • mako shark steaks • mullets (whole) • porgy (whole) • sablefish fillets • salmon fillets • sturgeon fillets • swordfish steaks • tilefish fillets • trout (whole) • tuna steaks • whitefish (whole)

or shellfish such as

mussels • oysters • scallops • shrimp

Note: Small fish can be split or butterflied and spread open for smoking. Other fish can be filleted or cut into steaks. Smoke oysters on the half shell and leave shrimp unpeeled.

⅔ cup salt
1 cup brown sugar
½ tablespoon freshly ground black
*   pepper*
½ teaspoon cayenne
4 tablespoons packaged pickling
*   spices or bottled shrimp and crab*
*   boil or a mixture of 1 teaspoon*
*   coriander seeds, 1 teaspoon*
*   mustard seeds, 1 teaspoon*
*   allspice, 1 teaspoon fennel seeds,*
*   2 dried chili peppers (seeds*
*   removed), and 3 bay leaves*
*   roughly crushed in a mortar*
*   with a pestle or for a few*
*   seconds in a coffee grinder*

1 head garlic, halved horizontally
*   and crushed with the flat of a*
*   knife*
Juice of 1 lemon
4 to 5 pounds seafood

1. Mix all the ingredients except the seafood together with 2 quarts (8 cups) water in a nonaluminum pot or dish large enough to cover the seafood.
2. To preserve seafood, brine between 1 hour and 24 hours. If you are eating right away, don't bother to brine at all, unless you want to give extra flavor to the seafood. I recommend brining ½-inch-thick fillets for 4 hours.
3. Rinse seafood in cold water for 5 minutes. Pat it dry with paper towels or a dishcloth.
4. Put the seafood on a rack and dry it in the wind (or use an electric fan) for 10 to 30 minutes, until you see a shiny skin form on the seafood.
5. Smoke from 10 minutes to 8 hours. I recommend smoking for 1 hour at 300 degrees F.
6. Check doneness (see page 94).
7. If you lightly smoked the seafood, eat it right away or within 2 days

(refrigerated). If you smoked it to an internal temperature of 180 degrees for 30 minutes, you can keep it up to 4 weeks in the refrigerator. When the seafood is cool, wrap it in several layers of plastic wrap before refrigerating or freezing.

SERVES 10 TO 12

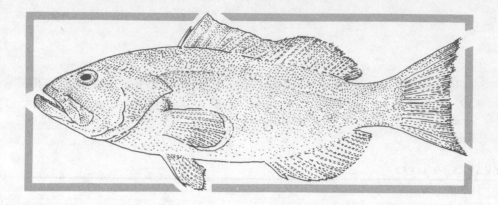

Microwave Seafood Cookery

MICROWAVE COOKERY IS HERE TO STAY; IT IS A NEW METHOD FOR SOME, BUT WE ARE LEARNING fast. Good, healthful seafood dishes can be cooked in the microwave oven, and of course all steaming, bake-poaching, and stewing recipes work particularly well cooked this way. For dishes in which the seafood is meant to have crisp or brittle skin or a colorful glaze, conventional methods such as broiling, grilling, barbecuing, roasting, baking, frying, sautéing, or deep frying are still preferable.

Seafood doesn't take long to cook by conventional methods, but then speed is not the main purpose of using the microwave oven in fish and shellfish cookery. Although we must be careful to avoid overcooking seafood in the microwave oven (as when using any cooking method), the precision timing the microwave oven offers can help cook seafood just right—tender and moist. The microwave oven can be set to cook for a few seconds to a few minutes, so we can't forget about a dish for a few critical moments as we can with conventional methods. Overcooking is a disaster for seafood—it becomes unappetizing, loses moisture, falls apart, or, in the case of shellfish, becomes rubbery—so when using a microwave oven, undercook the seafood at first and turn it halfway through cooking. If it is undercooked, set the oven to cook further at 30-second intervals until the seafood is cooked through.

Many of the recipes in this book for steaming and bake-poaching can be adapted for the microwave, although the amounts of liquid ingredients must be drastically reduced. Use microwavable dishes and microwave-proof plastic wrap to cover the seafood, leaving an open vent at one edge. Any juice that accumulates in the dish can be poured off to make a sauce. Or cover the dish with a paper towel if you want the moisture to be absorbed.

You won't achieve an attractive glaze on the seafood, as with other cooking methods, but when that is desirable, you can finish off the dish under the broiler for a minute or two. Also, you can begin cooking a whole fish or a large fish in the microwave oven and finish it by broiling or grilling.

I find the microwave oven useful in conjunction with broiling or grilling whole fish. If the fish is in danger of being burned under the broiler or over the coals before it is cooked through, or if an open fire dies on you, finish cooking the fish in the microwave oven. (Of course, you can also do this in a conventional oven, though it probably will take longer.) Be sure to wrap a piece of foil over the eyes when cooking head-on fish in the microwave, for they tend to explode. Also wrap tails with foil.

It's good to have a round or oval shallow casserole dish to put seafood in. Place the seafood around the inside edge of the dish with the thicker parts facing outward. If the seafood is thick all the way through, it will have to be moved around or turned over halfway through to achieve even cooking. You can prepare dazzingly handsome creations on platters or plates (depending on the size of the oven), with seafood, vegetables, and sauce all cooked at the same time. The only drawback is that if the microwave oven is small, you can only cook one plate at a time.

You can use the microwave to defrost seafood, but Marcia Cone and Thelma Snyder, in *Mastering Microwave Cookery* (Simon and Schuster, 1986), advise that you take the seafood out before it is defrosted all the way through. Leave it at room temperature to finish defrosting, otherwise you may be starting to cook the outside before the inside is defrosted.

Microwave ovens range in power from 500 to 700 watts. In the following recipes the longer cooking time listed is for the less powerful microwave ovens. All times are approximate; use the shorter cooking time to avoid overcooking. Most fish and shellfish should be cooked at the High setting; only small whole fish, such as trout, will cook on Medium.

BASIC MICROWAVE RECIPES

MICROWAVED SOLE WITH ENDIVES AND BÉCHAMEL

Preparation time: 10 minutes
Cooking time: 29 to 37 minutes

SPECIAL EQUIPMENT: Small oval micro-wavable casserole dish
Microwavable plastic wrap

You will need to cook the endives and a béchamel sauce, then wrap the sole around the endive, cover it with béchamel, and cook it for a few minutes before finishing it under the broiler.

2 large, fat endives or 4 medium leeks, trimmed
Salt to taste
1 cup milk
1 bay leaf
6 black peppercorns
¼ teaspoon salt
Pinch ground nutmeg
⅛ teaspoon freshly ground white pepper

2 tablespoons unsalted butter or margarine
3 tablespoons all-purpose flour
2 6- to 8-ounce fillets of sole (various) or flounder
Juice of ½ lemon
1 tablespoon finely chopped parsley

1. Trim any brown leaves from the endives or leeks and make a crisscross cut at the root end of each. This should prevent the root ends from bulging out during cooking.

2. Put the endives or leeks in a small oval microwavable casserole dish and add ¼ cup water and salt.

3. Cover the casserole dish with microwave plastic wrap, leaving an open vent at one edge.

4. Cook at the High setting for 12 to 15 minutes, depending on the strength of your microwave oven.

5. Put the milk, bay leaf, peppercorns, nutmeg, salt, and pepper in a 4-cup microwavable measuring cup.

6. Cook on High for 2 to 4 minutes. It should not boil.

7. Take it out of the oven, stir, and let stand 5 minutes.

8. Strain the mixture into another container, like a small saucepan or bowl.

9. Put the butter or margarine in the 4-cup measuring cup and cook it at High for 50 to 60 seconds to melt it.

10. Add the flour to the melted butter or margarine and whisk until smooth.

11. Stir in the warm milk mixture and whisk thoroughly.

12. Put this mixture in the oven and cook on High for 3 to 5 minutes until it has thickened, stirring well every 2 minutes.

13. Using the same oval dish that you cooked the endives or leeks in, wrap the endives or leeks with the sole fillets, sprinkle the fillets with lemon juice, and cover them with the béchamel sauce.

14. Preheat the broiler.

15. Put the oval dish in the microwave oven and cook at the High setting for 4 to 5 minutes, until sauce is bubbling.

16. For a nice brown glaze, put the dish under the broiler for less than a minute.

17. Sprinkle with parsley and serve.

SERVES 2

SEAFOOD STEW WITH TOMATO AND GREEN PEPPER

Preparation time: 20 to 30 minutes
Cooking time: 15 to 20 minutes

SPECIAL EQUIPMENT: Small oval micro-wavable casserole dish
Microwavable plastic wrap

I have listed specific kinds of seafood in the recipe below, but all you need is 2 pounds of seafood for 6 people, all cut about the same size (the fish should be cut in cubes) so substitute as you like, according to your taste and what is appealing in the market that day.

Choose firm fish that you can cut into 1-inch cubes, such as

blackfish • catfish • dolphinfish (mahi-mahi) • grouper • mako shark • monkfish • red snapper • sand shark (dogfish)

or choose shellfish such as

clams · crabmeat · mussels · sea scallops · shrimp · squid

3 tablespoons mild olive oil
1 very finely chopped medium
    onion (1 cup)
2 cloves garlic, finely minced
1 green pepper, cored and chopped
    into ¼-inch dice
3 medium tomatoes, peeled and
    chopped (nearly 2 cups)
½ cup red wine
2 tablespoons tomato paste
Salt to taste
Freshly ground black pepper to
    taste

1 teaspoon fresh thyme or ½ tea-
    spoon dried thyme
Good pinch cayenne
12 mussels (approximately 1
    pound), cleaned
½ pound dolphinfish (mahi-mahi),
    skinned and cut in 1-inch cubes
½ pound squid, cleaned and cut in
    ¼-inch rings
2 tablespoons chopped parsley

1. Put the olive oil, onion, garlic, and green pepper in a casserole. Cover with microwave plastic wrap, leaving a vent, and cook at the High setting for 4 to 6 minutes, stirring after 3 minutes.
2. Add the tomatoes, red wine, tomato paste, salt, pepper, thyme, and cayenne. Cover again with wrap, leaving a vent, and cook at the High setting for 1½ to 2 minutes, then uncover, stir, and cook for 1½ to 2 more minutes.
3. Add the mussels and cook for a total of 6 to 8 minutes, until they open. They need to be moved around in the dish every 2 minutes. After 2 to 3 minutes of cooking the mussels add the dolphinfish (total cooking time 4 to 5 minutes), and then 1 to 2 minutes after adding the dolphinfish add the squid (total cooking time 1½ to 3 minutes). Stir and test for doneness. If the seafood is just on the verge of being cooked, remove it from the oven and let it stand for 2 minutes.
4. Sprinkle with parsley and serve.

SERVES 6

BREADED SHELLFISH WITH SWEET RED PEPPER SAUCE

Preparation time: 20 minutes
Cooking time for sauce: 12 to 14 minutes
Cooking time for seafood: 2 to 3 minutes, depending on size of seafood and power of microwave oven

SPECIAL EQUIPMENT: 6-inch thin wooden brochette sticks *or* long toothpicks

This dish resembles tempura, but without the deep-frying. The seafood is spread with mayonnaise, which gives color and some crispness to the coating, before being coated with bread crumbs. I like to use the Japanese bread crumbs called *panko*, which are available at Japanese stores. (They look like shredded coconut.) I got the tip for using mayonnaise in this recipe from *Mastering Microwave Cookery* by Marcia Cone and Thelma Snyder.

Choose shellfish such as

sea scallops • shrimp

½ recipe Sweet Red Pepper Sauce
(see page 230)
Good pinch cayenne
½ cup Japanese bread crumbs or
dry bread crumbs
1 tablespoon salt
Freshly ground white pepper to
taste
½ to ¾ pound large shrimp

(16 to 35 per pound), shelled
and deveined as per instructions
on page 407
or
½ to ¾ pound sea scallops (¾ inch
thick), small tough muscle
removed
½ cup mayonnaise
1 kirby cucumber

1. First make the Sweet Red Pepper Sauce in the microwave oven, adding cayenne to taste to the recipe.
2. Put the bread crumbs in a bowl and mix with salt and pepper.
3. Insert brochette sticks or toothpicks through the middle of the shrimp so they lie straight. Some of the brochette stick or toothpick will protrude from the head end of each shrimp. No need to use brochette sticks or toothpicks on the scallops.
4. Spread the shrimp or scallops with mayonnaise, and spoon the bread-

crumb mixture all over them. Place a microwavable paper towel on a plate with the shrimp or scallops on top. Cover them loosely with another paper towel.

5. Microwave for 2 to 3 minutes on High. Check for doneness (see page 94).

6. Pour the Sweet Red Pepper Sauce onto two serving plates.

7. Slice the cucumber on a strong diagonal into thin slices and fan them out on the plate, leaving enough room for the shrimp or scallops to lay on the sauce. Serve.

SERVES 2

FISH FILLETS WITH SPINACH AND GINGER

Preparation time: 20 minutes
Cooking time: 9 to 11 minutes

SPECIAL EQUIPMENT: Shallow microwavable casserole dish
Microwavable plastic wrap

Choose flatfish fillets, or fillets of other fish not more than ½ inch thick, such as

baby coho salmon • blackfish • black sea bass • cod, scrod • gray sole • lingcod • mackerel • orange roughy • rainbow trout • red snapper • sole (various) • weakfish (sea trout)

¾ pound fresh spinach
¾ to 1 pound fish fillets, skin off and pin bones removed
2 tablespoons mild olive oil
1 tablespoon unsalted butter
1 clove garlic, finely minced

1 tablespoon finely chopped ginger
Salt to taste
2 scallions, finely sliced on the diagonal
2 slices lemon for garnish

1. Wash the spinach, remove stalks, and dry in salad spinner.

2. If using flounder or sole, cut the fillets in half lengthwise and fold them in thirds. Use appropriate-sized spinach leaves to partially cover each fillet.

3. Put oil, butter, garlic, and ginger in a shallow microwavable casserole dish or plate. Cover with microwave plastic wrap, leaving a vent open at the side, and cook for 1 to 2 minutes on High.

4. Place the rest of the spinach on the flavorings and turn the leaves over in them with your hands so they get somewhat coated by the mixture. Sprinkle with salt to taste. Re-cover with plastic wrap, leaving a vent open at the side, and cook for 1 to 2 minutes on High.

5. Lay the fillets with the spinach on them around the outside edge of the dish (on top of the wilted spinach), with the thickest part of each fillet facing the outside. Re-cover with plastic wrap, leaving a vent open at the side. Cook for 5 to 7 minutes on High.

6. After 2 to 3 minutes of cooking, sprinkle with the scallions. Check for doneness (see page 94).

7. Cook for 30 seconds longer if necessary.

8. Garnish with lemon.

SERVES 2

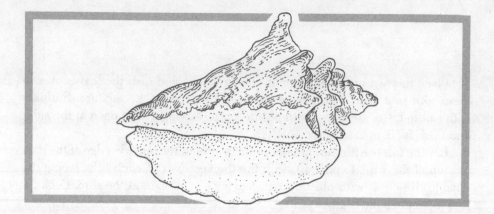

Seviche, Escabèche, and Other Ways to Marinate Seafood

WE MARINATE FISH AND SHELLFISH FOR THREE DIFFERENT PURPOSES. ALL THREE BRING DIF-ferent flavors to the seafood and the finished dish.

One purpose is to "cook" raw seafood with the acid of lime and lemon juices. Seafood prepared this way is called, variously, *seviche*, *cebiche*, and *ceviche* in Central and South America and the Caribbean.

The second purpose is to preserve and flavor cooked seafood—that is, fried or poached seafood—with vinegar, possibly mixed with wine or water. Seafood prepared this way is called *escabèche* or *caveach*. You can also use cider instead of vinegar, or ale to dilute the vinegar, when "sousing" seafood (see page 215).

The third purpose is to flavor seafood before it is cooked or give it a nice glaze as it cooks.

SEVICHE

Seviche is "cooked" raw seafood in lime juice or a mixture of lime and lemon juices. Basically Latin American and Caribbean (in the Caribbean, limes are used primarily), this preparation makes cooking with heat unnecessary—the seafood is served chilled or at room temperature. Flavorings are added to the juice to make an intriguing dish favored both by those who like raw fish and those who don't. Raw lean fish, such as flounder and sole, and shellfish, such as conch and scallops, are marinated in the juice and you can add other flavorings as you wish, such as chopped scallions, garlic, jalapeño or serrano peppers, fresh coriander, fresh parsley, a little ginger, a little chopped tomato, and salt and pepper to taste.

The time it takes to "cook" the seafood will depend on the acidity of the juices and the temperature of the kitchen. The more acidic the fruit and the warmer the kitchen, the speedier the "cooking" process. The acidity of limes and lemons differs, as does the temperature of different kitchens, so just to be sure, leave the seafood in the marinade in a nonmetal bowl for at least 4 hours at room temperature and then overnight in the refrigerator.

You can tell the seafood is "cooked" when it is opaque all the way through, just as with cooked fish.

Note: The seafood will exude moisture into the marinade if you leave it in too long—it will shrink and become "overcooked." Before serving seviche, and also when storing it, stop the "cooking" process by draining off most of the juice and adding a little olive oil. You can usually keep it another 24 hours in the refrigerator.

All white lean-fleshed fish do well by this method. Choose fish that are not prone to containing parasites (see page 17). Parasites can be killed by either freezing the fish for two days or cooking it to 140 degrees F. The acidity of the lime or lemon juice will not kill them. Fillet fish and cut it into strips ½ to 1 inch wide or into ½- or 1-inch cubes. Sea scallops (cut into quarters or thin wafers) and whole bay scallops do fine, as does freshly garnered conch (I am now dreaming of Key West!), but the flesh of squid and shrimp is too dense and cannot be "cooked" by this method. I like to add squid and shrimp to the seviche so I blanch them in a poaching liquid (see page 168) until they are opaque all the way through. I then throw them into ice water to stop further cooking, then drain them and toss them in a little oil before adding them to the marinade. This is a tip from Chef Felipe Rojas-Lombardi—tossing them in a little oil will prevent their color from being bleached out by the acid of the lemon or lime juice.

Escabèche, or caveach, introduced to Europe by the Moors in the fourteenth century, is cooked fish preserved and flavored with vinegar. More recently, in Central and South America and the Caribbean, cooks have greatly developed this preservation method, bringing more flavor to any number of escabèche dishes. I think vinegar has great affinities with the basic sweetness of seafood. Celts, Irish, Scots, and Welsh all have their versions of escabèche too—for example, "soused" herrings cooked in vinegar. Even the Japanese have their version, using rice vinegar and mirin (sweet cooking wine made from rice).

First, seafood is lightly cooked, then vinegar that has been diluted with water or wine and cooked with additional flavors is poured over the seafood. This flavors and preserves it. You can eat the dish right away or leave it to stand an hour or so at room temperature. You can also chill it.

This is an especially good way to preserve fish when you are given a great deal of fish or shellfish, or if you catch a lot at one time. In any case it is a good idea to make a large batch. Store it in the refrigerator where it will last a few days (up to a week). It's great being able to delve in the refrigerator over the next few days and treat yourself to a piece of cold seafood. You can also reheat it (gently) if you like.

MARINATING FOR FLAVOR OR GLAZE

Marinades for raw seafood that will be cooked are various. Some people claim milk sweetens, whitens, and tenderizes fish such as shad, whiting, and herring, and also white-fleshed fish such as cod, but I find them tender enough already not to need such treatment. Others, like Frank Davis, author of *The Frank Davis Seafood Notebook* (Pelican Press, 1983), like to marinate soft-shell crabs in milk to make them even richer in taste—a good idea!

Olive oil and lemon juice make a good marinade for cubes of fish like tuna, swordfish, and mako shark that you might want to put on brochette sticks. Another good one for the meaty tuna is a light mixture of dry white wine, molasses, and soy sauce. This gives the cooked flesh a nice glaze when broiled or barbecued.

Note: When marinating with acids such as lime juice, lemon juice, wine, or vinegar, be sure to do so only for a short time—20 minutes will suffice.

Otherwise you might find that the fish is halfway "cooked" before you are ready to cook it with heat.

HEALTH

Seviche is a healthy way to eat seafood for there is little oil in the marinade. Freeze seafood before making it into seviche, as a health precaution (see page 24).

Escabèche can have a light or heavy coating, or none at all, before the fish is fried, sautéed, or deep-fried. The heavier the coating, the less healthy it is.

Some marinades, such as oil and wine, produce a healthy glaze; much of the oil will remain in the utensil or disappear when grilling or barbecuing.

BASIC MARINATED SEAFOOD RECIPES

SEVICHE

Preparation time: 15 minutes or 1 hour if using shrimp or squid
"Cooking" time: 12 to 24 hours

SPECIAL EQUIPMENT: 4 to 6 wooden brochette sticks (optional)

Make this recipe the day before needed.

Choose fillets, with skin off of fish, such as

baby coho salmon • blackfish • black sea bass • flounder • grouper • monkfish • orange roughy • red snapper • rockfish • salmon* • salt cod (rehydrated) • sole • swordfish • tilapia • tilefish • trout • tuna • wolffish

or shellfish such as

conch • mussels • raw littleneck clams • sea or bay scallops • shrimp • squid

(continued)

---

* previously frozen for 2 days—see page 24.

1 pound fish fillet, cut into strips ½
  to ¾ inch wide by 2½ inches
  long, or into ¾-inch cubes
        or
1 pound one or more kinds of
  shellfish, such as:
  conch, very finely sliced,
        or
  mussels, steamed open and
  shucked (see page 178),
        or
  raw shucked littleneck clams,
        or
  sea or bay scallops, wafered (cut
  horizontally into thin slices) if
  large and small tough muscles
  removed,
        or
  shrimp or squid, previously
  poached (see page 172)

(Note: Toss the shrimp and squid in
  a little corn or olive oil before
  marinating for a minimum of
  one hour.)
½ cup lime juice
¼ cup lemon juice
1 scallion, thinly sliced
1 clove garlic, finely minced
1 inch ginger, scraped and finely
  grated
1 jalapeño pepper, seeded and
  finely chopped
¼ cup chopped fresh coriander
  leaves
1 small tomato, diced
2 tablespoons mild olive oil
Salt to taste
Freshly ground white pepper to
  taste
4 to 6 Boston or Bibb lettuce leaves

1. Put the fish or shellfish in a nonmetallic bowl and cover with the lime and lemon juices.
2. Let stand at room temperature for 4 hours and then put in the refrigerator overnight.
3. Add all the other ingredients (except the lettuce) and stir.
4. Serve the seafood on a lettuce leaf.

Variation: Instead of serving the seafood on a lettuce leaf, string it on brochette sticks for variety.

SERVES 6 AS AN APPETIZER OR 4 AS A MAIN COURSE

ESCABÈCHE

Preparation time: 15 minutes
Cooking time: 45 minutes

SPECIAL EQUIPMENT: Earthenware, Pyrex, or ovenproof china casserole dish with 2- to 3-inch-high edges

Steps 1–4 of this recipe can be done beforehand and the marinade can be reheated.

Choose whole small fish such as

baby coho salmon • black sea bass • herring • mackerel • perch • pompano • porgy • red snapper • rockfish • sardine • smelt • trout

or fillets or steaks of fish such as any of the above or

blackfish fillets • bluefish fillets • cod fillets or steaks • dolphinfish (mahi-mahi) fillets • grouper fillets or steaks • halibut fillets or steaks • lingcod fillets or steaks • ocean perch fillets • orange roughy fillets • salmon fillets or steaks • salt cod (rehydrated fillets) • shad fillets • southern kingfish fillets or steaks • sturgeon fillets or steaks • swordfish steaks • tilefish fillets or steaks • wolffish fillets

or shellfish such as

sea scallops • shrimp

3 cups white wine vinegar or white distilled vinegar
1½ cups dry white wine
½ teaspoon saffron threads and/or 1 small carrot, scraped and coarsely grated or sliced
4 bay leaves
1 medium onion, finely sliced
4 garlic cloves, finely sliced
Mild olive oil or vegetable oil as needed
1½ teaspoons sugar

½ cup flour
1 teaspoon salt plus salt to taste
½ teaspoon freshly ground black pepper
1 tablespoon paprika
4 small fish weighing between 1 and 1½ pounds each, with heads on or off, gutted and scaled and with gills removed, left whole, boned out or not or butterflied or split
or

(continued)

*4 fish fillets with pin bones removed
    or steaks weighing 6 to 8 ounces
    each
    or
1½ pounds large shrimp (16–35
    per pound), shelled and deveined
    or sea scallops, small tough
    muscle removed*

*2 scallions, sliced lengthwise, cut
    in 2-inch lengths, or 1 finely
    sliced sweet red, yellow, or green
    pepper
⅛ teaspoon cayenne
Freshly ground white pepper to
    taste
4 thin slices lemon*

1. Bring the vinegar, wine, the saffron and/or carrot, and bay leaves to the boil in a saucepan over high heat.

2. Turn the heat to moderate and cook for about ½ hour until the mixture is reduced to 2 cups.

3. In the meantime sauté the onion and garlic in 3 tablespoons of oil in a skillet over moderate heat. Add the sugar and cook until they are well browned.

4. Add the onion and garlic to the vinegar-wine mixture as it is reducing.

5. While the marinade is reducing, mix the flour, salt, pepper, and paprika together and put on a plate.

6. Coat the fish or shellfish with the flour seasoned with the salt, pepper, and paprika.

7. Heat 4 more tablespoons of oil in a skillet over moderately high heat.

8. When the oil is hot, fry the fish or shellfish on both sides until golden brown.

9. When the seafood has taken on good color, place it in a nonmetallic dish or casserole dish with 2-inch sides. (*Note:* The seafood need not be cooked all the way through, because when the hot vinegar is poured on, the seafood will continue to cook.)

10. Add the scallions, salt to taste, cayenne, and white pepper to the boiling vinegar-wine mixture. Cook for another 2 minutes or until the scallions are limp.

11. Pour the hot vinegar and vegetable mixture over the seafood and decorate each piece of seafood with a lemon slice.

12. Let stand for at least 10 minutes before eating. Eat warm or at room temperature. To store: cool and refrigerate, covered. Reheat gently in a 300 degree F oven if you want to eat the escabèche hot.

SERVES 4

SOUSED OR MARINATED FISH

Preparation time: 5 minutes
Cooking time: 20 to 45 minutes
Cooling time: 12 hours

SPECIAL EQUIPMENT: Earthenware, Pyrex, or ovenproof china casserole dish with 2- to 3-inch-high edges

Choose whole small fish such as

baby coho salmon • brook or rainbow trout • croaker • herring • ling • mackerel • perch • porgy • sardine • smallmouth or largemouth bass • whiting

4 small fish weighing 4 to 6 ounces each (2 per person) with heads on or off, gutted and scaled and with gills removed, left whole, boned out or not or butterflied or split
or
2 whole fish weighing 8 to 12 ounces each (1 per person), prepared as above

2½ cups white wine vinegar or distilled white vinegar
1 small onion, finely sliced
1 tablespoon salt
Freshly ground black pepper to taste
2 bay leaves
2 sprigs thyme or ¼ teaspoon dried thyme

1. Preheat oven to 400 degrees F.
2. Lay fish in an earthenware, Pyrex, or ovenproof china casserole dish.
3. Add the rest of the ingredients plus 2½ cups water, draping the sliced onion over the fish and making sure that the liquid just covers the fish.
4. Cover the dish with foil and put it in the oven.
5. Cook small fish for 20 to 25 minutes; cook larger fish for 45 minutes. Or insert an instant-read thermometer—when it reads 120 degrees the fish is ready to be taken from the oven. The fish need not be cooked completely because it will continue to cook in the liquid after it has been taken out of the oven.
6. Let the fish cool in the casserole dish to room temperature, then refrigerate overnight.

Variations: You can use apple cider instead of the vinegar and water; if so, use 1 tablespoon of fresh tarragon (or 1 teaspoon of dried tarragon) in place of the bay leaves and thyme. You can use dark brown ale in place of the water; if so, use 8 cloves in place of the thyme.

SERVES 2

MARINADE FOR BROILED, GRILLED, OR BARBECUED SEAFOOD

Preparation time: 3 minutes
Marinating time: 20 minutes

This marinade is suitable for fish such as

albacore (fillets or cubes) • **bluefish (whole or fillets)** • **dolphinfish (mahi-mahi) (fillets or cubes)** • **lingcod (cubes)** • **mackerel (fillets)** • **mako shark (cubes)** • **marlin (fillets or cubes)** • **porgy (whole)** • **sablefish (cubes)** • **tuna (cubes)**

or shellfish such as **shrimp (shelled and deveined).**

½ cup vegetable oil, such as peanut oil
3 tablespoons soy sauce
3 tablespoons balsamic or malt vinegar
Juice of ½ lime (¼ cup)

1 ounce (1½ inches) fresh ginger, peeled and cut in very fine julienne strips
Freshly ground black pepper to taste

1. Mix all the ingredients together in a bowl with a wire whisk.
2. Place the seafood in one layer in a nonmetallic casserole dish. Pour the marinade over the seafood.
3. Marinate the seafood for 20 minutes, turning occasionally.
4. Drain the seafood before cooking, but heat the marinade to a low boil before basting with it or serving it as a sauce for the seafood.

Variation: You can add ¼ teaspoon hot and spicy (Szechwan-style) oil to the marinade to give it some spice.

MAKES 1 CUP MARINADE, ENOUGH FOR 2 POUNDS OF SEAFOOD

GLAZE FOR BROILED, GRILLED, OR BARBECUED SEAFOOD

Preparation time: 1 minute
Marinating time: 5 minutes

This recipe is suitable for any cubed or filleted fish or shellfish that you are going to broil, grill, or barbecue.

¼ cup dry white wine
2 tablespoons molasses
2 tablespoons soy sauce

Freshly ground black pepper to taste

1. Mix all the ingredients together in a bowl with a wire whisk.
2. Marinate seafood in the mixture for 5 minutes only.
3. Drain the seafood before cooking, but use the glaze to baste it.

MAKES ½ CUP MARINADE, ENOUGH FOR 1 POUND OF SEAFOOD

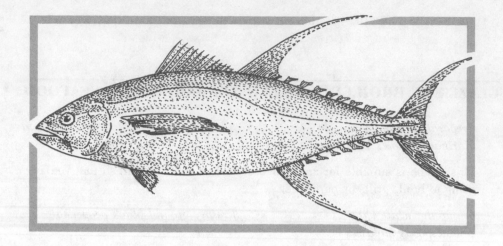

Raw Seafood

ALL OF US FLIRT WITH THE IDEA OF EATING RAW SEAFOOD AND MANY OF US ACTUALLY ENJOY it very much, even though it can pose slight health risks. The Japanese have, in recent years, made us aware of the beauty of eating raw seafood, not only for its exquisite taste but for the attractive way they serve it.

Several restaurants serving French and Italian dishes such as steak tartare and carpaccio are now making them with fish—salmon or tuna tartare and tuna carpaccio are some of the most recent variations.

To be eaten raw, seafood must be extremely fresh—that goes without saying. Avoid eating raw freshwater fish because of the parasites they may carry; this also applies to salmon, which spend part of their life in fresh water. Parasites carried by seafood are mostly harmless and very few people have been affected by them in the United States (see page 17). Parasites are killed when seafood is heated to 140 degrees F or when it has been frozen for at least two days. They are not killed when seafood is "cooked" with lime and lemon juices, as in seviche, nor are they necessarily killed when seafood is brined, smoked, cured, or pickled. Parasites look distasteful and some fish more than others carry parasites at times. Cod is such a fish. When cod, haddock, and other members of the cod family are processed in big plants, they are "candled," which means that the fillets are passed over translucent plastic shelves lit from below. Any imperfections or parasites that show are removed (see Tips for Careful Seafood Cooking, page 24).

SUSHI AND SASHIMI

Sushi, which translates as "vinegared rice," is one kind of raw seafood served by the Japanese. In one sushi preparation, rice, seafood, and vegetables are rolled up in dried seaweed (called *nori* in Japanese and "dried laver" in English). In another, rice is shaped into mounds that are about 2½ inches long and 1 inch wide, and raw seafood is then laid on top. I particularly like the sushi preparation in which the roll is made inside out: The seafood is enclosed in seaweed, the seaweed is surrounded by rice, the rice is rolled in sesame seeds, and the roll is then cut into logs.

Sashimi is made of raw seafood without rice.

Sushi and sashimi are served with pickled ginger, *wasabi* paste, a soy dipping sauce, and a number of artfully cut or decorated vegetables. All are delicious accompaniments.

Some of the kinds of seafood that can be used for sushi and sashimi are tuna, fluke, red snapper, bass, tilefish, bonito, salmon (it is not advisable to use salmon unless it was previously frozen to kill parasites), mackerel, yellowtail, geoduck, squid, octopus (cooked), abalone, scallops, shrimp (cooked or raw), sea urchin roe, flying fish roe, salmon roe, and crabs or crab sticks.

Some of the cuts that can be used include

- ¼-inch-thick slices of fish fillets, cut against the grain
- strips made from such slices, tangled up in a ball
- very thin slices of fish fillets, cut on a strong diagonal
- ½-inch cubes of fish fillets
- ¼-inch-thick slices of squid or cuttlefish, scored in a crisscross fashion with a knife

• slices of geoduck, octopus, or abalone cut ⅛ inch thick or thinner, then cut into slices 3 inches long and 1 inch wide, and finally tenderized gently with a mallet or scored in a crisscross fashion with a knife
• shrimp cut from the underside to make butterflies

As the handling of the raw seafood is so critical in these Japanese dishes, I think it best to put myself in the hands of one of the many expert sushi chefs presiding in reputable Japanese restaurants. If the restaurants are well attended, you can be sure that the seafood is as fresh as it can be and is uncontaminated. Besides, it is so fascinating to watch and learn from these experts. Sometimes I have fun and make my own sushi and sashimi when I know I can get very fresh seafood, especially if I or others have just caught the fish or shellfish. I'll take the precaution of freezing it for two days if it is fish from fresh water or other seafood that might be affected by parasites (see page 24).

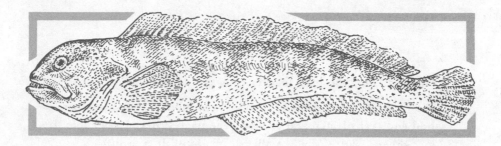

Seafood Salads

MADE WITH COOKED (LEFTOVER) FISH AND SHELLFISH, THESE SALADS ARE SUPER FAST TO assemble and delicious on hot days. Another recipe for shellfish salad is in the poaching section (see page 172).

BASIC SEAFOOD SALAD RECIPES

FISH SALAD I

Preparation time: 25 minutes
Cooking time: none unless leftover fish is not available; 15 to 30 minutes if you must steam, bake, or bake-poach raw fish

(continued)

221

Choose lean, white-fleshed, leftover cooked fish such as

bass • blackfish • catfish • cod • grouper • red snapper • salted cod (rehydrated and cooked—see page 290) • sea robin • sheepshead • skate • tilefish • whitefish • wolffish

1 recipe tomato or tomatillo salsa (see pages 225 and 226)
4 cups roughly flaked cooked fish, skin and bones removed if any
or
2 pounds steamed or baked fish fillets, skin and pin bones removed if any
or

4 pounds steamed or bake-poached whole fish, skin and bones removed
Salt to taste
Freshly ground black or white pepper to taste
Boston lettuce leaves or radicchio leaves or endive leaves for decoration

1. Combine all the ingredients (except the salad leaves) in a bowl, being careful not to let the fish flake too much.
2. Line a platter with the salad leaves and place the fish salad in the middle.

SERVES 6

FISH SALAD II

Preparation time: 30 minutes
Cooking time: 20 minutes, plus 15 to 30 minutes if you must steam, bake, or bake-poach raw fish

Choose leftover cooked or smoked fish such as

blackfish • bluefish • bonito • haddock • mackerel • mullet • porgy • sheepshead • trout • tuna • whitefish

¾ pound small red-skin potatoes
3 cups roughly flaked cooked or
   smoked fish, skin and bones
   removed if any
   or
1½ pounds steamed or baked fish
   fillets, skin and pin bones
   removed if any
   or
3 pounds steamed or bake-poached
   whole fish, skin and bones
   removed
1 small carrot, scraped and grated
   coarsely

1 celery stalk, chopped into ¼-inch
   pieces
3 tablespoons chopped fresh dill
   weed or parsley
¼ cup mild olive oil
¼ cup lemon juice
Salt to taste
Freshly ground black pepper to
   taste
Boston lettuce leaves or radicchio
   leaves for decoration

1. Boil the potatoes in their skins for 20 minutes, until just tender, not falling apart. Run cold water over them, then drain and cut in quarters.

2. Combine all the remaining ingredients (except the salad leaves) in a bowl, being careful not to flake the fish too much.

3. Line a platter with the salad leaves and place the fish salad in the middle.

SERVES 4

SHELLFISH SALAD II

Preparation time: 10 minutes
Cooking time: none

Choose cooked shellfish, out of shell, such as

bay or sea scallops (see page 172) • crabmeat (picked over for cartilage) • crawfish (tail meat, available frozen) • lobster meat (cut in ½-inch chunks) (see page 179) • medium-sized shrimps (peeled, deveined, and cut in ½-inch chunks) (see page 172)

(continued)

8 to 12 ounces cooked shellfish
   meat such as: lobster, crab,
   shrimp, sea or bay scallops, or
   crawfish
1 or 2 celery stalks, trimmed and
   finely chopped in ¼-inch dice
2 tablespoons finely chopped sweet
   red pepper dice
¼ cup mayonnaise (see recipe on
   page 227) or low-fat yogurt
2 teaspoons Dijon-style mustard
   (only for crabmeat salad)

2 tablespoons lemon juice
1 tablespoon chopped dill or basil
   or coriander
Pinch cayenne or 6 drops Tabasco
Salt to taste
Freshly ground white pepper to
   taste
Boston lettuce leaves or radicchio
   leaves or endive leaves for
   decoration

1. Combine all ingredients (except the salad leaves) in a bowl.
2. Serve the shellfish salad on salad leaves on individual plates.

SERVES 2

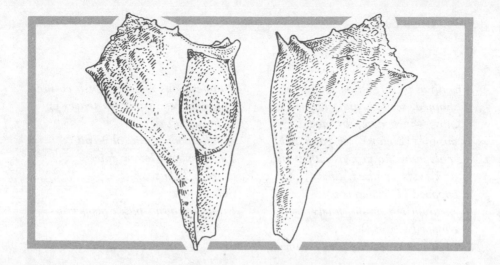

Sauces and Condiments

BASIC SAUCE AND CONDIMENT RECIPES

TOMATO SALSA

Preparation time: 15 minutes
Cooking time: none, except you must
    boil water to skin tomatoes

Tomato salsa can accompany many fish dishes, particularly those using lean, white-fleshed fish and all fried or deep-fried fish dishes—it is far superior to ketchup and quite different!

Note: This salsa recipe is incorporated into the fish salad recipe on page 222.

3 medium to large ripe tomatoes,
  skinned, seeded, and chopped
  into ¼-inch dice, drained 15
  minutes (2 cups) (see page 241)
1 small jalapeño pepper with stems
  and seeds removed, finely
  chopped (1 tablespoon)
¼ medium red onion, finely
  chopped (½ cup)
2 small cloves garlic, finely minced

3 tablespoons chopped fresh coriander leaves or parsley leaves or
  basil leaves
3 tablespoons mild olive oil
3 tablespoons lemon juice
8 drops Tabasco
Salt to taste
Freshly ground black pepper to
  taste

Mix all the ingredients together and refrigerate, cover with plastic wrap for 20 minutes before using.

MAKES 2 CUPS

TOMATILLO SALSA

Preparation time: 15 minutes
Cooking time: 2 to 3 minutes

You will find tomatillos—"green" tomatolike vegetables from Mexico or California—in specialty produce stores and some Spanish supermarkets. They give a slightly more acidic—and distinctive—tomato taste to salsa than tomatoes. Tomatillos are covered by papery husks, which are easily removed. They are really too acidic to eat raw and are best quartered and cooked until just tender.

Use the same ingredients as for
  Tomato Salsa, except use 1½
  pounds tomatillos instead of
  tomatoes

1. Remove the husks and rinse the tomatillos.
2. Cut them in quarters and put them in a saucepan with 1½ cups of water, salt to taste, and 1 teaspoon of sugar.

3. Bring them to the boil over moderate heat and cook them for 2 or 3 minutes only until they lose a little of their green color and are tender.
4. Drain them immediately and cool over ice water.
5. Put them on a board and chop them roughly before proceeding with the Tomato Salsa recipe.

MAKES 2 CUPS

BASIC MAYONNAISE

Preparation time: 10 minutes
Cooking time: none

1 large egg yolk
1 tablespoon Dijon-style mustard
⅓ cup mild olive oil
⅔ cup vegetable oil such as peanut,
*   sunflower, safflower, or corn oil*

Salt to taste
1 tablespoon lemon juice
1 or 2 tablespoons warm water, if
*   necessary*

1. Using a wire whisk or an electric beater, beat the egg yolk and mustard together until the mixture starts to turn a pale yellow.
2. Place the oils in a pouring measure or pitcher.
3. Add the oils, very gradually at first, in a thin stream. Then, as the mixture emulsifies and thickens, pour faster. (*Note:* If the mixture separates and curdles, start with another yolk in a clean bowl. Gradually introduce the curdled mixture and you will see that it emulsifies again.)
4. Add salt and lemon juice and beat. Add a little warm water (1 or 2 tablespoons) if the mayonnaise needs thinning.
5. Taste for seasoning, adding more lemon juice and salt if necessary.
6. Place the mayonnaise in a clean bowl or container and cover before refrigerating.

MAKES 1 CUP

MAYONNAISE FOR LOBSTER

Preparation time: 15 minutes
Cooking time: none

When cooking a female lobster, find the roe or coral and break it up a little to separate, then mix it into the Basic Mayonnaise recipe.

MAKES 1¼ CUPS

A SPICY GREEN MAYONNAISE

Preparation time: 30 minutes
Cooking time: none

*6 tablespoons finely chopped parsley
   or coriander
1 small clove garlic, finely minced,
   then mixed and mashed with ¼
   teaspoon salt*

*1 teaspoon finely grated ginger
1 small jalapeño pepper, seeded
   and finely minced
1 recipe Basic Mayonnaise*

Add the above ingredients together and mix well.

MAKES 1¼ CUPS

HARLEQUIN MAYONNAISE

Preparation time: 30 minutes
Cooking time: none

*1 medium ripe tomato, skinned,
   seeded, and chopped into ¼-inch
   dice, drained 15 minutes
   (¾ cup) (see page 241)
1 medium yellow pepper cut in
   ¼-inch dice (1 cup)*

*10 Spanish olives (stuffed with pi-
   mientos), diced (4 tablespoons)
2 tablespoons parsley or tarragon
1 recipe Basic Mayonnaise*

Add the above ingredients together and mix well.

MAKES 3 CUPS

AIOLI

Preparation time: 35 minutes
Cooking time: none

Aioli is a garlic mayonnaise that is an integral part of the fish soup called *bourride* (see page 188), and it is also particularly tasty with steamed, grilled, broiled, and deep-fried fish. For a delicious variation, you can spread it on fish fillets and broil, bake, or steam them.

½ teaspoon saffron
2 tablespoons dry white wine
4 cloves garlic, peeled and crushed
   with the flat side of a heavy
   chef's knife
½ teaspoon coarse kosher salt
2 large egg yolks
¾ cup mild olive oil
1¼ cups vegetable oil such as
   peanut, sunflower, safflower, or
   corn oil

3 tablespoons lemon juice
1 or more tablespoons warm water,
   if necessary
Salt to taste
Freshly ground white pepper to
   taste

1. Dissolve the saffron in the wine for 15 minutes.
2. Put the crushed garlic and coarse salt in a mortar (or a medium-sized bowl) and work them together with a pestle (or the back of a spoon) until you have a coarse paste.
3. Transfer the garlic paste to a bowl and add the egg yolks.
4. Using a wire whisk or an electric beater, beat the garlic paste and egg yolks together.
5. Place the oils in a pouring measure or pitcher.
6. Add the oils, very gradually at first, then in a thin stream. Then, as the mixture emulsifies and thickens, pour faster. (*Note:* if the mixture separates and curdles, start with another yolk in a clean bowl. Gradually introduce the curdled mixture and you will see that it emulsifies again.)
7. Add the lemon juice and the saffron and wine mixture, and beat. Add a little warm water (1 or more tablespoons) if the aioli gets too thick.
8. Add salt and pepper to taste.
9. To serve, place the aioli in a clean bowl or container.

MAKES 2¼ CUPS

LIME AND DILL VINAIGRETTE

Preparation time: 15 minutes
Cooking time: none

1 small clove garlic, finely minced
½ teaspoon salt
⅛ teaspoon freshly ground white
   pepper
½ large egg yolk

2 tablespoons lime or lemon juice
½ cup olive oil
2 tablespoons finely chopped dill or
   tarragon

1. Put everything except oil and dill or tarragon in a small bowl. Using a wire whisk or electric beater, beat together until light and frothy.
2. Add the oil in a thin stream until an emulsion is formed, then add it faster.
3. Finally, add the dill or tarragon.

**MAKES ⅔ CUP (ENOUGH FOR SEAFOOD SALAD FOR 6
AS A MAIN COURSE—SEE PAGE 172)**

SWEET RED PEPPER SAUCE

Preparation time: 15 minutes
Cooking time: 40 to 45 minutes (12 to
   14 minutes in a microwave oven)

SPECIAL EQUIPMENT: Small microwavable bowl *or* casserole dish (if using a microwave oven)
Microwavable plastic wrap (if using a microwave oven)

This sauce goes perfectly with all kinds of seafood for it is piquant—not hot and spicy, but sweet-sour. It has a wonderful color and it can be made in exactly the same way with yellow peppers. This sauce can be made in advance and will keep, covered in the refrigerator, for three days.

3 (1 to 1½ pounds) sweet red pep-
   pers, with stems, ribs, and seeds
   removed, cut in 1½-inch squares
3 shallots, peeled and cut in half,
   or 1 small onion, roughly
   chopped
3 cloves garlic
¼ cup mild olive oil

1 tablespoon water or dry white
   wine (optional)
1 tablespoon apple cider vinegar or
   raspberry vinegar
1 tablespoon lemon juice
¼ teaspoon salt
Freshly ground white pepper to
   taste

1. Put the red peppers, shallots or onion, garlic, and oil in a medium-sized saucepan and cover.

2. *To cook on a stovetop:* Put over low heat and cook for 40 minutes, stirring occasionally, until all the vegetables are soft. Add 1 tablespoon of water or dry white wine if the vegetables get dry. *To microwave:* Put red pepper, shallots or onion, garlic, and oil in a small microwavable bowl or casserole dish and cover with plastic microwavable wrap, leaving a vent at the edge. Cook for 12 to 14 minutes on High.

3. Process the red pepper mixture in a food processor or blender until very smooth, about 1 minute.

4. Add the vinegar, lemon juice, salt, and pepper; blend for another 5 seconds.

MAKES 1½ CUPS

NEW ORLEANS–STYLE BARBECUE SAUCE

Preparation time: 5 minutes
Cooking time: 15 minutes

This sauce is hot and spicy and suits a variety of seafood dishes. Serve this sauce as a dip with grilled, broiled, or poached shrimp. You'll love it when you taste it!

6 tablespoons (¾ stick) unsalted butter or 4 tablespoons mild olive oil (use butter if serving hot and oil if serving at room temperature)
3 cloves garlic, finely minced
¾ cup (6-ounce can) tomato paste
4 tablespoons Dijon-type mustard
1¼ cups cold water
½ teaspoon dried thyme

1 teaspoon dried oregano
1 teaspoon freshly ground black pepper
½ teaspoon cayenne
2 tablespoons Worcestershire sauce
2 tablespoons lemon juice
10 basil leaves, rinsed and dried if necessary, finely shredded at the last moment

1. Melt the butter or heat the oil in a 10-inch frying pan over moderate heat. When the butter or oil is hot, add the garlic and cook for 10 seconds.

2. Lower the heat and add the tomato paste, mustard, and 1¼ cups cold

water, stirring with a wire whisk. It will take a little time for these particular ingredients to mix together, but persevere!

3. Add all the remaining ingredients except the basil.
4. Cook for 10 to 12 minutes over low heat, stirring occasionally.
5. Sprinkle on the shredded basil before using.

MAKES 2 CUPS

BASIC TOPPING FOR STEAMING, BROILING, AND BAKING, OR FOR USE AS A STUFFING I

Preparation time: 15 minutes
Cooking time: none

2 tablespoons minced garlic
2 tablespoons scraped and fine grated ginger

2 tablespoons chopped jalapeño pepper (seeded)
2 tablespoons finely chopped fresh coriander or basil leaves

Mix all together and spread on seafood before cooking, or use as a stuffing for fish.

MAKES ½ CUP, ENOUGH FOR 2 POUNDS OF SEAFOOD

BASIC TOPPING FOR STEAMING, BROILING, AND BAKING, OR FOR USE AS A STUFFING II

Preparation time: 2 minutes
Cooking time: none

2 tablespoons lemon rind, finely grated

2 tablespoons finely chopped parsley
1 teaspoon minced garlic

Mix all together and spread on seafood before cooking or use as a stuffing for fish.

MAKES ¼ CUP, ENOUGH FOR 1 POUND OF SEAFOOD

HONEYCUP MUSTARD SAUCE

Preparation time: 10 minutes
Cooking time: none

The ingredients for this sauce are a little unusual, but it is worth finding them, for the taste is highly addictive!

¼ *cup honeycup mustard*
1½ *teaspoons balsamic vinegar*
½ *cup mild olive oil*
Freshly ground white pepper to
    taste

1 *tablespoon finely chopped dill,*
    fully packed

1. Place the honeycup mustard and balsamic vinegar in a bowl.
2. Place the oil in a pouring measure or pitcher and add it slowly, whisk as if you were making a mayonnaise.
3. Add 1 tablespoon water and the pepper.
4. Finally, fold in the chopped dill.

MAKES 1 CUP

LIME, GINGER, AND CORIANDER SAUCE

Preparation time: 10 minutes
Cooking time: none

SPECIAL EQUIPMENT: Cheesecloth (optional)

1 *tablespoon Dijon-type mustard*
1 *tablespoon lime juice*
Grated zest of 1 lime
1 *tablespoon finely grated ginger*
¾ *cup mild olive oil*

Salt to taste
Freshly ground white pepper to
    taste
1 *tablespoon finely chopped*
    coriander, fully packed

1. Place the mustard, lime juice, and zest in a bowl. Put the grated ginger in cheesecloth or a dishcloth and squeeze the juice into the bowl.
2. Using a wire whisk or electric beater, beat the mixture until opaque.
3. Place the oil in a pouring measure or pitcher and add it to the mixture in a fine stream, as if you were making mayonnaise.
4. Add salt and pepper to taste. Finally, add the chopped coriander.

MAKES 1 CUP

CORIANDER PESTO

Preparation time: 15 minutes
Cooking time: none

Unlike pesto made with basil leaves, this coriander pesto does not need pine
nuts and cheese to enrich it.

2 bunches coriander leaves picked
* from stalks, rinsed and dried*
1 tablespoon lemon juice
1 clove garlic, finely minced
¼ teaspoon salt
¼ cup mild olive oil

1. Place the coriander leaves, lemon juice, garlic, and salt in the blender or
food processor.
2. Blend or process for a minute or so until a fairly smooth puree is formed.
3. Finally, add the olive oil in a fine stream.

MAKES ⅔ CUP

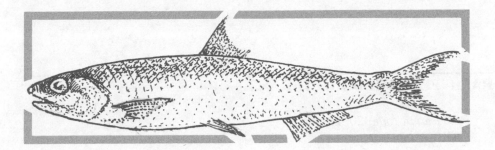

Flavored Butters

FLAVORED BUTTERS CONSIST OF DIFFERENT FLAVORS FOLDED OR BEATEN INTO SOFT BUTTER OR margarine. The butters complement baked, broiled, grilled, steamed, or poached seafood.

Here is a basic recipe followed by recipes for five flavored butters. It is very easy to make these butters in a food processor; an electric beater or wire whisk can also be used. You can make some recipes up yourself—be as creative as you like, but be generous with the added flavorings because the butter absorbs more flavor than you would think.

To serve a flavored butter, you can pipe or spoon it onto cooked fish fillets or shellfish right away, or shape the soft mixture into a log 1½ inches in diameter and roll it up in plastic wrap to be refrigerated and used later. (Flavored butters will generally keep a week in the refrigerator. They can also be frozen.) When the log is fully chilled, you can cut it into wafers and place them on top of the cooked seafood, where they will melt and add zest and taste to the dish. You can also place the butter on the side of the seafood, where it will melt as long as the plate is hot.

235

BASIC FLAVORED BUTTER

Preparation time: 20 minutes
Cooking time: none

*2 sticks (8 ounces) unsalted butter
or margarine, each stick cut into
5 pieces
2 tablespoons lemon juice*

*½ teaspoon salt or more to taste
Freshly ground black or white
pepper to taste*

1. Take the butter or margarine out of the refrigerator to soften it. Butter can be softened in the microwave oven.
2. When the butter or margarine is soft, put it in the food processor and process it until it gets airy and lightens in color.
3. Add the lemon juice, salt, and pepper. (*Note:* Do not add salt if salty ingredients such as anchovies or soy sauce are added.)
4. Unless otherwise noted, add flavorful ingredients of your choice and process until well blended, or scrape the butter into a bowl and *fold in* the other ingredients with a plastic spatula or spoon.
5. Use right away or place on plastic wrap and shape into a log before storing in the refrigerator.

MAKES 1 CUP

ANCHOVY BUTTER

Preparation time: 20 minutes
Cooking time: none

*2 sticks (8 ounces) unsalted butter
or margarine, each stick cut into
5 pieces
2 tablespoons lemon juice
Freshly ground black or white
pepper to taste*

*1 2-ounce can of anchovies or 15
anchovies drained of most of
their oil
25 mint leaves, finely chopped
Salt only to taste—the anchovies
will salt the butter*

Using the food processor, follow the Basic Flavored Butter recipe through step 3, then add the rest of the ingredients.

MAKES 1¼ CUPS

SNAIL BUTTER (GARLIC AND PARSLEY BUTTER)

Preparation time: 20 minutes
Cooking time: none

*1 stick (4 ounces) unsalted butter
or margarine, each stick cut into
5 pieces
1 tablespoon lemon juice
½ teaspoon salt*

*Freshly ground white pepper to
taste
3 garlic cloves, finely minced
3 tablespoons finely chopped parsley*

1. Using the food processor, follow the Basic Flavored Butter recipe through step 3, then add garlic.
2. Fold in the parsley with plastic or rubber spatula.

Variation: For a milder, sweeter garlic taste, boil un-peeled garlic cloves for 10 minutes in water. Drain and peel cloves, then mash with the flat side of a knife.

MAKES ¾ CUP

GARLIC, BASIL, AND TOMATO BUTTER

Preparation time: 25 minutes
Cooking time: none

*1 stick (4 ounces) unsalted butter
or margarine, each stick cut into
5 pieces
1 tablespoon lemon juice
1 teaspoon salt
Freshly ground black pepper to
taste*

*3 garlic cloves, finely minced
4 tablespoons finely chopped basil
3 tablespoons tomato concasse (see
page 241)*

1. Using the food processor, follow the Basic Flavored Butter recipe through step 3, then add garlic.
2. Fold in the basil and tomato with plastic or rubber spatula.

MAKES ¾ CUP

CHIVE AND TOASTED SESAME SEED BUTTER

Preparation time: 15 minutes
Cooking time: none

Note: Salt and pepper are not used in this recipe.

1 stick (4 ounces) unsalted butter
  or margarine, each stick cut into
  5 pieces
1 tablespoon lemon juice
2 teaspoons (Oriental-type) sesame
  oil

1 tablespoon soy sauce
2 tablespoons finely chopped chives
2 tablespoons toasted sesame seeds

1. Using the food processor, follow the Basic Flavored Butter recipe through step 3, then add the sesame oil and soy sauce.
2. Fold in the chives and sesame seeds with plastic or rubber spatula.

MAKES 1 CUP

SHRIMP OR CRAWFISH BUTTER

Preparation time: 15 minutes
Cooking time: 13 minutes

2 sticks (8 ounces) unsalted butter
  or margarine, each stick cut into
  5 pieces
4 cups uncooked shrimp shells
  collected from peeled raw shrimp
  (collect them yourself or ask
  your fishmonger for them)
  or
4 cups crawfish shells, collected
  from cooked crawfish, ground up
  in the food processor

½ cup dry white wine
½ teaspoon paprika
1 teaspoon salt
Freshly ground white pepper to
  taste
⅛ teaspoon cayenne

1. Heat one stick of butter or margarine in a frying pan over moderate heat. Add the shellfish shells and cook slowly, stirring occasionally for 7 to 10 minutes.

2. Put shells and butter or margarine in the bowl of a food processor.

3. Deglaze the pan with the white wine and stir in the paprika, salt, pepper, and cayenne. Add this to the mixture in the food processor.

4. Process for a minute, then add the second stick of butter or margarine and blend, scraping the sides of the bowl every now and again.

5. Push the mixture through the fine mesh of a food mill or strainer (with a spatula).

6. Place it on plastic wrap and shape it into a log before storing it in the refrigerator.

MAKES 1¼ CUPS

Some Cooking Techniques

HOW TO JULIENNE CARROTS, LEEKS, AND CELERY

A JULIENNE OF VEGETABLES IS A PRETTY AND APPETIZING ACCOMPANIMENT TO MANY DISHES. YOU need to achieve very thin matchstick or strawlike lengths of vegetable, about 2 or 3 inches long and although it is a little tedious to do, the end result is most attractive. The thinner the julienne the better!

CARROTS

1. Scrape or peel a carrot.
2. Cut off the ends of the carrot and cut it into 2- or 3-inch lengths.
3. Cut the carrot into very thin lengthwise slices and then cut these slices, stacked a few at a time, into thin julienne.

LEEKS

1. Trim a leek at the bottom root end and cut off the tough part of the green leaves.
2. Cut the leek in half lengthwise and rinse it thoroughly.
3. Now cut the leek in 2- or 3-inch lengths.
4. Take a piece of the leek and put it on the board, inside down, and press it flat.
5. Cut it into very thin julienne.

CELERY

This is the most difficult of the three to cut in a fine julienne.

1. Trim both ends of a celery stalk and cut it into 2- or 3-inch lengths.
2. Holding the celery stalk in your left hand, with the inside of the stalk facing you, cut the stalk lengthwise into very thin slices or slivers and then cut these into very thin julienne.

HOW TO SKIN, SEED, AND CHOP TOMATOES (TOMATO CONCASSE)

Preparation time: Approximately 4
    minutes per each tomato
Cooking time: 30 seconds

Chopped tomato without skin, seeds, or juice is a must for some of the recipes in this book. Use ripe tomatoes, preferably sun-ripened. In the winter I resort to using plum tomatoes if they are the ones with the most color and flavor.

1. Bring a saucepan of water to the boil.
2. Immerse tomatoes in the water for 30 seconds.
3. Take the tomatoes out of the water with a slotted spoon and place them under cold running water.
4. Now peel off the skins and cut out the cores.

5. Cut the tomatoes in half crosswise and squeeze out the seeds and juice. Cut the flesh into ¼-inch-wide slices, ¼-inch-wide lengths, and then into ¼-inch dice.

CLARIFIED BUTTER

Preparation time: 1 minute
Cooking time: 15 minutes

Clarified butter is useful for frying and sautéing fish; because the milk solids and water are removed, it can take high heat without burning. It is a good idea always to have some on hand; once made, clarified butter will keep for a week or so in the refrigerator.

Remember, clarified butter does not have the same flavor as whole butter.

2 sticks (8 ounces) unsalted butter

1. Cut each stick of butter into 5 pieces and put the pieces in a saucepan over low heat.
2. When the butter is melted, take it off the heat and let it stand 5 minutes.
3. Using a large spoon, spoon off the milk solids from the top.
4. Pour off the clarified butter into a bowl until you see the water content at the bottom of the saucepan. Carefully spoon off the rest of the clarified butter.
5. Cool before refrigerating.

MAKES ¾ CUP

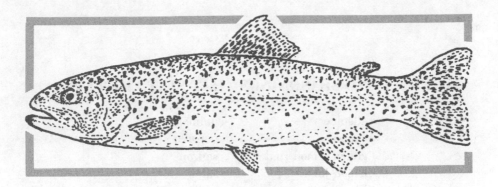

Herbs and Spices

THESE LISTS ARE ONLY SUGGESTIONS. HERBS AND SEASONINGS ARE A QUESTION OF PERSONAL taste.

HERBS THAT SUIT LEAN FISH

basil	dill
bay leaf	parsley
chervil	tarragon
coriander	thyme

SPICES AND SEASONINGS THAT SUIT LEAN FISH

allspice	nutmeg
cumin	paprika
grated lemon rind	saffron
lemon juice	salt
lime juice	white pepper
mustard	

HERBS THAT SUIT FATTY FISH

basil	oregano
dill	rosemary
marjoram	savory
mint	thyme

(Some of these herbs are mild, such as dill, but if used in quantity they more than make up for their mildness.)

SPICES AND SEASONINGS THAT SUIT FATTY FISH

allspice	lemon juice
black pepper	lemon rind
chili peppers	lime juice
cumin	mustard
dark or light Worcestershire sauce	onion
fennel seed	paprika
garlic	salt
ginger	soy sauce
ground coriander	teriyaki

When using fresh herbs such as parsley, basil, coriander, mint, and dill, rinse the leaves, shake them free of water, even pat them dry and then take the leaves off the stems before chopping. Sprigs are very decorative and can be used on the finished plate.

It is impossible to gauge how hot fresh chili peppers will taste by looking at them. Different chili peppers taste different—some are definitely hotter than others. Cross-pollination with a milder pepper may inadvertently cause some to lack heat altogether. The only reliable thing to do is to taste a very small piece of a chili pepper before using it. Use rubber gloves if you like when seeding and chopping hot peppers. Bottled and canned jalapeño peppers are perfectly all right to use, if you cannot get them fresh.

I like the flat-leaf Italian parsley for flavor and looks. Curly parsley has its own character and is useful too. Do not chop these parsleys into a green dust—there is nothing worse. Chop finely, but recognize that parsley is an herb. Separate parsley leaves picked off sprigs are a lovely decoration also.

I prefer using kosher salt when I cook, for it is pure and unadulterated. I have two pepper grinders, one for black peppercorns, the other for white peppercorns.

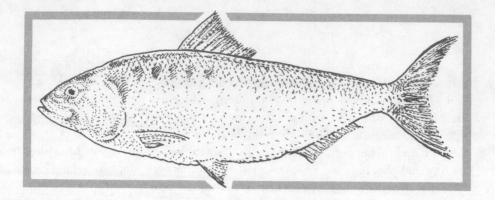

Accompaniments with Seafood

SOME VEGETABLES, FRUITS, AND HERBS ENHANCE THE CHARACTER OF FISH AND SHELLFISH MORE than others. Here's what I contemplate while deciding what goes alongside the seafood:

First there are the traditional companions. A squeeze from a wedge, slice, or curl of a lemon or lime is nearly always essential to a fish dish—the acidity balances the sweet flavors of fish. Chopped parsley, or even whole sprigs, may enhance the visual appeal of the dish, although other herbs often add more interesting flavors. I use garlic in many seafood recipes because I consider its flavor important in practically any cooking. Peeled, steamed, and turned potatoes are time-honored and always appealing—in fact, potatoes cooked by any method are delicious with seafood, as are simple rice and pasta dishes. Legumes are good companions because of their mild taste; white navy beans especially suit a tuna salad.

When planning the rest of the meal, think of vegetables whose taste will not overwhelm the seafood. Because fish is often sweet-tasting, serve vegetables that sweeten as they cook, and remember that roasting is one of the best cooking methods to bring out the sweetness.

246

I suppose onions and tomatoes—both raw and cooked—are my favorite vegetables to serve with fish. They are easily prepared, and can be cooked on top of, underneath, or on the side of fish. The pale purple color and mild, sweet flavor of red onions, for example, make them wonderful with practically any seafood. Yellow tomatoes—the delicious acid-free variety available in the summer months—are also favorites. I have cooked them along with broiled cod and then strewn them with a few anchovies and purple basil leaves with dramatic results. Tomatillos—those little green tomatolike vegetables with papery husks—make a great salsa to go with fish (see page 226). Cook some wedges with shallots or chopped onion for a slightly acidic accompaniment to an oilier or grilled fish.

Fennel bulb, or anise (again, either cooked or raw), is a delicious choice. The licorice taste is an elixir with fish. If you can find dried fennel stalks, buy them, because they make a fantastic bed for a roast fish, and will flavor whatever is cooking on an open grill.

I find that corn goes very well with steamed or grilled lobster and other shellfish dishes. Asparagus, by the same token, particularly suits lobster as well as other firm, sweet-fleshed fish and shellfish, and is pretty too. And don't overlook grilled or sautéed eggplant—its slight bitterness does not overpower most fish.

Sliced cool cucumbers, crisp jicama, and daikon work as foils to the soft texture of fish. These may be raw or lightly sautéed. Snow peas, green beans, lima beans, and sugar snap peas are all appropriate and pleasant for the same reason.

Sweet red, green, and yellow peppers may be sautéed or roasted and served with practically any fish. See page 230 for a delightful sweet red pepper sauce. The various hot chili peppers—both fresh and dried—are indispensable for bringing heat to a sauce, soup, or stew, but they should be used sparingly or you will cancel out the flavor of the seafood itself.

Sliced or whole baby carrots work well sautéed, steamed, or roasted with any seafood. A combination of leeks and celery cut into julienne slices and then blanched are perfect as a bed for a fish fillet or steak. Chopped celery definitely belongs in shellfish salads, particularly those featuring lobster or tuna.

Lemongrass works well in the same dishes as celery, although its lemon-lime taste is not at all similar. The tender inside can be thinly sliced and the dry grassy top is superb in soups and stews.

Then there's an elusive, thin, asparaguslike grass that grows in saline marshes both here and in Europe, known in France as *pousse-pierre*, in England and the United States as samphire or glasswort, and in the Latin by the genus name *Salicornia*. It is a spectacular vegetable to serve with seafood—slightly salty, with a taste of fennel—and looks extremely pretty. Just steam it for a few minutes. Glasswort is usually available in the spring and summer in specialty produce stores.

Scallions can be added to fish salads and salsas or grilled along with seafood. Leeks have a pronounced sweetness that complements especially sweet-tasting seafood such as crab and scallops as well as flounder and sole.

Sorrel, sometimes seen in produce markets but often found in vegetable gardens, is enjoyable with salmon in particular. The taste of sorrel is sharp and acidic, so it should either be used sparingly or mixed with spinach, which blunts its sharpness. Spinach, similarly, has a certain sharp flavor that counteracts the blandness of some fish. Steamed endive is featured with sole in the recipe on page 202. It is a fascinating counterpoint to this potentially bland fish.

Some of the common leafy vegetables go better with fish than others. Cabbages such as savoy cabbage may be very thinly sliced into a chiffonade and steamed. Savoy cabbage is a great accompaniment to a sweet-tasting fish such as monkfish. Lightly sautéing bok choy and Chinese cabbage brings out their sweet flavors; these cabbages are a delight with any fish dish. However, I find kale, mustard greens, collards, and turnip greens a little too strong to place alongside most seafood.

Broccoli and broccoli rabe—either sautéed or steamed—are colorful, crisp additions to any plate. Because broccoli rabe is rather bitter, it goes well with stronger, oilier fish. Cauliflower is also fine with seafood, especially if prepared with something acidic, like lemon or tomato.

Squashes of all kinds are sweet and attractive. They are best with baked or roasted fish. On the other hand, parsnips and yams are really so sweet that I don't recommend them with fish.

Because cooked mushrooms have a texture very similar to that of fish, I avoid using them as a sole accompaniment to fish. However, some dried wild mushrooms work well in sauces.

A few fruits go well with seafood. I like the tropical flavors of orange, mango, and papaya. Serve them raw or lightly sautéed.

For additional garnishes on the plate, try fennel fronds, or assorted greens such as radicchio, arugula, or mâche.

Remember to select the accompaniments to seafood dishes with the same care you use in selecting the seafood itself. Look for the freshest, most attractive vegetables, fruits, and herbs.

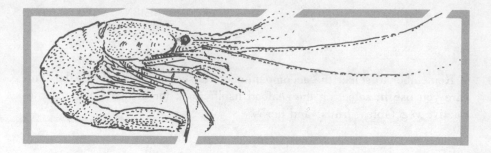

Wines

WE USUALLY DRINK WHITE WINES WITH SEAFOOD DISHES, BECAUSE THEY COMPLEMENT EACH other particularly well. Dry, light white wines go very well with delicately flavored seafood but heavier whites such as the big rich chardonnays go beautifully with the stronger-flavored seafood, especially shellfish. Oysters deserve crisp, dry whites and the spicy white wine Gewürztraminer stands up to smoked salmon, trout, and mackerel. A cold dry sherry such as a Fino or Manzanilla marries well with shrimp dishes. I also find that a light Chianti (red wine) is a wonderful complement to, for instance, a smoked haddock soufflé. A merlot or Beaujolais, also red wines, are just fine as well. These red wines can be treated as white wines and chilled if you want.

There are many fine white wines from all over the world at varying prices and quality, no doubt your local liquor store will have a large variety to choose from and to recommend.

The following gives some idea of the types of wines that go with the different tastes of fish and shellfish and their cooking methods. Some wines are listed by the name of the grape and others are named by type, but rarely by the particular name of the producer. It is best to avoid general brand names for they usually denote large production of an inferior wine.

SIMPLY PREPARED, DELICATELY FLAVORED	CREAM AND BUTTER PREPARATIONS
Vinho Verde (Portugal)	White burgundies (France)
Galestro (Italy)	White Riojas (Spain)
Vernaccia (Italy)	Torres Viña Sol (Spain)
Bourgogne Aligoté (France)	Long Island chardonnays
Bordeaux Sauvignons (France)	Californian chardonnays
Muscadet (Loire, France)	
Pouilly-Fumé (Loire, France)	
Very dry, ultra brut and brut sauvage champagnes (France)	
Edelzwicker (Alsace)	
New Zealand sauvignons	
Oregon sauvignons and chardonnays	
Washington sauvignons	

PREPARATIONS FOR RICH FATTY FISH	SMOKED FISH AND RICHLY PREPARED, SUCH AS GRILLED
Sonoma chardonnays (U.S.A.)	Gewürztraminer (Alsace)
Pinot grigio (Italy)	Tokay (Alsace)
Sancerre (Loire, France)	Riesling (Alsace)
New Zealand chardonnays	Riesling (Germany)
Chianti (Italy)	Sylvaner (Germany)
Beaujolais (France)	Australian dry semillion
Merlot (France, Italy, U.S.A.)	

HOT AND SPICY PREPARATIONS

Chianti (Italy)
Beaujolais (France)
Australian chardonnays
Riesling spatlese (Germany)

In addition here is a list of some wines I have enjoyed, particularly with fish and seafood dishes, in recent years.

France

Burgundy Chardonnays such as the delectable, crisp, elegant Chablis (not to be confused with the generic types), and fuller wines such as; Pouilly-Fuissé, Meursault, Puligny-Montrachet, Chassagne-Montrachet, Corton-Charlemagne from Burgundy, and on the lighter side, Mâcon-Villages, Bourgogne Aligoté, Montagny, and Moreau Blanc.

Bordeaux Dry graves, Entre-deux-Mers, and sauvignon blancs.

Loire Pouilly-Fumé, dry Vouvray, Saumur, Sancerre, Saint Pourçain-sur-Sioule, and Muscadet de Sèvre et Maine. These wines have been developed so that they are perfect with the freshwater fish of the Loire Valley and the shellfish from the nearby Atlantic coast.

Provence White and rosé Bandol, white Cassis, Côtes de Provence

Midi Listel—Vin des Sables from the Camargue and Blanquette de Limoux, a sparkling dry white wine

Alsace Dry gewürztraminers, rieslings, muscats, tokays, and the reasonably priced edelzwickers

From the United States

California The most appropriate wines from California are from Sonoma county and the lower Napa Valley, where the lighter wines come from. Sauvignon blancs, pinot blancs, and chardonnays from Chateau St. Jean, Grgich-Hills, Stag's Leap, Trefethen, Wente, Robert Mondavi, Firestone, Sterling, Simi, Fetzer, Heitz, Stony Hill, Kalin, Domaine Michel, Silverado, and Souverain.

Oregon Chardonnays, pinot gris, dry muscats, and pinot noir blancs from Knudsen Erath, Eyrie, and Tualatin

Idaho Chardonnay and chenin blanc from Ste. Chapelle

Washington Riesling, sauvignon blanc, and semillon from Château Ste. Michelle

New York Chardonnays, rieslings, and seyval-villards from Dr. Frank Konstantin, Heron Hill, Bully Hill, and Wagner (Finger Lakes, New York State)

Sauvignons and chardonnays from Hargrave, Lenz and Palmer (North Fork, Long Island), and Bridgehampton (South Fork, Long Island)

Pennsylvania Chardonnay, riesling, and seyval blanc from Chaddsford Winery (Chadds Ford)

Other Countries

Italy From Northern Italy in the Alto Adige area (by the Alps) come the light, fresh, crisp pinot grigios and pinot blancs. Other northern wines from the Veneto region are proseccos and the better soaves from Pieropan and Anselmi. From Tuscany come other fresh, light wines such as the Vernaccia di San Gimignano and the lovely orvietos such as Orvieto Bigi. Also from this area come Chiantis both red and white. Look for the white Chianti called Galestro.

Far south there are fuller white wines, such as the frascati from near Rome and the verdicchios from the Adriatic coast. See the Verdicchio Castelli Gesi.

Portugal Vinho Verde, particularly good when young, when it has a little spritz in it.

Spain White Riojas: Marqués de Cáceres, Marqués de Riscal, and Marques de Murrieta (best to drink when young)

Penedes, Torres Viña Sol; Sherries: Fino and Manzilla

Germany Kabinett, quality riesling and silvaner. Look for trochen (dry) on the label (particularly in the Baden area).

Australia Chardonnays, rieslings and muscats from Brown
Bros., Rosemount and Lindemans, and a dry semillion from Hunter Valley

New Zealand Chardonnay and sauvignon blanc from Corbans. There are many exciting new wines being imported now from New Zealand. The temperate climate makes them fresh and fragrant—in particular those made with the sauvignon blanc grape—and excellent with simply cooked seafood.

Part
III

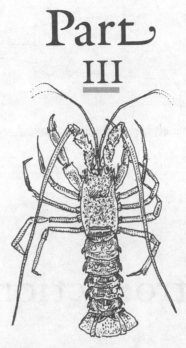

PROFILES

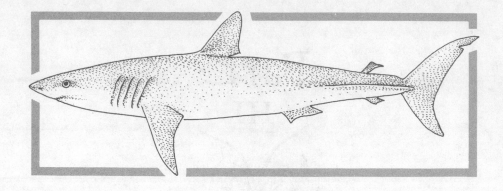

Introduction

FOLLOWING ARE PROFILES OF THE KINDS OF FISH AND SHELLFISH YOU ARE MOST LIKELY TO SEE at the fish store. All but a few of the profiled seafood varieties are caught or garnered in fresh and sea waters in and around the United States; the rest are European species that are marketed here.

The profiles are meant to help you distinguish varieties of fish and shellfish easily and learn how to prepare and cook them best. The profiles reveal that similar varieties of seafood can be cooked by similar methods and that an individual variety can be cooked in many different ways. This versatility makes seafood so appropriate for everyday cooking.

Some of the profiles group together related species of fish or shellfish. One profile, for example, discusses the various members of the cod family; another discusses drums, croakers, and other members of the same family, including weakfish (sea trout); still another groups together all the flatfish—several salmon, many trout, and so on—although they are not a family. If you have difficulty finding a particular variety of fish and shellfish, the index will direct you.

Each entry begins with the most common name of a fish, shellfish, or group of related varieties, followed by the scientific name; this is the surest means of identification, since it is the most consistent. Other names are also given, whether they are scientifically accurate or not, if they are commonly used by fishmongers.

Wherever possible, the profiles list statistical information relating to health—amounts of cholesterol in milligrams, omega-3 fatty acids and fat in grams per 100 grams (3½ ounces) raw seafood. Omega-3 fatty acids include only EPA (eicosapentaenoic acid) and DHA (docosahexaenoic acid) only. N/A indicates information is not available.

In addition, each profile designates the variety of seafood as low, moderate, or high in fat—low fat means less than 5 percent, moderate fat is between 5 and 10 percent, high fat is more than 10 percent.

Each profile notes the forms (other than whole) in which the fish or shellfish is usually found in the fish store, or the forms you can ask the fishmonger to prepare for you—fillets, steaks, split, pan-dressed, chunks. (See "Useful Terms You Will Need to Know," page 29).

Each profile also provides a description of the taste and texture of the fish or shellfish when cooked. Keep in mind that these descriptions are relative—I have described only some kinds of seafood as "mild," but in fact all seafood is mild-tasting when raw or cooked, although some varieties have more flavor than others. (If seafood tastes really strong, it is probably old and should be thrown away, although strong tastes can also come from curing with salt or salty brines.) I have also described some kinds of fish as "firm," not because they never flake, but because they do not flake as easily as other varieties. (All fish will eventually flake if overcooked.)

A description is given of each variety of fish or shellfish including its usual marketed size, its colors and availability, and where it can be found or caught. Seafood is available year-round from one body of water or another. Generally speaking, a number of kinds of fish become more available from south to north up the East Coast (to take an example) as the waters warm during spring and summer. Of course, seafood thrives in cold, temperate, and tropical waters.

For most of the profiled seafood varieties there is a table listing available forms or cuts, cooking methods for these cuts, and suggestions of how much to buy for how many people. Each profile ends with a choice of recommended recipes from Part II.

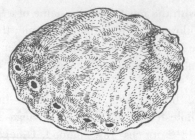

ABALONE

Genus Haliotis

Cholesterol 85 • Omega-3 .04 • Fat 0.8

Fat Content: low
Form Usually Prepared: slices
Taste: sweet and buttery
Texture: firm but melting

THE ABALONE IS A UNIVALVE. WE EAT THE FLESH THAT LIES INSIDE ITS SINGLE BEAUTIFUL SHELL. The shell is iridescent mother-of-pearl inside and the outside of it ranges in color from pink to red, green, or black. The flesh is much treasured because it is so delicious; it is unfortunately also hard to come by nowadays, which probably adds to its attraction.

Abalone are found in the Pacific Ocean off Alaska, California, Chile, and Southeast Asia. In the Pacific, not only has mankind overfished them, but the otters that populate the West Coast of the United States relish them. The supply of abalone is also suffering because supplies of the seaweeds upon which they live are dwindling.

A European abalone called the ormer is found off Jersey in the Channel Islands.

Baby abalone are farmed in Hawaii. They are also farmed by John Mc-Mullen at Ab Lab in Port Hueneme, California. These flavorful little morsels make a delightful appetizer. Save the shells—they are very decorative. Most recently, Alaskan waters have begun producing some varieties of abalone that are small but slightly larger than those farmed farther south. These have red shells and the flesh inside weighs about 4 ounces, enough for a main course.

Abalone are usually available at Japanese fish stores and at other specialty fish stores. They are usually sold in the shell at a set price per piece. They should be alive when you buy them. If there is some reaction when you touch the dark fringe and flesh in the shell of an abalone, then it is alive. The flesh of a commercially available abalone weighs from 1 to 8 ounces.

How to Shuck Abalone

• Push a wide wooden or metal spatula or a knife under the abalone flesh to detach it from the shell. Once the flesh is out of the shell, use a sharp knife to cut off the dark fringe that surrounds the flesh and scrape off any dark skin. Cut away the dark intestinal vein. Now you should have a nice piece of slightly off-white flesh.

You can eat abalone raw or cook it very briefly. To eat it raw, cut the flesh (downward if the abalone is large and horizontally if it is small) into very thin slices. To cook it, cut the flesh into slices ¼ inch thick and pound gently with a smooth-headed mallet—be careful not to pound too hard or you will tear the flesh. Or cut slices ⅛ inch thick and do not pound them. Fry them only for a few seconds. The flesh becomes unusually sweet and flavorful when cooked.

COOKING METHODS

CUT	COOKING METHODS	SUITABLE FOR	HOW MUCH TO BUY
Thin slices	Frying	1	4 ounces
Thin slices	Sushi and sashimi	1	4 ounces

CHOICE OF RECIPES

Fried Abalone *à la Meunière*, page 151
Sushi and Sashimi, page 219

ANCHOVY

Family Engraulidae

Canned or salted
Cholesterol 108 · Omega-3 2.0 · Fat 9.7
Fresh
Cholesterol N/A · Omega-3 1.4 · Fat 4.8

Fat Content: high (canned or salted anchovies); low (fresh anchovies)
Forms Usually Prepared: fillets (canned or salted); whole (fresh)
Taste: strong, salty (canned or salted); mild (fresh)
Texture: firm (canned or salted); flaky (fresh)

ANCHOVIES ARE HARVESTED WORLDWIDE. THOSE NATIVE TO THE UNITED STATES ARE FOUND IN both the Atlantic and the Pacific. There are many species, and most are caught too small to do anything with other than deep-fry whole, ungutted, as you would with whitebait. However, larger anchovies—like those from the Mediterranean and, on rare occasion, from U. S. waters—can be gutted (pull out the gills; see page 55 for instructions) and then grilled. They are delicious little silvery streamlined creatures. Those anchovies that are not sold fresh or canned are used for bait or made into fish meal.

Of course, we usually buy canned anchovies, either in oil or salted. By the way, anchovies are not naturally salty; the salt is part of the cure. Either people like these flavorsome fish or they don't, but they can be intriguing in many dishes and they are practically unrecognizable when cooked into a meat or game stew to deepen flavor. Be sure to tell people that the anchovies are there, for some dislike them intensely and others are allergic to them. They do well as a garnish for salade niçoise, with roasted red peppers, on top of a pizza, or in a cheese pie. Rinse canned salted anchovies before using.

Anchovies are also made into a paste, which is a handy way of using them in some dishes. Anchovy butter, a mixture of butter and ground-up canned or salted anchovies, is a great accompaniment to many fish—for example, sardines, or even milder lean white-fleshed fish such as red snapper. (See the recipe on page 236.)

COOKING METHODS

CUT	COOKING METHOD	SUITABLE FOR	HOW MUCH TO BUY
Whole	Grilling	1	¾ to 1 pound
Whole	Broiling	1	¾ to 1 pound
Whole	Deep-frying	1	6 to 8 ounces

CHOICE OF RECIPES

Broiled Whole Roundfish, page 125
Grilled Whole Fish or Shellfish, page 134
Deep-Fried Seafood, Variation I, page 160

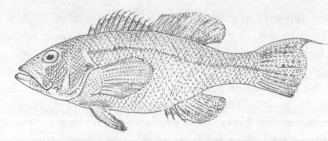

BASS, BLACK SEA

Family Serranidae, *Centropristis striata*

Cholesterol 55 • Omega-3 0.4 • Fat 2.0

Fat Content: low
Forms Usually Prepared: fillets, butter-
    flied, and split fish
Taste: mild
Texture: flaky

THE BLACK SEA BASS, WHICH IS OFTEN JUST CALLED THE SEA BASS, IS A MAGNIFICENT FISH. ITS
flesh is on a par with or very similar in excellence to that of red snapper and
striped bass. It is a wonderful-looking fish, black with light coloring under
each scale and beautiful articulated spiny fins, also black, striated with white
markings. It's one of my favorite fish. Black sea bass tastes sweet and its flesh
is firm, lean, and white.

The black sea bass is fished from the Atlantic from Maine down to Florida.
It usually weighs between 1 and 3 pounds when caught, but it does grow to 5
pounds. By the way, don't confuse the black sea bass with the blackfish, also
called the tautog or tog which is another species altogether (see page 267).

At the fish store, black sea bass are usually sold whole. Of course, you can
ask the fishmonger to fillet one for you or split it—that is, butterfly it—as
described on page 67. The beauty of this fish's skin is retained not only when

it is cooked whole, but also when it is cooked in filleted form with the skin showing.

Black sea bass can be prepared by many cooking methods.

COOKING METHODS

CUT	COOKING METHODS	SUITABLE FOR	HOW MUCH TO BUY
Whole	Roasting	4	3 pounds
Whole	Broiling or grilling	1 to 4	1 to 3 pounds
Whole, pan-dressed	Frying	1	¾ to 1 pound
Whole	Deep-frying	1	¾ to 1 pound
Whole	Poaching	1	1 pound
Fillets	As listed below	1	6 to 8 ounces
Butterflied or split	As listed below	1	8 to 10 ounces

CHOICE OF RECIPES

Baked Lean Fish Fillets, page 100
Bake-Poached Fish Fillets, page 101
Oven-Steamed Seafood *en Papillote*, page 105
Roast Whole Fish, page 115
Broiled Whole Roundfish, page 125
Broiled Fillets, Butterflied or Split Fish, Steaks, Escalopes, or Medallions, page 127
Grilled Whole Fish or Shellfish, page 134
Grilled Fish Fillets, Butterflied or Split Fish, Steaks, Medallions, or Shellfish, page 137
Fried Whole Fish or Pan-Dressed Fish, page 153
Fish Croquettes and Crab Cakes, page 154
Deep-Fried Seafood, Variation II, page 162
Poached Small Whole Fish or Fish Portions, page 170
Steamed Seafood, page 176
Fish Stock, page 187
Fish Soup (*Bourride*), page 188
Seafood Stew or Pasta Sauce, page 192
Fish Fillets with Spinach and Ginger, page 206
Seviche, page 211
Escabèche, page 213
Fish Salad I, page 221

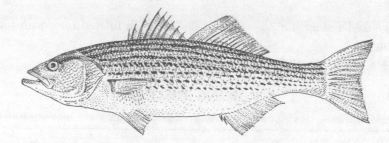

BASS, STRIPED

Family Percichthyidae, *Morone saxatilis*

Cholesterol 80 • Omega-3 0.8 • Fat 2.3

> *Fat Content:* low
> *Forms Usually Prepared:* fillets and steaks
> *Taste:* sweet
> *Texture:* firm

ALAS, THIS FISH FROM THE ATLANTIC COAST, ALSO CALLED THE STRIPER AND THE ROCKFISH DOWN Chesapeake Bay way, cannot be marketed at the time of this writing—at least not below Cape Cod—because of overfishing and pollution in the rivers where it is hatched before it migrates to the ocean. Sportsmen, however, are allowed to catch those fish that measure 36 inches and up. Striped bass have been successfully transplanted to the Pacific off California, where they are important in recreational fishery.

Some smart farmers are breeding a hybrid freshwater striped bass, which is some consolation. White bass or white perch (freshwater fish) have been interbred with striped bass to produce this hybrid (*M. chrysops* × *M. saxatilis* and *M. americanus* × *M. saxatilis*), which has excellent flesh—firm and sweet but a little bland in overall taste. It is incorrectly called white bass in the

Chesapeake area. In my opinion, this breed is just not the same and can't compare with the lovely striped bass that we used to eat from the Atlantic Ocean, which has such a fine yet firm texture and an exquisite taste. Treat the freshwater striped bass much like other bass, red snappers, or rockfish.

Whole striped bass, when available, grow up to 125 pounds, though they are usually caught at less than 50 pounds. Freshwater hybrid striped bass are only available at weights ranging from 1½ to 3 pounds, usually ungutted.

COOKING METHODS

CUT	COOKING METHODS	SUITABLE FOR	HOW MUCH TO BUY
Whole	Roasting	2 to 14	1½ to 9 pounds
Whole	Broiling or grilling	1 to 8	1 to 6 pounds
Whole (freshwater striped bass only)	Frying	1	1 pound
Chunks (wild striped bass only)	Roasting	2 to 8	1½ to 4 pounds
Fillets	As listed below	1	6 to 8 ounces
Steaks (wild striped bass only)	As listed below	1	6 to 8 ounces

CHOICE OF RECIPES

Baked Lean Fish Fillets, page 100
Bake-Poached Fish Fillets, page 101
Roast Whole Fish, page 115
Roast Stuffed Fish Chunk, page 118
Broiled Whole Roundfish, page 125
Broiled Fillets, Butterflied or Split Fish, Steaks, Escalopes, or Medallions, page 127
Grilled Whole Fish or Shellfish, page 134
Grilled Fish Fillets, Butterflied or Split Fish, Steaks, Medallions, or Shellfish, page 137
Fried Fish Fillets or Steaks *à la Meunière*, page 151
Fried Whole Fish or Pan-Dressed Fish, page 153
Fish Croquettes and Crab Cakes, page 154

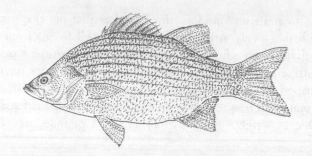

BASS, WHITE

Morone chrysops

Cholesterol 68 • Omega-3 0.6 • Fat 3.7

Fat Content: low
Form Usually Prepared: pan-dressed fish
Taste: mild
Texture: flaky

THIS FRESHWATER FISH COMES FROM THE LAKES, RESERVOIRS, RIVERS, AND ESTUARIES OF THE United States and Canada from the East Coast across to the Mississippi. It's a small fish but a good fighter and a favorite with sports fishermen. The flesh is white and firm and can be treated like black sea bass, striped bass, snapper, or rockfish. The fish is silvery and is marketed at weights from ½ pound to 1 or 2 pounds; it is essentially a pan fish.

There are numerous other freshwater fish called bass, such as the smallmouth, largemouth, redeye, rock, and spotted varieties. These are actually members of the sunfish family (see page 424). White sea bass from the Pacific, also called white bass and corbina (the Spanish name for the croaker), and channel bass from the Gulf of Mexico are members of the drum and croaker family (see page 311). Also see the discussion of sea bass of the grouper family (page 332).

COOKING METHODS

CUT	COOKING METHODS	SUITABLE FOR	HOW MUCH TO BUY
Whole pan-dressed	As listed below	1	¾ to 1 pound
Fillets	As listed below	1	6 to 8 ounces
Butterflied or split	As listed below	1	8 to 10 ounces

CHOICE OF RECIPES

Broiled Whole Roundfish, page 125
Broiled Fillets, Butterflied or Split Fish, Steaks, Escalopes, or Medallions, page 127
Grilled Whole Fish or Shellfish, page 134
Grilled Fish Fillets, Butterflied or Split Fish, Steaks, Medallions, or Shellfish, page 137
Fried Whole Fish or Pan-Dressed Fish, page 153

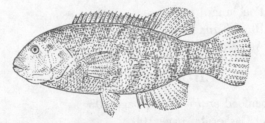

BLACKFISH

Tautoga onitis

Cholesterol N/A • Omega-3 N/A • Fat 0.2

Fat Content: low
Form Usually Prepared: fillets
Taste: mild
Texture: slightly firm

THE BLACKFISH IS A MEMBER OF THE WRASSE FAMILY (LABRIDAE). IT IS ALSO CALLED BY THE American Indian name *tautog* or just plain *tog*. This creature with mottled coloring has thick lips (the male has thicker lips than the female), a set of four long, very humanlike teeth in the front of its mouth, and more molars behind. With these teeth it eats its diet of crustaceans and mollusks.

Blackfish are caught in the Atlantic from Cape Cod down to the Carolinas and are available most of the year, although they are most plentiful during the summer. It is fun to catch them with hook and line around rocks.

The usual size of a blackfish is 2 to 5 pounds. Blackfish are sold whole and in filleted form. The flesh is white and firm but fairly bland, and it needs a flavorsome sauce or accompaniment such as a sweet red pepper sauce (see page 230) or one of the other sprightly mixtures to brighten its taste. The skin can be lifted off easily when serving. I like to poach blackfish whole with head and tail, to show off their blotchy skin and strange teeth.

COOKING METHODS

CUT	COOKING METHODS	SUITABLE FOR	HOW MUCH TO BUY
Whole	Poaching	6	5 pounds
Fillets	Blackening	1	8 to 10 ounces
Fillets	As listed below	1	6 to 8 ounces

CHOICE OF RECIPES

Oven-Steamed Seafood *en Papillote*, page 105
Baked Fish Fillet Casserole, page 108
Casserole of Fish Fillets with Potatoes and Coriander Pesto, page 113
Baked Cajun Fish Casserole, page 111
Broiled Fillets, Butterflied or Split Fish, Steaks, Escalopes, or Medallions, page 127
Grilled Whole Fish or Shellfish, page 134
Grilled Fish Fillets, Butterflied or Split Fish, Steaks, Medallions, or Shellfish, page 137
Fried Fish Fillets or Steaks *à la Meunière*, page 151
Fish Croquettes and Crab Cakes, page 154
Blackened Fish Fillets, page 156
Poached Whole Fish, page 169
Steamed Seafood, page 176

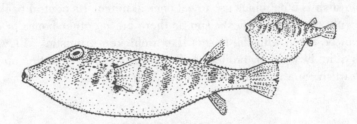

BLOWFISH

Spheroides maculatus

**Cholesterol 113 • Omega-3 N/A •
Fat (Cooked flesh) 0.7**

Fat Content: low
Form Usually Prepared: skinned tail
  pieces
Taste: sweet
Texture: flaky

BLOWFISH, ALSO KNOWN AS NORTHERN PUFFERS, PUFFERFISH, SEA SQUABS, SWELLFISH, SWELL toads, blow toads, and chicken of the sea, live in the waters along the eastern Atlantic coast. They are easy to catch in inshore waters, but they are not always available, for their appearance in these waters comes and goes. They are usually caught when they are 3 to 8 inches long.

Blowfish have white bellies and are brown on top (this color changes to yellow), and they have powerful teeth. They puff up their prickly skin when in danger. If you catch a blowfish yourself, handle it with rubber gloves. Cut off the head and turn the skin inside out to expose the flesh. Dispose of the guts and it is ready to cook; you do not need to fillet it. Under no circumstances should the skin, roe, or digestive system of a blowfish be eaten, because there is toxin in them. Blowfish are available in fish stores already skinned and ready to cook. (See page 78.)

The blowfish is a delicious fish to eat once skinned. Its central backbone is covered with sweet, moist flesh, and as there are no other bones to contend with it can be eaten with the fingers like a chicken drumstick. Blowfish are delicious quickly sautéed, broiled, grilled, or braised. Depending on the size of the blowfish, one person can eat up to 5 pieces.

COOKING METHOD

CUT	COOKING METHOD	SUITABLE FOR	HOW MUCH TO BUY
Whole, skinned, tail pieces	As listed below	1	6 to 8 ounces

CHOICE OF RECIPES

Broiled Fillets, Butterflied or Split Fish, Steaks, Escalopes, Medallions, page 127
Grilled Whole Fish or Shellfish, page 134
Sautéed Shrimp, Scallops, Soft-Shell Crabs, Squid, or Blowfish, page 155
Braised Fish Fillets or Steaks with Provençale Sauce, page 184

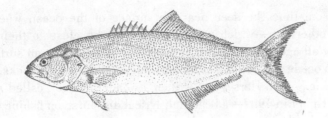

BLUEFISH

Pomatomus saltatrix

Cholesterol 60 • Omega-3 1.2 • Fat 6.5

> *Fat Content:* moderate
> *Forms Usually Prepared:* fillets and chunks
> *Taste:* mild
> *Texture:* soft and flaky

THESE FINE FISH ARE FAVORITES OF MINE, ESPECIALLY IN THE SUMMER. THEY ARE ATTRACTIVE-looking fish, with their silvery-blue skin and streamlined bodies, and they have rich and flavorful flesh. What a delight they are to cook and eat!

Bluefish are caught year-round along different parts of the western Atlantic Coast, from Cape Cod down to Florida, most notably between North Carolina and Massachusetts, where large and small ones appear in the late spring and summer as the waters grow warmer. Bluefish are also found in the eastern Atlantic, especially in the Mediterranean, off the coast of South Africa, as well as off the east coast of Australia.

Many of these fierce and lively fighting fish are caught by sports fishermen, who sell them to commercial markets or give them away to friends if they have caught more than they need—many friends have given me freshly caught bluefish during the summers on Long Island. Bluefish travel in large schools, and can sometimes be seen near the surface of the ocean when they are pursuing other fish—which may, incidentally, be close to their own size. Anglers of all ages have fun catching bluefish from the ocean surface as well as in deep ocean waters, in fast-running inlets, and even off docks, when they are "running." John Hersey has written a wonderful book called *Blues*, published by Knopf in 1987—a beautiful, lyrical discourse on fishing for bluefish in New England waters.

Bluefish are voracious eaters, and consequently they grow fast. They arc caught at weights up to 20 pounds, although they are usually sold weighing 1 to 10 pounds. Young bluefish weighing a pound or two are called snappers; when larger, they may be called choppers, or harbor blues. Snappers have lighter, sweeter flesh, probably because they are young.

Bluefish are sold whole or as skin-on fillets. They are very reasonable in price. Even more than most fish, they are at their most delicious when they are fresh. The flesh of bluefish is somewhat soft and perishable, so I eat only extremely fresh blues. Their flesh should look firm and translucent, and be a light blue-gray with a brownish tinge. They should be gutted as soon as possible to help forestall deterioration. I cannot stress this enough—amateur fishermen should be aware that this is the first consideration. A properly, promptly gutted bluefish is a wonderful gift—a carelessly treated one, a damn shame!

The bone structure of a bluefish is simple so the fish is easy to eat when cooked whole or filleted. It is easy to pull the pin bones out of a raw fillet of a small bluefish using pin-nose pliers; these bones can be cut out of a large bluefish.

Although the flesh of a large bluefish is quite dark and oily, it lightens up when it is cooked. It can take strong herbs, such as rosemary, in small quantities, and lemon or lime juice will counteract the oiliness of the flesh. Bluefish is excellent broiled, roasted, or baked. It can also be cooked over charcoal on an open grill.

Small bluefish are wonderful cooked over charcoal in an oiled, two-sided hinged grill, or pan-dressed and fried.

A fish salad made with bluefish is a breeze. The cooked flesh flakes easily and the addition of grated carrot, chopped cooked small red potatoes, lemon juice, dill, and other seasonings is all that is needed.

A note on health: Many people worry about eating bluefish because of reports that these fish may be contaminated with dangerous amounts of polychlorinated biphenyls (PCBs). Bluefish spawn at sea, where they are not likely to be affected by PCBs, but they are at the top of the food chain, and they eat other fish that may be affected by PCBs. Larger bluefish may absorb significant quantities of PCBs, but it is certainly fine to eat bluefish that weigh less than 6 pounds, and in fact there is no government health advisory against doing so. When toxic material is present in a bluefish, most of it collects in the dark red, fatty band that stretches along the lateral line on the side of the fish (this is also where the omega-3 fatty acids lie), and you can cut this muscle out if you want. As the benefits of eating fish outweigh the dangers—as heart disease kills more Americans than cancer and omega-3s do so much good—I don't believe there is any harm in eating bluefish a few times a year. It's a difficult debate.

COOKING METHODS

CUT	COOKING METHODS	SUITABLE FOR	HOW MUCH TO BUY
Whole	Roasting	Part of a buffet for 25	2 6-pound fish
Whole	Roasting	Dinner for 8	6 pounds
Whole	Grilling on an open fire	Dinner for 8	6 pounds
Whole	Bake-poaching	Dinner for 8	6 pounds
Chunks	Roasting	4	3 pounds
Whole snappers (small bluefish)	Grilling on an open fire	1	¾ to 1 pound fish
Fillets	Blackening	1	8 to 10 ounces
Fillets	As listed below	1	6 to 8 ounces

CHOICE OF RECIPES

Baked Fatty Fish Fillets, page 98
Bake-Poached Fish Fillets, page 101
Bake-Poached Whole Fish, page 102
Oven-Steamed Seafood *en Papillote*, page 105
Baked Fish Fillet Casserole with Light Tomato Sauce, page 109
Baked Cajun Fish Casserole, page 111
Roast Whole Fish, page 115
Roast Stuffed Fish Chunk, page 118
Broiled Whole Roundfish, page 125

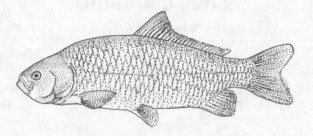

BUFFALOFISH

| SMALLMOUTH BUFFALOFISH | *Ictiobus bubalus* |
| BIGMOUTH BUFFALOFISH | *I. cyprinellus* |

Cholesterol N/A • Omega-3 N/A • Fat 16.6

> *Fat Content:* high
> *Form Usually Prepared:* fillets
> *Taste:* mild
> *Texture:* firm

SMALLMOUTH AND BIGMOUTH BUFFALOFISH, WHICH BELONG TO THE SUCKER FAMILY, LIVE IN fresh water. They are found in large lakes and rivers of North America. They have a slight hump where their shoulders are, which undoubtedly prompted someone to find a resemblance to a buffalo. The smallmouth has the more pronounced hump and is the preferred species of buffalofish.

Both buffalofish and incidentally carp look like large goldfish, although buffalofish are colored a dull gray to olive brown. Its internal structure is not quite as bony as the carp's, but it does have tiny, free-floating bones shaped like the letter Y in its upper part—its back—which are a nuisance. Learn to cut them out of the flesh if they are a bother to you. The scales are large, like those of the carp, and can be removed with the skin in one piece. To do this, insert a knife under the skin at the tail end of the fish and gradually loosen the skin from the flesh. The scales are embedded in the skin, and you can peel them off as a single armored sheet. This is a neat trick that I learned from my local fishmonger, Paul Diminio.

Buffalofish weigh 2 to 10 pounds when caught, although the bigmouth variety can grow to 50 pounds. Buffalofish are sold fresh or frozen whole. The fish are cheap; supply exceeds demand. The flesh is firm, sweet and pink, and turns white when cooked. It's very filling and has high fat content, so it lends itself well to being smoked.

COOKING METHOD

CUT	COOKING METHOD	SUITABLE FOR	HOW MUCH TO BUY
Fillets	As listed below	4	1½ to 2 pounds

CHOICE OF RECIPES

Baked Fatty Fish Fillets, page 98
Baked Fish Fillet Casserole with Light Tomato Sauce, page 109
Broiled Fillets, Butterflied or Split Fish, Steaks, Escalopes, or Medallions, page 127
Grilled Fish Fillets, Butterflied or Split Fish, Steaks, Medallions, or Shellfish, page 137

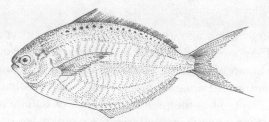

BUTTERFISH

Family Stromateidae, *Peprilus triacanthus*

Cholesterol 65 • Omega-3 N/A • Fat 8.0

HARVESTFISH

P. alepidotus

Cholesterol N/A • Omega-3 N/A • Fat N/A

> *Fat Content:* high
> *Forms Usually Prepared:* pan-dressed and split fish
> *Taste:* sweet
> *Texture:* flaky

BUTTERFISH ARE SMALL, ROUND FISH WITH COMPRESSED BODIES. THEY ARE SILVERY BLUE IN color. They are known also as dollarfish, as they are round, silver, and flat.

Butterfish are found in the Atlantic Ocean, from New York down to Florida. Most butterfish are between 4 and 9 inches long when caught and weigh a few ounces to half a pound.

Butterfish are ideal for smoking, as their flesh is oily. They are also delicious pan-dressed and then fried. Butterfish can also be broiled or grilled. Their gray flesh turns white when cooked.

In the summer in Montauk, Long Island, I have heard the fishermen say that a shortage of butterfish accounts for a shortage of tuna—butterfish are among the tuna's favorite foods, along with squid.

Harvestfish are sold as star butterfish at New York's Fulton Fish Market. They are similar, but are another species altogether.

COOKING METHOD

CUT	COOKING METHOD	SUITABLE FOR	HOW MUCH TO BUY
Whole pan-dressed	As listed below	1	8 to 10 ounces

CHOICE OF RECIPES

Broiled Whole Roundfish, page 125
Grilled Whole Fish or Shellfish, page 134
Fried Whole Fish or Pan-Dressed Fish, page 153
Hot-Smoking (Smoke-Cooking), page 197

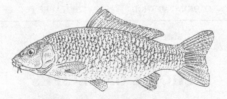

CARP

Cyprinus carpio

Cholesterol 69 · Omega-3 0.5 · Fat 5.6

> *Fat Content:* moderate
> *Form Usually Prepared:* fillets
> *Taste:* mild
> *Texture:* firm

CARP RESEMBLE LARGE GOLDFISH. THEY ARE GOLDEN TO BROWN IN COLOR AND HAVE LARGE scales. Carp are cultivated in ponds and reservoirs, and they also grow in rivers, streams, lakes, and swamps all over the United States. They have been known to live forty years or more, although most live twenty years if not caught before then.

The carp that are commercially available weigh up to 10 pounds. Their scales and skin, like those of buffalofish, can be peeled off in one piece (see page 275).

Carp can be cooked whole or filleted. As the carp is fatty, I remove the dark, fatty streak of flesh next to the skin along its lateral band before cooking it in filleted form. Since the flesh is very meaty, tough, and bony, a little goes a long way.

Carp are traditionally used to make gefilte fish, which is eaten at the seder at Passover time. The flesh is ground up which makes it less bony; long cooking softens the bones.

` COOKING METHOD

CUT	COOKING METHOD	SUITABLE FOR	HOW MUCH TO BUY
Fillets, steaks	As listed below	1	6 to 7 ounces

CHOICE OF RECIPES

Broiled Fillets, Butterflied or Split Fish, Steaks, Escalopes, or Medallions, page 127

Grilled Fish Fillets, Butterflied or Split Fish, Steaks, Medallions, or Shellfish, page 137

Braised Fish Fillets or Steaks with Provençale Sauce, page 184

Hot-Smoking (Smoke-Cooking), page 197

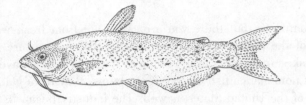

CATFISH

Family Ictaluridae

Freshwater
Cholesterol 52 • Omega-3 0.6 • Fat 4.4
Ocean
Cholesterol 58 • Omega-3 0.7 • Fat 2.9

Fat Content: low to moderate
Forms Usually Prepared: fillets, steaks,
   and nuggets
Taste: sweet
Texture: firm

IF SOME HOLD THAT *CATFISH* IS AN UNBECOMING NAME, THE NAME DOES SUIT, FOR THESE FISH have streamlined bodies and "whiskers" (barbels) around their mouths. I don't think they are ugly, and I like the fine, firm texture of their flesh.

There are twenty-five hundred species of catfish in the world, and I will list some of them here.

Brown bullhead *Ictalurus nebulosus*
White catfish *I. catus*
Channel catfish *I. punctatus*
Flathead catfish *Pylodictus olivaris*
Gafftopsail catfish *Bagne marinus*
Hardhead catfish *Arius felis*

All very confusing, but there you are. Most are from fresh water, with the exception of the gafftopsail and hardhead catfish, which are from the sea.

Catfish taken from rivers in the southern states have been favorites for many a year, but now that catfish are raised on farms, they have gained popularity in the rest of the United States as well. The industry began in 1965 and has grown enormously since 1974. Mississippi produces the most farm-raised catfish; other farms are in Arkansas, Alabama, Louisiana, Georgia, Idaho, California, North Carolina, and South Carolina. Up to five thousand pounds of fish can be produced from a one-acre pond and the fish are now available all year round. Farm-raised catfish are excellent—no more can we complain of a muddy taste, for they are farmed in fresh water in large ponds on flat land that holds groundwater well. The flesh of farm-raised catfish is pure white and the taste is sweet. They are high in protein and low in calories, fat, and cholesterol.

Catfish weigh 1½ pounds and up. Most commonly, they are skinned and their heads are removed. Much catfish flesh is filleted and sold fresh or frozen. Fillets usually weigh between 5 and 20 ounces, in my experience. Catfish fillets are also smoked. Catfish can also be bought as steaks or as diagonally cut strips of flesh called nuggets. Farm-raised catfish are processed right after they are taken from the pond, so we generally do not have the bother of skinning or filleting them ourselves.

Catfish are often deep-fried with a coating of cornmeal and served with a piquant or spicy sauce, but they can be cooked by various other methods—in fact, I can't think of any cooking method that does not suit them, except roasting whole. The firm, sweet flesh is conducive to strong flavorings as well as mild ones. I like to bake them in a casserole dish, where the fillets, or sliced fillets, retain their shape beautifully. The firmness of the flesh is a great feature and lends itself nicely to this method of cooking.

COOKING METHODS

CUT	COOKING METHODS	SUITABLE FOR	HOW MUCH TO BUY
Whole, head-off, skinned	Deep-frying	1	12 ounces
Fillets	Blackening	1	8 to 10 ounces
Fillets	As listed below	1	6 to 8 ounces

CHOICE OF RECIPES

CLAMS

Fat Content: low
Form Usually Prepared: in
    shell
Taste: sweet and slightly salty
Texture: soft

CLAMS, CLAMS, CLAMS. THERE ARE SO MANY DELICIOUS SPECIES OF CLAMS. THESE BIVALVE (double-shelled) mollusks are found in both the shallow and deep cool waters of the Atlantic and Pacific. They live a pretty stationary life in the sand or mud on the floor of the ocean. Quahogs (hard-shell clams), some razor clams, and soft-shell clams are from the Atlantic, while butter, Manila, common Pacific littleneck, geoduck, and other razor clams are found in the Pacific.

Many clams are found in shallow sandy bays or freshwater inlets, and it is fun to collect them (but watch out for razor clams—they can cut your toes). Large Atlantic surf or bar clams are dredged up commercially from deeper waters.

Hard-shell clams are sold by the dozen. Other clams are sold by the pound. All clams must be alive when you buy them. Make sure that the shells are tightly closed, except for soft-shell, razor, and geoduck clams, which gape naturally. If hard-shell clams do gape a little, give them a good knock, and if they close, all is well, they are alive. As with all bivalves, you must be sure they are fished from clean waters. Here you have to trust your fishmonger. If you collect your own, check for local laws that set limits on your take and make sure that the water is considered clean by the local office of the Environmental Protection Agency, or by local health authorities.

QUAHOGS (HARD-SHELL CLAMS)   *Mercenaria mercenaria*

Cholesterol 34 · Omega-3 0.24 · Fat 1.0

The smallest of the hard-shell quahog clams are the little-necked clams. They have hard off-white shells with striations (fine ridges) encircling them. You must scrub and rinse these and other clams to rid them of sand. These clams are delicious eaten raw, but they can be briefly sautéed until their shell opens or put, at the last moment, into a fish soup or even a paella. They will toughen if they are cooked too long. It's best to eat them as soon as their shells open.

Cherrystones are the next-largest hard-shell clams. They are also delicious eaten raw or chopped for chowders.

As quahog clams grow larger they are called chowder clams. Their flesh gets tougher and needs to be ground or chopped and then cooked.

Ocean quahogs (Arctica islandica), also called mahogany or black clams, are large clams, up to 4 inches wide. These clams are used to make chowder and may also be called chowder clams. They are also minced and canned.

Atlantic surf clams (*Spisula solidissima*) also called bar or sea clams are even larger—4 to 7 inches wide. They are usually cut into strips and fried—Howard Johnson restaurants couldn't exist without them!

SOFT-SHELL CLAMS *Mya arenaria*

Cholesterol 25 • Omega-3 0.24 • Fat 1.2

Soft-shell clams—also called steamers, softs, gapers, squirts, or even "pissers"!—have soft shells, that is, shells that are brittle and break easily. A soft-shell clam's shell never closes completely because the neck or siphon sticks out. Steam soft-shell clams open and serve them with broth and melted butter, or dip them in a batter and deep-fry them.

These clams are nirvana for me, and you must know that I hunt up and down the highways for the stand or small restaurant serving the best fried clam rolls whenever I visit Long Island or Cape Cod, where these rolls are popular. They have to be coated with a light batter and must be supercrisp. I specify that I want bellies, not just fried strips—the bellies burst with sweet flavor in my mouth.

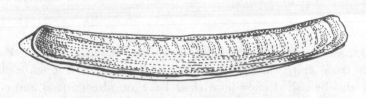

RAZOR CLAMS   Family Solenidae

Cholesterol 107 • Omega-3 0.26 • Fat 1.5

The Atlantic and Pacific razor clams are shaped like lozenges, up to 6 inches long. Other species such as the common razor (from the Atlantic) and the jackknife clams (from the Atlantic and Pacific) look like the old-fashioned strap razors and grow as long as 10 inches. They have sweet flesh and can be prepared in the same way as soft-shell clams. In some markets they may be sold by the pound already shucked.

MANILA CLAMS   *Tapes phillippinarium*

Manila clams, which are native to the western Pacific but are now also found in the Pacific off British Columbia, are wonderful little mollusks that are best cooked, in my opinion. They need only be sautéed with a little oil, garlic, fresh herbs, and wine for a few minutes until they open. You can make a great pasta sauce with them or add them to fish soups such as the *Bourride* on page 188. The Manila clam is thin-shelled, but not as brittle as a soft-shell clam, and is light to dark brown with striations that extend from its hinged part of the clam to the edges of its shells. Manila clams are small and round, about 1¼ to 1½ inches in diameter.

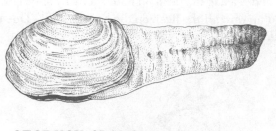

GEODUCK CLAMS   *Panopea generosa*

Geoduck clams, large relatives of soft-shell clams, weigh 1 pound or more. They are harvested from the Pacific Northwest. The geoduck clam has a very long siphon or neck that protrudes at great length from the shell, and it is lewd-looking to say the least! Lewd-looking or not, it has the most delicious, sweet, rich flesh inside. We eat the peeled neck and the strip of flesh that runs around the belly. Japanese fish stores sell the geoduck already prepared. Eat it raw or cooked, but cook it ever so briefly, otherwise it will toughen.

How to Shuck Clams

• Before eating clams, whether raw or cooked, scrub them under cold running water with a scrub brush and put them in a bowl of cold water for 20 to 30 minutes where they can rid themselves of any sand they may have in their bodies. Don't soak them any longer than that, for fresh water will eventually kill them.

• As you shuck clams, work over a clean empty bowl that has a fine sieve or cheesecloth in it, so you can catch the juice and free it of sand or pieces of shell. Pick up each clam and put it in your left hand (your right if you are left-handed) with the hinged thick part of the clam in your palm near your thumb. Take a clam knife that has a blunt tip or a thin paring knife and insert it where you can easily see the division between the shells. If it is difficult or even impossible to insert the knife, you can resort to putting the clam in the freezer (for ½ hour) until it gives up and opens its shells a little, or try twirling the clam on a board—to make it dizzy and give up resistance! When your knife is between the shells, don't let it go in too far, because you might cut the clam in half inadvertently. Using just the tip of the knife, slide it up close to the inside of the shells so that you cut the two muscles holding the shell together. Open the clam and release the flesh on both shells by sliding your knife under it—you will end up with all the flesh on the bottom shell. This is called a clam *on the half shell*.

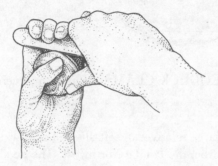

• If you are serving clams raw, pull the top shell of each clam off and display the flesh on the lower shell. Pour some of the strained juice you have collected on the flesh. Serve with lemon wedges.

• Always save the clam juice—it helps to flavor soups and chowders. You can freeze it if you like. When you are going to cook clams for a chowder or a sauce, you can put them in a hot oven for a few minutes until they open, or steam them open using very little water.

How to Prepare Geoduck Clams

• Loosen the flesh from its shell with a thin knife and put the whole creature in a bowl of hot water for five minutes. Then rinse it in cold water. Peel off the skin from the siphon and the strip surrounding the belly. Discard the belly. You are left with the siphon and the strip that was around the belly.

• Cut the siphon away from the strip and trim off the tip. Cut the siphon

lengthwise but not all the way through. You will see that the siphon is hollow like a pipe. Spread it open and cut it into very thin slices on the horizontal. Cut across the slices every 1¼ inches and you will have little butterfly shapes.
• You can tenderize geoduck clams by pounding them very gently with a smooth mallet, or, as the Japanese do by making very fine incisions in the flesh.

COOKING METHODS

FORM	COOKING METHODS	SUITABLE FOR	HOW MUCH TO BUY
Little-neck or cherrystone clams	On the half shell	1	6 to 9
Same	Soup	1	2
Same and razor	Chowder	6	2 cups shucked (20 to 30)
Soft-shell	Deep-frying	1	¾ to 1 pound
Soft-shell	Steam	1	¾ to 1 pound
Geoduck sliced	Frying	1	4 ounces
Geoduck chopped	Chowder	6	2 cups (2 pounds)
Geoduck sliced	Raw	1	4 ounces
Manila	Frying	1	6 to 8 ounces

CHOICE OF RECIPES

Clams or Mussels Steamed in Aluminum Foil on the Grill or in the Oven, page 146

Fried Goeduck Clam Slices *à la Meunière*, page 151

Deep-Fried Seafood: Variation III, page 162

Steamed Mussels or Soft-Shell Clams *Marinière*, page 178

Fish Soup (*Bourride*), page 188

Creamy Seafood Chowder, page 190

Seafood Stew or Pasta Sauce, page 192

Seafood Stew with Tomato and Green Pepper, page 203

Seviche, page 211

Sushi and Sashimi, page 219

Also: Littlenecks or cherrystones on the half shell (serves 6 to 9 per person)

COD

Family Gadidae

> *Fat Content:* low
> *Forms Usually Prepared:* fillets and steaks
> *Taste:* mild
> *Texture:* flaky

THE COD FAMILY INCLUDES ATLANTIC AND PACIFIC COD, HADDOCK, WHITE HAKE, RED HAKE (ling), European whiting, pollock, Atlantic pollock, and cusk.

Cod and its family are lean, white-fleshed creatures that are marvelous for our health; the flesh is low in fat and calories and high in protein. Although similar to each other in many ways, there are differences within the cod family as you will find out by reading the following profile.

Cod can be deep-fried, broiled, baked in a casserole or in a baking pan, bake-poached, steamed, braised and stewed, used in a salad, or made into croquettes (fish cakes), just to name a few methods of preparation.

Fillets from larger fish have firmer flesh with large flakes. The smaller fish produce softer, flakier flesh. For this reason cod cannot be grilled with much success.

ATLANTIC COD   *Gadus morhua*

Cholesterol 42 • Omega-3 0.2 • Fat 0.7

Cod has made men rich on both sides of the northern Atlantic, and indeed there is nothing to compare with its pearly white flesh, which is lean, sweet, flaky, and delicious. Hardy fishermen battle the North Atlantic in all weathers to catch these cold-water fish.

William Warner, in his book *Distant Water* (Atlantic Monthly, Little, Brown and Company, 1977), describes the start of a week of cod fishing on the trawler *Tremont* out of Boston:

> After supper the breeze stiffens and a quarter moon, waxing, hangs halfway up the night sky. Cables sway and the net gear shifts and clanks, tugging at stop lines, on the spray-swept steel of the main deck. To the south the distant flashes of Cape Cod lighthouses are easily seen on the horizon. Race Point, Highland, Nauset Beach—each conjures up its full share of summer memories. But the *Tremont* is hurrying along at twelve knots, pushed by quartering seas, and the lights fall off fast to starboard. Soon they are no more than smudged and irregular twinkles, frequently obscured by heaving seas. A pyramidal wave rises up in the dark, showing a large white crest, and slams hard against the *Tremont*'s side. Water explodes through the crack of a hinged scupper and hisses across the deck. It is reminder enough. We are going somewhere else. And summer is over.

Huge amounts of Atlantic cod are caught off Georges Bank (United States and Canadian fishing territory) and the Grand Banks (Canadian territory), sand formations on the continental shelf teeming with fish. Most of this cod is gutted at sea, then iced down and landed fresh. Much of it is then frozen in the Northeast before being sent off to the rest of the country.

The Atlantic cod lives close to the bottom of the ocean. It has olive-green to gray skin that changes to white at the belly. It has a whitish lateral line from its head to its tail and a hooked barbel (a fleshy, whiskerlike protuberance) under its jaw. Its belly is large; when emptied of the guts, the belly leaves a large hollow. There is little flesh covering the rib bones, except on a heavy fish.

Codfish up to 200 pounds have been caught, but the average cod taken weighs 10 pounds or less. The names *scrod* and *schrod* used to refer to codfish and other members of the same family weighing less than 3½ pounds. Nowadays the terms are used rather loosely for any size cod or any member of the same family.

In the fish trade, the name *market cod* refers to cod with head and tail on, and *steak cod* is the name used when the head of the cod is cut off. You seldom see a whole codfish in the store, because so much is processed and filleted before it reaches us. Boneless filleted cod is, after all, the way most cod lovers like their fish.

Cod fillets and steaks are sold fresh or frozen. I don't care for the frozen fillets or steaks because they exude an unnecessary amount of moisture as they defrost and they tend to dry out when cooked. Let's hope we get to see whole fish and fresh, not frozen, fillets more often.

Salt cod, popular in regions around the world as diverse as the warm Caribbean, the Mediterranean countries, and the cold countries of Scandinavia, is nowadays mostly produced by Canada, Iceland, Spain, and Norway and exported across the world. It is called, variously, *bacalhau* in Portugal, *baccalà* in Italy, *morue* (*seche*) in France, and *bacalao* in Spain and the West Indies.

Many other fish of the cod family are salted and dried and may also be called salt cod. The actual name of the fish that has been salted, such as pollock, cusk, or haddock, should be on the package.

Salt cod can be prepared in different ways: Some are dried on the bone, and some are prepared boneless and skinless. Some are salted down and partially dried, so they come to us in a somewhat moist condition. Another preparation entails salting it and then drying it out until it becomes hard as wood and sometimes has to be cut with a saw. The Norwegians use this method.

Stockfish (*stoccafisso* in Italy) is a similar product, but it is not salt cod. Stockfish is preserved by drying—no salt is used.

How to Prepare Salt Cold for Cooking

• All salt cod must be soaked, for a number of hours or overnight, in running water or several changes of water so that it loses its salt and its flesh is reconstituted. The length of time will depend on the method by which the cod was salted and dried. Obviously, the drier the cod, the longer it takes to rehydrate it. When buying salt cod, you can judge for yourself if it will need a long soaking time: Very dry fish will require longer soaking than moist fish.
• When the flesh is soft, put it in a saucepan of cold water. Bring it to the boil, lower the heat, and simmer it for 10 minutes, or until tender. Strain. Cut it

into slices or flake it according to the recipe you are using. The saltiness of the cod is usually washed away during the rinsing period and you may find that you have to add salt to your dish—but be sure to taste it before adding salt.

Salt cod can be used to make a delicious variety of dishes, such as those listed on page 295.

Cod is often smoked instead of haddock to make finnan haddie. It's good either way.

Cod roe is edible—it can be delicious fried—but it is more popular in Europe than in North America. It is sold both canned and fresh. Cod roe is also smoked, and it can be used successfully to make the lovely Greek spread or dip called taramasalata.

If you can find cod cheeks, buy them, for they are wonderful small morsels of tender flesh, which can be quickly sautéed and served with brown butter.

PACIFIC COD   *Gadus macrocephalus*

Cholesterol 37 · Omega-3 0.2 · Fat 0.6

This cod is also known as the gray cod because of its coloration, although it is colored brown to gray. It is also called the true cod to distinguish it from the lingcod, rock cod, and black cod, which are also from the Pacific, and are not of the cod family at all.

It is caught in the Pacific from Oregon to Alaska and can weigh up to 10 pounds.

It is sold whole and in filleted form, and its flesh is similar to that of Atlantic cod. Cook this fish as you would the Atlantic cod.

HADDOCK   *Melanogrammus aeglefinus*

Cholesterol 57 · Omega-3 0.18 · Fat 0.7

Haddock is found in much the same waters as Atlantic cod. Its skin is gray to purplish gray. It has a thin, black lateral stripe along its body with a dark smudge behind the pectoral fin. Its body is more streamlined than the cod's;

its flesh is so similar to the cod's that all the cod recipes listed on page 294 can be prepared with haddock. It appears in the fish store in cuts similar to those used for cod, but it commands a higher price.

Haddock smokes well. Smoked haddock is called finnan haddie, after a town called Findon in Scotland, where very good smoked haddock is produced. The flavor of smoked haddock on the bone is definitely superior to that of smoked haddock fillets, but the former is not always available.

WHITE HAKE   *Urophycis tenuis*

Cholesterol 39 • Omega-3 0.22 • Fat 0.5

White hake, also called hake, is caught at weights up to 50 pounds from Newfoundland down to North Carolina. Its flesh is white and it is usually sold filleted. Often there is a line of beige muscle running along the center and sides of a white hake fillet. This fish has a large stomach cavity and therefore a fairly low yield of flesh. Nearly all white hake is landed dressed so the consumer doesn't have to worry about yield. It is sometimes sold as cod or scrod. Don't confuse it with the European hake, page 334.

RED HAKE   *U. chuss*

The red hake is also called the squirrel hake and the ling. It is smaller than the white hake, growing to only about 3 pounds. It is caught off the coasts of New England, Canada, and the mid-Atlantic region. In the mid-Atlantic states it is sold whole and dressed. It is also salted or canned. Not to be confused with the European hake, page 334 or lingcod page 339.

EUROPEAN WHITING   *Merlangius merlangus*

Fished in great quantities from northern European waters and the Mediterranean, this is a popular fish in Europe. The whiting found in American waters is profiled on page 334.

ATLANTIC POLLOCK   *Pollachius virens*

Cholesterol 58 • Omega-3 0.37 • Fat 0.9

The Atlantic pollock, also known incorrectly as the Boston bluefish and the blue cod in the United States and as the saithe and the coley in England, is a fine fish that resembles cod (its skin is darker, without the light spots) but is sold at half the price, probably because the flesh is gray-pink before it is cooked. The flesh does turn white when cooked, and it has a mild flavor. The average Atlantic pollock sold is between 4 and 8 pounds. These fish are taken from the northern Atlantic in great quantities.

The Atlantic pollock should not be confused with the walleye pollock (*Theragra chalcogramma*), which is caught in huge quantities in the Bering Sea and the Gulf of Alaska. The walleye pollock is smaller and has white flesh. Much is frozen at sea and then reprocessed to make surimi, which, with the addition of flavorings, is made to resemble crab, scallops, shrimp, and even lobster. I can't say I like the taste of surimi, for processors add sugar and monosodium glutamate to it.

Atlantic Pollock is sold whole, in chunks, in fillets, and occasionally in steak form. It is often frozen. I used to feed my gorgeous Persian cat this fish in England, but now the fish is better appreciated—the price is up and it can only be considered food for a rich cat! It can be baked, fried, broiled, grilled, and stuffed and roasted. It is often salted down like salt cod, and it is good smoked.

CUSK   *Brosme brosme*

Cholesterol 41 • Omega-3 N/A • Fat 0.7

Cusk, important to the Maine fishing industry, is sold mainly in New England. It is available year-round and has white flesh, reminiscent of cod. The fish has one dorsal fin and one anal fin; they stretch all the way down to its tail in one continuous line.

Cusk is sold in filleted form and can be cooked like cod.

COOKING METHODS

CUT	COOKING METHODS	SUITABLE FOR	HOW MUCH TO BUY
Cod			
Whole	Roasting	6 to 8	6 pounds
Chunks	Roasting	4 to 5	2 pounds
Fillets and steaks	As listed below	1	2 to 8 ounces
Red hake and whiting			
Whole	Roasting	1	¾ to 1 pound
Whole	Grilling	1	¾ to 1 pound
Whole	Deep-frying	1	¾ to 1 pound
Whole	Sousing	1	¾ to 1 pound
Fillets and steaks	As listed below	1	2 to 8 ounces

CHOICE OF RECIPES

Cod

Baked Lean Fish Fillets, page 100
Bake-Poached Fish Fillets, page 101
Oven-Steamed Seafood *en Papillote*, page 105
Baked Fish Fillet Casserole, page 108
Baked Fish Fillet Casserole with Light Tomato Sauce, page 109
Casserole of Fish Fillets with Potatoes and Coriander Pesto, page 112
Roast Whole Fish, page 115
Roast Stuffed Fish Chunk, page 118
Broiled Fillets, Butterflied or Split Fish, Steaks, Escalopes, or Medallions, page 127
Grilled Fish Fillets, Butterflied or Split Fish, Steaks, Medallions, or Shellfish, page 137
Fish Fillets Steamed in Aluminum Foil on the Grill, page 144
Fried Fish Fillets or Steaks *à la Meunière*, page 151
Fish Croquettes and Crab Cakes, page 154
Deep-Fried Seafood: Variation I, page 160
Steamed Seafood, page 176
Braised Fish Fillets or Steaks with Provençale Sauce, page 183
Fish Stock, page 187

Fish Soup (*Bourride*), page 188
Creamy Seafood Chowder, page 190
Seafood Stew or Pasta Sauce, page 192
Hot-Smoking (Smoke Cooking), page 197
Fish Fillets with Spinach and Ginger, page 206
Escabèche, page 213
Marinade, page 216
Fish Salad I, page 221

All the above recipes can also be prepared using other members of the cod family, including European Hake, except smaller members such as the red hake (ling) and European whiting (recipes suitable for these fish are listed below).

Salt Cod

Fish Croquettes and Crab Cakes, page 154
Fritters, page 164
Braised Fish Fillets or Steaks with Provençale Sauce, page 184
Creamy Seafood Chowder, page 190
Seviche, page 211
Escabèche, page 213
Fish Salad I, page 221

Red Hake (Ling), European Whiting, and American Whiting

Bake-Poached Fish Fillets, page 101
Roast Whole Fish, page 115
Grilled Whole Fish or Shellfish, page 134
Grilled Fish Fillets, Butterflied or Split Fish, Steaks, Medallions, or Shellfish, page 137
Deep-Fried Seafood: Variation II, page 162
Fish Stock, page 187
Soused or Marinated Fish, page 215

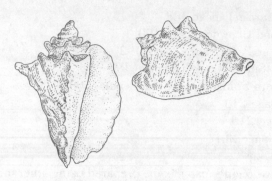

CONCHS

Family Strombidae

WHELKS

Genus Buscyon

Cholesterol 65 • Omega-3 N/A • Fat 0.4

Fat Content: low
Form Usually Prepared: shucked
Taste: smoky
Texture: firm

THE CONCH (PRONOUNCED "CONK" OR "CONCH") IS FOUND IN THE WARM WATERS OFF THE FLOR-ida Keys and in the Caribbean. Queen conch (*strombus gigas*) is the best known in the United States. The pretty single shell of this mollusk is shaped a bit like that of a snail, with a pointed, striated turret or crown at one end. The shell is thick and the flesh spirals up into the turret. Once extracted from the shell, the flesh is a delight to eat raw with lime juice. Getting the flesh out without giving into an urge to break the whole shell to pieces on the nearest rock is tricky.

Knobbed and channeled whelks, often called conch or scungilli (from the Italian word for "conch"), are similar in shape and are found down the East Coast from Rhode Island to the Gulf of Mexico. Whelks consume other shell-fish and fish. The whelk manages to break open the shells of oysters, clams, and mussels with its knobbed turret and extract the flesh with its "tongue." Conch are herbivorous.

Conch and whelks have fascinating sweet flesh with a slightly smoky taste; the flesh is smooth and chewy when cut. You can slice the flesh and pound it to tenderize it, or cook it whole. Be sure a conch or whelk is alive if you want to eat it raw: Tap the operculum (a thin hard covering at the opening) and if there is some movement or response, the creature is alive. Before you eat a conch or whelk raw, the flesh must be shaved into very thin slices. You can tenderize these thin slices by making very fine incisions in the flesh or by pounding it lightly. The queen conch is better than the whelk for eating raw.

Conch and whelks are sold by the piece when alive in their shells. Conch meat is often sold frozen. Whelk meat is usually partially or fully cooked and then frozen. This meat is not like the fresh article, but is perfectly fine for making fritters or stews. Conch and whelk meat—cooked or raw, fresh or frozen—is sold by the pound.

Scungilli marinara, a fine southern Italian dish much appreciated in the United States as well, is made with conch or whelk.

How to Extract the Flesh from a Conch or Whelk Shell

Method 1

• It is easier to extract the meat from a conch or whelk shell after dunking it in boiling water for a minute or two. When its muscles relax, pull on the flesh from the opening and extract it.

Method 2

• The flesh of a conch or whelk is attached to a spiral column inside the pointed, conical spire at the top or turret, and it is necessary to detach this muscle to extract the flesh. Make a hole in the turret about one inch from the top. Insert a sharp, pointed knife in the hole and scrape the muscle free. Put the tip of the knife under the operculum (the thin hard covering) at the opening of the shell and pull the flesh out. Cut off the operculum and the long, tough pointed appendage (its tongue). Clean off the intestines and peel off any tough skin, especially if you will be eating the conch or whelk raw.

• If you are going to cook the conch or whelks whole, put the extracted flesh in boiling water without cleaning off the intestines and cook it in lightly salted boiling water until tender. Remove the intestines and skin the flesh before using it.

COOKING METHOD

FORM	COOKING METHOD	SUITABLE FOR	HOW MUCH TO BUY
Out of shell	As listed below	1	6 to 8 ounces

CHOICE OF RECIPES

Grilled Fish Fillets, Butterflied or Split Fish, Steaks, Medallions, or Shellfish, page 137
Fritters, page 164
Creamy Seafood Chowder, page 190
Seafood Stew or Pasta Sauce, page 192
Seviche, page 211

CRABS

Fat Content: low
Forms Usually Prepared: various
Taste: sweet
Texture: flaky

AS ANYONE WHO FREQUENTS THE SHORES OF THIS COUNTRY KNOWS, MANY SPECIES OF CRAB ARE available in shallow waters, bays, and estuaries. These feisty creatures, which may tickle your toes or even nip you with their meaty claws, are most delicious to eat. Other notable crabs are found in very deep waters.

West Coast people think the Dungeness crab is the best, East Coast and Gulf people love their blue crabs and stone crab claws, and I like them all, for their different qualities are wonderful. Dungeness and blue crabmeat are mild, sweet, and so tender. Stone crab claw meat tastes like lobster and crabmeat all at once. Picked crabmeat can be made into all sorts of delicious hot or cold preparations, such as crab cakes, deviled crab, and crab salads.

On the East Coast you can buy live hard- and soft-shell blue crabs. Some fish stores in the East also have live Dungeness crabs from the Pacific in tanks; these crabs are also sold cooked and frozen in the East. On the West Coast you can buy live Dungeness crabs and, sometimes, live snow crabs kept in tanks. Some live hard- and soft-shell blue crabs can survive the journey from the East Coast and may be for sale in the West. Packaged, picked-cooked blue crabmeat travels well also, either pasteurized or frozen.

Snow and king crab legs are available on the West Coast cooked and frozen; their sweet meat makes a delicious treat. On the East Coast cooked legs and shoulders of Atlantic and Pacific snow crabs are available, as well as legs and claws of northern Pacific king crabs. Also available in the East are cooked blue crab claws, as well as cooked claws from stone crabs, which are taken from Florida waters and the Gulf of Mexico.

On both coasts fresh or frozen crabmeat picked from cooked crabs is sold in different grades. (See page 33 for details.) Cooked crabmeat is picked over for cartilage before it is sold, but it is worth picking it over again when you get it home, because it is not pleasant to find bits of shell in your mouth.

When alive, crabs have various colorings, including green, brown, red, and blue, but they turn orange-red when cooked.

BLUE CRAB   *Callinectes sapidus*

Cholesterol 78 • Omega-3 0.32 • Fat 1.0

Blue crabs are found along the Atlantic Coast from Cape Cod down the eastern seaboard into the Gulf of Mexico, with a large concentration in the

Chesapeake and Delaware Bay areas off Maryland and Virginia. A wonderful book called *Beautiful Swimmers* by William Warner, to whom I am beholden for a lot of information, tells in a delightful way much more about these crabs than I can cover here.

The blue crab has a green-brown body with blue claws and a shell measuring 5 to 9 inches across. The female can be distinguished by her orange-red–tipped claws. When cooked the crabs turn orange-red all over. The immature female, called a *she-crab*, has a V-shaped tail (apron) on the underside of her body; after her last molt, when she is ready for mating, her apron becomes round with a tiny V shape on the top, and then she is a mature *sook*. The male crab, called a *jimmy*, has a very small apron. Live blue crabs are steamed or boiled. Chesapeake people choose to eat jimmies, for they contain a slightly higher yield of flesh than the females. They usually cost more. New Yorkers choose to buy the females with their pretty orange-red–tipped claws.

In the summer blue crabs are fairly easy to catch. Even young children can have the fun of baiting up some string with a piece of chicken or fish, for instance, and pulling in a blue crab. As soon as you know you have a crab on

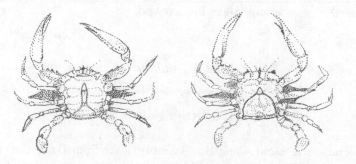

the bait, use a net to get it into a tall container—crabs can pinch and come out fighting, seemingly all claws. As a rule blue crabs are trapped in pots baited with bits of fish such as menhaden, or with trotlines (lines stretched two thousand feet or so between buoys), from shallow saline estuarine water during the summer months in the Chesapeake Bay area. In the winter they are dredged from this area; in the Gulf of Mexico they can be trapped all year round.

An acquaintance of mine who lives in Washington, D.C., and goes crabbing on weekends tells me that he usually uses eel as bait on his trotline. However, when eel gets too expensive he alternates it with pieces of cow or ox lips—he says he is tempting the crabs with "surf and turf"!

Live blue crabs are sold by the dozen or by the piece. They stay alive in bushel baskets for up to five days.

The soft-shell blue crab season, happily, is nice and long; from about May 15 to September 15. Soft-shell crabs are best sautéed, broiled, or grilled. A soft-shell blue crab is a hard-shell blue crab that is caught within 6 hours after it has shed its hard outer shell. All crabs do this periodically so that they can grow larger. During the season, "peelers" ready to shed their shells are sold to soft-shell crab producers who keep them in pens, pick them out as they molt, and sell them at fish markets. (Crayfish and lobsters also shed their hard shells periodically.)

Soft-shell blue crabs are graded and priced according to size. (See page 33 for details.) They are packed with seaweed or straw in flat boxes where they stay alive for three to four days. Many are frozen, but I like to see signs of life in the soft-shell crab before I prepare them for cooking.

ROCK CRAB   *Cancer irroratus*
JONAH CRAB   *C. borealis*
RED CRAB   *Geryon quinquidens*

Other crabs from the northern Atlantic are the rock and Jonah crabs. Most of their meat is contained in their claws, which resemble those of the stone crab but have black tips. Most body meat of the Jonah crab is picked and canned in Maine. A company in Virginia sells a small number of soft-shell rock crabs during the winter months when blue "softies" are out of season. Until more become available, they will continue to be expensive.

The deep-sea red crab, also from the Atlantic, is processed on board and is marketed as picked meat, legs, and claws.

STONE CRAB   Family Xanthidae, *Menippe mercenaria*

There are three species of stone crab, two from the Gulf of Mexico and one from Chile. The stone crab's claws are very popular, for their flesh tastes like a marvelous cross between crab and lobster. One large, smooth, rounded claw is picked off each stone crab and then the crab is returned to the water to grow another. The missing claw gradually grows back, and then the other claw may be picked off. The claws are cooked right away and are sold fresh, frozen, or defrosted. Stone crab claws are priced according to their size—the largest ones are the most expensive. They are bright orange-red with black tips when cooked. Stone crabs are in season all year round in the Gulf of Mexico and from November to May in Florida waters.

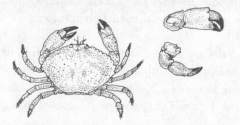

Cooked stone crab claws must be cracked with a mallet or nutcracker and can be served with lemon or lime wedges or mayonnaise or lime and dill vinaigrette (page 230).

DUNGENESS CRABS   *Cancer magister*

Cholesterol 59 • Omega-3 0.3 • Fat 1.0

Dungeness crabs come from the northern Pacific. They are large crabs, weighing 1 to 3 pounds, with a high yield of the most delicious meat. Buy them

live and steam them yourself, then eat them hot, or cold in a salad. You should beware of their strong claws when they are alive, although they are usually held together with rubber bands.

KING CRABS

Cholesterol 42 • Omega-3 N/A • Fat 0.6

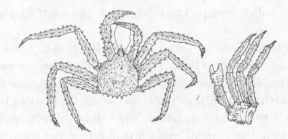

King crabs also come from the northern Pacific. There are three king crabs, two of the genus *Paralithodes*, the red king crab (*P. camtschatica*) and the blue king crab (*P. patypus*), and one of the genus *Lithodes*, the golden or brown king crab (*L. aequispina*). King crabs have long legs, and it is there we find the meat. The legs and claws are cooked and then sold whole or split, fresh or frozen. Picked king crab meat is also sold canned or frozen. King crab meat is excellent in salads, or reheated under the broiler or on the grill.

King crabs have spiny shells.

SNOW CRABS   *Chionoecetes bairdi* and *C. opilio*

Cholesterol 55 • Omega-3 0.37 • Fat 1.2

Snow crabs, also called tanner and queen crabs, come from the northern Atlantic and the Pacific. They have long legs. The claws, legs, and shoulders are cooked and then sold in clusters, fresh or frozen, or as picked meat. Snow crabs have smoother shells than king crabs. Prepare snow crab like king crab.

How to Eat Whole Steamed Blue, Dungeness, Rock, or Jonah Crabs

• You will need plenty of napkins, a wooden or plastic board, a nutcracker or a small wooden mallet, a nutpick or lobster pick (optional), and a container for the empty shells.

• First remove the tail (apron) under the main body, then break off the claws and legs so you can eat them later. Pull the top shell that covers the body off from the rear end. (You can stuff the shell with cooked crabmeat and serve it hot or cold.) Brush off the feathery gills and break the body in two. Break the two halves again so you have quarters. You can use your fingers or a pick to take out the meat. Use a small wooden mallet or a nutcracker to crack the claws and legs. Of course, you can use your teeth to crack the softer legs and suck the meat out.

• A few beers and a side plate of coleslaw will complete the feast!

How to Prepare Hard-Shell Crabs for Deep-Frying or Grilling

• Follow instructions on page 180, but steam the crabs for only a minute or two, or until they stop moving. Rinse them in cold water. Take off the top shell of each crab, clean the insides, and cut each crab in half.

How to Prepare Soft-Shell Crabs for Cooking

• Fresh soft-shell crabs should be alive shortly before being cooked. A "softy" cannot really hurt you, but you may want to use rubber gloves when preparing one. First remove the tail (apron) from under the main body. Then lift up each pointed side of the body and remove the feathery gills with scissors or your fingers. Cut off the face, which includes the eyes and mouth. Behind this opening you will find a little sac that is like a bubble—pull it out and discard it.

• You can ask your fishmonger to clean soft-shell crabs for you. Frozen soft-shell crabs are already cleaned. Be sure to defrost them in a colander or sieve so they shed some of the moisture accumulated during the freezing process.

COOKING METHODS

TYPE OF CRAB	COOKING METHODS	SUITABLE FOR	HOW MUCH TO BUY
Blue crabs	Steaming	1	2 to 6 in shell, depending on size
	Soup		
Soft-shell blue crabs	Grilling	1	2 to 4 in shell, depending on size
	Deep-frying		
	Sautéing		
	Soup		
	Stew		
Dungeness crabs	Steaming	1	1 pound in shell
King and snow crabs	As suggested on page 303	1	½ to 1 pound in shell
Stone crab claws	As suggested on page 302	1	¾ to 1 pound
Picked crabmeat	Croquettes (crab cakes)	1	4 to 8 ounces
	Fritters		
	Chowder		
	Stew		
	Salad		

CHOICE OF RECIPES

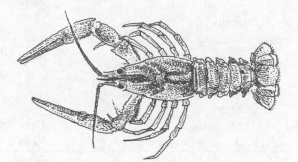

CRAWFISH

LOUISIANA RED SWAMP CRAWFISH   *Procambarus clarkii*

LOUISIANA WHITE RIVER CRAWFISH *Procamborus acutus*

PACIFIC NORTHWEST CRAWFISH *Pacifasticus leniusculus*

Mixed Species
Cholesterol 139 • Omega-3 0.17 • Fat 1.06

> *Fat Content:* low
> *Form Usually Prepared:* tail meat
> *Taste:* sweet
> *Texture:* tender

CALLED *CRAYFISH* UP NORTH, *CRAWFISH* OR *CRAWDADS* IN THE SOUTH, THESE SMALL FRESHWATER creatures look like miniature lobsters. In Louisiana, where most of them come from, they live in streams, swamps, bayous, and rice fields, they are harvested in the wild and farmed. Crawfish are also harvested in the wild and from farms in Oregon, California, and Washington State. They grow in streams and rivers all over the country and can be caught by hand.

Crawfish 3 to 5 inches long are marketed. They are shipped to market very tightly packed in string bags or boxes where, out of water but in a cool environment, they survive nicely for several days.

If you want fresh crawfish, you'll need to order them in advance, unless, of course, your fish store is close to the source. Be sure to buy them live. (It's easy to tell—they will splay their claws as you pick them up and even try to nip you.) Do not cook dead crawfish, for their flesh deteriorates quickly. Some stores sell crawfish already cooked with a spicy coating.

Crawfish are highly decorative on a plate. As with lobster, the meat is mostly in the tail, which contains a wonderful tidbit of sweet meat, but there is also a small amount in the claws.

You can boil whole crawfish, and they can be served hot or cold. You can enjoy the tail and claw meat and suck out the juices and fat from their heads. You'll need a finger bowl, napkins, and a bowl for the discarded shells. Unless the crawfish are large, you won't need a nutcracker or mallet—you can crack the shells with your teeth and extract the meat easily.

You can pick the meat from crawfish and make a salad or pie from it. You can also use the meat to make crawfish bisque, a sumptuous soup; you'll also need the shells for flavor.

Crawfish tail meat is available, usually in frozen packages. This is what is used to make Cajun popcorn, a popular snack or appetizer.

Soft-shell crawfish are now available to restaurants and specialty fish stores. They are simply delicious deep-fried.

How to Clean Crawfish

• Put the crawfish in a bowl of running water, and with a long wooden spoon stir them around for a few minutes. When they are clear of mud, drain them through a colander and run more water over them for a minute. Discard any dead crawfish.

How to Shell and Devein Boiled Crawfish

• Boil and drain crawfish (see page 173). When they are cool enough to handle, break the tail end of each crawfish away from the head; with it will come the orange-yellow "fat" (tomalley). Peel the tail, leaving on the fins at the end of the tail. Straighten the tail with one hand, take hold of the middle fin with finger and thumb, and give it a nice twist and pull. The vein should come out all in one piece. If it doesn't, cut a very shallow groove down the top of the tail meat and extract it.

• The twisting and pulling technique of ridding the crawfish of the vein is somewhat fancy, but it keeps the tail meat intact. Once you get used to the procedure, it can be done quickly.

COOKING METHODS

FORM	COOKING METHODS	SUITABLE FOR	HOW MUCH TO BUY
Whole	Boiling	1	6 to 12 (½ to 1 pound)
Tail meat	Deep-frying	1	6 to 8 ounces
	Salad		

CHOICE OF RECIPES

Deep-Fried Seafood: Variation I, page 160
Boiled Crawfish, page 173
Shellfish Salad II, page 223

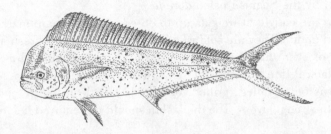

DOLPHINFISH (Mahi-mahi)

Coryphaena hippurus

Cholesterol 73 • Omega-3 108 • Fat 0.7

Fat Content: low
Form Usually Prepared: fillets
Taste: sweet
Texture: firm

DOLPHINFISH, NOW MORE COMMONLY KNOWN BY THE HAWAIIAN NAME *MAHI-MAHI*, ARE NOT THE mammals we call dolphins. They are brilliantly colored fish with blue to turquoise backs, iridescent emerald-green bodies, and yellowish bellies. Most of their color fades, however, as they die: Their skin turns a silvery gray the longer they are out of water.

> . . . Parting day
> Dies like the dolphin, whom each pang imbues
> With a new colour as it gasps away,
> The last still loveliest, till—'tis gone—and all is grey,

wrote Lord Byron. The bodies of dolphins are very compressed and the males have high foreheads.

Dolphins come from all over the world, inhabiting the tropical waters of the Pacific from one side to the other, the Atlantic Ocean from Long Island down to the Caribbean and the Gulf of Mexico, and the Central and South American waters of Costa Rica, Ecuador, Peru, and Brazil. (In Latin America they are also known by the Spanish name *dorado*.)

Dolphins are caught at weights up to 88 pounds. They are marketed at 15 pounds and under. They are sold whole and in filleted form, fresh and frozen. Fillets are of even thickness. The texture of dolphin flesh is firm; it is dark along the lateral line and off-white elsewhere, but it lightens up as it cooks.

Dolphin is best broiled, grilled, or baked. The flesh is firm enough to be braised with strong flavors. The thick skin should be removed before cooking.

COOKING METHODS

CUT	COOKING METHODS	SUITABLE FOR	HOW MUCH TO BUY
Fillets	Blackened	1	8 to 10 ounces
Fillets	As listed below	1	6 to 8 ounces

CHOICE OF RECIPES

Baked Lean Fish Fillets, page 100
Baked Fish Fillet Casserole, page 108
Baked Cajun Fish Casserole, page 111
Casserole of Fish Fillets with Potatoes and Coriander Pesto, page 112

DRUMS AND CROAKERS

Family Sciaenidae

Fat Content: low
Forms Usually Prepared: fillets and split fish
Taste: sweet and mild
Texture: soft and flaky

DRUMS AND CROAKERS ARE SO NAMED BECAUSE THEY ARE CAPABLE OF MAKING GRUNTING OR drumming noises in the water.

REDFISH   *Sciaenops ocellatus*

Cholesterol 65 • Omega-3 0.5 • Fat 1.0

The redfish, a member of the drum family, is also called the channel bass, red drum, puppy drum, spottail bass, and red bass. It is found along the

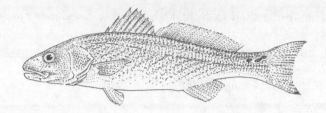

southeastern coast of the United States and in the Gulf of Mexico. It has been overfished and its catch is now prohibited in most waters, at least partly as a result of the popularity of blackened redfish, the dish made famous by Chef Paul Prudhomme of New Orleans. The redfish has reddish-bronze skin with one or two spots on its tail, and pinky-white flesh that turns white when it is cooked.

WHITE SEA BASS   *Atractoscion nobilis*

Cholesterol N/A • Omega-3 N/A • Fat N/A

The white sea bass is a member of the croaker family found in the Pacific from California down to Chile. White sea bass weighing up to 10 pounds are caught.

In Central and South American countries, white sea bass are called *corbinas* (Spanish for "croakers"). White sea bass flesh is similar to that of striped bass or grouper and can be treated as such.

BLACK DRUM   *Pogonias cromis*

Cholesterol N/A • Omega-3 0.2 • Fat 1.5

NORTHERN KINGFISH   *Menticirrhus saxatilis*

Cholesterol N/A • Omega-3 N/A • Fat N/A

SOUTHERN KINGFISH *M. americanus*

Cholesterol N/A • Omega-3 N/A • Fat N/A

Other members of the drum family include the black drum, also the northern kingfish (Maine to Florida) sometimes sold as whiting in Virginia and the southern kingfish from the Gulf of Mexico, also known as the Gulf kingfish. All have white, lean flesh. Northern and southern kingfish are not related to the king mackerel, which is sometimes also called the kingfish.

WEAKFISH (SEA TROUT) *Cynoscion regalis*

Mixed Species
Cholesterol 83 • Omega-3 0.37 • Fat 3.6

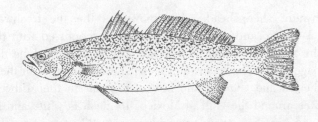

The weakfish, also called the squeateague or gray sea trout, is a silvery fish with small speckles on its skin. Its flesh is gray before it is cooked, but then turns white. The name *weakfish* does not refer to the texture of the flesh, but rather to the fish's weak mouth, which is easily torn by fishhooks. Weakfish are caught all along the Atlantic Coast, from Massachusetts to Florida; they are in season much of the year. Weakfish weighing up to 40 pounds are caught, but those sold usually weigh 2 to 10 pounds. They can be cooked whole or in filleted form, and they are very good to eat. Interestingly enough, they have no pin bones.

SPOTTED SEA TROUT   *C. nebulosus*

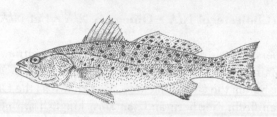

The spotted sea trout, also called the speckled trout or southern spotted weakfish, is prized in the South, where it is fished from the waters of the southeastern coast and the Gulf of Mexico. It has firmer flesh than the weakfish. Its skin is silvery in color, and it is spotted.

FRESHWATER SHEEPSHEAD   *Aplodinotus grunniens*

The freshwater sheepshead—also known as the the freshwater drum, gasperou, gaspergoo, and graybass—is not to be confused with the sheepshead from the Sparidae family, a saltwater fish that lives along the Atlantic Coast (see page 403). The freshwater sheepshead is caught in the lakes and rivers of America and Canada and is very popular in the Midwest and the southern states around the Gulf of Mexico. Its flesh is white and flaky when cooked. Freshwater sheepsheads weighing up to 20 pounds are caught, but those marketed usually weigh 1 to 5 pounds.

SPOT   *Leiostomuis xanthurus*

Cholesterol N/A • Omega-3 0.8 • Fat 6.1

The spot, also called the Lafayette, goody, and Norfolk spot, is a croaker. Spots are caught mainly along the southeastern coast. Most are small—they usually weigh ¼ pound each—but they can grow to as much as a pound. They have lean, flaky flesh and are best pan-fried.

ATLANTIC CROAKER   *Micropogon undulatus*

Cholesterol 61 • Omega-3 0.22 • Fat 3.2

The Atlantic croaker, also called the hardhead (a name also applied to catfish), is a pretty little fish with silvery-bronze skin, a dark back, and reddish-brown spots that form lines going down to a white belly. Atlantic croakers are fished along the mid-Atlantic coast. They weigh as much as a pound in the summer, but are caught at 2 or 3 pounds in the fall. They are sold whole and can be pan-dressed or filleted and fried. They have a lot of taste; their flesh is firm and makes small flakes when cooked.

COOKING METHODS

CUT	COOKING METHODS	SUITABLE FOR	HOW MUCH TO BUY
Redfish			
Fillets	Blacken	1	8 to 10 ounces
Fillets	As listed below	1	6 to 8 ounces

(continued)

COOKING METHODS

CUT	COOKING METHODS	SUITABLE FOR	HOW MUCH TO BUY
Southern Kingfish			
Fillets	As listed below	1	6 to 8 ounces
Steaks	As listed below	1	6 to 8 ounces
Weakfish (sea trout)			
Whole	As listed below	1	¾ to 1 pound
Fillets	As listed below	1	6 to 8 ounces
Spotted Sea trout			
Fillets	As listed below	1	6 to 8 ounces
Spot			
Whole pan-dressed	As listed below	1	¾ pound
Atlantic Croaker			
Whole pan-dressed	As listed below	1	¾ pound

White bass
Cook like grouper or striped bass (see pages 333 and 265).
Black drum
Seldom marketed; cook small individuals like Atlantic croaker
Northern Kingfish
Cook like European or American whiting (see pages 295 and 337).

CHOICE OF RECIPES

Redfish

Baked Cajun Fish Casserole, page 111
Broiled Fillets, Butterflied or Split Fish, Steaks, Escalopes, or Medallions, page 127
Grilled Fish Fillets, Butterflied or Split Fish, Steaks, Medallions, or Shellfish, page 137
Blackened Fish Fillets, page 156

Southern Kingfish

Broiled Fillets, Butterflied or Split Fish, Steaks, Escalopes, or Medallions, page 127
Grilled Fish Fillets, Butterflied or Split Fish, Steaks, Medallions, or Shellfish, page 137
Escabèche, page 213

Weakfish (Sea Trout)

Spotted Sea Trout

Freshwater Sheepshead

Spot

Atlantic Croaker

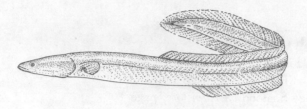

EELS

**Mixed species other than conger eels
Cholesterol 126 · Omega-3 1.2 · Fat 15.8**

Fat Content: high
Forms Usually Prepared: fillets and
  steaks
Taste: sweet and mild
Texture: firm

EELS ARE LONG AND SNAKELIKE, WITH CONTINUOUS DORSAL AND ANAL FINS STRETCHING THE
length of their brownish cylindrical bodies. A cross section of the eel's bone
structure resembles the symbol of a Mercedes-Benz.

AMERICAN EEL   Family Anguillidae, *Anguilla rostrata*

American eels, also known as freshwater eels, are catadromous—that is,
they spawn in the ocean and grow up in fresh water. They are found in waters
from Newfoundland down to the West Indies, and also inland in rivers,
streams, reservoirs, lakes, and brackish water.

The American eel spawns in the Atlantic Ocean and the young are helped
to the East Coast of the United States by ocean currents. It is an astonishing
story, for it seems that both the European and American eels spawn in the
same area, the Sargasso Sea, but each finds its way back to its own homeland.
The trip for the young European eel takes longer than a year. The small eels
that take a year to reach our shores in the springtime are called elvers. Mature

eels contain high levels of fat and are extremely fine food when smoked. They are good fried and used in soups or stews.

Baby European eels are called *angulas* in Spain, where they are a great delicacy. The baby eels are rinsed, dried, and quickly fried in oil with garlic. Some Spanish restaurants in New York serve them when they are in season. A typical English dish is jellied eel, which I find delicious.

Other species of eels are found in Japan and New Zealand, but not along the West Coast of the United States.

AMERICAN CONGER EEL Family Congridae, *Conger oceanicus*

Cholesterol 49 · Omega-3 N/A · Fat N/A

This silvery-gray eel, which grows much larger than the American eel, is found in the Atlantic along the East Coast of the United States. It is not catadromous. It does not reach many fish markets, for it is not commonly caught and there is little demand for it. It is closely related to the European conger eel (*Conger conger*) which is a fine fish. When the American conger eel is available, buy it, for its flesh is most suitable for cooking in stews, braising, or frying. It is firm, white, and not as fatty as the smaller eel.

COOKING METHODS

CUT	COOKING METHODS	SUITABLE FOR	HOW MUCH TO BUY
Whole	Smoking	6	1 pound (appetizer)
Skinned Steaks	As listed below	1	7 ounces
Skinned Fillets	As listed below	1	7 ounces

CHOICE OF RECIPES

Broiled Fillets, Butterflied or Split Fish, Steaks, Escalopes, or Medallions, page 127

Grilled Fish Fillets, Butterflied or Split Fish, Steaks, Medallions, or Shellfish, page 137

Braised Fish Fillets or Steaks with Provençale Sauce, page 184

Hot-Smoking (Smoke-Cooking), page 197

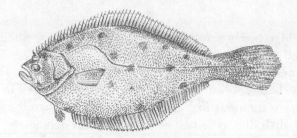

FLATFISH

Order Pleuronectiformes; Families Soleidae, Bothidae,
Pleuronectidae

**Mixed flounder, sole species
Cholesterol 48 · Omega-3 0.2 · Fat 1.2**

> *Fat Content:* low
> *Forms Usually Prepared:* fillets and
>   steaks
> *Taste:* bland to mild and sweet
> *Texture:* flaky to soft

FLATFISH ARE SO CALLED BECAUSE THEIR BODIES ARE COMPRESSED LATERALLY INTO FLAT OVAL shapes. A flatfish starts life swimming in a vertical position, as other fish do. Gradually it begins to swim in a "flat" (horizontal) position, and it is during this time that the eye on its bottom side joins the eye on its top side. The eyes of a flatfish may be on the left or right side of its head. Most flatfish caught in U. S. waters are right-eyed. Knowing the difference between left-eyed and right-eyed flatfish is important in identifying species.

The upper part of a flatfish is colored variously from sandy brown to reddish brown, brown, green, gray, and black. With the exception of the gray sole (witch flounder) and Greenland turbot, flatfish are white or nearly white underneath. The dark top skin is a flatfish's camouflage: Because of it, flatfish can hide or bury themselves on the ocean floor in the sandy, rocky, or muddy soil where they live.

Every flatfish has continuous dorsal and anal fins, starting at its head and running along its body down to its tail. The tail is rounded on a small flatfish and convex on larger flatfish such as the halibut.

European flatfish include the Dover sole (the true sole), plaice, turbot, and brill. Flatfish from the United States and Canada include the flounder, fluke, plaice, dab, and halibut from both the cold and warm parts of the Atlantic and Pacific oceans. Many flatfish are called "sole" in the United States, even though there are no commercially important true soles in North American waters. In the North Atlantic flatfish are part of a group of fish called ground-fish, which includes cod, haddock, pollock, hake, and ocean perch. All of which are caught from one of the world's richest sources for fine fish, the relatively shallow cold water above the continental shelf on Georges Bank (United States and Canadian fishing territory) and Grand Bank (Canadian fishing territory).

Flatfish are very desirable, lean fish. They cook beautifully on the bone (when you see a small, gutted whole flatfish in your store, buy it and try cooking it under the broiler) as well as in filleted form, although we see more filleted than whole flatfish in fish stores. The sparkling double fillets, which weigh a few ounces to a pound each and are usually skinned, are cut by suppliers or fishmongers from whole flatfish such as flounder, fluke, plaice, and "sole." The fillets are boneless because the skeletal construction of a flatfish is very simple (see page 72). As flatfish are not round-bodied, their flesh is more evenly distributed than the flesh of roundfish, which is an advantage if you are cooking fillets. Fillets from different species have slightly different textures, although most are smooth, with firm flesh. Flatfish flesh is translucent white to light gray when raw. However, note that the fillet from the top of a flatfish (the dark-skinned side of the fish) is thicker than the bottom fillet and is usually slightly off-white in color. Flatfish fillets turn white and opaque when cooked and the flesh flakes easily.

On the East Coast, flatfish fillets are not usually identified by the actual names of the fish from which they are cut. Various flounders are called fillets of flounder, sole, lemon sole, or gray sole.

Fillets of blackback (winter) flounder are called variously fillet of flounder and fillet of sole. When it weighs more than 3 pounds it is called lemon sole.

Gray sole fillets come from the witch flounder.

ATLANTIC SOLE   Family Soleidae

There are a few species of true sole along the East Coast that have some amusing names. They are naked, fringed, lined, and scrawled sole. There is also one called the hogchoker (which has been known to make its way into fresh water)! All these fish are small and commercially insignificant.

The true sole from the northeast Atlantic is the Dover sole, available from the North Sea, Channel Islands, and the Bay of Biscay. This fish is much prized for its firm texture, sweet taste, and lean flesh. It's a pity it does not inhabit the western part of the Atlantic, because it is a particularly fine eating fish. This sole is flown over to the United States from Europe. You can find them in a few fish markets, but you are more likely to see them served up in restaurants.

ATLANTIC FLOUNDER, FLUKE, "SOLE," AND PLAICE
Family Pleuronectidae (right-eyed), Family Bothidae (left-eyed)

Flounders and fluke from the west Atlantic are often called "sole" but they are technically flounder. There are many species of flounder available from the western Atlantic, up and down the East Coast of the United States. They have white, mild-tasting, fine flesh and are very popular, for their fillets are boneless. They are easy to cook and can be prepared in countless ways, both simple and elaborate.

The species listed below are all members of the Pleuronectidae family, with the exception of the summer flounder and the southern flounder, which are members of the Bothidae family.

BLACKBACK FLOUNDER   *Pseudopleuronectes americanus*

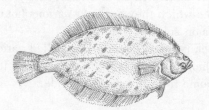

This right-eyed fish is also called the winter flounder; when it weighs over 3 pounds it is called the lemon sole. It is available nearly all year from the northwest Atlantic, mostly from Canadian and New England waters. Fillets of blackback flounder are variously called fillets of flounder, sole, or lemon sole at the fish store.

WITCH FLOUNDER   *Glyptocephalus cynoglossus*

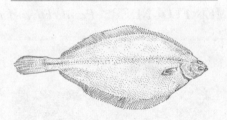

This fish, known as the gray sole, has dark gray skin. It is found in cold water from Labrador down to North Carolina. Fillets of witch flounder are usually more substantial than other flounder fillets but not as wide. The fillets lie very much in the middle of the fish on top of the backbone, and they do not stretch across the fish to the dorsal and anal fins as on other flatfish.

SEA DAB   *Hippoglossoides platessoides*

The sea dab (also know as American plaice) is reddish brown and is caught in waters from the Grand Banks down to Rhode Island. Sea dabs weigh up to 14 pounds. The fillets are sold as flounder in fish stores.

YELLOWTAIL FLOUNDER   *Limanda ferruginea*

This fish, caught in Canadian and New England waters, is yet another flounder, not to be confused with the yellowtail, a member of the jack family (see page 447).

GREENLAND TURBOT   *Reinhardtius hippoglossoides*

This fish is also called the Greenland halibut, although, since it is not a halibut, use of that name is illegal. Not all Greenland turbot are caught near Greenland—they are caught in both the northern Atlantic and the Pacific. Greenland turbot have a high fat content compared to flounders. Most are filleted and then frozen.

SUMMER FLOUNDER   *Paralichthys dentatus*

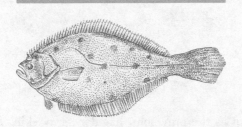

This fish, also known as the fluke, is left-eyed. It can weigh up to 25 pounds, but those sold usually weigh up to 5 pounds. The summer flounder is available in the winter from Virginia and North Carolina waters and in the summer from waters as far north as Massachusetts. The Japanese like to use this heavy flatfish for sushi and sashimi.

SOUTHERN FLOUNDER   *Paralichthys lethostigma*

This left-eyed flounder is fished from the southeastern Atlantic, from North Carolina to Florida and into the Gulf of Mexico.

Gulf flounder are found in the same waters, although the landings are small.

PACIFIC SOLE, FLOUNDERS, AND DABS   Family Pleuronectidae (right-eyed), Family Bothidae (left-eyed)

Some flatfish species from the Pacific are described below. Most of these fish are sold in filleted form and are equally good broiled, fried, deep-fried, bake-poached, baked, or steamed.

The species listed below are all members of the Pleuronectidae family, with the exception of the Pacific Sand Dab and the California Halibut, which are members of the Bothidae family.

WEST COAST DOVER SOLE   *Microstomus pacificus*

The West Coast Dover sole is usually sold at weights ranging from 2 to 6 pounds, but it can grow larger.

ENGLISH SOLE   *Parophrys vetulus*

The English sole, also called the lemon sole, is a small fish that ordinarily weighs ¾ pound but can grow larger.

BUTTER SOLE   *Isopsetta isolepis*

Sometimes available in the fish store, this fish weighs under 1¼ pounds.

PETRALE SOLE   *Eopsetta jordani*

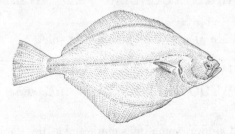

The petrale sole, also called the sand sole, is the best of the Pacific flatfish, a 1- to 8-pound fish with thick, flavorsome fillets.

REX SOLE   *Glyptocephalus zachirus*
PACIFIC SAND DAB   *Citharichthys sordidus*

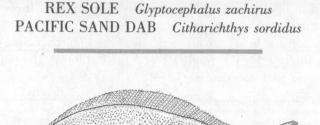

The rex sole, also known as the brill sole, and the Pacific sand dab are small fish that cook well whole and in fillets. The Pacific sand dab is left-eyed.

ROCK SOLE   *Lepidopsetta bilineata*

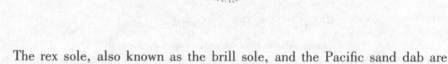

The rock sole is considered to have excellent flesh and is usually filleted.

YELLOWFIN SOLE   *Limanda aspera*
CURLFIN SOLE   *Pleuronichthys decurrens*
STARRY FLOUNDER   *Platichthys stellatus*

These flounders are also sold as flounder or sole.

ARROWTOOTH FLOUNDER   *Atheresthes stomias*

The arrowtooth flounder, sometimes marketed as the Pacific turbot, does not have consistently good flesh—the flesh tends to be very soft when cooked, so it falls apart. It is mostly used for mink food.

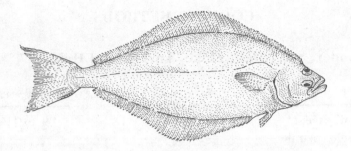

HALIBUT

ATLANTIC HALIBUT   *Hippoglossus hippoglossus*
PACIFIC HALIBUT   *H. stenolepis*
CALIFORNIA HALIBUT   *Paralichthys californicus*

Mixed Species (Atlantic and Pacific)
Cholesterol 32 • Omega-3 0.36 • Fat 2.3

Halibut are large flounder, harvested in both the Atlantic, from New York up to Greenland, and the Pacific, from Oregon to the Bering Sea. Atlantic halibut weighing 10 to 400 pounds are sold, although females can grow to 750 pounds! The Pacific halibut grows to 500 pounds, but is usually caught at weights up to 10 pounds. The smaller California halibut, not a true halibut, is closely related to the East Coast fluke, which makes it a West Coast fluke! It is caught in California and northern Mexico and grows up to 50 pounds, although most are sold at weights under 10 pounds.

Halibut are usually cut into steaks in the store. A halibut can be filleted easily and a "roast" can be made with the tail end of the fish. Halibut has lean, firm, sparkling white flesh that can be broiled, grilled, bake-poached, or steamed. It is ideal flesh for skewering on brochettes because of its firmness. Be sure to have steaks cut at least 1 inch thick, preferably 1¼ inches thick; these steaks can then be cut into 1¼-inch cubes for brochettes.

COOKING METHODS

Flounder, Sole, Dab, Fluke, Turbot, and Halibut

CUT	COOKING METHODS	SUITABLE FOR	HOW MUCH TO BUY
Whole (all except gray sole, petrale sole, and turbot)	Broiling	1	1 to 1¼ pounds
Tail ends (halibut)	Roasting	4	3 pounds
Steaks (halibut)	As listed below	1	6 to 8 ounces
Fillets	As listed below	1	6 to 8 ounces

CHOICE OF RECIPES

A recipe that includes a flatfish as one of its ingredients can generally be made with any other flatfish. (An exception is halibut, which is much larger than other flatfish and therefore has a distinct recipe list.) Note, however, that gray sole and petrale sole have thicker and firmer fillets than other flatfish.

Flounder, Lemon Sole, Sole, Sand Dab, Turbot

Oven-Steamed Seafood *en Papillote*, page 105
Broiled Whole Flatfish, page 123
Broiled Fillets, Butterflied or Split Fish, Steaks, Escalopes, or Medallions, page 127
Grilled Fish Fillets, Butterflied or Split Fish, Steaks, Medallions, or Shellfish, page 137
Fish Fillets Steamed in Aluminum Foil on the Grill, page 144
Fried Fish Fillets or Steaks *à la Meunière*, page 151
Deep-Fried Seafood: Variation I, page 160
Steamed Seafood, page 176
Fish Stock, page 187
Microwaved Sole with Endives and Béchamel, page 202
Fish Fillets with Spinach and Ginger, page 206
Seviche, page 211

Gray and Petrale Sole

Fluke

All of the above recipes for Gray and Petrale Sole.

Halibut

GOOSENECK BARNACLE

Pollicipes polymerus (North and South America),
Mitella pollicipes, also known as *Pollicipes cornucopia*
(Spain, Portugal, and North Africa)

Cholesterol N/A • Omega-3 N/A • Fat N/A

Fat Content: low
Form Usually Prepared: in shell
Taste: sweet
Texture: firm to soft

ALTHOUGH MANY EDIBLE BARNACLES ARE FOUND IN THE ATLANTIC AND PACIFIC, THE MOST appealing and best-tasting is the gooseneck barnacle, also known as the leaf barnacle. Gooseneck barnacles grow in dense clusters on boats, rocks, buoys, and pilings that are washed by the tides. They also grow on whales and floating logs.

The gooseneck barnacle is a remarkable-looking creature. Its neck can be up to 6 inches long (the reason for its name), on top of which it has a configuration of pointed, naillike plates that fit closely together and look a lot like a collection of pointed hooves or big-toe nails. Feathery appendages extend between the plates when the barnacle is gathering food.

Gooseneck barnacles are popular in Spain and Portugal, and as they are now scarce there, people in British Columbia are exporting them there. Some are also supplied to restaurants in the Pacific Northwest, and some others are dropped off in New York restaurants, where I first had the opportunity to cook and eat them.

Barnacles should show signs of life before being rinsed in cold water. They should be steamed above boiling water for 3 to 5 minutes—no longer than that. The peeled little pink necks are what we eat—when they are cool enough to handle, peel the skin off each neck to expose a pink-orange stem. You can dip barnacle necks in a container of melted butter and lemon, or a garlic sauce, though I find they are quite wonderful on their own. I think they taste like mussels, though others say they taste like crab, shrimp, and lobster.

Gooseneck barnacles are not generally available in retail fish stores yet, but if you live in the Northwest you can garner them yourself from coastal rocks with a little effort. Check with the local health and fish and game authorities before harvesting them.

My friend Bruce Stutz has written a short, amusing piece of history about the gooseneck barnacles called "Goosefeathers" in *Natural History* magazine. He recounts that "Irish priests were caught eating geese during Lent. Because they had never seen the arctic nests of these migrating birds, the priests believed they arose from the goose-necked shells with the feathery tendrils. So they considered them seafood, not fowl." In 1215 the pope had forbidden the eating of geese during Lent, but likewise a rabbi in France decided that if the geese did indeed grow from the gooseneck barnacles, Jews should be forbidden to eat them as they were considered shellfish!

COOKING METHOD

FORM	COOKING METHOD	SUITABLE FOR	HOW MUCH TO BUY
In shell	Steaming	1	½ to ¾ pound

CHOICE OF RECIPE

Steamed Seafood, page 176

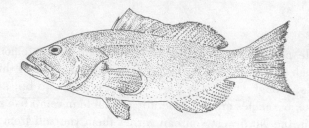

THE GROUPER AND SEA BASS FAMILY

Family Serranidae, Genera *Epinephelus*, *Myctoperca*, and *Paranthias*

Mixed Species
Cholesterol 37 • Omega-3 0.3 • Fat 1.0

> *Fat Content:* low
> *Form Usually Prepared:* fillets
> *Taste:* mild to sweet
> *Texture:* quite firm

THIS LARGE FAMILY OF FISH INCLUDES GROUPERS AND SEA BASS. (ALSO SEE THE PROFILE OF THE black sea bass on page 262.)

Most groupers and sea bass are fished in temperate and tropical waters. There are 385 species of grouper worldwide: To name but a few, Atlantic Ocean groupers include the yellowfin grouper, Nassau grouper, black grouper, red grouper, rock hind, red hind, speckled hind, gag, scamp, Warsaw groupers, and giant jewfish, while Pacific Ocean groupers include the California sea bass and the cabrilla.

The jewfish can grow to 800 pounds, and other groupers have been known to grow to 1,200 pounds—in Queensland, Australia, for instance. I expect you have seen those huge monsters of the deep in aquariums; they are so large they take a few minutes to swim by you. In the fish stores we see groupers weighing from 2 to 20 pounds, and they are just fine for eating.

Some groupers are as colorful as their names, but most have brown-gray skin. The red grouper, popular on the East Coast, has a reddish hue. They have large heads and spiny dorsal fins. Their excellent flesh is similar to that of red snapper—it is firm, sweet, white, and lean. Whole groupers, both large and small, are very good roasted; filleted groupers are good baked, broiled, or grilled. Cook them as you would red snapper or black sea bass.

COOKING METHODS

CUT	COOKING METHODS	SUITABLE FOR	HOW MUCH TO BUY
Whole	Roasting	4	3 pounds
Whole	Roasting	Part of a buffet for 15	9 pounds
Fillets	Blackening	1	8 to 10 ounces
Fillets	As listed below	1	6 to 8 ounces

CHOICE OF RECIPES

Baked Lean Fish Fillets, page 100
Bake-Poached Whole Fish, page 102
Baked Fish Fillet Casserole, page 108
Baked Fish Fillet Casserole with Light Tomato Sauce, page 109
Baked Cajun Fish Casserole, page 111
Roast Whole Fish, page 115
Broiled Whole Roundfish, page 125
Broiled Fillets, Butterflied or Split Fish, Steaks, Escalopes, or Medallions, page 127
Grilled Whole Fish or Shellfish, page 134
Grilled Fish Fillets, Butterflied or Split Fish, Steaks, Medallions, or Shellfish, page 137
Fried Fish Fillets or Steaks *à la Meunière*, page 151
Blackened Fish Fillets, page 156
Poached Whole Fish, page 169
Steamed Seafood, page 176
Fish Stock, page 187
Fish Soup (*Bourride*), page 188
Seafood Stew or Pasta Sauce, page 192
Seafood Stew with Tomato and Green Pepper, page 203
Seviche, page 211
Escabèche, page 213
Fish Salad I, page 221

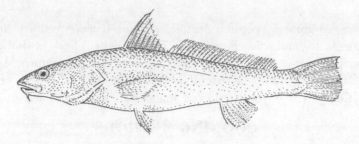

EUROPEAN HAKE AND AMERICAN WHITINGS

European Hake
Cholesterol N/A · Omega-3 N/A · Fat N/A

American Whiting
Cholesterol 67 · Omega-3 0.22 · Fat 1.3

Fat Content: low
Forms Usually Prepared: fillets and
    steaks
Taste: mild
Texture: flaky

EUROPEAN HAKE   *Merluccius merluccius*

The European hake and the U.S. whiting used to be considered members of the cod family, but it is now established that they belong to a separate family called Merlucciidae.

Hake is called *merluza* in Spain, *pescada* in Portugal, and *merlu* or *colin* in France. Hakes are caught off the Bay of Biscay and the Irish coast. Prized in Spain and Portugal, they are used often in soups and stews. They can also be baked, fried, or deep-fried. The Spanish also smoke hake. The flesh, when cooked, resembles that of cod, so hake can be used in recipes that call for cod (see page 294).

AMERICAN WHITING   *M. bilinearis*

Also called the silver hake, New England hake, and frostfish, this fish abounds in the northwestern Atlantic. It is silvery brown with a dark lateral line.

The flesh of American whiting is made up of small flakes, because it is usually quite a small fish. It is off-white before it is cooked, but turns clear white when cooked. The taste is quite bland. Because whiting is small, it makes good individual helpings, either whole or filleted. It can be fried, deep-fried, or used in stews (in steak form). One wonderful method of cooking it is to place its tail in its mouth, fix the tail there with its very sharp teeth, then souse it (see page 215) or deep-fry it.

It is easy to remove the fillets from a cooked whiting. When you have taken the first fillet off, just pull the skeleton free from the rest of the flesh.

Whiting is usually very cheap, and I often use it to make a light fish stock when other, richer fish bones are not available.

Cook whiting like red hake (ling) or European whiting (see page 295).

PACIFIC WHITING   *M. productus*

Caught abundantly in the northeastern Pacific, this fish does not often reach the fish stores because it is used primarily for fish meal.

HERRING

Family Clupeidae

ATLANTIC HERRING   *Clupea harengus harengus*

Cholesterol 60 · Omega-3 1.5 · Fat 9.04

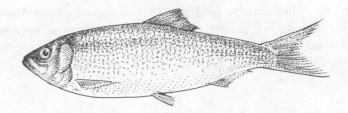

PACIFIC HERRING   *C. harengus pallasi*

Cholesterol 77 • Omega-3 1.6 • Fat 13.9

> *Fat Content:* moderate to high
> *Forms Usually Prepared:* fillets, split
>   fish, and butterflied fish
> *Taste:* mild to strong
> *Texture:* soft

HERRING ARE CAUGHT BOTH IN THE NORTHERN ATLANTIC AND IN THE PACIFIC FROM CALIFORNIA to Alaska. These silvery blue elongated creatures have moderately fat flesh that is delicious, especially when broiled or grilled.

Herring are sold at weights up to about 8 ounces. When fresh and young, small Atlantic herring are sold as sardines, and most of them are canned as such. Many herring are frozen or cured in some form or other: When smoked, they are called kippers, when pickled in brine or flavored vinegars, they are called rollmops, matjes herring, schmaltz herring, bismarck herring, and soused herring.

The flesh of herring is soft and tends to spoil quickly, so it is fairly rare that one finds a fresh herring to cook in this country.

When herring are available fresh (or defrosted), whole, and ungutted, they can be split or butterflied from the back. The fishmonger is used to doing this with herring and should be willing to do it for you. Another good way to serve them is gutted through the head (see page 56). They can also be filleted like other roundfish.

Herring roe is important to the Japanese. It is exported from Alaska, where roe-bearing herring are caught. A very limited season is imposed so the herring can maintain their population—but who knows how they have fared since the terrible oil spill in Alaska in April 1989?

COOKING METHODS

CUT	COOKING METHODS	SUITABLE FOR	HOW MUCH TO BUY
Whole	Roasting	1	½ to ¾ pound
Butterflied or split	As listed below	1	½ to ¾ pound
Fillets	As listed below	1	6 to 8 ounces

CHOICE OF RECIPES

Roast Whole Fish, page 115
Broiled Fillets, Butterflied or Split Fish, Steaks, Escalopes, or Medallions,
    page 127
Grilled Whole Fish or Shellfish, page 134
Grilled Fish Fillets, Butterflied or Split Fish, Steaks, Medallions, or Shellfish,
    page 137
Escabèche, page 213
Soused or Marinated Fish, page 215

JACKS
Family Carangidae

PACIFIC CREVALLE JACK   *Caranx Caninus*

Cholesterol N/A • Omega-3 N/A • Fat 2.2

AMBERJACK   *Serida rivoliana*

Cholesterol N/A • Omega-3 N/A • Fat 8.7

JACKMACKEREL   *Trachurus symmetricus*

Cholesterol N/A • Omega-3 N/A • Fat N/A

> *Fat Content:* moderate
> *Form Usually Prepared:* fillets
> *Taste:* sweet
> *Texture:* firm flake

THERE ARE MANY SPECIES OF JACKS ROAMING THE TROPICAL AND WARM TEMPERATE WATERS OF the world. They are bright silvery creatures with compressed bodies. Some sport yellow or orange tinges on their sides. All of them have forked tails and many have a row of bony scutes (hard bony scales) on each side.

The best known jacks from the Atlantic are the Florida pompano (see page 373), the permit, and the palometa. Other important jacks are the Pacific crevalle jack, the amberjack, the yellowtail (which is farmed in Japan for sushi and sashimi and is also caught off the California coast—see page 447), and the Pacific jackmackerel. Large species may contain ciguatera toxin, which can cause food poisoning (see page 25).

Apart from the Florida pompano, jacks are not as yet available in many fish markets. As more jacks appear in fish markets, take advantage of the firm, sweet flesh. Remove the dark oily flesh along the lateral line of the fillets before cooking.

Cook crevalle jack like pompano—see page 374.

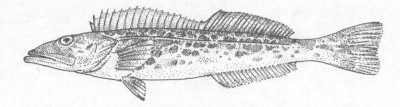

LINGCOD

Ophiodon elongatus

Cholesterol 52 • Omega-3 N/A • Fat 1.1

Fat Content: low
Forms Usually Prepared: fillets and
steaks
Taste: mild
Texture: firm

LINGCOD, ALSO INCORRECTLY CALLED CULTUS COD, GREEN COD, LEOPARD COD, AND BUFFALO cod, is not related to the Atlantic cod but is part of the greenling family. It inhabits the waters of the Pacific from Alaska down to California; most lingcod is caught off Alaska and British Columbia.

This brownish-green mottled and spotty creature looks similar to a cod, although it has a more elongated body. It can weigh up to 70 pounds, although 10 to 40 pounds is more usual. Its flesh when cooked is white, firm-textured, and mild-tasting. Its scales are negligible because they are so small and smooth.

Lingcod is sold whole and as fillets and steaks. It is available fresh, frozen, and smoked.

Cook lingcod like cod—see page 294.

LOBSTERS

> *Fat Content:* low
> *Forms Usually Prepared:* Northern Lobsters: alive and cooked;
> *Cooked lobster meat:* pasteurized, canned, and frozen lobster meat;
> *Spiny Lobsters:* alive and cooked. Frozen tails.
> *Taste:* sweet
> *Texture:* firm

NORTHERN LOBSTER   *Homarus americanus*

Cholesterol 95 • Omega-3 0.2 • Fat 1.5

The northern or American lobster is a fascinating-looking crustacean with large claws, an armored head and tail, and antennae as long as its body. It is black with dark brown, red, or green hues; when cooked, it turns a lovely bright orange-red. Its flesh is white with red tinges.

These lobsters thrive in the cold waters of the North Atlantic. They are caught in wooden traps from Labrador down to Virginia. The largest supplies come from waters off the coasts of Canada, Massachusetts, and Maine: most of the rest come from waters off Rhode Island, New Jersey, New York, and Connecticut.

Although they can live to a grand old age and can grow to as much as 45 pounds, lobsters are generally sold at weights ranging from 1 pound to about 5 pounds. Those that weigh 1 to 1½ pounds are suitable for individual helpings. Larger lobsters—those that weigh 3 pounds and up—have meat that is just as flavorful as that of smaller lobsters, and a steamed or broiled lobster this size can be shared by two people, since it can easily be cut in half. Lobsters command high prices, which are affected by supply and demand.

Lobsters must be kept alive in tanks of aerated salt water until shortly before they are cooked. In some fish stores they are kept on ice, but it's not a very efficient way to keep them alive. Be sure a lobster shows real signs of life before you buy it: The claws and tail should splay out when it is picked up. The tail may also curl tightly under when it is picked up. If your lobster dies on the way home, cook it immediately and eat it as soon as possible. If it is a lively lobster, you can keep it for a few hours or even overnight in an open paper or plastic bag in the refrigerator. Make sure it is covered with a damp dishcloth or paper towels, or nestle it in seaweed.

Lobsters have firm, high-quality meat. You don't want to let lobster meat dry out—it becomes firm naturally as it cooks and it must not lose any moisture, or it will toughen. Lobsters are best simply steamed or boiled, then served with melted butter and lemon juice (or lemon juice alone). Your fishmonger may sell cooked lobsters or be willing to steam a lobster for you—be sure to choose a lively one. Broiling or grilling a lobster is tricky but not impossible, and the cooked shell does impart a very special flavor to the meat when cooked by these methods. Follow the accompanying instructions if you want to prepare a lobster for broiling or grilling, if you want to make a dish such as lobster *a l'americaine* that calls for lobster in sections, or if you need raw lobster meat for a terrine or ravioli stuffing. These instructions are not for the squeamish! You can also ask your fishmonger to prepare lobsters for you in these ways.

Apart from the shell, the only parts of a lobster that are not edible are the little sac found behind the eyes and the feathery gills found at the base of the legs inside the body. The vein (which incidentally is edible, but unsightly) running down the back of the tail meat, usually shrinks up when cooked and nearly disappears. If, when you cut the tail lengthwise, you see the vein, pull it out before serving. Among the edible parts of a lobster are the tomalley (pancreas and liver), a lovely, creamy, light green substance found in all lobsters, and the coral (rue), a dark green substance that turns bright red when cooked and is found only in the female. (You can tell the sex of a lobster by looking under the tail at the tiny claws nearest the body—if these claws are very thin and feathery, the lobster is a female, whereas if the lobster is a male the claws will be thick and bony.) I think cooked tomalley and coral are delicious eaten along with the lobster meat, or sieved when raw into a sauce to thicken it. Cooked coral added to a mayonnaise served with the lobster, gives added dimension to the mayonnaise.

In addition to whole lobsters, your fishmonger may also sell cooked lobster meat, which you can use to make a nice salad, and lobster meat that is pasteurized, canned, and frozen.

How to Kill a Lobster for Broiling, Grilling, or Sectioning

• Always pick up the lobster by its body. Put the lobster on a board in the sink and pierce it with the point of a heavy chef's knife where there is a little crease halfway down the back of the body. This will kill the lobster instantly, but the nervous system will continue to cause movement for a few minutes, so leave the lobster alone until it is still.

How to Prepare a Lobster for Broiling or Grilling After Killing It

• Put the lobster on its back and cut through the middle of its body lengthwise. *Do not cut all the way through the back shell.* Use kitchen scissors to cut

through the middle of the shell on the underside of the tail. Spread the two halves apart with your hands, leaving the lobster partly joined at the back.
• Remove the little sac from behind the eyes. Leave the pale green tomalley and the dark green coral (if there is any) inside the body.
• It is not absolutely necessary to remove the intestinal vein that runs along the back of the tail, but it can be unsightly if it is exposed when cooked. Here are two methods for removing it from a raw lobster (if you don't succeed, leave it in—you can easily discard it as you are eating):

1) I have to say that this method does not always work, because the vein is fragile, but give it a try! Straighten out the uncooked tail with one hand, twist the middle tail fin, and pull gently: The vein should come out in one piece.
2) Take hold of the vein from inside the body and pull it out gently. Now you are ready to broil or grill the lobster.

How to Section a Lobster After Killing It

• To obtain lobster sections, first sever the tail from the body. (It's easy to remove the vein now.) Twist off the claws, cut the body in two lengthwise, remove the little sac behind the eyes, pull off the leg sections, and remove the feathery gills near the base of the legs. You now have two halves of tail, two leg sections, two claws, some tomalley, and some coral (if any).

How to Kill a Lobster to Obtain Raw Meat

• Kill the lobster by putting it in boiling water for 1 or 2 minutes, making sure the lobster shell turns red all over. The preliminary heating of the shell helps separate the flesh from the shell so that extraction of the raw meat will be easier.
• To extract the raw meat, first twist off the claws. Cut the body (not the tail) in two lengthwise. Using scissors, cut the underside of the tail shell down its length. Do not cut the tail meat. Prize open the tail shell and pull out the flesh in one piece. Remove the vein running down the back of the tail meat. Collect the coral (if there is any) and the tomalley and put them in a bowl. Crack the claws with a mallet or nutcracker and extract the flesh. Pick the meat out of the body where the legs are attached.

SPINY LOBSTERS   Family Palinuridae
WEST INDIES LOBSTER   *Palinurus argus*
CALIFORNIA SPINY LOBSTER AND OTHER SPECIES
P. interruptus

Mixed Species
Cholesterol 70 • Omega-3 0.37 • Fat 1.5

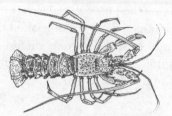

West Indies spiny or rock lobsters are fished in warm waters from the Florida Keys down to Brazil. On the West Coast of North America, California spiny lobsters are caught from Los Angeles and San Diego down to Baja California. Other spiny lobsters are caught in Hawaiian waters and in the cold waters of Australia and New Zealand.

Live spiny lobsters have a reddish-brown color mottled with yellow, orange, green, and blue. They may be called crawfish, but they should not be confused with those little freshwater crustaceans.

Spiny lobsters are clawless. They are known for their tail meat, which is often sold frozen. Spiny lobster tails are graded by size, and prices differ accordingly—cold-water tails are more expensive then warm-water tails.

DUBLIN BAY PRAWN   *Nephrops norvegicus*

Cholesterol N/A • Omega-3 N/A • Fat N/A

Dublin Bay prawns are neither shrimp nor prawns, but miniature lobsters. They have claws about 4 to 6 inches long and are colored pink to white. They are fished from the east Atlantic, the North Sea, and the Mediterranean. They are called *langoustines* by the French and *scampi* by the Italians. In the United States these lobsters are sometimes available at restaurants and are rarely found in retail fish stores.

COOKING METHODS

FORM	COOKING METHODS	SUITABLE FOR	HOW MUCH TO BUY
Northern Lobster			
Whole live	Broiling	2	2 1¼ pounds
		(see table, page 51)	
	Grilling	2	2 1¼ pounds
		(see table, page 51)	
	Steaming	(see table, page 51)	
Sectioned, raw	Braise	4	2 2 to 2½ pounds
Cooked lobster meat	Salad	2	8 to 12 ounces
Spiny Lobster			
Whole	Steaming	2	2 1½ pounds
Tails	Broiling	1	6 to 8 ounces
	Grilling	1	6 to 8 ounces

CHOICE OF RECIPES

Broiled Lobster, page 128
Grilled Lobster, page 142
Steamed Lobster, page 179
Braised Fish Fillets or Steaks with Provençale Sauce, page 184
Shellfish Salad II, page 223

MACKEREL

Family Scombridae

Fat Content: high
Forms Usually Prepared: fillets, split
    fish, and butterflied fish
Taste: mild
Texture: flaky

THE MACKEREL FAMILY CONSISTS OF FORTY-NINE SPECIES, INCLUDING ALL THE TUNAS. SOME mackerels we are familiar with are the Atlantic, Spanish, king, chub, and Pacific varieties. All have beautifully shaped and colored bodies and are excellent to eat when fresh. Their flesh is gray (sometimes pink), soft, and oily before it is cooked and is best broiled, grilled, or baked. Once cooked, the flesh firms up and turns off-white.

ATLANTIC MACKEREL   *Scomber scombrus*

Cholesterol 70 • Omega-3 1.1 • Fat 13.9

These beautiful fish, also known as Boston mackerel, have silvery blue, streamlined bodies and greenish backs that are striated with dark, uneven, wavy little stripes. The "mackerel" sky, with its thin, unevenly waved clouds, undoubtedly takes its name from the skin of Atlantic mackerel. These fish seem to be scaleless—their scales are so minute and smooth as to be negligible. They range in size from ½ pound to 7 pounds.

Atlantic mackerel are available from both sides of the north Atlantic. On this side of the Atlantic, they are primarily available in the spring, when they migrate from south to north between Cape Hatteras and Labrador, and in the autumn, when they return south. During the summer they are found in the Gulf of Maine and the Gulf of Saint Lawrence.

The Atlantic mackerel is a soft-fleshed fish and must be eaten when very fresh. It is sold whole, usually ungutted. You have to ask the fishmonger to gut it and split, butterfly, or fillet it for you, or do these things yourself. One of the best ways to gut a small Atlantic mackerel (called a tinker in England and a *lizette* in France) is through the head (see page 56).

Smoked Atlantic mackerel is available, imported from Europe. Fillets of Atlantic mackerel, sometimes both smoked and peppered, can be used for a cold lunch or brunch, or can be made into a smoked mackerel pâté.

PACIFIC AND CHUB MACKEREL *S. japonicus*

Cholesterol N/A • Omega-3 N/A • Fat N/A

These fish are identical. They look like the Atlantic mackerel but are smaller. They are very plentiful in the Pacific and found in the Atlantic, where they are called chub mackerel. They can be cooked like Atlantic mackerel.

SPANISH MACKEREL *Scomberomorus maculatus*

Cholesterol 76 • Omega-3 1.3 • Fat 6.3

This colorful mackerel has a silvery body and yellow to deep orange spots on its sides. It is available in waters from the Chesapeake Bay area down to southern Florida and the Gulf of Mexico. It can be treated like Atlantic mackerel, although it has paler flesh and is not as strong-tasting.

KING MACKEREL   *S. cavalla*

Cholesterol 53 • Omega-3 N/A • Fat 2.0

King mackerel, also called kingfish (but not to be confused with the kingfish of the drum family), come from the warm waters off Florida and the Gulf Coast. They grow large, up to 100 pounds. Cook them as you would Atlantic mackerel. They are usually sold as steaks at the fish store.

COOKING METHODS

CUT	COOKING METHODS	SUITABLE FOR	HOW MUCH TO BUY
Whole	Roasting	1	¾ to 1 pound
Whole	Broiling	1	¾ to 1 pound
Whole	Grilling	1	¾ to 1 pound
Whole	Sousing	1	8 to 12 ounces
Split	As listed below	1	6 to 8 ounces
Fillets	As listed below	1	6 to 8 ounces

CHOICE OF RECIPES

Baked Fatty Fish Fillets, page 98

Bake-Poached Fish Fillets, page 101

Oven-Steamed Seafood *en Papillote*, page 105

Baked Fish Fillet Casserole with Light Tomato Sauce, page 109

Roast Whole Fish, page 115

Broiled Fillets, Butterflied or Split Fish, Steaks, Escalopes, or Medallions, page 127

Grilled Whole Fish or Shellfish, page 134

Grilled Fish Fillets, Butterflied or Split Fish, Steaks, Medallions, or Shellfish, page 137

Hot-Smoking (Smoke-Cooking), page 197

Fish Fillets with Spinach and Ginger, page 206

Escabèche, page 213

Soused or Marinated Fish, page 215

Marinade, page 216

Fish Salad II, page 222

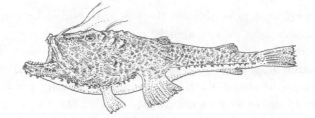

MONKFISH

Family Lophiidae

Cholesterol 25 • Omega-3 N/A • Fat 1.5

> *Fat Content:* low
> *Form Usually Prepared:* fillets
> *Taste:* mild
> *Texture:* firm

THE MONKFISH, ALSO KNOWN AS GOOSEFISH AND AT LEAST FOURTEEN OTHER NAMES, IS AN excellent fish to eat, but hardly easy to look at in its natural state. Most of the names given to it refer to its looks and its habits: *Anglerfish* and *fishing frog* allude to the fact that fish are enticed into its extraordinarily large mouth by a dorsal spine that sports a fleshy tab on its tip, which resembles a bit of food. This little "fishing rod" protrudes above the head, and when lowered over the mouth the tissue acts as bait or lure. The monkfish will eat nearly anything, including fish, shellfish, and water birds, and it has an insatiable appetite, hence the name *bellyfish.* Its mouth is very wide and the fish is ugly, hence the names *bullmouth, allmouth, frogfish, bellowsfish,* and *devilfish.* As for the names *monkfish, abbotfish,* and *lawyerfish,* these are beyond my comprehension, unless they refer to the silken, mottled, dark brown skin and side appendages that "enrobe" the monkfish. My friend Richard Lord suggests that the fish might have attained the name *monkfish* because they were fish taken by monks who used to go through the catch discarded by fishermen. Who knows? There is room for speculation.

One species of monkfish (*Lophius americanus*) is fished in the Atlantic from North Carolina up the entire East Coast to Newfoundland. A European monkfish (*L. piscatorius*) is caught in the eastern Atlantic and the Mediterranean. Other monkfish species are caught near Japan.

Monkfish is popular in France, where it is called *lotte* and *baudroie*, in Spain, where it is called *rape*, and in Italy where it is called *coda di rospo* and *rana pescatrice*. In Japan it is much appreciated for its delicious liver (sometimes served here in Japanese restaurants) as well as its flesh. In America, monkfish has only recently found a market. Enterprising people have discovered its culinary merits and it is now relatively well known and still reasonably cheap to buy.

The monkfish can weigh up to 50 pounds. We seldom see the entire fish, for the head is nearly always cut off and discarded before the fish reaches the market, although in Europe the head is used to make stock. As a rule, we eat only the tail section of the fish, which consists of firm white flesh surrounding a central backbone that has no rib bones protruding from it. I have handled monkfish tails that weighed as much as 10 pounds and others that weighed less than a pound.

The fish should be skinned, the pinkish-purplish dark outer flesh should be removed; what remains is flesh that is pearly white. Thereafter it should be extremely easy for you to cut fillets from each side of the backbone (see page 80); and the tough fiber on the side of the fillet that was nearest to the backbone should also be cut away.

If you like, you can then cut the fillets into individual portions, depending on the size of the tail. Cubes can be cut and cooked in stews or skewered for grilled or broiled brochettes. Using the whole tail end for a braised dish is one of my favorite ways of preparing monkfish. Even though they are easy to cut, monkfish steaks are not practical, for the flesh contracts and shrinks around the central backbone in cooking, and the backbone protrudes, making it impossible to cook the steak evenly on both sides.

The flesh is firm, white, and lean. It will not flake unless cooked for a long time, so it is perfect for soups, stews, and brochettes. It can be braised, fried, steamed, broiled, or grilled. It tastes sweet and its texture is like that of lobster meat, so it is sometimes called "the poor man's lobster." The flesh loses quite a bit of moisture as it cooks and shrinks, so you must buy a little more of this fish than you usually would of other fish, and when cutting fillets, you should cut the portions larger than usual.

The flesh absorbs flavors readily, so you can use many delicious ingredients, such as garlic, tomatoes, fresh herbs, wine, and stocks, to flavor it.

When monkfish cheeks are available, buy them, for they are wonderfully easy to prepare, and are skinned before being sold. They are beautiful little round nuggets of firm white flesh. You need 3 or 4 per portion.

COOKING METHODS

CUT	COOKING METHODS	SUITABLE FOR	HOW MUCH TO BUY
Whole tail ends	Braising	Part of a buffet for 20 to 30	10 pounds
Whole tail ends	Braising	Dinner for 2	1½ pounds
Fillets	As listed below	1	8 ounces
Slices or medallions	As listed below	1	8 ounces
Cubes (brochettes)	Grilling or broiling	1	6 to 8 ounces

CHOICE OF RECIPES

Broiled Fillets, Butterflied or Split Fish, Steaks, Escalopes, or Medallions, page 127

Grilled Fish Fillets, Butterflied or Split Fish, Steaks, Medallions or Shellfish, page 137

Grilled or Broiled Seafood Brochettes, page 139

Grilled or Broiled Seafood and Vegetable Brochettes, page 141

Fried Fish Fillets or Steaks *à la Meunière*, page 151

Steamed Seafood, page 176

Braised Monkfish Tail, Dolphinfish (Mahi-mahi) Fillets, or Sand Shark, page 183

Braised Fish Fillets or Steaks with Provençale Sauce, page 184

Fish Stock, page 187

Fish Soup (*Bourride*), page 188

Seafood Stew or Pasta Sauce, page 192

Seafood Stew with Tomato and Green Pepper, page 203

Seviche, page 211

MULLET, STRIPED

Mugil cephalus

Cholesterol 49 · Omega-3 0.3 · Fat 3.8

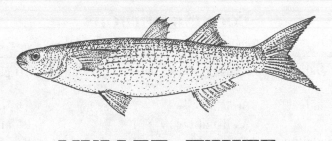

MULLET, WHITE

M. curema

Cholesterol N/A · Omega-3 N/A · Fat N/A

> *Fat Content:* low
> *Form Usually Prepared:* fillets and split fish
> *Taste:* mild
> *Texture:* flaky

THERE ARE SEVERAL SPECIES OF MULLET, OF WHICH TWO ARE THE STRIPED MULLET, ALSO called the jumping mullet, and the white mullet, also called the silver mullet. Long but stout-bodied, with silvery blue skin and large, loose scales, they are herbivorous and often inhabit brackish waters. They form large schools and may be seen jumping from the water.

Striped mullet are found worldwide in warm waters. They are important as food fish. White mullet are caught in the Atlantic from Cape Cod down to Florida, in the Gulf of Mexico and on down to South America. Some are farmed in ponds.

Mullet are marketed weighing up to 5 pounds. They are sold whole and in filleted form.

Mullet flesh is firm, mild, and nutty-tasting. Both the flesh and roe smoke well.

You can all but eliminate the muddy taste a mullet may have by skinning it and removing the dark lateral strip of fatty flesh.

COOKING METHODS

CUT	COOKING METHODS	SUITABLE FOR	HOW MUCH TO BUY
Whole	Roasting	1	¾ to 1 pound
Fillets	As listed below	1	6 to 8 ounces

CHOICE OF RECIPES

Baked Lean Fish Fillets, page 100
Bake-Poached Fish Fillets, page 101
Roast Whole Fish, page 115
Broiled Fillets, Butterflied or Split Fish, Steaks, Escalopes, or Medallions, page 127
Grilled Fish Fillets, Butterflied or Split Fish, Steaks, Medallions, or Shellfish, page 137
Fried Fish Fillets or Steaks *à la Meunière*, page 151
Fish Croquettes and Crab Cakes, page 154
Hot-Smoking (Smoke-Cooking), page 197
Fish Salad II, page 222

MUSSELS

Fat Content: low
Form Usually Prepared: live in shell and sometimes frozen; cooked and shucked fresh, bottled, or canned
Taste: sweet
Texture: soft to firm

BLUE MUSSEL *Mytilus edulis*

Cholesterol 28 • Omega-3 0.44 • Fat 2.2

This attractive bivalve has become widely popular in the United States relatively recently, but why it took so long I don't know. Europeans have enjoyed mussels for centuries for their distinctive taste and versatility. Their near-black shells are attractive in many dishes and their flesh, though briny, is rich and sweet.

A wild mussel affixes itself to a rock, pier, or pole by means of its *byssus* (also known as its "beard"), a tuft of dark threads that it makes itself. Mussels are also farmed: Farmers dangle ropes from large rafts above the ocean floor, and the mussels attach themselves to these ropes. Great quantities of mussels are gathered commercially in the northern Atlantic from North Carolina up to Canada, and in the Pacific from Alaska to California; in addition, the aquaculture of mussels is a large, expanding business.

You can also collect your own mussels, but be sure they are from clean, uncontaminated water—check with the local department of health or fish and game department. Red tides that occasionally invade some Atlantic and Pacific coastal waters are dangerous to humans who eat bivalves, and these shellfish should not be picked when such tides are present.

Mussels that are sold commercially range up to 3 inches in length, although they may grow larger. Mussels in their shells are sold by the pound, fresh or sometimes frozen; mussels are also cooked, shucked, and then canned or bottled.

Mussels must be alive shortly before they are prepared. If the shells are tightly closed, you can be sure they are alive. Throw out any that are broken or gaping open, or any that are extra heavy—they may be filled with only sand or mud. (If you suspect that a mussel is filled with mud or sand, try sliding the shells apart with your finger and thumb. When the shells slide apart easily it is probably filled with only mud or sand, but if there is flesh inside there will be resistance. Wild mussels are often washed before going to the consumer, but some may have barnacles on them or may be sandy inside. This is a nuisance, but they can be cleaned easily—see the instructions that follow. Cultivated mussels are usually far cleaner than wild mussels; their shells are thin and light and they are less prone to grow "pearls" or be sandy.

How to Clean Mussels

• Put the mussels in a large bowl, bucket, or sink under cold running water. Discard any broken, gaping shells or shells filled with mud or sand (see above). Rub the mussels together vigorously for 2 to 3 minutes until you rid them of barnacles and sand (you might want to wear rubber gloves for this). It is the rubbing together that cleans them. If some stubborn barnacles do not rub off, take a paring knife or wire brush to scrape them off.
• Put the cleaned mussels in a container of cold, lightly salted water and sprinkle them with a teaspoon of flour so they plump up and disgorge any sand that may be inside them. (This is not absolutely necessary for farmed mussels that are usually free of sand.) Leave them to stand for up to 1 hour (no longer, for the fresh water will kill them), then pull off the beards just before cooking them or serving them raw. The mussels will die within hours without their beards. You can tell they are dead when their shells gape open.

You can use mussels cold in salads or hot in soups; you can bake them on the half shell or add them to a risotto. One simple way to cook mussels is to put them in a shallow covered skillet with a little dry white wine, fresh herbs, shallots, and parsley and steam them just until their shells open. This only takes 4 to 5 minutes, and then they are ready to eat. (Incidentally, you can never tell what color their flesh is going to be once it's cooked—it can vary from a bright orange to a dull gray. I'm told that this may have to do with their sex or what they are feeding on.) If you are going to use the mussels cooked and shucked, shuck them as soon as they are cool enough to handle and put them in their own juice, so they won't dry out and shrivel.

Incidentally, it is best to eat mussels during the fall, winter, and spring, before they spawn. After they spawn, their flesh is depleted, and you will not find the plump morsels for a while.

GREEN-LIPPED MUSSEL

Cholesterol N/A • Omega-3 N/A • Fat N/A

The green-lipped mussel, imported from New Zealand, is another wonderful mussel. Green-lipped mussels not only look beautiful, but their orange and white flesh is exquisite to eat. Their shells are usually larger than those of blue mussels; they range in color from light brown at one end to bright green at the tip, and they are striated with thin dark brown stripes. Their inside shells are iridescent mother-of-pearl.

Green-lipped mussels are farmed and arrive in this country perfectly clean. You are likely to find them on restaurant menus. They are not generally available in fish stores, but some supermarkets carry them already cooked and frozen.

The best way to cook these beautiful mussels is to steam them open like blue mussels and savor their unique flavor, either hot or cold.

COOKING METHOD

FORM	COOKING METHOD	SUITABLE FOR	HOW MUCH TO BUY
In shell	As listed below	1	¼ to 1 pound

CHOICE OF RECIPES

Broiled Mussels with Garlic, Basil, and Tomato Butter, page 130
Clams or Mussels Steamed in Aluminum Foil on the Grill or in the Oven,
    page 146
Shellfish Salad, page 172
Steamed Mussels or Soft-Shell Clams *Marinière*, page 178
Fish Soup (*Bourride*), page 188
Creamy Seafood Chowder (use smoked mussels), page 190
Seafood Stew or Pasta Sauce, page 192
Hot-Smoking (Smoke-Cooking), page 197
Seafood Stew with Tomato and Green Pepper, page 203
Seviche, page 211

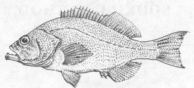

OCEAN PERCH

Sebastes marinus

DEEPWATER REDFISH

S. mentella

Mixed Species
Cholesterol 42 • Omega-3 0.29 • Fat 1.6

Fat Content: low
Form Usually Prepared: fillets
Taste: mild
Texture: flaky

OCEAN PERCH—ALSO KNOWN AS GOLDEN REDFISH, ATLANTIC REDFISH, REDFISH, ROSEFISH, deep-sea perch, and red perch—are found in the cold northeastern waters of the Atlantic off the coasts of the United States and Canada. They are members of the rockfish family, Scorpaenidae.

Ocean perch are commercially important fish for Canada, the United States, and other countries. Most weigh up to 3 pounds when caught, although they grow larger. They have fine, attractive red to orange skin and small scales.

Ocean perch are sold whole and filleted; the fresh skin-on fillets are pink in tone. The flesh has a fine, flaky texture and is mild-tasting.

Deepwater redfish, marketed as ocean perch, have large eyes, which are probably distended because the fish are taken from very deep water.

COOKING METHOD

CUT	COOKING METHOD	SUITABLE FOR	HOW MUCH TO BUY
Fillets	As listed below	1	6 to 8 ounces

CHOICE OF RECIPES

Oven-Steamed Seafood *en Papillote*, page 105
Baked Fish Fillet Casserole with Light Tomato Sauce, page 109
Broiled Fillets, Butterflied or Split Fish, Steaks, Escalopes, or Medallions, page 127
Fried Fish Fillets or Steaks *à la Meunière*, page 151
Steamed Seafood, page 176
Escabèche, page 213

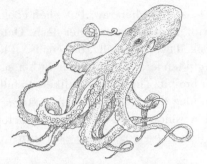

OCTOPUS

Family Octopodidae

> *Fat Content:* low
> *Form Usually Prepared:* fresh or frozen,
>   raw or partially cooked
> *Taste:* mild
> *Texture:* firm

THE OCTOPUS HAS A SCARY REPUTATION AS AN EIGHT-ARMED CREATURE THAT CAN ENFOLD ITS victims in its tentacles and puff out black ink to avoid being seen. It is terrifying to some, but delicious eating for others! Indeed, octopus do grow large, but those available to us weigh a pound up to 3 or 4 pounds. They are found worldwide. Octopus, like squid, are cephalopods, that is, "head-footed," meaning that their tentacles or legs are attached to their heads.

In this country, most octopus are sold partially cooked and then frozen, or frozen raw. Many are imported from Portugal. However, fresh whole octopus are available in November and December on the East Coast. Most of these are sold cleaned. The octopus has a delicate ink sac embedded in its head that is obtainable only if it has not been cleaned, so if you are buying a cleaned whole octopus and you want to use the ink (it is a marvelous flavoring for sauces, and can also be used for a risotto), arrange in advance for your fishmonger to remove the sac.

Octopus skin may look gray when raw, but when cooked it turns a purplish color that contrasts with the solid white inner flesh. Octopus flesh is firm and flavorful. It can be cooked ever so briefly, or because it toughens quickly, boil it for an hour or so until tender. Then finish it with a sauce, put it in a stew, marinate it, grill it, or broil it. The flesh is unlikely to fall apart; however, take care not to cook it so long that it loses its firm texture.

The Japanese have a wonderful way of preparing octopus: They rub it with salt and then pickle it in rice vinegar. The skin turns a bright, deep, nearly unreal purple.

The people of the Mediterranean use this creature in many dishes and I have seen the Greeks tenderize the octopus by repeatedly throwing it on a rock. Of course, I would imagine that the ink is lost during this operation.

COMMON ATLANTIC OCTOPUS   *Octopus vulgaris*

Cholesterol 48 • Omega-3 0.16 • Fat 1.04

The Atlantic octopus is found in U.S. waters from Connecticut all the way to Mexico.

How to Prepare Octopus for Cooking

• Turn the head inside out and clean it under running water. You will find the delicate ink sac inside—carefully free it from the attached membrane and save it. Turn the head right side out and cut off the part where the eyes are.

How to Cook Octopus

This is the way octopus is cooked at the Ballroom restaurant in New York City:

• Bring a pot of water (enough to cover the octopus) to the boil with

1 head of garlic, cut in half horizontally
3 inches fresh ginger, sliced
4 dried chili peppers
1 tablespoon whole allspice
6 bay leaves
salt to taste

• Add the octopus and cook slowly for 40 minutes. Then turn off the heat and let stand for 40 minutes before draining.

• After the octopus is cooked, scrape and pull off the outside layer of purplish skin from the head and tentacles with your fingers and cut it in suitable-sized pieces.

COOKING METHOD

CUT	COOKING METHOD	SUITABLE FOR	HOW MUCH TO BUY
Previously cooked and cut into pieces	As listed below	1	6 to 8 ounces

CHOICE OF RECIPES

Broiled Fillets, Butterflied or Split Fish, Steaks, Escalopes, or Medallions, page 127

Grilled Fish Fillets, Butterflied or Split Fish, Steaks, Medallions, or Shellfish, page 137

Seafood Stew or Pasta Sauce, page 192

Sushi and Sashimi, page 219

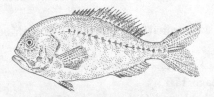

ORANGE ROUGHY

Hoplostheus atlanticus

Cholesterol 20 • Omega-3 N/A • Fat 0.3

> *Fat Content:* low
> *Form Usually Prepared:* fillets
> *Taste:* mild
> *Texture:* flaky

THE ORANGE ROUGHY IS A RELATIVE NEWCOMER TO THE COMMERCIAL FISH SCENE. EVEN THE name had to be invented! (*Roughy* is pronounced "ruffy.") Only discovered in marketable quantities in 1975 and only marketed since 1979, it is fished from the Tasman Sea in the South Pacific and off the coasts of New Zealand and Australia. It has bright red-orange skin and firm white flesh. It is usually frozen at sea, thawed on shore, and then filleted and refrozen.

The market for this fish has grown enormously, as has the price, in recent years. It is exported all over the world in large quantities. This excellent if somewhat bland fish can be cooked in many ways.

COOKING METHOD

CUT	COOKING METHOD	SUITABLE FOR	HOW MUCH TO BUY
Fillets	As listed below	1	6 to 8 ounces

CHOICE OF RECIPES

Broiled Fillets, Butterflied or Split Fish, Steaks, Escalopes, or Medallions, page 127

Grilled Fish Fillets, Butterflied or Split Fish, Steaks, Medallions, or Shellfish, page 137

Fish Croquettes and Crab Cakes, page 154

Steamed Seafood, page 176

Fish Fillets with Spinach and Ginger, page 206

Seviche, page 211

Escabèche, page 213

Also see the suggested recipes for cod (fillets) on page 294 and for red snapper (fillets) on page 417.

OYSTERS

EASTERN OYSTER   *Crassostrea virginica*

Cholesterol 55 • Omega-3 0.44 • Fat 2.5

PACIFIC OYSTER   *C. gigas*

Cholesterol 47 • Omega-3 0.68 • Fat 2.3

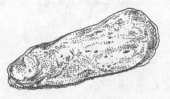

OLYMPIA OYSTER   *Ostrea lurida*

Cholesterol N/A • Omega-3 0.45 • Fat 2.5

BELON OYSTER   *O. edulis*

Cholesterol N/A • Omega-3 0.24 • Fat 1.7

> *Fat Content:* low
> *Form Usually Prepared:* shucked
> *Taste:* salty, sweet to flinty
> *Texture:* soft

THESE CRAGGY BIVALVES, EACH OF WHICH CONTAINS A PLUMP, MEATY MORSEL, ARE MUCH appreciated the world over. Supplies may come and go, but many oysters are commercially grown nowadays and production seems to be keeping up with demand.

The above listed oysters are those that are harvested in U.S. and Canadian waters. Common eastern oysters are found in the Atlantic from the Gulf of Saint Lawrence down the East Coast to the Gulf of Mexico, in brackish waters close to shore. They vary greatly in shape, size, taste, and name, according to the region they come from. Everyone has favorites. The best-known of the eastern oysters are the Apalachicola (Florida), Blue Point (Long Island), Bristol (Maine), Caraquet (New Brunswick), Chatham (Massachusetts), Kent Island (Chesapeake Bay), Chincoteague (Maryland and Virginia), Cotuit and Wellfleet (Cape Cod), Malpeque (Prince Edward Island), Louisiana, and Texas Gulf.

Pacific oysters, introduced from Japan, are found in the Pacific from northern California up to British Columbia. Their shapes, sizes, tastes, and names differ according to the region. Some of the best-known Pacific oysters are the Golden Mantle (British Columbia), Hog Island Sweetwater and Tomales Bay (north of San Francisco, California), Kumamoto (Washington and California), Penn Cove (Washington), Quilcene (Washington), Rock Point (Dahob Bay, Seattle, Washington), Westcott Bay (Washington), Willapa Bay (Washington), and Yaquina Bay (Oregon).

Belon oysters, indigenous to France, are now farmed off the coasts of Maine, New Hampshire, California, and Washington.

Olympia oysters are harvested off the coast of Washington State.

Some oysters are marketed fresh and sold by the pound (in Cape Cod), by the piece, or by the dozen. Others are shucked and sold by volume (pint, quart, or gallon). Still others are cooked, smoked, and canned.

Be sure you obtain your oysters from reliable fish stores or eat them in good restaurants, for they can become contaminated by tainted water. Be sure that oysters are alive and have tightly closed shells if you are going to eat them raw, and store them in an open container in the refrigerator with a damp towel, paper towel, or seaweed.

Oysters spawn as the waters warm, so it is best to avoid eating oysters during the summer months—they get milky and tasteless, and they tend to perish more quickly out of water at this time. However, the time to eat the Malpeques from Prince Edward Island, the Caraquets from New Brunswick, and the Bristols from Maine is from May to November—they are harvested when the ice melts, and the cold water they come from keeps them in good condition for eating in the summer. The triploid oysters from the West Coast never spawn and therefore they are plump and good to eat all year round.

The saltiness of oysters can vary a lot, from mild to strong. They usually have a full sweet flavor with a delicious flinty overtone. Surely the best way to eat them is on the half shell with a squeeze of lemon juice. Warmed oysters are also a delight, but only warm them until they plump up, or, if you cook them, cook them only until their edges curl. If you deep-fry them, use good oil at the right temperature (375 degrees F) and cook them for a minute only.

Incidentally, oysters have far less cholesterol than previously thought, which is encouraging. It turns out that in their calculations scientists were mistakenly including the plant sterols contained in oysters—in fact, these sterols work against cholesterol accumulation.

How to Shuck Oysters

• You will need an oyster knife to shuck oysters—no other knife will do. This is a strong pointed knife available in fish stores or kitchen supply stores; it usually has a guard. I like simple, sturdy, narrow-pointed oyster knives with or without a guard.

• Scrub the oysters with a wire or plastic brush in running water just before shucking. Wrap a dishcloth around your holding hand so that you can hold the oyster down firmly and protect your hand in case the knife slips. With the rounded shell down, find the hinged, pointed end of the oyster and push the tip of the knife into it, between the shells. When you get inside, twist the knife a little to loosen the shell—you'll hear a click. Insert the knife and scrape close to the top shell to cut the muscle that keeps the shells together. Discard the top shell. Slide your knife under the oyster so it sits freely on the bottom shell. Retain as much juice as you can, and strain out any pieces of broken shell before serving.

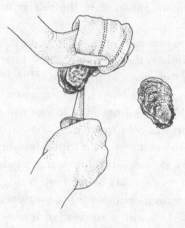

• If you need shucked oysters without shells, break the thin end of each shell with a hammer, then slide your knife around the shell and release the oyster.

COOKING METHODS

FORM	COOKING METHODS	SUITABLE FOR	HOW MUCH TO BUY
Shucked or half shell	Raw or hot-smoking	1	6 to 9
Shucked	Deep-frying	1	12 (½ to 1 pint)
Shucked	Fish Soup	1	2 to 3

CHOICE OF RECIPES

Deep-Fried Seafood: Variation III, page 162
Fish Soup (*Bourride*), page 188
Hot-Smoking (Smoke-Cooking), page 197
or raw on the half shell

PERCH FAMILY

Family Percidae

Mixed Species
Cholesterol 90 · Omega-3 0.25 · Fat 0.9

> *Fat Content:* low
> *Form Usually Prepared:* fillets
> *Taste:* mild
> *Texture:* flaky

ALL OF THE FOLLOWING FISH ARE LEAN AND CAN BE TREATED LIKE PIKE (SEE PAGE 372):

YELLOW PERCH   *Perca flavescens*

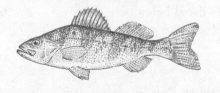

Yellow perch are small freshwater fish caught in lakes, streams, rivers, and low-saline estuaries from Canada down to South Carolina. These are colorful creatures with brown bands of color striping their backs. In the winter they are caught through the ice by hardy fishermen. Fun!

WALLEYE *Stizostedion vitreum vitreum*

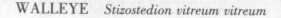

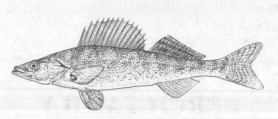

Walleyes, also called pickerel, walleye pike, or walleyed pike (although no relative of pike), are freshwater fish variously colored yellowish to greenish. They have large, glassy-looking eyes. They are much treasured as game fish, have excellent fine white flesh, and grow up to 20 pounds.

SAUGER *S. canadense*

The sauger is a smaller version of the walleye, but can grow to 8 pounds in, for instance, the Missouri River.

COOKING METHODS

CUT	COOKING METHODS	SUITABLE FOR	HOW MUCH TO BUY
Whole perch	Frying	1	¾ pound to 1 pound
Whole perch	Soused or marinated	1	8 to 12 ounces
Whole walleye	Roasting	4	3 pounds
Fillets	As listed below	1	6 to 8 ounces

CHOICE OF RECIPES

Oven-Steamed Seafood *en Papillote*, page 105
Baked Fish Fillet Casserole with Light Tomato Sauce, page 109
Roast Whole Fish, page 115
Broiled Fillets, Butterflied or Split Fish, Steaks, Escalopes, or Medallions, page 127

Grilled Fish Fillets, Butterflied or Split Fish, Steaks, Medallions, or Shellfish,
   page 137
Fried Fish Fillets or Steaks *à la Meunière*, page 151
Fried Whole Fish or Pan-Dressed Fish, page 153
Fish Croquettes and Crab Cakes, page 154
Escabèche, page 213
Soused or Marinated Fish, page 215

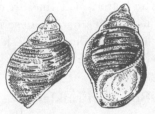

PERIWINKLE, COMMON

Littorina littorea

Cholesterol N/A • Omega-3 N/A • Fat 2.3

Fat Content: low
Form Usually Prepared: in shell
Taste: smoky
Texture: firm

THE COMMON PERIWINKLE, CALLED A WINKLE IN ENGLAND AND A *BIGORNEAU* IN FRANCE, IS JUST
one of many species of the periwinkle family (Littorinidae). Common periwinkles
look like little sea snails and live on pilings and rocks up and down the
Atlantic Coast. They are colored a brownish, grayish black, and they come
about 40 to 60 to the pound. Although they are not often sold in retail fish
stores, you can collect your own from safe, clean waters.

Make sure periwinkles are alive when you buy them: Touch the lid or operculum and if it moves slightly, the periwinkle is alive. They should also smell good, with just a slight aroma of the sea.

You can eat periwinkles hot or cold in a stew or a salad, or just plain steamed; they can also be used as a pretty and highly edible garnish for other dishes. You must have patience when eating them. After you've prepared them, push off the tiny hard lid (operculum) of each and then with a long tailor's pin, lobster pick, or fork pull out the little creature. You can dip periwinkles in lemon, garlic butter, malt vinegar, or balsamic vinegar.

Periwinkles are delicious, but it's hard to describe their flavor—they are inevitably a little rubbery in texture, but their flesh is nutty and a bit smoky. They are particularly good when boiled in cayenne-flavored water.

How to Clean and Boil Periwinkles

1. Wash the periwinkles in cold water until the water runs clear. Rub them together with your hands.

2. Put the clean periwinkles in a pot and cover them with cold water.

3. Optional: Add ¼ teaspoon cayenne or 4 dried chili peppers to each pound of periwinkles.

4. Bring to the boil for 3 minutes, then drain and put under cold running water for a few seconds.

5. Remove the tiny thin foot (operculum) from each periwinkle with a tailor's pin, the point of a small, sharp knife, or a small lobster pick or fork.

6. Extract the meat with the tailor's pin or lobster pick or fork.

COOKING METHOD

FORM	COOKING METHOD	SUITABLE FOR	HOW MUCH TO BUY
In shell	Steaming	1	4 to 8 ounces

CHOICE OF RECIPES

Hot and spicy periwinkles—as above
Steamed (as above) and served with a balsamic vinaigrette

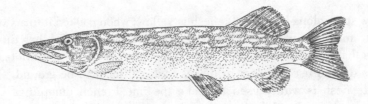

PIKE

Family Esocidae

Northern Pike
Cholesterol 39 • Omega-3 0.1 • Fat 0.7

Fat Content: low
Form Usually Prepared: fillets
Taste: sweet to bland
Texture: flaky

PIKE LIVE IN THE LAKES, STREAMS, AND RIVERS OF THE CENTRAL AND SOUTHERN UNITED States. Varieties of pike include the redfin pickerel (*Esox americanus*), chain pickerel (*E. niger*), northern pike (*E. lucius*), and muskellunge, or muskie (*E. masquinongy*). Their large mouths, which are like the bills of spoonbills, are full of teeth that they use to satisfy their large appetite for fish. Because pike are voracious eaters and can live for years, they can be the scourge of a stream or river. For this reason, and also because of their size (northern pike are caught at weights up to 20 pounds, while muskellunge are caught at weights up to 60 pounds), these fish are prize catches for the sports fisherman—particularly as their demise gives other fish a chance to live and be caught!

Pike are not widely distributed. When available, they are sold whole, usually with heads off, at weights of ½ pound and up, or in filleted form.

The northern pike has a silvery brown belly with a dark back and pale yellow spots along its sides. Its flesh is yellow; when cooked it turns very lean, sweet, and white with small flakes. The upper half of the fish has tiny floating bones that are a nuisance. Either be patient and bone out the fillets, or do as others do and use the meat in dishes that call for it to be ground.

Pike flesh is widely used to make the fine French dumplings known as *quenelles de brochet*. Pike is also used (along with whitefish and carp) to make gefilte fish.

The other members of the pike family are similar in looks, although their coloring differs slightly.

COOKING METHODS

CUT	COOKING METHODS	SUITABLE FOR	HOW MUCH TO BUY
Whole	Roasting	4	3 pounds
Fillets	As listed below	2	6 to 8 ounces

CHOICE OF RECIPES

Baked Lean Fish Fillet, page 100
Roast Whole Fish, page 115
Broiled Fillets, Butterflied or Split Fish, Steaks, Escalopes, or Medallions, page 127
Grilled Fish Fillets, Butterflied or Split Fish, Steaks, Medallions, or Shellfish, page 137
Fried Fish Fillets or Steaks *à la Meunière*, page 151

POMPANO, FLORIDA

Family Carangidae (Jacks), *Trachinotus carolinus*

Cholesterol 50 • Omega-3 0.56 • Fat 9.5

> *Fat Content:* moderate
> *Form Usually Prepared:* fillets
> *Taste:* sweet
> *Texture:* firm-flaked

THIS MARVELOUS-LOOKING FISH COMES PRIMARILY FROM THE WATERS OFF FLORIDA. RELATED species include the round pompano (*T. ovatus*) and the gafftopsail pompano (*T. glaucus*), which are mostly fished from waters off the Carolinas and Florida and from the Gulf of Mexico as far west as the Texas coast. Other related species are the permit (*T. falcatus*) and the palometa (*T. goodei*), which are fished in waters from Massachusetts to Argentina, and another gafftopsail pompano (*T. rhodopus*), which is fished in Pacific waters from southern California to Peru.

The Florida pompano is a smallish fish weighing ¾ pound to 2 pounds. It has a blue back and a silvery belly when it has just been taken from the water; after it dies, it turns silver all over with tinges of yellow and blue. The Florida pompano is extremely flat-bodied for a roundfish, with a compact small head, a tiny mouth, and a forked tail. Its scales are negligible and so it does not need to be scaled.

The Florida pompano is particularly suited to being halved before cooking (see page 70); it can also be cooked whole or in filleted form. Broiling, baking, grilling, bake-poaching, and roasting are good cooking methods for this firm-fleshed fish. The anatomy of this fish is much like that of a flatfish such as flounder, so it is easy to eat when cooked on the bone. Always try, if you can, to show the skin because it is very beautiful. The flesh of this fish is much appreciated, as it is sweet and firm.

COOKING METHODS

CUT	COOKING METHODS	SUITABLE FOR	HOW MUCH TO BUY
Whole	Roasting	2	1½ to 2 pounds
Fillets	As listed below	1	6 to 8 ounces
Halved	Broiling, Grilling	1	6 to 8 ounces

CHOICE OF RECIPES

Bake-Poached Fish Fillets, page 101
Oven-Steamed Seafood *en Papillote*, page 105
Roast Whole Fish, page 115
Broiled Whole Roundfish, page 125
Broiled Fillets, Butterflied or Split Fish, Steaks, Escalopes, or Medallions, page 127
Grilled Fish Fillets, Butterflied or Split Fish, Steaks, Medallions, or Shellfish, page 137
Escabèche, page 213

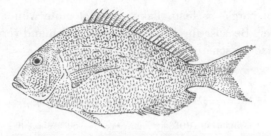

PORGY, NORTHERN

Family Sparidae, *Stenotomus chrysops*

Cholesterol 38 • Omega-3 N/A • Fat 2.7

> *Fat Content:* low
> *Forms Usually Prepared:* split and pan-
>   dressed fish
> *Taste:* sweet to mild
> *Texture:* flaky

NORTHERN PORGIES, ALSO KNOWN AS SCUPS, ARE MEMBERS OF THE SEA BREAM FAMILY. Related species include the whitebone porgy, also called the chocolate porgy; the knobbed porgy, also called the Key West porgy; and the red porgy, also called the pink porgy or silver snapper. Northern porgies are caught in waters from Cape Hatteras down to Florida and also in the Gulf of Mexico. They are easily caught, even by children, with a stout rod and a bent pin.

Porgies are flat-bodied. They are colored silver to gray, and they have spiny fins. Some porgies weighing more than 8 pounds have been caught, but most porgies sold weigh ½ pound to 3 pounds.

Porgies are usually cheap. They are more than likely to be sold pan-dressed (scaled and gutted with heads and tails removed). You can ask for them to be split also. If you catch your own, you can do your own pan-dressing.

The flesh of porgies is lean, flaky, and not quite white; when cooked, it becomes whiter. Because the flesh of porgies is lean and very flavorful, it can be accompanied by some strong flavors.

COOKING METHODS

CUT	COOKING METHODS	SUITABLE FOR	HOW MUCH TO BUY
Whole	Roasting, broiling, sousing	2	1½ to 2 pounds
Pan-dressed or split	Grilling, frying, broiling, or hot-smoking	2	1½ to 2 pounds
Fillets	As listed below	1	6 to 8 ounces

CHOICE OF RECIPES

Roast Whole Fish, page 115
Broiled Whole Roundfish, page 125
Broiled Fillets, Butterflied or Split Fish, Steaks, Escalopes, or Medallions, page 127
Grilled Whole Fish or Shellfish, page 134
Grilled Fish Fillets, Butterflied or Split Fish, Steaks, Medallions, or Shellfish, page 137
Fried Whole Fish or Pan-Dressed Fish, page 153
Fish Croquettes and Crab Cakes, page 154
Seafood Stew or Pasta Sauce, page 192
Hot-Smoking (Smoke-Cooking), page 197
Escabèche, page 213
Soused or Marinated Fish, page 215
Marinade, page 216
Fish Salad II, page 222

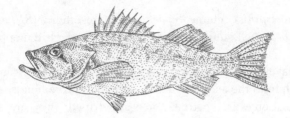

ROCKFISH

Family Scorpaenidae, *Sebastes* spp.

Mixed Species
Cholesterol 35 • Omega-3 0.3 • Fat 1.6

> *Fat Content:* low
> *Form Usually Prepared:* fillets
> *Taste:* mild
> *Texture:* flaky

ON PAGE 357 I DISCUSS TWO MEMBERS OF THE SCORPAENIDAE FAMILY, THE ATLANTIC OCEAN perch (*Sebastes marinus*) and the deepwater redfish (*S. mentella*), but there are numerous species of rockfish worldwide—approximately 330. I will now discuss Pacific rockfish.

Fishing for rockfish is a major industry on the West Coast: In the Pacific, rockfish are harvested from southern California up to Oregon, Washington, British Columbia, and Alaska. There are sixty-five species found there and I would need to write a separate volume to describe them all.

Rockfish are colorful, and different species are named for all the colors of the rainbow—species include black (*S. melanops*), copper (*S. caurinus*), brown (*S. auriculatus*), blue (*S. mystinus*), canary (*S. pinniger*), vermilion (*S. miniatus*), and yelloweye (*S. ruberrimus*) rockfish. Indeed, these fish are accurately named. Other popular species are the widow (*S. entomelas*), bocaccio (*S. paucispinis*), china (*S. nebulosus*), rosethorn (*S. helvomaculatus*), tiger (*S. nigrocinctus*), quillback (*S. maliger*), and chili pepper (*S. goodei*) rockfish.

Rockfish have heavily armored gill covers, and they are somewhat similar in looks to fish from the snapper family, with their large heads, spiny fins, and colorful skins. Some are spotted, some are striped; they are a very colorful bunch! Put them together and we have numerous clowns for a fish circus!

Rockfish weigh up to 15 pounds, but are usually sold at weights ranging from 1½ pounds to 5 pounds. They are sold whole and as fillets.

Rockfish flesh is lean, white, and flaky—it is similar to the flesh of fish from the snapper family and some bass. These fish can all be cooked in similar fashion. Some rockfish have firmer flesh than others and can be eaten in filleted form, while others with softer flesh will do better by being cooked whole; your fishmonger should be willing and able to guide you on this. The Chinese steam or deep-fry whole rockfish with added flavorings such as ginger, soy sauce, and scallions.

A word of warning: As I have stated before, the red-skinned rockfish are shamelessly labeled red snapper, or Pacific red snapper, which is actually legal in California, but not elsewhere.

COOKING METHODS

CUT	COOKING METHODS	SUITABLE FOR	HOW MUCH TO BUY
Whole	Roasting	4	3 pounds
Fillets	As listed below	1	6 to 8 ounces

Also see the tables for black sea bass and red snapper (pages 263 and 416).

CHOICE OF RECIPES

Baked Lean Fish Fillets, page 100
Bake-Poached Fish Fillets, page 101
Baked Fish Fillet Casserole, page 108
Baked Fish Fillet Casserole with Light Tomato Sauce, page 109
Baked Cajun Fish Casserole, page 111
Roast Whole Fish, page 115

Also see the recipes for black sea bass and red snapper (pages 263 and 417).

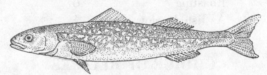

SABLEFISH

Anoplopoma fimbria

Cholesterol 49 • Omega-3 1.4 • Fat 14.2

Fat Content: high
Forms Usually Prepared: fillets, steaks, and chunks
Taste: sweet and rich
Texture: flaky

THE SABLEFISH, ALSO KNOWN AS THE BLACK COD, AND (IN THE LOCAL FISH STORES) AS THE butterfish when in filleted form, is not a member of the cod family but of the skilfish family. It is a sleek fish that ranges in color from blue-black to gray, and is commercially available at weights ranging from 5 to 100 pounds. It is fished in the Pacific from California to the Bering Sea off the coast of Alaska.

The flesh is white with large flakes. It is very oily and is eminently suitable for smoking—a great deal of it is marketed this way as smoked Alaskan black cod or sablefish. I can recommend smoked sablefish, and you can, if you want, have the pleasure of smoking your own (see page 197).

Sablefish fillets and steaks are fine grilled, broiled, or baked. A large chunk or roast can be roasted.

COOKING METHODS

CUT	COOKING METHODS	SUITABLE FOR	HOW MUCH TO BUY
Steaks	Grilling, broiling	1	6 ounces
Chunks	Roasting	6	4 pounds
Fillets, steaks	As listed below	1	6 ounces

CHOICE OF RECIPES

Roast Stuffed Fish Chunk, page 118
Broiled Fillets, Butterflied or Split Fish, Steaks, Escalopes, or Medallions, page 127
Grilled Fish Fillets, Butterflied or Split Fish, Steaks, Medallions, or Shellfish, page 137
Creamy Seafood Chowder, page 190
Hot-Smoking (Smoke-Cooking), page 197

SALMON

ATLANTIC SALMON   *Salmo salar*

Cholesterol 55 • Omega-3 1.4 • Fat 6.3

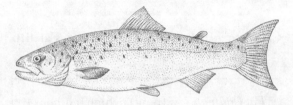

CHINOOK SALMON (KING SALMON)   *Oncorhynchus tshawytscha*

Cholesterol 66 • Omega-3 1.5 • Fat 10.4

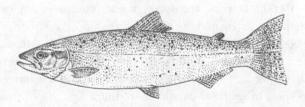

CHUM SALMON (DOG OR KETA SALMON)   *O. keta*

Cholesterol 74 • Omega-3 1.1 • Fat 4.2

COHO SALMON (SILVER SALMON)   *O. kisutch*

Cholesterol 39 • Omega-3 1.0 • Fat 6.0

PINK SALMON (HUMPBACK SALMON OR HUMPIE)
O. gorbuscha

Cholesterol 62 • Omega-3 1.0 • Fat 3.4

SOCKEYE SALMON (RED OR BLUEBACK SALMON)
O. nerka

Cholesterol 62 • Omega-3 1.3 • Fat 8.6

Fat Content: low (pink) to high (chinook)
Forms Usually Prepared: fillets, steaks, and chunks
Taste: rich and buttery
Texture: flaky

THE SALMON IS A BEAUTIFUL FISH, ALL SILVER, BLACK, AND SHINY. ONE CAN IMAGINE THE hidden strength it uses in making arduous sea and river journeys during its lifetime. Its body is perfectly proportioned to move swiftly through the water or fly into the air as it makes its way up waterfalls or fast streams to spawn or to grab at an angler's teasing flyhook. You are fortunate indeed if you can obtain the freshest of salmon, caught by rod and fly.

Wild salmon are anadromous, that is, they spend most of their lives in the sea but return to the streams and rivers of their birth to spawn. Most wild salmon are fished on their return to fresh or coastal waters.

Salmon flourish in both the northern Atlantic and the Pacific, not only in the wild state but also farmed: In this aquaculture, young salmon bred from large, fecund females are transferred to controlled areas, which may be inland lakes or protected sea pens. Farming of Atlantic salmon in Norway, Canada, Scotland, and Ireland is extensive and accounts for some of the best salmon available. Atlantic and coho salmon are farmed in Chile; other salmon are farmed in Australia and New Zealand. In the United States, some chinook and coho salmon have been successfully introduced into the Great Lakes.

Most of the salmon fished in the United States come from Alaskan waters, the rest coming from Washington State, Oregon, and California. Chinook salmon from the Pacific (with flesh the color of a blood orange) have good texture and taste and command the highest price; coho salmon cost somewhat less. Some chinook salmon have white flesh; these fish are much treasured, especially by the Japanese. Chum salmon have pale pink flesh, sockeye salmon have bright orange-red flesh, and pink salmon have pale pink flesh. Most chum, sockeye, and pink salmon are canned, but nowadays some chum and sockeye are available fresh and frozen.

Atlantic salmon have moist flesh and a beautiful, rich pink color. They are well handled by the farmers, so they usually reach the fish store in pristine condition. Wild Atlantic salmon are rarely available nowadays.

Salmon trout are sea-run rainbow, brown, or brook trout. For a discussion of trout, which are related to salmon, see page 432.

Also available nowadays are farm-raised baby coho salmon with pink-orange flesh from the West Coast and silver coho from Chile. They are the size of trout, weighing 8 to 10 ounces. They are sold boned out and butterflied, ready to cook, and are quite delicious.

When filleting salmon, notice that the pin bones are thin and feathery and can easily be pulled out with pin-nose pliers or tweezers.

The taste of cooked salmon appeals to almost everyone. The pink to red flesh is moist and tender when properly prepared. It is important just to cook the flesh through, and perhaps leave it a tiny bit underdone to ensure that it does not dry out. Take into account that the fish will continue to cook in its own heat once it is removed from the stove or grill.

You can cook salmon by many methods. Broiling, grilling, and baking give the pink-orange flesh added color; poaching and roasting are favorite ways to cook salmon and the flesh retains an inviting, unadulterated blush color.

It is not a good idea to eat salmon raw, as some restaurants serve it, either in the form of sushi or as salmon tartare, because no matter how fresh the fish is, a wild salmon has spent some of its life in fresh water and many contain parasites. (You can freeze salmon for a couple of days to kill any parasites—see page 24.) I like the way the Japanese prepare salmon skin: broiled and then wrapped around rice, in the manner of the seaweed sheets called *nori*. Of course, these fatty skins have the benefit of being rich in omega-3 fatty acids.

Salmon is marvelously suitable for smoking—witness the popularity of smoked salmon. The Swedish preparation known as *gravead lax*, which is salmon cured with salt, sugar, and dill and lox are both very popular. Lox is not necessarily smoked salmon; rather, it is salmon cured in a salted brine for up to a year, rinsed, and then only sometimes smoked.

Most everyone has his own particular taste when it comes to choosing smoked salmon—I can only say that the intensity of the brine and method of smoking make the difference. The flavor you prefer seems to depend on the salt content, the oiliness, and the moisture. I prefer moist, sweet, slightly salty smoked salmon. In any case, before buying smoked salmon—whether Scotch, Norwegian, Irish, Canadian, Pacific, or nova—you must decide for yourself by tasting a little piece.

When preparing a whole side of smoked salmon, you will usually need to shave off a thin layer of the flesh or skin that has formed from the brine and smoking and then pull out the pin bones before slicing it.

COOKING METHODS

CUT	COOKING METHODS	SUITABLE FOR	HOW MUCH TO BUY
Whole	Roasting	Part of a buffet for 20	8 pounds
Whole	Poaching	Dinner for 10 to 12	8 pounds
Whole	Bake-poached	1	½ to ¾ pound
Chunks	Roasting	5 to 6	3 pounds
Fillets, steaks, escalopes, and medallions	As listed below	1	6 to 8 ounces
Smoked salmon	———	Appetizer for 1	2 to 4 ounces

CHOICE OF RECIPES

Baby Coho Salmon (8 to 10 ounces each)

Oven-Steamed Seafood *en Papillote*, page 105
Broiled Fillets, Butterflied or Split Fish, Steaks, Escalopes, or Medallions, page 127
Grilled Whole Fish or Shellfish, page 134
Grilled Fish Fillets, Butterflied or Split Fish, Steaks, Medallions, or Shellfish, page 137

Salmon

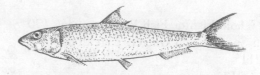

SARDINE

Family Clupeidae

ATLANTIC HERRING   *Clupea harengus*
PACIFIC HERRING   *C. pallasi*
PACIFIC SARDINE   *Sardinops sagax*
EUROPEAN SARDINE   *Sardina pilchardus*

Mixed Species
Cholesterol 52 • Omega-3 1.5 • Fat 6.8

Fat Content: moderate
Form Usually Prepared: butterflied fish
Taste: mild to strong
Texture: flaky

SARDINES THRIVE ON BOTH SIDES OF THE ATLANTIC AND PACIFIC. THE EUROPEAN PILCHARD IS A member of the herring family, which when young is called a sardine. In the western Atlantic there are no pilchards, but the Atlantic and Pacific herrings are called sardines when juvenile. On the East Coast in Maine these sardines are mostly canned. In Europe the sardines are also canned, but can be found fresh, frozen, or defrosted from the Mediterranean and the East Atlantic. If you can find them in specialty fish markets on the East Coast, by all means buy them, for they are delicious grilled or broiled. I don't find American sardines (Atlantic herring) as flavorful as European sardines (pilchards). I can't help it—all I can think of are those delicious fat sardines, grilled outdoors on charcoal, that one can eat in Spain, Portugal, and France. (Pacific sardines are no longer a viable commercial catch because the stock is depleted, and those few that are caught are usually used for bait.)

The sardine is a silvery, bullet-shaped fish that grows to only about 8 inches long. The fresh sardines that are commercially available weigh up to 5 ounces or so.

You can gut sardines through the head (see page 56), brush off the loose scales, oil them lightly, roll them in coarse salt, and broil, grill, or roast them. The flesh of sardines is fat and oily, so they need a good squeeze of lemon when cooked and a nice crust bread to accompany them. They can also be boned out (fiddly work), rolled up, and baked; if you want to bone out and butterfly sardines, follow the instructions on pages 67 and 69.

Brisling (sprats), pilchards, and silds are very similar to sardines and like sardines are mostly available canned. All these fish are delightful in sandwiches and salads and are full of healthy minerals and calcium, if you eat the bones.

COOKING METHODS

CUT	COOKING METHODS	SUITABLE FOR	HOW MUCH TO BUY
Whole	Grilling, roasting, broiling, sousing, or as escabèche	1	¾ to 1 pound
Boned out, butterflied, or split	Broiling, grilling	1	6 to 8 ounces

CHOICE OF RECIPES

Roast Whole Fish, page 115
Broiled Whole Roundfish, page 125
Broiled Fillets, Butterflied or Split Fish, Steaks, Escalopes, or Medallions, page 127
Grilled Fish Fillets, Butterflied or Split Fish, Steaks, Medallions, or Shellfish, page 137
Escabèche, page 213
Soused or Marinated Fish, page 215

SCALLOPS
Family Pectinidae

SEA SCALLOP   *Placopecten magellanicus*

Cholesterol 36 • Omega-3 0.2 • Fat 0.8

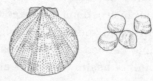

BAY SCALLOP   *Aequipecten irradians*

Cholesterol N/A • Omega-3 0.13 • Fat 0.06

CALICO SCALLOP   *A. gibbus*

Cholesterol N/A • Omega-3 0.13 • Fat 0.06

> *Fat Content:* low
> *Form Usually Prepared:* shucked
> *Taste:* sweet
> *Texture:* quite firm

THE SEA SCALLOP IS A BIVALVE MOLLUSK THAT THRIVES IN DEEP ATLANTIC WATERS FROM Canada down to North Carolina. Other scallops are found worldwide—in Alaskan, Peruvian, Icelandic, Central American, and Japanese waters, as well as in other waters off the coast of the United States.

Unlike other mollusks that stay sedentary, most scallop species swim by snapping their shells together, using the muscle in the center of their shells. This large, round, white muscle, called the adductor muscle, is the sweet, rich, scallop meat we eat.

We buy scallop meat by the pound. (Scallops are sold by the piece and by the pound in Europe.) Scallops can be sautéed, broiled, grilled, baked in the shell, and made into salads and seviche. They are highly successful when placed on brochette sticks, because they keep their shape.

Use high heat when cooking scallops. When sautéing, do a few at a time so the temperature of the fat does not drop. Scallops are cooked when they are opaque all the way through.

Scallop shells are seldom seen nowadays because scallops are shucked at sea, but we all know the shape from the Shell gasoline logo, for example, or from Botticelli's *Birth of Venus*, in which Venus stands on a large scallop shell. Many decorators and architects have made use of this shell in decorating doors and mantelpieces through the ages.

It is useful to have a few sea scallop shells around, for many a delightful dish can be baked in them. Even though the Atlantic sea scallops have smoothish shells, other more attractive grooved shells are available from Europe and other parts of the world. The small pink scallops from the Pacific Northwest are nicknamed "singing scallops." They come with their roe and are cooked in their shells. After eating the sweet little morsels, we can keep the charming pink shells.

Unfortunately, usually the scallop's roe, or coral, is discarded at sea by American fishermen, mostly because it can cause the meat to spoil during the long trip at sea. In Europe the roe is prized for its color and flavor and is sold with the scallop on the half shell. Scallops with roe are imported from France, Holland, the Isle of Man, and New Zealand. Some fishermen on the East Coast are now selling the roe with scallops; the female roe is coral-colored, while the male roe is less colorful, a pale gray.

Sea scallops have shells up to 8 inches wide. The white meat inside is round like a drum, measuring up to 2½ inches in diameter and 2 inches high. The flesh is sweet and firm when cooked.

How to Prepare Sea Scallops for Cooking

• Remove the tough little muscle from the side of each scallop before cooking. If the scallops are of very different sizes, wafer them (cut them crosswise) so they are the same thickness.

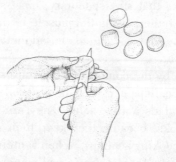

Bay scallops, the small cousins of the sea scallops, have an even sweeter, more delicate flavor than sea scallops. Try eating them raw when they are fresh—they taste as sweet as candy. They are wonderful sautéed quickly over high heat, when steamed and added to salads, or when made into seviche.

Calico scallops are southern bay scallops harvested off Florida. Steam-shucked at processing plants, they are usually not as sweet as other scallops. Cook these scallops like bay scallops.

COOKING METHOD

FORM	COOKING METHOD	SUITABLE FOR	HOW MUCH TO BUY
Shucked	As listed below	1	4 to 8 ounces

CHOICE OF RECIPES

Sea Scallops

Oven-Steamed Seafood *en Papillote*, page 105
Casserole of Large Sea Scallops with Potatoes and Coriander Pesto, page 112
Broiled Fillets, Butterflied or Split Fish, Steaks, Escalopes, or Medallions, page 127
Grilled Whole Fish or Shellfish, page 134

Bay and Calico Scallops

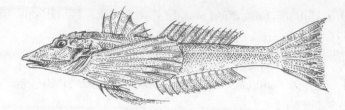

SEA ROBIN

Family Triglidae

Cholesterol N/A · Omega-3 N/A · Fat N/A

> *Fat Content:* low
> *Form Usually Prepared:* fillets, steaks
> *Taste:* mild
> *Texture:* quite firm

THE SEA ROBIN, CALLED THE *GRONDIN* IN FRENCH AND THE *CAPONE* IN ITALIAN, IS POPULAR IN Europe for its delicate flavor. In the United States, where it is also known by the English name *gurnard* and is sometimes incorrectly referred to as the angelfish, the sea robin is not much favored: On the eastern seaboard, sea robins are caught along with flukes and flounder, but are often thrown back or used as bait for larger fish; a few are marketed in the United States, however, and they can sometimes be found in ethnic fish stores. The two species most likely to be seen in the Northeast are the striped sea robin and the northern sea robin.

When these creatures are hooked, they flutter and fly and even squeal in indignation. They appear, to some, to be prehistoric or medieval-looking—and a little scary-looking for they have rays that jut out and spiny, winglike fins that they use to swim, find food, or hide in the sandy seabed. They have wide, flat, bony heads and bodies that taper off to very narrow tails. Different species can be colored orange, red, gray, or brown; some are mottled and others are striped. They grow to weights of as much as 3 pounds.

Sea robin flesh is firm, lean, flavorful, and sweet, but you do want to get rid of the skin, for it is rough and unpleasant. The fish is bony: The rib bones extend into the flesh, and you can see the ends of them sticking out when you fillet the fish. The best way to get rid of these bones is by pulling them out with pin-nose pliers. Alternatively, since the flesh is firm when cooked, you can cook it by poaching or baking, for instance, then flake the flesh and pick out the bones at the same time.

Sea robin cut into steaks can be added to fish soups, as it is in a French bouillabaisse. Poached sea robin can be made into a salad. Sea robin can be grilled or steamed.

How to Prepare Sea Robin for Cooking

• Gut the fish by making a cut from the anal vent toward the head, bypassing each side of the Y-shaped flat bone behind the mouth, at the base of the head.
• Turn the fish over, cut the head off, and discard it. The guts will come away with the head. Cut off the spiny fins. Rinse the fish.

How to Remove the Skin of a Sea Robin

• Loosen the skin at the head end with a sharp-pointed knife and then pull it off with your fingers or pliers (I find it easier with pliers).
• *Or* blanch the fish in boiling water for 10 seconds, then rinse it in cold water and peel the skin off with a knife or your fingers.

How to Fillet Sea Robin

• Cut down each side of the backbone. You will feel the knife cutting through the rib bones. When you have two fillets, feel for the rib bones with your fingertips. Pull these out with pliers or tweezers.

COOKING METHODS

CUT	COOKING METHODS	SUITABLE FOR	HOW MUCH TO BUY
Whole, skinned	Grilling	1	½ to 1 pound
Fillets, steaks	As listed below	1	6 to 8 ounces

CHOICE OF RECIPES

Broiled Fillets, Butterflied or Split Fish, Steaks, Escalopes, or Medallions, page 127

Grilled Whole Fish or Shellfish, page 134

Grilled Fish Fillets Butterflied or Split Fish, Steaks, Medallions, or Shellfish, page 137

Fish Croquettes and Crab Cakes, page 154

Steamed Seafood, page 176

Fish Stock, page 187

Fish Soup (*Bourride*), page 188

Seafood Stew or Pasta Sauce, page 192

Fish Salad I, page 221

SEA URCHIN

Class Echinoidea

Cholesterol 498 • Omega-3 • Fat 3.21

> *Fat Content:* low
> *Form Usually Prepared:* Gonads
> *Taste:* sweet
> *Texture:* unctuous

VARIOUS SPECIES OF SEA URCHINS INHABIT THE ATLANTIC OCEAN, FROM CANADA DOWN THROUGH the West Indies, and the Pacific, from Canada down to Baja California. Sea urchins have spherical shells, called tests, that measure up to 6 inches in diameter and are covered with spines like the bodies of porcupines. Those from U.S. waters can be red, green, or purple. Sea urchins grow on rocky shores, eat kelp, and can be a nuisance to swimmers.

In the United States, we eat the gonads of these creatures, also called roe, which are a delicious treat. There is nothing quite like them—they are bright orange-yellow and shaped like little tongues, and they taste sweet and unctuous at the same time. Europeans are also keen on sea urchin gonads and cook them in a number of dishes—for example, they mix them in eggs, a preparation that is very high in cholesterol indeed.

Sea urchin gonads develop during spawning season and urchins must be harvested prior to spawning. In the Pacific, and particularly on the British Columbian coast near Vancouver, mostly red sea urchins thrive; their season is from October to May. Harvested by humans, they are also favored by sea otters, who are quite capable of cracking large ones on rocks. The gonads of the British Columbian red sea urchins are mostly exported to Japan on shallow trays, in very fresh condition, as they are eaten raw in sushi. I particularly like the preparation *uni-maki* (*uni* is the Japanese word for "sea urchin").

The green urchins from the Atlantic are in season from November to March on the East Coast of the United States. I enjoy eating the gonads of green urchins straight out of the shell, especially at the Oyster Bar in New York City's Grand Central Station.

The little trays of sea urchin gonads prepared for Japanese consumption are fortunately available in Japanese food stores in large cities of the United States. They are very convenient to use and contain ½ pound of gonads.

If you buy whole sea urchins, choose those that show some signs of life before extracting the gonads. The spines should be erect, and if they move when you touch them, the sea urchin is alive.

How to Extract Sea Urchin Roe or Gonads

• Wear heavy gardening or rubber gloves so the spines do not pierce the skin of your fingers. Hold the sea urchin so the "mouth" side of the shell (the bottom) is uppermost. Insert scissors into the shell about 1½ inches below the mouth and cut around it so you have a lid. Discard the lid and with a small spoon scoop out the orange-yellow gonads, avoiding the brown viscera. There are five little gonad sacs to each sea urchin, and you will need between ten and twenty gonad sacs to obtain ½ pound of roe.

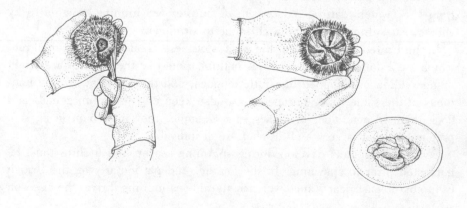

PREPARATION METHOD

FORM	PREPARATION METHOD	SUITABLE FOR	HOW MUCH TO BUY
Raw gonads	Sushi or sashimi	1	Up to 4 ounces

CHOICE OF RECIPE

Sushi and Sashimi, page 219

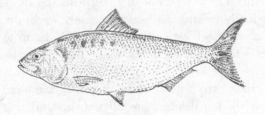

SHAD

Family Clupeidae

AMERICAN SHAD

Alosa sapidissima

Cholesterol 49 • Omega-3 N/A • Fat 13.8

Fat Content: high
Form Usually Prepared: fillets and roe
Taste: sweet
Texture: quite flaky

SHAD, WHICH ARE MEMBERS OF THE HERRING FAMILY (CLUPEIDAE), ARE ANADROMOUS—THAT is, they are hatched in fresh water, go out to sea to grow, and return later to spawn in the rivers in which they were born. Shad are marvelous to look at, sporting bright silver coloring, small heads, and compressed bodies. They weigh as much as 4 to 5 pounds.

The American shad and the hickory shad (*Alosa mediocris*) are related species that inhabit the rivers that spill into the Atlantic, from the Gulf of Saint Lawrence down to Florida. American shad is the important food fish. The American shad season along the East Coast is from February to May, when the fish return to the rivers of their birth to spawn. The season starts down south, gradually moving north as the waters warm up. American shad are also caught along the West Coast, from California up to Alaska. One of their home rivers is the Columbia River, where they return to spawn from May through July.

Fishmongers rarely carry whole shad—these fish are nearly always sold in filleted form. It is the females that are filleted, and filleting them is an art, known only to a few patient and skillful people. The shad has an inordinate amount of bones in its bone structure: I'm told by a man who fillets shad at the Fulton Fish Market in New York that there are 365 bones in this fish! Whether there are or not, we do know that there are double rows of bones in each fillet—I know because I own a piece of a skeleton that was given to me by the ichthyology department of the American Museum of Natural History. I do not fillet my own shad—I leave this task to others.

It is perfectly possible to cook a split shad or its fillets without boning it completely, for with long cooking the bones will eventually soften. The softening process can be helped along by sprinkling the shad or fillets with lemon juice or another acid. Shad from the Delaware River in Pennsylvania are pickled without being boned out.

The sweet-fleshed, boned-out fillets are best broiled, baked, or fried. The precious roe has to be cooked gently, only until firm all the way through, so that it does not dry out and so that the membrane that surrounds the eggs is not split.

Planking, an American Indian specialty, is an interesting way to cook shad: The shad is fastened to a board spread-eagled (butterflied), a few pieces of bacon are stretched across it, and then the board is set at an angle in front of an outdoor fire.

COOKING METHODS

CUT	COOKING METHODS	SUITABLE FOR	HOW MUCH TO BUY
Fillets	As listed below	1	6 to 8 ounces
Roe	Frying	1	1 pair

CHOICE OF RECIPES

Shad

Baked Fatty Fish Fillets, page 98

Oven-Steamed Seafood *en Papillote*, page 105

Baked Fish Fillet Casserole, page 108

Broiled Fillets, Butterflied or Split Fish, Steaks, Escalopes, or Medallions, page 127

Grilled Fish Fillets, Butterflied or Split Fish, Steaks, Medallions, or Shellfish, page 137

Fried Fish Fillets or Steaks *à la Meunière*, page 151

Hot-Smoking (Smoke-Cooking), page 197

Escabèche, page 213

Shad Roe

Fried Fish Fillets or Steaks *à la Meunière*, page 151

SHARKS

Order Selachii, Class Chondrichthyes

Mixed Species
Cholesterol 51 • Omega-3 0.84 • Fat 4.5

Fat Content: mostly low
Forms Usually Prepared: fillets and steaks
Taste: mild
Texture: firm

SHARKS INHABIT ALL THE OCEANS WORLDWIDE. BECAUSE OF THEIR VORACIOUS APPETITES, WE have been somewhat reluctant to think of sharks as food. But, not too late, we have found out that many species, including the larger mako, blacktip, and thresher sharks and the smaller species of dogfish, are highly edible.

The sharks I want to see more of in the markets and on restaurant menus are the smooth dogfish (*Mustelus canis*), also called the sand shark, and the spiny dogfish (*Squalus acanthias*), also called sand shark and grayfish. These two sharks are very similar in looks: Both have light gray to brown backs and white bellies. The spiny dogfish has short spines on its fins and is sometimes spotted. The flesh of this shark happens to be fattier than other shark (11.4 milligrams per 100 grams raw fish). These sharks weigh up to 10 pounds and are caught up and down the Atlantic Coast and in the Pacific. They are easily obtainable in Europe (lightly battered and deep-fried, they are among the fish used for England's famous fish and chips) and are such good eating. Unfortunately, they are rarely available in fish stores here, for there is not a big enough demand for them presently. Many that are caught on the East Coast, as an incidental catch along with other fish, are thrown away because they are a nuisance to the fishermen (who cannot get a good price for them) and because they tend to mess up fishing nets. We must change this situation, for the fish are delicious. I like sand shark fried (coated only with seasoned flour); it is also good baked or braised in a casserole with tomatoes.

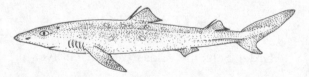

From the Pacific and the Atlantic oceans we have angel sharks (*Squatina californica*), which have small "wings" like skates. They weigh up to 60 pounds and constitute a large part of the shark catch in California. They are sold in the form of fillets and steaks.

Blacktip sharks (*Carcharhinus limbatus*) and spinners (*C. brevipinna*) from the requiem family (Carcharhinidae) of sharks are found worldwide in temperate waters. They weigh up to 80 pounds. They are gray with black tips on each fin.

Mako sharks (*Isurus glaucus*) are caught in the Atlantic from Massachusetts down to the Gulf of Mexico and in the Southern Hemisphere too.

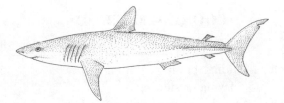

Threshers (*Alopias vulpinus*) are found worldwide. Soupfin (*Galeorhinus zyopterus*) and bonito (*Isurus oxyrinchus*) sharks, are found in the Pacific off California.

The flesh of the larger shark that we eat—like angel, blacktip, soupfin, mako, and thresher—is white to pink with red tinges when raw that turns nearly white when cooked. The flesh is similar to that of swordfish, but is not quite as flaky or sweet. Sand shark flesh is quite different from that of other sharks: Because sand sharks are smaller, their flesh is softer and has small flakes. It is firm, sweet, and white when cooked, although it is pink when raw.

All sharks have cartilaginous skeletons and no rib bones or other smaller bones to bother the cook. They must be bled within minutes after they are caught, for the urea in their blood, flesh, and skin will produce an ammonia smell. If a shark has a strong ammonia smell, don't buy or use it, but if the smell is faint, soak it in acidulated water (for example, a mixture of vinegar and water or lemon juice and water) or milk for an hour or so.

When you catch a sand shark, it is best to cut the gills if you can, or quickly cut the tail off, or at least cut to the backbone at the tail end to bleed it. Remove the head, gut the shark, then ice it down.

The larger sharks, such as mako and thresher sharks, are cut into loins or wheels and then into steaks or cubes for brochettes. Sand sharks are skinned and then cut in steaks, fillets, or cubes for brochettes.

How to Skin a Sand Shark

• Cut off the fins and make a slit in the skin along the back, from head to tail. Loosen the skin from the flesh at the head end of the fish and use pliers to pull it off down to the tail end. Repeat with the other side of the fish. You can cut off and discard the belly flaps if you wish—they are very fatty, though they are often exported to Europe, where they are smoked.

• Now you can fillet the fish—this is easily done by cutting along both sides of the cartilaginous "backbone"—or you can simply cut the fish into 1-inch-thick steaks (cut across the grain of the fish) or 3-inch-long chunks.

COOKING METHODS

CUT	COOKING METHODS	SUITABLE FOR	HOW MUCH TO BUY
Sand shark fillets	Baking, broiling, grilling frying or stewing	1	6 to 8 ounces
Sand shark steaks	Frying, broiling, grilling, stewing, or braising	1	6 to 8 ounces
Mako or thresher steaks	Broiling, grilling, or hot-smoking	1	8 to 10 ounces
Mako or thresher cubes	Broiling, grilling, soup, or stew	1	4 to 6 ounces

CHOICE OF RECIPES

Sand Shark Fillets

Baked Fish Fillet Casserole, page 108
Baked Fish Fillet Casserole with Light Tomato Sauce, page 109
Baked Cajun Fish Casserole, page 111
Broiled Fillets, Butterflied or Split Fish, Steaks, Escalopes, or Medallions, page 127
Grilled Fish Fillets, Butterflied or Split Fish, Steaks, Medallions, or Shellfish, page 137
Fried Fish Fillets or Steaks à la Meunière, page 151
Seafood Stew or Pasta Sauce, page 192
Seafood Stew with Tomato and Green Pepper, page 203

Sand Shark Steaks

Broiled Fillets, Butterflied or Split Fish, Steaks, Escalopes, or Medallions, page 127
Grilled Fish Fillets, Butterflied or Split Fish, Steaks, Medallions, or Shellfish, page 137
Grilled or Broiled Seafood Brochettes, page 139
Grilled or Broiled Seafood and Vegetable Brochettes, page 141
Fried Fish Fillets or Steaks à la Meunière, page 151
Braised Monkfish Tail, Dolphinfish (Mahi-mahi) Fillets, or Sand Shark, page 183
Braised Fish Fillets or Steaks with Provençale Sauce, page 184
Seafood Stew or Pasta Sauce, page 192
Seafood Stew with Tomato and Green Pepper, page 203

**Steaks and Cubes of Mako, Thresher, and
Other Large Sharks**

Broiled Fillets, Butterflied or Split Fish, Steaks, Escalopes, or Medallions,
page 127
Grilled Fish Fillets, Butterflied or Split Fish, Steaks, Medallions, or Shellfish,
page 137
Grilled or Broiled Seafood Brochettes, page 139
Grilled or Broiled Seafood and Vegetable Brochettes, page 141
Fish Soup (*Bourride*), page 188
Creamy Seafood Chowder, page 190
Seafood Stew or Pasta Sauce, page 192
Hot-Smoking (Smoke-Cooking), page 197
Seafood Stew with Tomato and Green Pepper, page 203
Marinade, page 216

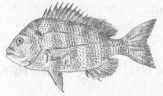

SHEEPSHEAD

Family Sparidae, *Archosargus probatocephalus*

Cholesterol N/A • Omega-3 N/A • Fat 2.4

> *Fat Content:* low
> *Form Usually Prepared:* fillets and split
> fish
> *Taste:* sweet
> *Texture:* firm flake

THE SHEEPSHEAD IS A ROUND, FLAT-BODIED SALTWATER PORGY. THE STRONG WIDE STRIPES THAT cross its body from back to belly inspired another name for it—the convict! Sheepshead have thick lips and extremely strong teeth, with which they eat all sorts of shellfish, including barnacles.

Sheepshead Bay in New York was named after these fish, but they are no longer found in its waters, which have turned too cool for them. Sheepshead are fished in the Atlantic, from New York down to the Florida Keys. They are also found in the Gulf of Mexico and off South America. They are caught at weights up to 15 pounds. They are sold whole or pan-dressed and a small quantity are filleted. Their flesh is white and firm when cooked.

I find sheepshead flesh delicious. I took a tip from Susan Herrmann Loomis, author of the *The Great American Seafood Cookbook* and mixed some steamed sheepshead fillet with a little crab seasoning. Voilà! It tasted like crab.

COOKING METHODS

CUT	COOKING METHODS	SUITABLE FOR	HOW MUCH TO BUY
Whole	Roasting	2	1½ pounds
Pan-dressed	Frying	2	1½ pounds
Fillets	As listed below	1	6 to 10 ounces

CHOICE OF RECIPES

Oven-Steamed Seafood *en Papillote*, page 105
Baked Cajun Fish Casserole, page 111
Roast Whole Fish, page 115
Broiled Fillets, Butterflied or Split Fish, Steaks, Escalopes, or Medallions, page 127
Grilled Fish Fillets, Butterflied or Split Fish, Steaks, Medallions, or Shellfish, page 137
Fried Whole Fish or Pan-Dressed Fish, page 153
Blackened Fish Fillets, page 156
Steamed Seafood, page 176
Fish Salad I, page 221
Fish Salad II, page 222

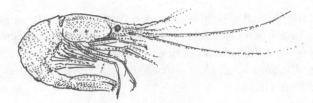

SHRIMP

Family Penaeidae and Pandalidae

Mixed Species
Cholesterol 152•Omega-3 0.48•Fat 1.73

Fat Content: low
Form Usually Prepared: headless, in
  and out of shell
Taste: mild
Texture: firm

SHRIMP DISHES ARE WIDELY POPULAR, AND NO WONDER. THERE ARE A MYRIAD OF WAYS OF preparing the delicately flavored shrimp and all of these methods are delicious as long as the shrimp are cooked well, that is, not too long, for they toughen and lose flavor.

Shrimp are found worldwide, and we import many from such diverse places as India, Bangladesh, Thailand, and most of the Central and South American countries, where many shrimp are farmed. The largest exporters of shrimp to the United States are Ecuador, China, and Mexico, in that order. Nearly all the shrimp from these countries are sold frozen with heads removed.

Several species of shrimp are found in our coastal waters. Northern shrimp (*Pandalus borealis*) are harvested from the waters off Maine from December through March. They are usually sold cooked, peeled, and frozen, but some are available fresh in the spring. Look out for them—they are pink when raw, small, and fragile and should be steamed whole as quickly as possible. They are great eating—don't forget to suck the head of a northern shrimp after you break it away from the tail for the delicious piece of "fat" (liver, pancreas, and roe) inside. *P. jordani*, another pink shrimp, is harvested from the waters of the Pacific near Oregon.

Brown (*Penacus aztecus*) and white shrimp (*P. setiferus*) are harvested in waters from South Carolina to the Gulf of Mexico. Pink shrimp (*P. duorarum*) are harvested from the Gulf of Mexico off southwest Florida. Most are sold frozen, but in some markets they are available fresh with heads on.

Another shrimp harvested from fresh water is called the blue prawn or sweet-water prawn (*Machrobrachium rosenbergii*). Similar in looks to other shrimp, blue prawns have marvelous-looking armored heads; they are blue with red tinges on their long antennae and claws. These prawns are farmed primarily in Hawaii, and also in Puerto Rico, Jamaica, Brazil, and the southern states. Blue prawns are rushed to restaurants for immediate cooking. They are most delicious.

Spot shrimp or prawns (*P. platyceros*) are an exceptionally well-flavored shrimp from the Pacific. It's best to buy and eat them when on the West Coast, for they are highly perishable.

Head-off shrimp are available in fish stores frozen or defrosted, cooked or raw, with shell on or peeled. Some fish stores sell shrimp that are peeled, deveined, and cooked. Frozen, cooked, and peeled shrimp are also sold in cans. Many chefs will only use fresh, not frozen, shrimp when they are in season; you should buy fresh local whole shrimp when you can, but know that the other shrimp you see (about 95 percent of the available shrimp) have been defrosted and should be cooked quickly. Be sure they smell fresh; that is, be sure they have no odor of ammonia. The color of raw shell-on shrimp can vary from a transparent light brown to gray to pink and orange and even to black (the color of oriental tiger prawns), but when shrimp are cooked the shells are nearly always pink to red and the flesh turns an attractive pearly white with pink and red shadings. Sometimes a pink-shelled shrimp may look cooked when it is actually raw. If you aren't sure, ask your fishmonger.

Shrimp are graded by size—the larger the shrimp, the higher the price. They range in weight from 400 to the pound (tiny shrimp that are peeled, cooked, and frozen called titi in the trade) to 8 to the pound (extra-colossal shrimp).

Incidentally, it is useful to know that in English-speaking countries the names *shrimp* and *prawn* refer to the same creature, though local usage may differ. In England tiny shrimp in cans are called shrimp, but all other larger shrimp are called prawns. Dublin Bay prawns (*Nephrops norvegicus*), however, are neither shrimp nor prawns, but miniature lobsters (see page 344). To add to the confusion, *scampi* is the Italian name for the Dublin Bay prawn, but in restaurants here in the United States, *shrimp scampi* refers to a dish of sautéed shrimp with a butter and garlic sauce.

The Why and How of Deveining and Peeling or Shelling Shrimp

• I have had to shell and devein thousands of shrimp in my life and it's really not such a chore, as some would have it.

• Every shrimp has a vein running down its back that is unsightly but edible— this is its digestive tract. All too often, however, just when I am trying to explain the deveining process during cooking demonstrations, I find empty-veined shrimp that look as if they are veinless! You can imagine my frustration, but I proceed to show the method anyway.

• Use a pair of scissors. Hold each shrimp with the head end toward you and insert the point of the scissors under the shell on the top (back) of the shrimp. Cut the shell down to the next to the last section before the tail. Now peel the shell off and discard it. You will see that the vein is exposed, so just pull it out and rinse the shrimp. Voilà! The shrimp is ready and it looks attractive with the tail shell still attached.

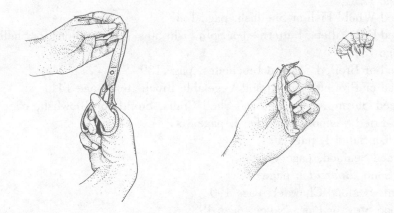

• It is my firm opinion that tiny headless shrimp need not be shelled or even deveined, for the vein will be negligible and the shell, which is soft and edible, will impart a special flavor to the flesh when it is cooked. Large shrimp

cooked in their shells are delicious, but you must be willing to peel them with your fingers, which I enjoy if I have plenty of napkins and a finger bowl!
• Cooking lightly marinated shell-on shrimp on an outdoor grill or even in a cast-iron frying or grill pan makes them taste fantastic. You can also poach peeled shrimp for salads, steam them with vegetables, broil them, braise them, or cook them in a stew, soup, paella, gumbo, or jambalaya.

How to Butterfly a Shrimp

• To butterfly a shrimp, peel and devein it, then make a cut down the back nearly all the way through and spread it open.

COOKING METHODS

FORM	COOKING METHODS	SUITABLE FOR	HOW MUCH TO BUY
Head-off	As listed below	1	4 to 8 ounces
Fresh head-on	Steaming	1	4 to 8 ounces

CHOICE OF RECIPES

Oven-Steamed Seafood *en Papillote*, page 105
Broiled Fillets, Butterflied or Split Fish, Steaks, Escalopes, or Medallions, page 127
Grilled Whole Fish or Shellfish, page 134
Grilled Fish Fillets, Butterflied or Split Fish, Steaks, Medallions, or Shellfish, page 137
Grilled or Broiled Seafood Brochettes, page 139
Grilled or Broiled Seafood and Vegetable Brochettes, page 141
Sautéed Shrimp, Scallops, Soft-Shell Crabs, Squid, or Blowfish, page 155
Deep-Fried Seafood: Variation I, page 160
Shellfish Salad I, page 172
Steamed Seafood, page 176
Fish Soup (*Bourride*), page 188
Creamy Seafood Chowder, page 190
Seafood Stew or Pasta Sauce, page 192
Hot-Smoking (Smoke-Cooking), page 197
Seafood Stew with Tomato and Green Pepper, page 203

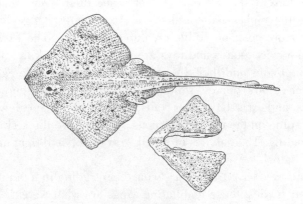

SKATES

Family Rajidae

RAYS

Cholesterol N/A • Omega-3 N/A • Fat 1.3

Fat Content: low
Form Usually Prepared: wings
Taste: sweet
Texture: tender, filamentous

THESE GRACEFUL CREATURES GLIDE THROUGH THE WATER LIKE FUTURISTIC AIRPLANES. IN U. S. waters, they are found in the Atlantic (from Canada to Florida) and the Pacific; in addition, many species inhabit the oceans of the world. Some of the better known are the big (*Raja binoculata*), thorny (*R. radiata*), smooth (*R. senta*), clearnose (*R. eglanteria*), and barndoor skates (*R. laevis*), the cownose rays (*Rhinoptera bonasus*), and many species of stingray. It is not easy to distinguish the different species when we only see their wings in the fish store.

Although the names *skate* and *ray* are used interchangeably, we usually refer to the more common edible creatures as skates. The French, however, use the name *raie*. Skates and rays are very similar-looking. They have cartilaginous skeletons and their young are hatched from little egg cases called mermaids' or sailors' purses, which we find along the seashore and beaches. Both skates and rays have long tails, and in some species, such as the stingray, a spine on the tail is poisonous. Skates have thick skins covered by a viscous coating. Their skin is brownish gray on top and light underneath like the skin of flatfish.

Skates and rays have triangular "wings" protruding in a fan shape from the sides of their bodies; these undulating wings are what we eat. The wings are enlarged pectoral fins, and skates and rays use them to swim and to burrow in the sand for food or hiding places. A wing can measure up to 2 inches thick at its thickest point and be near zero thickness at its edge. In some species, tiny thornlike spines stick out of the tops of the wings, hence the name given to one species—*the thorny skate.*

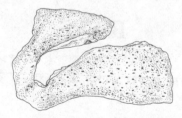

The composition of the flesh and cartilage is as follows: filaments or strands of flesh in one layer, then a layer of cartilage and more strands of flesh underneath. The thin part of the cartilage is soft and edible. The flesh easily slides off the layer of cartilage "bone." It is this flesh that is so delicious: It is sweet and white. I refuse to believe the story that is bandied about that people used to cut "scallops" out of the flesh and sell them as such. It is just not possible that anyone could be fooled by this deception because skate is made up of distinctly separate strands of flesh, tenously held together, that tend to separate easily after the flesh is cooked.

Skate wings are eaten all over Europe—*raie au beurre noir* is a marvelous French dish, using browned butter and capers as a sauce—and skate cheeks and livers are also favored. Unfortunately, in this country, skates are caught as a by-product to the catch of other groundfish and are often thrown back in the water. Very little skate is processed for the home market—most that is taken is exported to Europe. When the wings do reach the market, they are very cheap, and you should snap them up.

You can buy whole wings or parts of wings. Sometimes fishmongers fillet these wings, which I think is highly unnecessary, as the flesh falls so easily off the cartilaginous bones when cooked. Whole skate wings weigh 1 pound or more.

Unless skates are bled immediately, the urea in their flesh will produce an ammonia smell. The ammonia smell is a natural phenomenon with the shark and skate family, for they carry urea in their blood and tissue to keep a natural balance of salt in their bodies. Blanch skates in vinegar mixed with water, or soak them in salt water, milk, or lemon juice and water. Bleeding skate properly when first caught will also help to keep their flesh white.

How to Skin Skate Wings

• Prepare a poaching liquid with:

Water to cover the skate wings
½ cup dry white wine
1 carrot, peeled and sliced
½ teaspoon black peppercorns
2 celery stalks, roughly chopped

1. Bring the poaching liquid to the boil.
2. Turn the heat to low and simmer for 10 minutes.
3. Immerse skin-on skate wings in the liquid one at a time and cook over very low heat for 1 to 2 minutes, depending on how large they are. *Note:* If you want to poach the skate wings, cook them for another 4 to 5 minutes, until they are cooked all the way through. Insert a fork or knife and pull the flesh apart to see whether the flesh is opaque all the way through.

4. Lift the skate wings out of the water with wide spatulas and let them drain on a plate or dishcloth for a minute or so.

5. Use a thin pointed knife to remove the skin. It should come off easily. Also remove any part of the flesh that is dark so that all that is remaining is strands of completely white flesh. There is no need to pull the bottom (white) skin off.

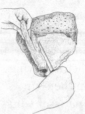

Raw skate wings can be skinned by pulling the skin of (across the wing) with heavy pliers.

You can broil, fry, grill, or steam skate. You can make lovely salads with it. Little wings look most decorous on a plate and the larger wings can be cut into portion-sized pieces or into little strips about 1½ inches wide that can be placed in a star pattern on the plate.

Skates need to be accompanied by a sauce or dressing with acid, such as the lime and dill vinaigrette on page 230. Tomatillo salsa, on page 226, is also a good accompaniment.

COOKING METHODS

CUT	COOKING METHODS	SUITABLE FOR	HOW MUCH TO BUY
Whole wings	As listed below	1	8 to 12 ounces
Fillets	As listed below	1	6 to 8 ounces

CHOICE OF RECIPES

Broiled Fillets, Butterflied or Split Fish, Steaks, Escalopes, or Medallions, page 127

Grilled Fish Fillets, Butterflied or Split Fish, Steaks, Medallions, or Shellfish, page 137

Fried Skate Wings *à la Meunière*, page 151

Poached Small Whole Fish or Fish Portions, page 170
Steamed Seafood, page 176
Fish Salad I, page 221

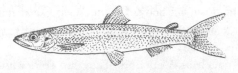

SMELT

Family Osmeridae

Rainbow smelt
Cholesterol 70 • Omega-3 0.6 • Fat 2.42

Eulachon
Cholesterol N/A • Omega-3 N/A • Fat N/A

Fat Content: low
Form Usually Prepared: butterflied fish
   (sometimes headless)
Taste: sweet
Texture: flaky

MOST OF THESE BEAUTIFUL, IRIDESCENT LITTLE FISH ARE ANADROMOUS (THOSE THAT LIVE IN THE sea, but spawn in rivers) and are caught when returning to fresh water to spawn. Others have adapted to life in fresh water and now inhabit cold-water lakes and streams; this means they are available for much of the year, which is good news for those who love to eat them. Most smelts are caught from the Atlantic, primarily off the coast of Canada, especially at New Brunswick, and also off the coast of Maine. They are also caught in the Pacific and the Great Lakes.

There are many species of smelt. Varieties include the eulachon (*Thaleichthys pacificus*), a West Coast fish that is also known as the icefish, frostfish, and candlefish because of its oiliness; and the rainbow smelt (*Osmerus mordax*), a pale olive-green fish with a yellow and silver belly and a bright silver lateral band running down its body. On the West Coast many fish are called smelts when they are actually from the silversides family, Atherinidae—jack smelts, for example, are silversides.

Smelts weigh as much as ⅓ pound. They are sold whole and gutted and sometimes beheaded, fresh and frozen. They are so small that they can be easily gutted through the head: Pull out the gills and the guts will follow (see page 56). If you feel roe inside the fish, either squeeze the fish gently like a toothpaste tube to get the roe out or leave it in. The roe is a delight to eat along with the fish.

The flesh of smelts is sweet with fine flakes when cooked. Deep-fry, fry, or broil them whole, filleted, or butterflied. I prefer to cook a whole smelt that has been gutted through the head. I eat it with my fingers, chewing up the bones and head if they are very small, and if they are larger I pull the flesh off either side of the backbone with my teeth to savor the delicious, sweet flesh!

COOKING METHODS

CUT	COOKING METHODS	SUITABLE FOR	HOW MUCH TO BUY
Whole	Roasting, deep-frying, or escabèche	1	8 to 12 ounces
Butterflied and fillets	Frying, broiling, grilling, or escabèche	1	6 to 8 ounces

CHOICE OF RECIPES

Roast Whole Fish, page 115

Broiled Fillets, Butterflied or Split Fish, Steaks, Escalopes, or Medallions, page 127

Grilled Fish Fillets, Butterflied or Split Fish, Steaks, Medallions, or Shellfish, page 137

Fried Fish Fillets or Steaks *à la Meunière*, page 151

Deep-Fried Seafood: Variation I, page 166

Escabèche, page 213

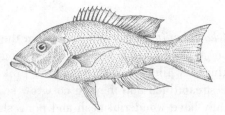

SNAPPER, RED

Lutjanus campechanus

Mixed Species
Cholesterol 37 • Omega-3 0.31 • Fat 1.3

> *Fat Content:* low
> *Form Usually Prepared:* fillets
> *Taste:* mild
> *Texture:* flaky

ALTHOUGH THERE ARE MANY MEMBERS OF THE SNAPPER FAMILY (LUTJANIDAE) BEARING MANY different names and 103 species of the *Lutjanus* genus, there is only one true red snapper, according to the Food and Drug Administration. Also called the American red or northern red snapper, this is truly a special fish that can command good prices. It is a handsome fish with spiny fins, a large head with a strong gill cover, large scales, eyes with red irises and black pupils, and beautiful pink-tinged skin. It is also a magnificent fish to taste. The red snapper is caught in the Atlantic in warm waters off North Carolina, down south off the Florida "snapper banks," off the coasts of Texas and Louisiana, and from the Campeche Bank off Mexico.

Around the world there are many other snappers with similar looks to the red snapper. Some are the mutton snapper (*Lutjanus analis*), blackfin snapper (*L. buccanella*), gray or mangrove snapper (*L. griseus*), lane snapper (*L. synagris*), and mahogany snapper (*L. mahagoni*). Silk snappers (*L. vivanus*), also incorrectly called queen snappers, whose eyes have yellow irises, are also called yelloweye snappers. Yellowtail snappers (*Ocyurus chryurus*) and vermilion snappers (*Rhombloplites aurorubens*) are from the same family but not the same genus; they are similar in looks, with yellow markings. The vermilion snapper is red-skinned while the red snapper is pink-skinned. Vermilion snappers are more streamlined and they do not grow so large.

Snappers generally have wonderful flesh and none should be shunned. A large number of snappers are imported from Central and South American waters nowadays; they are similar-tasting fish. They usually come to us already gutted and with gills removed. But look carefully for the true American red snapper—other snappers may be called by this name to justify a high price. Incidentally, on the West Coast a red-skinned rockfish may be called a red snapper to fetch a high price. This is allowed in California but not in interstate trade.

Red snappers weighing up to 30 pounds and more are caught, although we usually see 1- to 3-pounders at the fish store. True red snapper is sold whole and in filleted form, nearly always with its skin left on, for that is one of the main attractions of this fish and it also helps to identify the fish. (On the East Coast be suspicious of "skinned red or white snapper fillets"—they're probably tilefish!) When buying whole red snappers, keep in mind that true red snappers have large, heavy heads (the South American species have smaller heads).

Snappers are easy to fillet once you know how to fillet roundfish (see page 59). However, I prefer to roast these creatures whole: Take a snapper weighing 1 to 1½ pounds and roast it with a good variety of vegetables, or take one weighing 10 to 15 pounds that is stuffed very simply with fresh herbs and seasonings and roast it on a bed of sliced onions. Red snapper flesh is especially white, sweet, and lean when cooked.

The frames (heads, bones, and skin) of snappers make wonderful stock.

COOKING METHODS

CUT	COOKING METHODS	SUITABLE FOR	HOW MUCH TO BUY
Whole	Roasting, broiling, grilling, and frying	2	1½ to 2 pounds
Whole	Roasting	Dinner for 10	10 pounds
Whole	Roasting	Part of a buffet for 20	10 pounds
Whole	Bake-poaching	Dinner for 8 to 10	7 pounds
Fillets	As listed below	1	6 to 10 ounces

CHOICE OF RECIPES

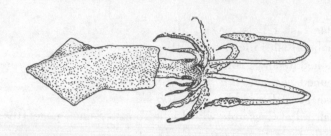

SQUID

SQUID, LONG-FINNED OR WINTER   *Loligo pealei*

Cholesterol 283 • Omega-3 0.24 • Fat 0.7

SQUID, SHORT-FINNED OR SUMMER   *Illex illecebrosus*

Cholesterol 260 • Omega-3 0.8 • Fat 1.8

SQUID, PACIFIC   *Loligo opalescens*

Cholesterol N/A • Omega-3 N/A • Fat 1.0

Fat Content: low
Form Usually Prepared: cleaned and
    uncleaned
Taste: mild
Texture: firm

SQUID ARE TENTACLED, "HEAD-FOOTED" CREATURES (CEPHALOPODS)—A SQUID'S EIGHT ARMS and two tentacles are attached to its head. Squid are also mollusks. A squid has a thin internal quill, or pen, that supports its soft body. It can swim at great speeds and therefore can migrate great distances.

Squid are caught in both the Atlantic and Pacific in some abundance. The biggest fisheries are in Japanese waters, off Argentina in the Pacific, and off Morocco in the Atlantic. Squid are also caught in the Mediterranean: There is nothing so good as the tiny squid of Greece, which, when I stayed there, we refused to eat if they were any larger than the first joints of our thumbs! On the East Coast of North America, the two main commercial species caught are the summer squid, also known as the short-finned squid, which is taken primarily from Canadian Atlantic waters, and the winter squid, also known as the long-finned squid, which is taken from the Atlantic waters of the United States. The biggest markets for squid are the Orient, Spain, Italy, and the United States.

In the fish store we see squid tubes (bodies) that range in size from 3 to 12 inches long, although squid grow to some 30 feet long. They are sold cleaned and uncleaned, with head, arms, and tentacles fresh and frozen. Much squid is processed at sea and even frozen on board. Look for creamy white flesh under a brown, mottled membrane on the summer squid, and the same pearly flesh on the winter squid with a membrane that turns purplish the longer it is out of the water.

Also known as *calamari* (Italian) or *calmars* (French), squid are often sold in restaurants as fried rings, stuffed, or in seafood salad. Because of their pocketlike shape, they are perfect for stuffing. Cut small, they make a flavorful addition to soups and stews. The arms and tentacles may be unsightly for some, but they can be chopped for stuffings or added to soups. Large giant squid are cut in round or oval "steaks" on the West Coast; they can be nearly an inch thick and are tenderized before being grilled or broiled.

Ink is usually found in a little sac in the body of a squid, although sometimes the sac is too small or nonexistent (perhaps the squid blew all its ink away in fright at being caught, or hadn't developed any yet). Squid ink is also available in little sachets at a reasonable cost in specialty stores. It is worth collecting to flavor sauces or a black risotto. Nowadays, some black pasta is made with squid ink.

How to Clean Fresh Whole Squid

• Gently pull the head, arms, and tentacles from the body. Remove the creamy-colored viscera and plasticlike quill from the inside of the body. Rinse

well for sand and pull off the outer membrane. Find the ink sac near the head and inside the eyes; reserve it if needed. Cut the arms and tentacles from the head and remove the small beak from it. (The beak is a little, hard, round ball with a beak like a bird's inside it.) Cut the large tentacles in two and use them for a stock, stuffing, soup, or stew.

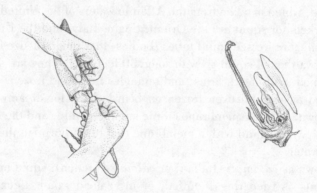

• Squid ink is very thick and viscous. Have a two-cup measure ready with ½ cup water in it. Squeeze the ink from the sac into the water and also rinse your fingers in the water. This way you will catch all the ink.

• If the squid has been "cleaned" by the processor or the fish store, you still need to rinse it well for sand and pull off the outer membrane if it is still on.

• Squid flesh will toughen easily with overcooking, so cook a small squid very quickly at high temperatures. If it toughens, you must then cook it until it gets tender again. This might take a long time. Large squid take slightly longer than small squid to cook.

COOKING METHODS

CUT	COOKING METHODS	SUITABLE FOR	HOW MUCH TO BUY
Cut in rings	As listed below	1	6 to 8 ounces (uncleaned squid)
Cut in rings	As listed below	1	4 to 6 ounces (cleaned squid)

CHOICE OF RECIPES

Sautéed Shrimp, Scallops, Soft-Shell Crabs, Squid, or Blowfish, page 155
Deep-Fried Seafood: Variation I, page 160
Shellfish Salad I, page 172
Steamed Seafood, page 176
Fish Soup (*Bourride*), page 188
Seafood Stew or Pasta Sauce, page 192
Seafood Stew with Tomato and Green Pepper, page 203
Seviche, page 211
Sushi and Sashimi, page 219

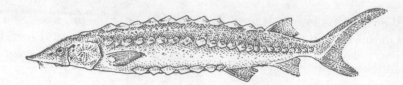

STURGEONS

Family Acipenseridae

Mixed Species
Cholesterol N/A • Omega-3 N/A • Fat 5.2

> *Fat Content:* low (ocean species),
>   high (lake species)
> *Forms Usually Prepared:* steaks and
>   fillets
> *Taste:* mild
> *Texture:* firm

THE ANADROMOUS STURGEONS ARE THE GRAND OLD PREHISTORIC FISH OF RIVER AND SEA. AS THE source of the best caviar (treated eggs or roe), they are precious to us. Their flesh is also in high demand, for it is delicious when cooked or smoked. Sturgeon flesh is better known as a smoked product, but that is changing as more people begin to appreciate it freshly cooked.

Sturgeons grow to a large size, a mature old age, and a great weight (nowadays they are caught at weights up to 350 pounds, although weights of 40 to 50 pounds are more common). Sturgeons have five rows of bony scutes (strong bony plates or scales) running along their bodies. The mouth is a long snout with whiskers on the bottom that are used to search for food in dark, sometimes muddy waters. They are colored olive-gray, brown, green, or gray. It has a primitive cartilaginous "backbone" that surrounds its notochord (spinal cord); the notochord can be removed by twisting and pulling it out all in one piece. Isinglass, used to clarify liquids, used to be prepared from air bladders of sturgeon, as well as from other fish.

As a consequence of overfishing, sturgeons are scarce and rigid fishing limitations have been set. The Atlantic sturgeon from Nova Scotia to North Carolina (*Acipenser oxyrhynchus*) and the shortnose sturgeon (*A. brevirostris*) from Cape Cod to Florida have been nearly fished out. The white sturgeon (*A. transmontanus*) and the green sturgeon (*A. medirostris*) are still found in rivers, bays, lakes, and coastal waters from California to Alaska; the Columbia River is the largest source of these West Coast sturgeons. Lake sturgeon (*A. fulvescens*) once inhabited the Great Lakes but are scarce nowadays. Shovelnose (*Scaphirhynchus platorhyncus*) and pallid sturgeons (*S. album*) inhabit the lakes and rivers of Mississippi Valley. Some sturgeons are also farmed in California.

The flesh of sturgeon is cut in fillets and also in steaks. It is a delightful taste treat if grilled or braised.

Salted American sturgeon eggs, or roe, can be sold as caviar as long as they are marketed as American caviar to distinguish them from the imported sturgeon caviars of Russia and Iran. Roe from other fish, such as whitefish and lumpfish, can also be treated and sold as caviar as long as the name of the fish is included in the name—for example, "golden whitefish caviar" or "black lumpfish caviar."

COOKING METHOD

CUT	COOKING METHOD	SUITABLE FOR	HOW MUCH TO BUY
Steaks, fillets	As listed below	1	6 to 8 ounces

CHOICE OF RECIPES

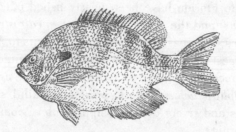

SUNFISH

Family Centrarchidae

Cholesterol 67 • Omega-3 N/A • Fat 0.7

Fat Content: low
Form Usually Prepared: pan-dressed
Taste: mild
Texture: flaky

SUNFISH ARE COLORFUL FISH THAT ARE CAUGHT IN FRESH WATER IN LAKES, RIVERS, AND streams all over the inland United States and southern Canada. There are many species of sunfish—bluegill, green, warmouth, pumpkinseed, redbreast, spotted, longear, and redear, just to name a few. Other very similar species are the black and white crappies. Largemouth and smallmouth bass are also members of the sunfish family.

Sunfish have lean and delicate flesh, and are best pan-fried, grilled, or roasted. Watch out for bones!

COOKING METHODS

CUT	COOKING METHODS	SUITABLE FOR	HOW MUCH TO BUY
Whole	Roasting or grilling	2	1½ to 2 pounds
Pan-dressed or split	Broiling, grilling, or frying	2	1½ to 2 pounds

CHOICE OF RECIPES

Roast Whole Fish, page 115

Broiled Fillets, Butterflied or Split Fish, Steaks, Escalopes, or Medallions, page 127

Grilled Whole Fish or Shellfish, page 134

Grilled Fish Fillets, Butterflied or Split Fish, Steaks, Medallions, or Shellfish, page 137

Fried Whole Fish or Pan-Dressed Fish, page 153

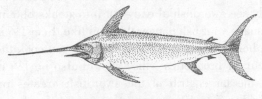

SWORDFISH

Xiphias gladius

Cholesterol 39 • Omega-3 0.6 • Fat 4.0

Fat Content: low
Forms Usually Prepared: steaks and cubes
Taste: mild
Texture: firm

RANGING THE WARM WATERS OF THE WORLD, THE SWORDFISH WHICH GROWS UP TO 1,000 pounds but is usually caught weighing about 250 pounds, is a favorite food of mine and probably yours. This fish, a member of the billfish "clan" also called the broadbill, is aptly named for the flat swordlike protrusion that extends from the upper part of the jaw; it uses this "sword" to swat and stun its diet of fish. The swordfish has a torpedo-shaped body that tapers off narrowly at the tail end and has strong fins that help get it through the water with speed.

Swordfish are caught in the Atlantic from Newfoundland (when the waters get warm) down to Argentina. In the Pacific they are found from Chile up to California. Swordfish are imported to America from places like Chile, Japan, Taiwan, Spain, Brazil, Ecuador, Portugal, and Greece (Spain is the largest producer), but Americans favor the swordfish caught off the East Coast (New England) because it is very well handled by the fishermen—that is, it is bled on board fishing boats and not stored too long on them.

Swordfish are usually beheaded at sea (some fishermen save and exhibit the swords if they are very large). When the fish are brought to shore, distributors cut them into large "wheels," which are cuts across the body. In the fish store you will most likely see swordfish already cut into steaks obtained from these wheels. Try to persuade your fishmonger that you like them 1¼ inches thick—this thickness will help to keep the steaks moist as you cook them. The same is true for cubes cut for brochettes—they should also be 1¼ inches square. (*Note:* Sometimes the large girth of the swordfish creates problems when cutting steaks weighing 7 to 10 ounces—the proper size for a portion. You may have to cut them less than 1¼ inches thick. If a swordfish steak is less than 1 inch thick, cook it very carefully.)

Swordfish flesh is firm, lean, and sweet. It can be gray, orange, white, or pink when raw, but it turns white when cooked. The only bothersome bone in a swordfish steak is the central backbone, which is large and easily avoided. There is a dark red muscle running through the fish that some feel they must cut out before cooking, but it is in fact edible.

COOKING METHODS

CUT	COOKING METHODS	SUITABLE FOR	HOW MUCH TO BUY
Steaks	Broiling, grilling, hot-smoking, or escabèche	1	7 to 10 ounces
Brochette cubes	As listed below	1	4 to 8 ounces

CHOICE OF RECIPES

Broiled Fillets, Butterflied or Split Fish, Steaks, Escalopes, or Medallions, page 127
Grilled Fish Fillets, Butterflied or Split Fish, Steaks, Medallions, or Shellfish, page 137
Grilled or Broiled Seafood Brochettes, page 139
Grilled or Broiled Seafood and Vegetable Brochettes, page 141
Fish Soup (*Bourride*), page 188
Creamy Seafood Chowder, page 190
Hot-Smoking (Smoke-Cooking), page 197
Seviche, page 211
Escabèche, page 213

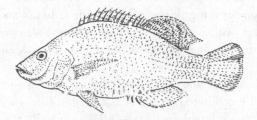

TILAPIA

Family Cichlidae; *Genus Orechromis, Sarotherodon,* or *Tilapia*

Cholesterol N/A • Omega-3 N/A • Fat 2.5

> *Fat Content:* low
> *Form Usually Prepared:* fillets
> *Taste:* mild
> *Texture:* firm

TILAPIA IS A GENERAL NAME GIVEN TO SEVERAL SPECIES OF FISH THAT HAVE BEEN BRED FOR years all over the world in freshwater ponds, although they can also grow in seawater. Africa (from Egypt down to the Cape of Good Hope), India, Bangladesh, Indonesia, Jamaica, Hawaii, and Taiwan are just a few of the places where these fish are bred. Israel has now started to farm and export tilapia, and recently many tilapia farms have been established all over the United States, primarily in southern states such as Florida, Texas, and Arizona.

The beauty of tilapia is that they can reach the table in a day or so, because they can be processed so quickly and efficiently from the ponds and they stay fresh longer than saltwater fish. These fish grow in great profusion in small ponds; when the ponds are kept clean, the tilapia produced are excellent food fish. Tilapia grow fast in warm water—80 degrees F produces large fish, though they cannot survive in water less than 60 degrees F or more than 85 degrees F. In the southern states of the United States where they are bred, it is easy to keep the water temperatures high; in other states, breeders use water from naturally warm springs or warm the water artificially.

Tilapia have good-looking skin which as a rule is black and white, like salt and pepper—black with light shadings where the scales were. Breeders in Florida, Texas, and Arizona have developed hybrids with an attractive pink-red skin.

Tilapia grow up to 3 pounds, but most of those marketed weigh less. They are available whole or filleted, fresh or frozen; the fillets weigh 3 ounces or more, and those bred in Israel are usually filleted with the skin on. The texture of the flesh is not unlike that of catfish—firm yet light and sweet when cooked.

Tilapia is most versatile for cooking. It will suit most cooking methods, but remember to feature its good-looking skin, whether it is black and white, or red.

A word of warning: Up to now the Food and Drug Administration has insisted that these fish be called tilapia, but some (for instance, some of the tilapia bred in Israel) can slip by as Saint Peter's fish in supermarkets. Some tilapia from Florida, Texas, and Arizona are given names such as sunshine snapper and cherry snapper, which are also not correct.

COOKING METHODS

CUT	COOKING METHODS	SUITABLE FOR	HOW MUCH TO BUY
Whole	Roasting	2	1½ pounds
Pan-dressed	Frying	1	¾ to 1 pound
Fillets	As listed below	1	6 to 8 ounces

CHOICE OF RECIPES

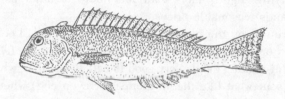

TILEFISH

Lopholatilus chamaeleonticeps

Cholesterol N/A • Omega-3 0.4 • Fat 2.3

> *Fat Content:* low
> *Forms Usually Prepared:* fillets and steaks
> *Taste:* mild
> *Texture:* flaky

THE TILEFISH, ALSO MOST APTLY CALLED THE GOLDEN TILEFISH AND THE RAINBOW TILEFISH, does bear all the colors of the rainbow. Its blue-green back extends to a blue head, which is tinged with rose and yellow. Its back and head are dotted with yellow and gold spots and its sides, which are pink and yellow, shade to a white-silver belly. Sadly, once out of water the fish tends to lose some of this fine coloring.

Although its colors might suggest that the tilefish belongs in tropical waters, it is fished in waters from the Gulf of Mexico up the East Coast to Cape Cod. Much tilefish is caught off the New Jersey coast year-round; Barnegat Light in New Jersey has been called the tilefish capital of the world. The usual weight is between 5 and 20 pounds, although tilefish weighing up to 60 pounds have been caught.

Tilefish are cut into steaks at the fish store or sold in filleted form. If you want a whole fish, know that the head is large and heavy (only the cheek is edible) and the relative percentage of flesh to bone is not large. Tilefish exudes a fair amount of moisture as it cooks, so there is some shrinkage. Compensate for this by buying slightly more than you would of other fish. At present, tilefish commands reasonable prices.

Pin bones run along the fillets to just short of the tail. Loosen them with pin-nose pliers or cut them away with a knife if they are hefty.

This splendid-looking fish is very good to eat. It has lean white flesh and a flaky texture (somewhat like that of grouper or even cod) when cooked. The flavor is quite sweet but bland, and you will need to use a cooking method and seasonings that will make it interesting. For this reason I find deep-frying, sautéing, broiling, and grilling good cooking methods for this fish, and I season it more strongly than others with fresh herbs and seasonings and flavorful sauces.

COOKING METHODS

CUT	COOKING METHODS	SUITABLE FOR	HOW MUCH TO BUY
Whole	Roasting	Part of a buffet for 15	10 pounds
Whole	Roasting or poaching	Dinner for 8	7 pounds
Chunks	Roasting	Dinner for 4 or more	10 to 12 ounces per person
Fillets, steaks	As listed below	1	6 to 8 ounces

CHOICE OF RECIPES

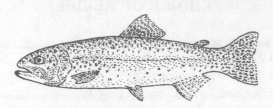

TROUT

Genus Oncorhynchus, Genus Salmo, and *Genus Salvelinus*

> *Fat content:* low to moderate
> *Forms Usually Prepared:* butterflied and
>   split fish
> *Taste:* mild
> *Texture:* flaky

TROUT ARE WONDERFUL FISH TO COOK, FOR THEY ARE SO VERSATILE. THESE ATTRACTIVE FISH are marketed at just the right size for individual servings. Those in the wild are a joyous catch for the fly fisherman or angler when they are caught in lakes, streams, and rivers.

Most trout and chars belong to the Salmonidae family (salmon). Some, such as lake trout, survive only in fresh water, while others are anadromous—that is, they spend some time in the sea before returning to their freshwater birthplace to spawn. Anadromous trout become silvery when they go to sea but regain their skin colors upon returning to fresh water. They also grow larger during their stay in the sea and become fat before entering the rivers to spawn.

Most of the trout we buy at fish stores have been farmed in spring-water-fed ponds. Rainbow trout is the predominant species that is farmed, but brook trout and brown trout are also farmed.

In the wild we have rainbow trout all over the United States, brook and brown trout in the eastern United States and the Canadian Atlantic states, lake trout from the northern United States and all over Canada, cutthroat trout, and Dolly Varden char from rivers to the sea on the West Coast, just to mention a few.

Salmon trout is a name that is given by fish suppliers to the rainbow, brown, or brook trout that go to sea. Rainbow trout gone to sea on the West Coast are not only called salmon trout, but more correctly steelhead. Some steelheads are bred to 8 to 12 ounces each. Steelhead is also the given name for some rainbow trout that live in the Great Lakes, who never get to the sea.

Farmed trout are most often marketed at 8 to 10 ounces (though they do grow larger). They are boned out (butterflied) or filleted and sold fresh or frozen.

Trout are delicate and mild in taste and must not be overwhelmed with strongly flavored sauces. A simple way to enhance trout is with a little butter, lemon, and parsley. The color of trout flesh ranges from white to pink, orange, and red. Take advantage of this lovely color when cooking this fish.

RAINBOW TROUT *Oncorhynchus mykiss*

Cholesterol 56 • Omega-3 0.5 • Fat 3.4

The rainbow trout is a freshwater fish that sports a lot of color: It has a green or blue back, silvery sides with a red strip along each side, a white belly, and little dark spots all over.

The West Coast steelhead trout, which is a rainbow trout that goes to sea, loses some of this color when in the sea and becomes silvery and very bright with a green and pink lateral band. Steelhead trout grow larger than inland rainbow trout, but they are also marketed at the same size (8 to 10 ounces) as rainbow trout.

Rainbow trout originated in the western part of the United States but are now farmed all over America—in fact, all over the world. Idaho has the largest number of trout farms in America. Most of them are located in the Magic Valley, which has a lot of natural spring water for the rainbow trout to grow in.

BROOK TROUT   *Salvelinus fontinalis*

Cholesterol 68 • Omega-3 0.3 • Fat 2.5

Brook trout are an angler's treat. These fish, also called eastern brook trout, grow in the wild in cool lakes and streams in the eastern United States and Canada; some are anadromous and go to sea.

The brook trout has a green-brown back and green sides, and its skin is mottled with yellow spots and red spots surrounded with blue halos. Fins on its lower body are outlined in black with white edges.

Aquafarmed brook trout are available in fish stores in the same form as rainbow trout.

BROWN TROUT   *Salmo trutta*

Cholesterol N/A • Omega-3 N/A • Fat N/A

The brown trout originated in Europe and was brought over by settlers. It now inhabits inland waters all over the United States and Canada; some brown trout go to sea (the Atlantic) and are known as sea or salmon trout. The fish is brownish with dark spots on its back and sides and a white belly.

LAKE TROUT   *Salvelinus namaycush*

Cholesterol 36 • Omega-3 1.4 • Fat 9.4

These trouts are not farmed but thrive in the cold-water lakes and rivers of the northern United States and all of Canada. They do not go to sea. They grow large and are colored brown and silver with yellow spots. They are very high in fat and do not have as much food appeal as other trout. I find them too oily.

COOKING METHODS

CUT	COOKING METHODS	SUITABLE FOR	HOW MUCH TO BUY
Whole or pan-dressed	As listed below	1	8 to 10 ounces
Butterflied or split	As listed below	1	6 to 10 ounces
Fillets	As listed below	1	2 3- to 4-ounce fillets

CHOICE OF RECIPES

Baked Fatty Fish Fillets, page 98

Oven-Steamed Seafood *en Papillote*, page 105

Casserole of Fish Fillets or Large Sea Scallops with Potatoes and Coriander Pesto, page 112

Roast Whole Fish, page 115

Broiled Fillets, Butterflied or Split Fish, Steaks, Escalopes, or Medallions, page 127

Grilled Whole Fish or Shellfish, page 134

Grilled Fish Fillets, Butterflied or Split Fish, Steaks, Medallions, or Shellfish, page 137

Fried Whole Fish or Pan-Dressed Fish, page 153

Poached Small Whole Fish or Fish Portions, page 170

Steamed Seafood, page 176

Creamy Seafood Chowder, page 190

Hot-Smoking (Smoke-Cooking), page 197

Fish Fillets with Spinach and Ginger, page 206

Seviche, page 211

Escabèche, page 213

Soused or Marinated Fish, page 215

Fish Salad II, page 222

TUNA

Family Scombridae

Fat Content: low to moderate
Forms Usually Prepared: steaks and cubes
Taste: mild to bland
Texture: firm flakes

TUNA ARE MEMBERS OF THE MACKEREL FAMILY, AND A LARGE NUMBER OF TUNA SPECIES ROAM the temperate and subtropical waters of the world. Many people know tuna only as a canned product, but for the rest of us fresh is best—there is no comparison. Fresh tuna has superb flesh, and it can be cooked or enjoyed raw in sushi or sashimi.

A typical tuna is silver with a bluish back, large round eyes lying flat against its head, and little finlets stretching down to the tail behind the dorsal and anal fins. It is capable of achieving great speed in the water—most tuna have voracious appetites, so they need speed and endurance for their long migrations away from their spawning grounds in search of food. A tuna's body is torpedo-shaped—just about round at the center and tapering off toward the head and tail ends. Its fins can be retracted into its body so it can become more streamlined and therefore swim faster. The differences among tuna species lie in the sizes they attain (bluefin tuna grow to 1,400 pounds, while yellowfin and bigeye tuna grow to around 400 pounds, blackfin, skipjack, albacore, and bonito weigh less than 100 pounds), the markings on their skin, and the sizes of their eyes.

The best varieties of tuna for eating raw or cooked are bluefin, bigeye, yellowfin, bonito, and blackfin. The Japanese, who buy up the best tuna for the sashimi trade from New England, New York, and other parts of the world and fly it fresh to their country, pay very high prices for bluefin; the bluefin catch has now been restricted because of overfishing, and consequently these fish are becoming very scarce. Skipjack and yellowfin are mostly canned as light tuna, while albacore is mostly canned as white tuna.

Tuna flesh differs in quality from fish to fish, and it takes years of experience to recognize the quality differences. The Japanese assign three grades to tuna: Grade-1 and grade-2 tuna are considered sashimi quality—they are fresh, have a high fat content, and are a glossy, translucent red (brownish tuna is oxidized)—while grade-3 tuna, which must be fresh but may have less color, is considered good enough for cooking. The quality of tuna flesh depends on the size of the fish, the time of the year when it was caught (the fat content varies with the season, and the fatter the flesh, the more delicious it is), the way it was caught, and its subsequent handling—tuna have been known to "cook" themselves in their struggle to survive when caught, and when this happens their flesh deteriorates quickly. Of course, the higher a tuna's grade, the more expensive it is.

As a rule, a tuna that is marketed is cut into four boneless loins. In the fish store we see these loins as well as steaks, chunks, and sometimes cubes cut from the loins. The tuna at your fish store may be fresh or defrosted.

When buying tuna for sashimi, you should look for deep red, glistening flesh—ask for a thin little slice and rub it between your fingers to make sure it is oily. (Incidentally, *toro*, the marbled flesh from the belly, is considered the most delicious part of the tuna, and I can attest to that.) If you are going to cook the tuna you need not be as fussy, but be sure the tuna is fresh and colorful. Buy steaks that are cut 1¼ inches thick—you are less likely to overcook them.

The dark red fatty muscle found near the skin along the lateral line has a different texture and is rich and flavorful, but you may want to remove it. You can cook tuna like swordfish or mako shark; you can also marinate it with oil and herbs and then grill or broil it, or you can sauté or braise it. You can for a change grill a thick (2-inch-thick) steak on an open fire or in a grill pan, then finish cooking it in the oven; this makes for a most impressive dish. Tuna flesh has large flakes when cooked and is flavorful and firm. It turns a light gray as it cooks. Be sure to undercook it slightly as it dries out easily. After cooking tuna, just add some freshly ground black pepper and a squeeze of lemon juice for flavor.

Tuna freezes well. The Japanese are experts at freezing tuna and may keep it frozen for up to a year.

BLUEFIN   *Thunnus thynnus*

Cholesterol 38 • Omega-3 1.17 • Fat 4.9

Bluefin tuna are found in the waters of the eastern Atlantic (from Norway to the Mediterranean), the western Atlantic (from Labrador to South America), and the Pacific. Atlantic bluefish grow to weights of 1,400 pounds; Pacific bluefish are smaller. Bluefins caught in the western Atlantic spawn in the Gulf of Mexico and the Mediterranean and swim north as the waters warm in the summer.

Bluefins have blue-black backs that shade to silver at the belly; their finlets are yellow outlined with black. Bluefin flesh is dark red. Although their catch is limited now that they have been overfished, bluefins command high prices for their high fat content, which occurs in the late summer and fall. They are very much sought after by the Japanese, who eat them raw. Bluefin tuna is sold fresh or defrosted.

YELLOWFIN   *T. albacares*

Cholesterol 45 • Omega-3 0.6 • Fat 0.95

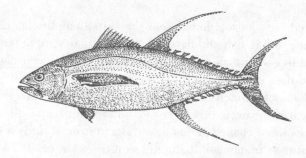

Yellowfin tuna are found worldwide in warm waters. They grow to weights of as much as 500 pounds. They look similar to bluefin tuna, but have yellow bellies, fins, and finlets.

BIGEYE *T. obesus*

Cholesterol N/A • Omega-3 N/A • Fat 1.6

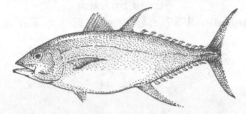

The bigeye tuna is found from Cape Cod down to Brazil. It is colored blue and silver, and has yellow finlets and large eyes. It grows to weights of 400 pounds, and is excellent eating.

BLACKFIN *T. atlanticus*

Cholesterol N/A • Omega-3 N/A • Fat N/A

Blackfin is another highly edible tuna. It is found in the Atlantic from Cape Cod to Brazil. It only grows to weights of about 40 pounds. It has a brownish stripe on its back and a silver belly.

ALBACORE *T. alalunga*

Cholesterol 38 • Omega-3 2.1 • Fat 7.2

Also called the longfin tuna, the albacore looks like other varieties of tuna, with its blue and silver coloring, but it has long pectoral fins. Albacore tuna grow to weights of 90 pounds. Most are caught in the Pacific, though they are also found in the Atlantic. Some albacore tuna goes in the can—albacore is the white meat of canned tuna, but albacore is delicious cooked fresh. Take care to keep it moist.

ATLANTIC BONITO   *Sarda sarda*
PACIFIC BONITO   *S. chiliensis*

Mixed Species
Cholesterol 37 • Omega-3 N/A • Fat 5.5

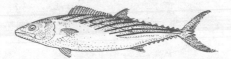

Bonitos are fished on both sides of the temperate Atlantic as well as in the Pacific. In looks they resemble small tuna with stripes on their backs, and they grow to weights under 20 pounds. Bonitos have dark red flesh; when they are bled, their flesh turns an apricot color. Japanese cooks sometimes broil bonitos very briefly and serve them uncooked at the center.

SKIPJACK   *Euthynnus pelamis*

Cholesterol 32 • Omega-3 0.5 • Fat 2.7

Similar in looks to other tuna, the skipjack has stripes on its belly and grows to weights of as much as 70 pounds. It is caught predominantly in the Pacific, but is also found in warm waters of the Atlantic. Much skipjack is canned or frozen.

LITTLE TUNNY   *E. alletteratus*

Cholesterol N/A • Omega-3 N/A • Fat N/A

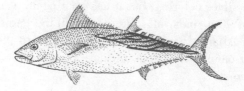

Also called the false albacore, the oceanic bonito, and the spotted bonito, the little tunny has spots on its belly under the pectoral fin and has wavy stripes on its back. It is fished abundantly in the warm waters of the Atlantic, mostly by sports fishermen.

COOKING METHODS

CUT	COOKING METHODS	SUITABLE FOR	HOW MUCH TO BUY
Brochette cubes	Grilling	1	6 to 8 ounces
	Broiling	1	6 to 8 ounces
Chunks	Braising	4	2 pounds
Steaks	As listed below	1	6 to 10 ounces

CHOICE OF RECIPES

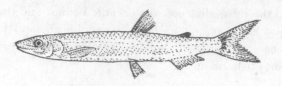

WHITEBAIT

Silversides Family Atherinidae
Sand Lances Family Amonodytidae

Cholesterol N/A • Omega-3 N/A • Fat N/A

> *Fat Content:* moderate
> *Form Usually Prepared:* whole
> *Taste:* mild
> *Texture:* flaky

WHITEBAIT ARE ANY VERY SMALL FISH FOUND IN WATERS WORLDWIDE THAT ARE AS TINY AS minnows; these include silversides and sand lances. Whitebait are practically transparent and silvery in color. They are sold in some fish stores, although restaurants seem to get most of them.

We eat whole whitebait, bones, eyes, and all. They are most delicious deep-fried after having been coated lightly with seasoned flour. (They should be rinsed in a colander with cold running water, then drained and patted dry before being coated.) Pile them up on the plate, sprinkle them with a little cayenne, and serve them with lemon wedges. This preparation is extremely popular in England.

COOKING METHOD

CUT	COOKING METHOD	SUITABLE FOR	HOW MUCH TO BUY
Whole	Deep-frying	1 as appetizer	6 to 8 ounces

CHOICE OF RECIPE

Deep-Fried Seafood: Variation I, page 160

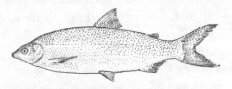

WHITEFISH

Family Coregonidae, Part of Family Salmonidae

Mixed Species
Cholesterol 60 • Omega-3 1.2 • Fat 5.9

> *Fat Content:* moderate
> *Forms Usually Prepared:* fillets and steaks
> *Taste:* mild to sweet
> *Texture:* flaky

LAKE, MOUNTAIN (*PROSOPIUM WILLIAMSONI*), AND ROUND (*P. CYLINDRACEUM*) WHITEFISH INHABIT the lakes and streams of the United States. Lake whitefish is the most important.

LAKE WHITEFISH *Coregonus clupeaformis*

Cholesterol 48 • Omega-3 1.3 • Fat 9.0

Lake whitefish, relatives of the salmon, have certain similarities to salmon, being freshwater fish with silver-colored skin and scales and streamlined bodies. Lake whitefish have more compressed bodies than salmon and very small heads, so they yield a lot more flesh than other fish.

Caught in cold freshwater lakes and rivers, lake whitefish are imported from Canada in considerable numbers. They are caught at weights up to 7 pounds and are sold whole or filleted. They can be broiled, fried, grilled, roasted, or baked. Their flesh is white, firm, and sweet-tasting. As they are moderately fatty fish, many are smoked very successfully.

Chub, a small freshwater fish, is also another name for a small smoked whitefish.

COOKING METHODS

CUT	COOKING METHODS	SUITABLE FOR	HOW MUCH TO BUY
Whole	Roasting	4	3 pounds
Fillets	As listed below	1	6 to 8 ounces

CHOICE OF RECIPES

Baked Fatty Fish Fillets, page 98
Oven-Steamed Seafood *en Papillote*, page 105
Baked Fish Fillet Casserole with Light Tomato Sauce, page 109
Roast Whole Fish, page 115
Broiled Whole Roundfish, page 125
Broiled Fillets, Butterflied or Split Fish, Steaks, Escalopes, or Medallions, page 127
Grilled Fish Fillets, Butterflied or Split Fish, Steaks, Medallions, or Shellfish, page 137
Fish Croquettes and Crab Cakes, page 154
Steamed Seafood, page 176
Creamy Seafood Chowder, page 190
Hot-Smoking (Smoke-Cooking), page 197
Fish Salad I, page 221
Fish Salad II, page 222

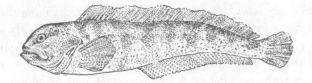

WOLFFISH

Anarhichas lupus

Cholesterol 46 • Omega-3 0.6 • Fat 2.8

WOLF-EEL

Anarrhichthys ocellatus

Cholesterol N/A • Omega-3 N/A • Fat N/A

Fat Content: low
Form Usually Prepared: fillets
Taste: mild to sweet
Texture: flaky

THE WOLFFISH IS INDEED AN INTERESTING IF NOT SOMEWHAT ASTONISHING CREATURE TO SEE AND deal with, for in many ways it does not resemble a marine fish: The head of a wolffish is round like the head of a cat (it is sometimes called the ocean catfish). It has large eyes, long front teeth, and powerful back teeth that allow it to eat shellfish, thereby creating delicious flesh. And then there is its body which has continuous dorsal and anal fins down to the tail, like an eel.

Some wolffish are dark gray or nearly black, while others are gray and black with darker strips and spots. Wolffish are scaleless.

There are two other species of wolffish in the Atlantic—the northern wolffish (*Anarhichas denticulatus*) and the spotted wolffish (*A. minor*). The wolf-eel

(*Anarrhichthys ocellatus*) is from the Pacific. The wolffish and the wolf-eel are extremely similar in looks and both are known to bite viciously when caught.

Wolffish is not widely marketed, which is a real shame, because once you get past its strange looks you will find it has marvelous flesh—white, sweet, lean, and firm with small flakes. A whole wolffish may weigh up to 20 pounds. Fishmongers usually sells fillets that can be fried, baked, broiled, or grilled.

COOKING METHOD

CUT	COOKING METHOD	SUITABLE FOR	HOW MUCH TO BUY
Fillets	As listed below	1	6 to 8 ounces

CHOICE OF RECIPES

Baked Fish Fillet Casserole, page 108
Baked Cajun Fish Casserole, page 111
Broiled Fillets, Butterflied or Split Fish, Steaks, Escalopes, or Medallions, page 127
Grilled Fish Fillets, Butterflied or Split Fish, Steaks, Medallions, or Shellfish, page 137
Fried Fish Fillets or Steaks, *à la Meunière*, page 151
Steamed Seafood, page 176
Fish Soup (*Bourride*), page 188
Seafood Stew or Pasta Sauce, page 192
Seviche, page 211
Escabèche, page 213
Fish Salad I, page 221

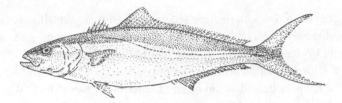

YELLOWTAIL

Seriola quinqueradiata

Cholesterol N/A • Omega-3 N/A • Fat 9.9

YELLOWTAIL, CALIFORNIA

S. lalandei

Cholesterol N/A • Omega-3 N/A • Fat N/A

> *Fat Content:* high
> *Form Usually Prepared:* raw slices
>   (yellowtail);
>   fillets (California yellowtail)
> *Taste:* sweet and mild
> *Texture:* flaky

THE YELLOWTAILS ARE MEMBERS OF THE JACK FAMILY, CLOSELY RELATED TO THE AMBERJACK. Their name can cause some confusion, for there are other fish bearing the same name: the yellowtail flounder (from the northern Atlantic), yellowtail rockfish (from the Pacific), and yellowtail snapper (from the southern Atlantic).

The species *S. quinqueradiata* is aquafarmed in Japan. It is expertly frozen, defrosted slowly, then cut in strong diagonal slices for sushi and sashimi when it is called *hamachi*. It has a delicious buttery flesh.

The California yellowtail, equivalent to the East Coast amberjack, is considered a game fish, and is not often obtainable in fish stores. When marketed it is sold whole and as fillets and steaks. Broil or grill it. (Remove the dark fatty flesh along the lateral line before you cook it.)

COOKING METHODS

CUT	COOKING METHODS	SUITABLE FOR	HOW MUCH TO BUY
Fillets	Broiling or grilling	1	6 to 8 ounces
Fillets	Raw	1	3 to 4 ounces

CHOICE OF RECIPES

Broiled Fillets, Butterflied or Split Fish, Steaks, Escalopes, or Medallions, page 127

Grilled Fish Fillets, Butterflied or Split Fish, Steaks, Medallions, or Shellfish, page 137

Sushi and Sashimi, page 219

Liquid and Dry Measure Equivalencies

CUSTOMARY	METRIC
¼ teaspoon	1.25 milliliters
½ teaspoon	2.5 milliliters
1 teaspoon	5 milliliters
1 tablespoon	15 milliliters
1 fluid ounce	30 milliliters
¼ cup	60 milliliters
⅓ cup	80 milliliters
½ cup	120 milliliters
1 cup	240 milliliters
1 pint (2 cups)	480 milliliters
1 quart (4 cups, 32 ounces)	960 milliliters (.96 liters)
1 gallon (4 quarts)	3.84 liters
1 ounce (by weight)	28 grams
¼ pound (4 ounces)	114 grams
1 pound (16 ounces)	454 grams
2.2 pounds	1 kilogram (1000 grams)

Oven Temperature Equivalencies

DESCRIPTION	°FAHRENHEIT	°CELSIUS
Cool	200	90
Very slow	250	120
Slow	300–325	150–160
Moderately slow	325–350	160–180
Moderate	350–375	180–190
Moderately hot	375–400	190–200
Hot	400–450	200–230
Very hot	450–500	230–260

Bibliography

Audubon Society Staff and Norman A. Meinkoth. *The Audubon Society Field Guide to North American Seashore Creatures*. New York: Alfred A. Knopf, 1981.

Audubon Society Staff et al. *The Audubon Society Field Guide to North American Fishes, Whales, and Dolphins*. New York: Alfred A. Knopf, 1983.

Commonwealth of Massachusetts. Division of Marine Fisheries. *The Northeast Seafood Book: A Manual of Seafood Products, Marketing and Utilization*. Boston: Division of Marine Fisheries, 1984.

Davidson, Alan. *North American Seafood*. New York: The Viking Press, 1980.

Eschmeyer, William N., and Earl S. Herald. *A Field Guide to Pacific Coast Fishes: North America from the Gulf of Alaska to Baja California*. Peterson's Field Guide Series. Boston: Houghton Mifflin, 1983.

Fletcher, Anne M. *Eat Fish, Live Better*. New York: Harper & Row, 1989.

Gosner, Kenneth L. *A Field Guide to the Atlantic Seashore*. Peterson's Field Guide Series. Boston: Houghton Mifflin, 1982.

Krzynowek, Judy and Murphy, Jenny. *Proximate Composition, Energy Fatty Acid, Sodium and Cholesterol Content of Finfish, Shellfish and Their Products*. National Oceanic and Atmospheric Administration Technical Report National Marine Fisheries Services 55. National Technical Information Service, Springfield, VA, July 1987.

Lamb, Andy, and Phil Edgell. *Coastal Fishes of the Pacific Northwest*. Madeira Park, B.C., Canada: Harbour Publishing, 1986.

Loomis, Susan Herrmann. *The Great American Seafood Cookbook*. New York: Workman Publishing, 1988.

Manooch, Charles S., III. *Fisherman's Guide: Fishes of the Southeastern United States*. Raleigh, N.C.: North Carolina State Museum of Natural Sciences, 1984.

McClane, A. J. *McClane's Field Guide to Freshwater Fishes of North America*. New York: Henry Holt & Co., 1978.

Morris, Percy A. *A Field Guide to Atlantic Coast Shells*. 3d ed. Peterson's Field Guide Series. Boston: Houghton Mifflin, 1973.

Nettleton, Joyce. *Seafood and Health*. Huntington Station, N.Y.: Osprey Books, 1987.

Ray, G. Carleton, and C. Richard Robins. *A Field Guide to Atlantic Coast Fishes*. Peterson's Field Guide Series. Boston: Houghton Mifflin, 1986.

U.S. Department of Agriculture. Human Nutrition Information Service. *Composition of Foods: Finfish and Shellfish Products*. Agriculture Handbook No. 8–15. Washington: U.S. Government Printing Office, 1987.

U.S. Department of Health and Human Services. Food and Drug Administration. *Food and Drug Administration Guide to Acceptable Market Names for Food Fish Sold in Interstate Commerce 1988*. Washington: U.S. Government Printing Office, 1989.

Warner, William W. *Beautiful Swimmers*. Boston: An Atlantic Monthly Press Book, Little, Brown and Company, 1976.

Index

451

About the Author

BORN IN LONDON, ENGLAND, SHIRLEY KING TRAINED AS AN ARTIST, BUT HAS SPENT THE LAST 20 years in the food business. She first catered in London and Provence, and later became a restaurant chef in London, East Hampton, and New York. She is the author of *Saucing the Fish and Dining with Marcel Proust*, and is featured in the video *A Guide to Seafood Cookery*. Her obsession with fish continues into this latest book.

Shirley King teaches cooking extensively in the New York metropolitan area, continues to write, and finds time to exhibit her photographic work.